The Cuban Revolution in the 21st Century

THE CUBAN REVOLUTION
IN THE 21st CENTURY

George Lambie

*To Antony
with best wishes
from
George
4 Dec. 2010*

PlutoPress
www.plutobooks.com

First published 2010 by Pluto Press
345 Archway Road, London N6 5AA and
175 Fifth Avenue, New York, NY 10010

www.plutobooks.com

Distributed in the United States of America exclusively by
Palgrave Macmillan, a division of St. Martin's Press LLC,
175 Fifth Avenue, New York, NY 10010

British Library Cataloguing in Publication Data
A catalogue record for this book is available from the British Library

ISBN   978 0 7453 3011 2   Hardback
ISBN   978 0 7453 3010 5   Paperback

Library of Congress Cataloging in Publication Data applied for

This book is printed on paper suitable for recycling and made from fully managed
and sustained forest sources. Logging, pulping and manufacturing processes are
expected to conform to the environmental standards of the country of origin.

10   9   8   7   6   5   4   3   2   1

Designed and produced for Pluto Press by
Chase Publishing Services Ltd, 33 Livonia Road, Sidmouth, EX10 9JB, England
Typeset from disk by Stanford DTP Services, Northampton, England
Printed and bound in the European Union by
CPI Antony Rowe, Chippenham and Eastbourne

This book is dedicated to my father George Thomas Lambie, who would be proud to know that I have continued to struggle for the ideals in which he believed.

Contents

Acknowledgements

Any form of intellectual production is never the work of one individual, but a collective process in which an author brings together the ideas and experiences learned from, and shared with, many people and presents them through his/her prism on the world. In this sense it is impossible to acknowledge all such influences on a body of work, because the list would be too long, and ideas and consciousness are neither formed in a linear nor predictable way. Those who receive mention therefore are the people, to the best of my memory, who have had a direct impact on my thinking or helped to shape this book. There are others, not acknowledged, who may also have played a role, but their contributions have been less tangible.

My first acknowledgement is to Professor Alistair Hennessy who introduced me to Cuba when I was an undergraduate at the University of Warwick. After my postgraduate studies he guided me as a research fellow and together we compiled and edited a book entitled *The Fractured Blockade: West European–Cuban Relations during the Revolution* (Macmillan 1993). He was one of the first British scholars to analyse the Revolution and remains today a leading authority on Cuba. Another Cuba specialist who has had a notable impact on my work is Ken Cole (University of East Anglia, retired). Over the years we have held many challenging and productive discussions on the nature and significance of the island's revolutionary process. Others in the UK who have influenced my thinking on Cuba are: Gareth Jenkins (formerly of *Cuba Business*); Antoni Kapcia (University of Nottingham); Stephen Wilkinson (International Institute for the Study of Cuba (IISC); London Metropolitan University); Professor Patrick Pietroni (IISC); Emily Morris (IISC); David Jessop (Caribbean Council, London) and David Thomas and Philip McLean (former British Ambassadors to Cuba). I should also like to thank my friends Jack and Fedelma Winkler for the many stimulating conversations we have had about Cuba and related subjects, especially in their fields of healthcare and nutrition. At my own university, De Montfort, I am grateful to my colleague Professor John Greenwood (retired) whose expertise in politics and public administration provided vital insights into Cuba's system of local government. In the US a key academic influence on my work has been Professor William Robinson of the University of California, Santa Barbara. His theory of global capitalism provides a powerful explanatory framework for understanding the current world order and the context in which Cuba finds itself in the 21st Century.

I first started going to Cuba in the early 1980s and between then and the completion of this book in June 2010 I visited the island over thirty times, as a researcher, project manager and member of the Cuba Initiative (yearly mission to Cuba organised by the Caribbean Council). During that period I met, and made friends with, many Cubans but for reasons of space can only mention a few. My first debt of gratitude goes to Dr José Luis Rodríguez, who in the 1980s was Deputy Director of the Centre for the Study of the World Economy (CIEM) in Havana. In this capacity he generously provided seminars for my students from the University of Warwick who visited Cuba, and also contributed a chapter for *The Fractured Blockade*. In 1991 Dr Rodríguez became Minister of Finance and played an important role in the negotiations with the European Commission which in 1995 led to the first major cooperation project with Cuba (Ministry of Finance). I had the honour of acting as co-director of this project with him. When Dr Rodríguez became Minister of the Economy and Planning in 1998, I had the privilege of knowing his special adviser the late Dr Alfredo González from whom I learned a great deal about the workings of the Cuban economy. While still engaged in the European Commission project in the late 1990s I worked with the new Minister, Dr José Manuel Millares, who like his predecessor was always helpful and supportive. During this period I developed a close cooperation with the Ministry's International Relations Officer Dr Alejandro Fuentes, whose kindness, wisdom and revolutionary commitment taught me what it means to be Cuban. There were many other people in the Ministry of Finance whom I came to know and regard as colleagues, including Armando Casado Castro, Ruben Toledo, Rafael González and Lázaro Pérez. Concerning my official contact with Cuban Government administration, my deepest gratitude goes to Doris Simons who, until 2005, worked as Officer for the UK in the Ministry of Foreign Investments (MINVEC). She was my champion for over ten years, giving support to many initiatives that I proposed. I should also thank Maria Teresa Rodríguez from the Ministry of External Relations (MINREX) for her invaluable assistance during the initial negotiations of the European Commission project.

The Commission project was delivered by a European Consortium named the Cuba Financial Reform Group (CFRG). From De Montfort University I am grateful for the support and assistance of all my colleagues who participated. I am especially indebted to Professor Gregory Wilkinson Riddle (retired), who was the technical coordinator, and played an important role in designing aspects of Cuba's new taxation system. Frances Wright, who managed the project, was not only an outstanding organiser, but also shared with me a wide ranging interest in Cuba and some of the ideas we discussed appear in this book. From our European partners I wish to make special reference to Dr Bernhard Seidel and Dieter Teichmann from the German Economic Research Institute (DIW) and Professor Ernesto Carrillo, from the Complutense University in Madrid. Among the independent consultants who contributed to the project Professor Allister Wilson should receive special mention for his valuable support. All of these people and many others who worked with the CFRG helped to enrich my knowledge of Cuba and give perspective to my thinking. In the European Commission I am particularly grateful to Manel Camos for his support and guidance through the intricacies of Brussels.

In my various capacities in Cuba I met many other people who either improved my understanding of the island or gave me assistance with my work. Among these I owe a particular thanks to José Antonio and his family; Carlos Alzugary; Haroldo Dilla; Fernando Martínez Heredia; and Dr Osvaldo Martínez, the Director of CIEM and Minister Ricardo Cabrisas who both read and commented on an early draft of the first two chapters of this book. Minister Cabrisas also kindly gave me a copy of *Fidel Castro. My Life* (2007), a biography based on 100 hours of interviews with Ignacio Ramonet, which I have cited extensively. Among the many other contacts and friends I have made in Cuba, I should like to make special mention of Vilda Figueroa and José Lama who run the Community Project for the Conservation of Organic Produce. Their exceptional initiative illustrates Cuban community participation at its best. Working with Cubans and sharing issues in their everyday lives was a wonderful experience and I am grateful to all of them.

Besides those who gave me academic or project-related assistance, I am especially grateful to my talented friend Judith Hinz who played an essential role in the development and completion of this book: first, for taking an interest in my ideas and work, and then going on to become editor, occasional researcher, and an endless source of support and encouragement.

Three individuals not directly involved with Cuba, but who have significantly influenced my thinking on globalisation and politics are Tony Benn, the late Ken Coates and Stuart Holland. I am very grateful to Tony (veteran Labour Party politician and former Minister) for granting me access to his Uncut Diaries and sharing with me his unique and valuable perspective on political issues past and present. Ken, a founder of the Institute of Worker's Control and MEP, contributed principally to my research into social democracy in the 1970s, but our discussions ranged widely and he inspired my thinking in many areas. He was, in my opinion, one of the most outstanding socialist intellectuals and activists in Europe. I shall miss him as a friend and mentor. I am also indebted to Stuart, formerly an adviser to Harold Wilson, an architect of Labour's progressive economic strategies in the 1970s, MP and collaborator of senior officials such as Willy Brandt and Jacques Delors, for bringing to our conversations on the current financial and economic crisis his extensive knowledge and experience, and offering his insights into global and European alternatives.

I should like to acknowledge with gratitude the support of the British Academy for awarding me a Small Research Grant in 2005 to investigate popular participation in Cuba.

As this book was nearing completion I received excellent advice and assistance from my publisher, Pluto Press. I am especially grateful to Anne Beech, the Director, who supported my project from the time it was first presented and played a major role in guiding the book to publication. Other staff at Pluto from whom I received invaluable support are Will Viney, Roger van Zwanenberg, Robert Webb, David Shulman and Dave Stanford.

All opinions and interpretations in this book, though influenced by many people, are entirely mine and for which I take full responsibility.

Finally, I hope that one day my daughters Jennifer and Rebecca will read the words that I have written and understand and appreciate the 'battle for ideas' they represent.

Introduction

The Cuban Insurrection of 1959 came as a surprise not only to the United States but also to the Soviet Union, which had paid scant attention to the island and knew very little about its internal affairs. Once Fidel Castro and his supporters had overthrown the corrupt Batista dictatorship and secured power, they embarked on a Revolution, which soon attracted the interest of the superpowers, sections of the media, and a number of academics; but it was not until the international trauma of the 1962 Missile Crisis that Cuba was projected onto the world stage. In the 1960s, the Cuban Revolution represented socialism reborn and a new hope for the political Left, especially when compared to the entrenched ideologies of the Cold War. Some believed that this small country was building the foundations of a new society, and Che Guevara's forays abroad in Africa and Latin America presented an image of socialism in action. After a few years of radical experimentation, it was Havana, rather than Moscow, that inspired the Left around the world. This was true not only for independence movements in developing countries, which hoped to emulate Cuba's revolutionary project, but also for the 1960s generation of European and American students, workers, and intellectuals. Perhaps most memorably, the European student and worker protesters of 1968 carried images of Che Guevara as their most prominent symbol. As David Caute (1988: 31) suggests, 'the legend of Cuba was inscribed on the hearts of the New Left'.

Despite Castro's vocal support for the Soviet invasion of Czechoslovakia in 1968, which put an end to the progressive reforms of the 'Prague Spring', and Cuba's decision to move into a closer relationship with the Soviet Union in the 1970s, the island's revolutionary image remained largely untarnished. The deployment of Cuban troops to support the Angolan liberation movement (MPLA) in the mid 1970s boosted its socialist internationalist credentials, and earned the small Third World country an international status and importance disproportionate to its size (Domínguez 1989). In 1988, after a protracted war, the Cuban army played the principal role in containing the Angolan opposition forces, fronted by South Africa, at the battle of Cuito Cuanavale. However, by the time of this extraordinary military achievement – which led to the withdrawal of all foreign troops from Angola, liberated Namibia, and contributed significantly to the end of apartheid in South Africa – the world had changed.

In the 1980s, despite continuing support in some quarters for the Cuban domestic 'model' (Zimbalist and Brundenius 1989), its wider revolutionary influence began to fade as the international Left lost ground to apolitical solidarity movements and neo-liberalism emerged as the New World Order. Cuba's relations with the Soviet Union also became increasingly uncertain. When the US invaded Grenada in 1983, raising concerns in Havana that Cuba would be next, Moscow gave virtually no response, leaving the island to feel that it was 'on its own' (Bengelsdorf 1994: 143). Then, under Gorbachev, the Soviet Union began an ideological shift which emphasised *perestroika*, *glasnost*, and market-orientated reforms; these were modifications to socialism that the Cuban government could not countenance, as they were seen to threaten the heart of the Revolution. Although disappointed by these changes, Cuba remained highly dependent on Soviet aid and trade. Facing an uncertain future, in 1986 Havana launched the Rectification of Errors and Negative Tendencies Campaign. This sought to roll back the Sovietised developmental model that had been pursued since the 1970s, and attempted a return to Guevara's 'moral economy' based on consciousness building, among other objectives (Cole 1998). But nothing could have provided adequate preparation for the Communist debacle at the end of the decade. By 1991 the question was no longer 'Could Cuba export its Revolution?', but rather 'Could Cuba survive?'

In 1989, when it was clear that Soviet-style Communism's days were numbered, Francis Fukuyama (1992: 4) made his triumphalist statement proclaiming the inevitability of neo-liberal globalisation:

> What we are witnessing is not just the end of the Cold War, or a passing of a particular period of post-war history, but the end of history as such: that is, the end point of mankind's ideological evolution and the universalisation of Western liberal democracy as the final form of human government.

Fidel Castro (2007: 386) recalls that, despite the island's appalling predicament at that time – facing economic catastrophe, isolation and increasing hostility from the international community – he continued to believe that history was on the side of the Revolution, not of capitalist globalisation: 'I was fully convinced that it was the other way around, and that it [globalisation] had to be resisted. This is the certainty I had then.' He, and the Cuban leadership, therefore decided to 'wait patiently, for globalisation to collapse'. Interestingly, as this book was being finalised in June 2010, two years into perhaps the worst financial crisis in modern history, one of the most perceptive commentators on globalisation, the billionaire and international financier George Soros, stated at a conference held at the Institute of International Finance in Vienna, 'The collapse of the financial system as we know it is real, and the crisis is far from over ... Indeed, we have just entered Act II of the drama.'

This book examines the diametrically opposed perspectives of Francis Fukuyama and Fidel Castro, with a view to assessing the possibilities and options for the Cuban Revolution in the twenty-first century. To undertake this task it is necessary to go beyond the specifics of Cuba and its current situation, and consider the wider world. Consequently, the following analysis will be of interest not just for students of Cuba, but for anyone wishing to understand the global order and the roots of its current crisis.

Against all odds, the Cuban Revolution has now survived for almost 20 years since the collapse of Communism. Yet the perception prevails that a Cuban transition from socialism to a market economy is inevitable. Over time, all that has changed is the view of how this is likely to take place. In the early 1990s, it was predicted that Cuba would be 'the next domino to fall'; in the mid to late 1990s, tentative market reforms were heralded as indications of an opening to capitalism; and most recently it has been assumed that the 'avalanche' will come when Fidel Castro and his brother Raúl have gone. A few years after the debacle of Soviet-style Communism, when it became clear that the Cuban Revolution's demise was not imminent, the problems surrounding a possible future 'transition' were dealt with in a study edited by Miguel Centeno and Mauricio Font, *Toward a New Cuba? Legacies of a Revolution* (1997). The authors, although sympathetic to Cuba's cautious approach to reform, ultimately see the Revolution as an obstacle to market integration. They, like others dealing with this topic, believe that a Cuban transition is unavoidable and necessary, and that it is only a matter of time before it will occur. The arguments put forward by such analysts are relevant in the context of a presumed shift from socialism to capitalism, but are largely misplaced if Cuba is attempting to build on its strengths in order to advance an alternative developmental model – one that differs from the market-dominated route that virtually all commentators seem to think the island must follow.

Based on the mainstream view of Cuba and its presumed future, most academic studies dealing with the contemporary period focus on the island's internal processes: the workings of a system that has endured against enormous odds and is still trying to adhere to its principles, but whose days are numbered. For instance, a recent survey of Cuba edited by Brenner et al. (2008), *Reinventing the Revolution. A Contemporary Cuba Reader*, concentrates on domestic developments in Cuba and Cuban–US relations as self-contained topics. Among the 49 chapters from different contributors, some of which are excellent in their own right, there is no mention of Cuba and globalisation that makes any sense, and the future of the Revolution in this context is not considered. Most remarkably, there is no reference to Cuba's relations with Latin America.

Some studies in the field of economics (Eckstein 2003; Ritter 2004) have made accurate observations on the Cuban situation and the resistance to change, but do not consider the model to be sustainable. Mainstream academics analysing political and social aspects of the Revolution, including López (2002) on democracy and Feinsilver (1993) on health care, as well as the sympathetic studies of Rosset and Benjamin (eds) (1994) on organic horticulture and Bengelsdorf (1994) on democracy and participation, do not link these processes clearly to a wider survival strategy. Only rarely do scholars writing on Cuba raise the possibility that Cuban socialism has a future (e.g. Cole 1998). However, a pragmatic study (Sweig 2007), prompted by Fidel Castro's poor state of health, has emerged from within the US academic establishment, which concluded that the Revolution may survive for some time after its 'maximum leader' has retired.

Fidel Castro's decision in February 2008 to step down as Head of State generated another round of speculation about Cuba's future. *The Economist* (2008a) predicted that 'real change in Cuba will only start after Fidel's death' and argued that there are only two options for this 'sad, dysfunctional island': transition or collapse. *Business Week* (Smith 2008) was a little more circumspect, raising the point that the Cuban economy is performing well and still has plenty of potential. Ultimately, however, transition and a rapprochement with the US are seen as the only way forward. This biased ideological approach is also reflected in mainstream media coverage of Cuba. For instance, in April 2010 major news networks were eager to report that the country's state-run barber shops and beauty salons are being handed over to their employees, who will now rent their spaces and be responsible for their own business, rather than receiving a state wage. On 13 April the UK's main morning news programme, Radio Four's *Today*, broadcast a report on this development which it saw as a 'small step' to wider market reform (Voss 2010). In contrast, Cuba's important contribution to the health aid effort that followed the January 2010 Haitian earthquake, which killed an estimated 220,000 people, injured 300,000 and left 1.5 million homeless, was hardly mentioned in the mainstream media, despite massive international coverage of the event. This omission must be more than an oversight, especially considering that Cuban medical personnel in Haiti treated more patients and performed more surgical operations than all of the other donor agencies and countries combined (Kirk & Kirk 2010). It would seem that Cuba's supposed moves towards an internationally failing free-market system are of more interest than the successes that apparently emerge from its socialist Revolution.

Because of the all-pervasive nature of the market myth (hegemony) which underpins these biased views, even the most fervent advocates of socialist Cuba hope only that it can survive longer than predicted by its detractors. Nearly all shades of opinion believe the island will have to adapt to global (market) conditions, with only the speed and nature of the change remaining in question. From this perspective, socialism is dead; but this resilient country and its tenacious leaders still hold the respect of many, even though their fate is presumed to have been decided by the course of history.

This study will turn the analytical telescope around and, rather than focusing directly on Cuba, will begin instead by viewing the wider perspective and posing different questions. The first, prompted by Fidel Castro's observation above, asks: Can the neo-liberal global order survive in its current form? This leads to the second: Does Cuban socialism offer possible alternatives and examples to those countries in which sections of society, and their leaders, have lost faith in market-orientated solutions? As Raby (2006: 9) states, 'The Cuban revolution is clearly the starting-point for contemporary Latin American revolutionary movements, yet remarkably little attention has been devoted to its political originality.'

It would be an exaggeration to suggest that history has come full circle and Cuba is once again on the revolutionary offensive. Indeed, no one knows for sure whether the Cuban Revolution can survive the global pressures that weigh upon it, or contain its own domestic tensions and challenges. But the actions of the Cuban government, both internally and in its foreign policy, do not indicate that the Revolution is in its death throes. Although Cuba has engaged in some market reforms, these actions appear to be guided by expediency rather than any long-term commitment. Despite many changes, it continues to be the revolutionary priorities – social welfare, encouraging grassroots participation in decision making, attempting to manage economic processes for the social good, and exporting the 'achievements' and philosophy of the Revolution through health care and technical assistance programmes – that remain the *raison d'être* of Cuba, not some incremental move towards the market. If neo-liberal globalisation was firmly established and had succeeded in producing a sustainable model of development, including the long promised 'trickle down' to the poor and marginalised who are the majority in many developing countries, then Cuba's stubbornness would indeed be anachronistic. But globalisation is in crisis, a problem that was foreseen by some of its own influential (reformist) advocates (Soros 1998; Stiglitz 2002). In his 2008 testimony to the US House of Representatives on the financial crisis, Soros questioned the dogma which allowed him to make his fortune, stating, 'Since market fundamentalism is built on false assumptions, its adoption in the 1980s as the guiding principle of economic policy was bound to have negative consequences.' Now the international financial debacle is having deep structural implications for the neo-liberal experiment, making its failures as a model more apparent. In this environment of growing inequality and injustice, Cuba is again becoming a symbol of resistance and hope.

In practical terms, decades of delivering cheap, effective and participatory social welfare in health, education, and more, both at home and abroad, has put the island in a good position to directly address the needs of those who have been marginalised by contemporary capitalism. Testimony to this is the work of more than 40,000 Cuban medical and educational personnel in the shanty towns of Venezuela, as part of a reciprocal agreement with Hugo Chávez's government, which for its part sends much-needed oil to Cuba. There are also Cuban health, education and aid workers in many other countries from which the island receives little or nothing in return, with Cuban support seen as part of its international mission, as in the case of Haiti mentioned above. Politically, Cuban participatory democracy, with its focus on establishing structures and social processes by which citizens can seek to resolve problems and conflicts and make their voices heard by government, all within a system whose objective is social and economic equality, has appeal for many of the new popular movements in Latin America. Cuba's inclusive democracy may also offer even more profound indications of how social change can be enacted and consolidated.

However, this book does not seek to present Cuba as an example to be copied, but rather aims to understand how the failure of neo-liberal globalisation is beginning to produce a counter-hegemony with which the Cuban socialist project can integrate. The Cuban Revolution, no matter how popular, or resilient, cannot survive globalisation alone; 'socialism in one country' is untenable in the long run, and in this its detractors are correct. But today there seems to be a growing synthesis between Cuba's resistance to the dominant market-driven order and the anti-neoliberal movements that are emerging in Latin America. As noted, on one level this is a material process, as Cuba contributes to radical alternatives in the region by providing support in social welfare, intelligence and organisation, but it also represents a coincidence of consciousness as more people reject market solutions to their problems and seek to build something new. In this context, the survival of Cuban socialism is not simply a question of how long the Revolution can endure on the island, but how, through a symbiotic link with a wider process of change, it can influence and ultimately be absorbed into a growing popular resistance that is emerging from within the core of globalisation. In the author's view, this is a far more important issue for the future of the Revolution than Cuba's relations with the US. Many Cuba sympathisers were initially encouraged by the apparently progressive stance towards the island of the newly elected US President Barack Obama, but this hope seems to have faded as Washington's policies have again hardened towards Havana. Besides, any significant rapprochement leading to an end of the embargo would serve to compromise Cuba and dilute its socialist objectives. It is only by being part of a counter-hegemony to global capitalism that the Revolution can follow its metier and its perceived destiny.

From this inverted optic, that of a global perspective on Cuba's contemporary position, the subsequent analysis will begin with critical studies of globalisation and capitalist democracy. Moving on to Cuba, it will then attempt to define the nature of the socialist trajectory that has been taken by the Revolution. This will be followed by an analysis of the crisis that was precipitated by the collapse of Communism and Cuba's determination to continue with its socialist project in the face of adversity. A brief assessment will then be made of the relevance of Cuba's involvement in the growing struggles in Latin America. Finally, the options that are open to Cuba will be considered.

It is important to emphasise that while this book will take a positive approach to Cuban socialism in the twenty-first century for the reasons stated above, it does not seek to be predictive or prescriptive. The objective is to highlight the possibilities for the socialist project, especially as nurtured and promoted by the Cuban Revolution, at the current juncture in the development of capitalist globalisation. If the Revolution collapses, or moves into transition, precipitated perhaps by a rapprochement with the US, this will not be the end of socialism's necessary contestation with capitalism. Nor will Cuba's experiment be rendered irrelevant, as it represents a stage in that process, one that already merits a place in history.

This study does not adopt a strict methodology or ideological approach, but contributing schools of thought include political economy, International Political Economy (IPE) and Marxism. Within this general framework, the main influence derives from the Italian intellectual Antonio Gramsci and his followers, particularly those of the 'New Italian School' such as Cox (1987), Gill and Law (1988) and Robinson (2004a). This branch of Gramscian analysis is associated particularly with extending the idea of 'hegemony' into the field of IPE. Within this tradition, Robinson elaborates a *Theory of Global Capitalism* which claims that globalisation represents a new epoch. In this period, the transnationalisation of finance and production is complemented by the rise of a global elite that includes not only international business leaders, financiers, officials in multinational agencies, etc., but also neo-liberal state managers who have taken over from their social democratic predecessors. Although the notion of a Transnational Capitalist Class and a Transnational State have been suggested by other authors (Sklair 2001; Cox 1993), Robinson brings these formations into a clear perspective with his theory by employing the concept of hegemony.

When analysing contemporary developments in Cuba and Latin America, academia tends to reject this new transnational dimension, or be unaware of it, and places too much emphasis on internal country processes rooted in history, culture, intellectual and popular tradition and national specificities. Although the resistance to neo-liberalism that is forming in many countries is unquestionably nourished and stimulated by these domestic influences, it is the external dynamic – globalisation and the transnationalisation of production, finance and ruling-class power – that is the engine which drives change and the reaction to it. Throughout its post-conquest history, Latin America has been heavily influenced by its external relations, but at no other time has its integration into a dominant world order been more complete. The tendency by academia to concentrate principally on national-level processes to analyse change is part of a post-Marxist trend to seek explanations for events in cultural and 'superstructural' formations, rather than by giving primacy to the 'base' factors such as the dominant mode of production and the international system in which its logic resides (Cox 1987). This is not to argue for a simple materialist approach, but to make the case for bringing material factors firmly back into the analytical equation. Most importantly, serious analysis, from Marxist and other perspectives, must acknowledge the interrelationships between base and superstructure if it is to make sense of certain situations.

Current theoretical models also encounter a problem with the nature of globalisation itself. In most mainstream disciplines – economics, politics, international relations, sociology, etc. – their underlying assumptions are still embedded in the nation-state phase of capitalism. However, the new global order, based on the deregulation of finance and production, has led to 'transnationalisation', which, as one author starkly proclaims, marks 'the end of geography' (O'Brian 1992). This has important implications for national and regional studies because transnationalising processes are penetrating into economic and social spaces in a way they have never done before.

Finally, the analysis will draw on the author's own experiences of Cuba as a researcher: as co-director of the European Union's first major co-operation project with Cuba from 1994 to 2000; as organiser of two smaller projects funded by the British Embassy (Havana) to provide assistance in banking regulation and agricultural development; and as a member, since 1998, of the Cuba Initiative Committee, an independent body which seeks to improve and support commercial and other reciprocal relations between the UK and Cuba.

Based on the questions, issues and approaches outlined above, the chapters are structured in the following way:

Chapter 1 will set the framework for the book by presenting globalisation as a new epoch in the development of capitalism. This begins with a historical description of the transition from a statist Keynesian-style world system to a transnationalised order of finance and production. From this perspective of structural change, an assessment will be made of the impact of such forces on the state, and the social arena, and how these, in turn, have interacted with globalisation.

To understand Cuba's position in the world today, it is not sufficient to assume an immutable 'end of history' neo-liberal global system in which this socialist anomaly continues to survive. Globalisation itself, like any other defined period of history and international political economy (e.g., the Pax Britannica and the post-war Keynesian consensus), is a process which, as it unfolds, reveals itself and its contradictions. Today, after over 30 years of neo-liberal restructuring, the stark battle between capital and labour, which lies at the heart of globalisation, is becoming sharper as inequality increases on a world scale. As reactions grow to this injustice, so does the conscious formation of a counter-hegemony. Many studies of globalisation see it as a quantitative, two-dimensional, linear process (Hirst & Thompson 1996; Held & McGrew et al. 1999, etc.), but it also has a qualitative and dialectical dimension. It is in this latter context that Cuba can be seen as actor, rather than simply survivor.

Chapter 2 considers the theory of modern democracy and its practical and ideological manifestation under neo-liberalism and globalisation. Although the post-Communist 'resurgence' of democracy has been celebrated by many authors (Diamond & Platter eds 1993; Axworthy 1992), its ability to deliver 'power to the people', or achieve even the more modest feat of ensuring a reasonable and fair distribution of goods and services, remains in question. How effective is 'procedural' democracy based on parliamentary liberalism, which offers few opportunities to challenge the global structures of power and wealth, in satisfying the needs and aspirations of the masses, especially in developing countries? But Cuba, despite its excellent record of development with social equality, is regarded by many analysts to be a dictatorship. Such a view can only be sustained through the unquestioned assumption that contemporary liberal democracy is the definitive model against which all other forms of political and social organisation have to be measured. This perspective must be challenged if any sense is to be made of, or relevance attributed to, Cuban 'democracy'. Without contextualising Cuba's distinctive approach to democracy, it remains an anomaly and cannot be comprehended as part of a counter-hegemonic process, nor can we interpret its possible significance for other anti-globalisation struggles in the world. To undertake this task, the historical trajectory of democracy is analysed from both its liberal and socialist perspectives. An assessment is then made of the ideological and ontological underpinnings of these different understandings.

Chapter 3 focuses on Cuba. Firstly, a study is made of the factors and trends that have served to legitimise the Revolution and give it resilience to external threats and non-socialist alternatives. One variable that analysts often omit in their studies of Cuba is how the revolutionary process established itself on a separate track to mainstream Communism. This is a significant issue if one is to understand, rather than simply describe, the complex blend of nationalism and socialism which has given Cuba its distinctiveness and its ability to survive. Out of this radical political process has emerged a strong current of popular involvement in the Revolution. This is realised through the mechanism of participation and the fostering of a socialist consciousness; a separate ontology that poses different priorities and questions concerning human development than those narrow perspectives which form the presumed immutable order of neo-liberalism. In this respect Cuba has hidden strengths that have not only secured its survival under duress, but might also offer a route through which it could construct a sustainable future.

Chapter 4 will firstly examine the immediate consequences for Cuba of the collapse of Communism. Then, based partly on the author's experience of working with the Ministry of Finance in the 1990s, an explanation and assessment will be made of the economic strategies that were used to confront the crisis. This will be followed by a study of the political and social developments that complemented these changes, with particular reference to the enhancement of democratic and participatory structures and processes. Finally, consideration will be given to the issues of Cuban youth and culture in the global era.

Chapter 5 will first consider the implications of the transfer of leadership from Fidel Castro to his brother Raúl. This is followed by an analysis of Cuba's attempts to project its socialist ideals into the global arena and build international solidarity through the export of health care to developing countries, and its more specific objective of providing assistance to governments in Latin America which are responsive to the popular rejection of neo-liberalism. In this latter context, Cuba's energies are particularly focused on assisting the government of President Hugo Chávez in Venezuela, and the regional anti-globalisation initiative called the Bolivarian Alternative for the Americas (ALBA). The chapter concludes with an analysis of the options for development that Cuba might follow.

The objective of this final chapter, and indeed the whole book, is to set a new framework for subsequent studies of the Cuban Revolution. These would concentrate less on Cuba as a socialist anomaly in a global capitalist world, a perception which invites detailed studies of the island's internal dynamics, and would instead seek to understand the Revolution as an important example of counter-hegemony in a failing international system.

1
Globalisation: Understanding the Rationale for an Alternative

To analyse Cuba's position today and its prospects for the future, especially as it strives to defend its Revolution and seeks to align and integrate its socialist experience with anti-neoliberal movements in Latin America, it is essential to understand the challenges, opposition and opportunities it faces in a globalising world system.

As noted in the Introduction, Fukuyama (1989:4) has argued that 'Western liberal democracy [is] the final form of human government'. From this perspective, the Cuban Revolution is an impossible and failed experiment, and the only way forward is for the country to abandon its past and try to catch up with the 'inevitable' trend that history has taken. For those who accept this view, there is no longer a debate regarding Cuba's future. The only issues at stake are how long the Castro brothers' leadership can survive, and how long the socialist system over which they preside can resist the logic of global market forces and democratisation (Eckstein 2003; López 2002). This view must be questioned if one is to make sense of the Revolution in the twenty-first century.

To undertake this task it is not enough to simply declare a political preference for the Cuban system or cite impressive social statistics, which some authors seem to think is sufficient. One must analyse, interpret and challenge the whole hegemonic worldview upon which is premised the certainty of Cuban socialism's demise. Moreover, to suggest that Cuba offers alternatives to the market creed, it is necessary to conceive of a counter-hegemony that can transcend globalisation.

Globalisation is a much-contested subject and invites many definitions and interpretations. However, this uncertainty resides in the application of inadequate analytical tools, rather than in the elusiveness of the subject. Economics, politics, business studies and many other academic disciplines can offer us insights into the globalisation process, but none alone can explain it. Therefore the approach taken by the author is International Political Economy (IPE), which seeks to understand globalisation as a 'totality':

an 'epochal shift' within capitalism which transforms virtually everything we do and experience. From this perspective it has a historical background. In economic terms it is principally associated with the deregulation of international finance, a technological revolution (especially in microelectronics), and the transnationalisation of production processes. Such developments are complemented and facilitated by ideological and political changes that took place during the last three decades of the twentieth century, principally the rise of neo-liberalism and the collapse of Soviet-style Communism.

   Combined, these trends have opened up the world to market forces. In this environment there appears to be a shift of power, away from the nation-state and towards a new community of international financiers, multinational corporations (MNCs) and multilateral agencies such as the World Trade Organisation (WTO), the International Monetary Fund (IMF) and the World Bank. To its advocates, globalisation represents the unshackling of the logic of capitalism, especially free markets, and its ascendancy into a supreme and inevitable world system. To its detractors, it is capitalism *in extremis*, temporarily unchallenged, and sense lies not in its existence but in its eventual demise. Between these two poles there are many intermediate interpretations and shades of opinion.

THE BACKGROUND TO GLOBALISATION: FROM CAPITALISM 'CONTROLLED' TO CAPITALISM UNLEASHED

In 1944, towards the end of the Second World War, the allied nations, headed by America and Britain, attended a conference at Bretton Woods in the US to discuss the post-war world economic order. The conference was dominated by a strong anti-free market (but not anti-free trade) ideological current led by the British economist John Maynard Keynes and the American Harry Dexter White. They believed that the liberal (free market) financial order of the 1920s, which had been dominated by speculative private financial interests and a blind faith in the market, had led to the Wall Street Crash of 1929. This in turn had resulted in a collapse of international capital markets, the abandonment of the gold standard, descent into recession, social and economic disorder in the capitalist powers and many peripheral nations, and, indirectly, the war. Addressing the conference, US Treasury Secretary Henry Morgenthau stated that an agreement should be reached at Bretton Woods that would 'drive the usurious money lenders from the temple of international finance' (cited in Helleiner 1994:4).

Since the early 1930s, all the major powers had used some form of state control to deal with the depression that followed the 1929 crash. Indeed, the most successful economies during the decade were the Soviet Union and Nazi Germany, which, although political polar opposites, had in common massive levels of state intervention. Regulation and the subjugation of finance to economic and political priorities increased in the late 1930s and during the war, especially in the US and Britain. This gave rise to a new alliance of state officials, industrialists and labour leaders, who assumed positions of power that had previously been held by the champions of laissez-faire business and private and central bankers. Intellectually, this new hegemonic bloc was wedded to Keynesian economic principles and believed that the reconstruction of the post-war world order should be state- rather than market-driven. This represented a radical shift in thinking which rejected the liberal financial policies that had predominated before 1931, and, as Keynes himself put it, 'What used to be a heresy is now endorsed as orthodox' (1980:17). But Keynes was not a socialist; on the contrary, he was dedicated to market principles in an environment of stability. As one analyst notes, 'Keynes, for all that he broke with classical economics, operated entirely within its framework. He was a heretic rather than an infidel' (Drucker 1983).

While most of Europe lay in ruins, the US emerged from the war with its economy intact and booming, and was the only power capable of leading a recovery of world capitalism:

> At the end of the war the USA controlled some 70% of the world's gold and foreign exchange reserves, and more than 40% of its industrial output while Europe and Japan had been devastated by war and the Third World was still locked into colonial servitude and contained less than 1% of the world's industrial capacity. (Brett 1985:63)

Bretton Woods established the US dollar, backed by gold, as the key world currency against which other currencies would be pegged in a system of semi-fixed exchange rates. The unquestioned hegemonic power of the US after the war gave it the 'exorbitant privilege' (Giscard d'Estaing, cited in Gourinchas & Rey 2005) of being able to print limitless paper certificates in the form of dollars, which could be exchanged for imports from other countries at no cost to the issuer. The former hegemon, Great Britain, had enjoyed a similar privilege in the nineteenth century, based on the gold standard and the international role of sterling. Although America's financial advantage can be see as a means to advance its imperial power, a dominant and stable 'fiat' currency was essential for world economic recovery and Bretton Woods represented the first ever attempt to establish an international financial and trading order among independent nation-states. The founding of the World Bank, the IMF, and the General Agreement on Tariffs and Trade (GATT) were also planned at the negotiations, as a means to regulate finance and trade in the post-war world economy.

The so-called Bretton Woods system that emerged was a watered-down Keynesian version of development that placed emphasis on the management of capitalism by international and state institutions. With Europe severely weakened and Communism on the doorstep, this was no time to leave the rebuilding of the economies of the Western world to the vagaries of the market. Fundamental to this view was that states had the right to impose capital controls in order to take charge of internal development strategies, and that the international system of semi-fixed exchange rates would promote world economic stability and curb speculation. Keynes stressed the importance of encouraging the function of 'productive' and 'legitimate' capital that supported real economic activity and trade, rather than speculative financial movements.

The Bretton Woods formula was given material substance through the European Recovery Programme (Marshall Plan 1948–52), when the United States pumped $12 billion into the economies of Europe and Japan to support their reconstruction and keep up demand for US industrial goods after the war's end. The plan was sold to the American public, and to Congress, as a means to turn the 'Red Tide' (perceived support for Communism), particularly in France and Italy, but there was little evidence that such a threat existed (Kunz 1994). Marshall aid certainly made an important contribution to post-war reconstruction. However, as Milward (1984) has suggested, European recovery was already underway by 1948 and Marshall dollars were needed not so much for the buying of goods, but rather to provide offsetting finance for purchases already made in the US, and to compensate for continuing private capital flight to America, despite regulatory controls. Because of these problems, and especially the weakness of the British economy, it was not until the late 1950s that international conditions were suitable for the full implementation of the Bretton Woods financial order based on the convertibility of currencies (Burnham 2003).

Although the establishment of Bretton Woods was problematic and delayed, the quarter century from 1945 to 1970 was the most successful period of economic development ever recorded, especially in the industrialised world. 'Between 500 and 1500 AD the world's income grew by 0.1% a year. Over that millennium 'world' Gross Domestic Production went up by 2.5–3 times. The world economy grew just as fast in only twenty years from 1950 to 1970 – and from a higher base' (Maddison 1982:4–5). Moreover, during this latter period, gains were made not only by those who owned capital and the means of production, but also by ordinary working people as welfare reforms, trade unions and national economic planning improved job security and standards of living. High levels of Keynesian-style domestic investment and a sustained increase in world trade drove the long boom of the post-war period. The aim of the system was full employment, growth, development, and limited wealth redistribution, all under the control of national elites and professional managers. A formula that would secure political stability in a divided world, in which Communism was presented as a threat to the capitalist West and its professed values.

There was also a general acceptance that 'development' must be a staged process in Third World countries, an idea that was mainly informed by 'modernisation' theory. In many respects this was the highest level of the nation-state phase of capitalism, characterised by domestic circuits of production ('auto-centric accumulation') linked to a wider system through international markets and nationally orientated capital flows that were tied to trade, aid and production. Nation-states, and particularly developed ones, had a significant degree of control over their economic activity, and governments were expected to regulate such spheres as employment, industrial policy and growth.

During more liberal phases of capitalist development in the nineteenth century and in the decades on either side of the First World War, the colonies were fundamental to the accumulation regimes of the industrialised European nations because they allowed for super-exploitation to take place abroad. This relieved some of the pressures on their own domestic working classes. However, the problems of economic depression, followed by wartime destruction of capitalist stock, decolonialisation and the rise of Communism, put pressure on national ruling elites to reach an accord with their subordinate classes. Fordist manufacturing techniques and Taylorist forms of work organisation permitted the centralisation of production and high levels of social control, but their continuing success was based on satisfying the material needs and welfare of the workers. Representative democracy along with Keynesian-style state controls allowed the popular classes to support political leaders who would act on their redistributive demands, and constrain the more aggressive aspects of capitalism. This arrangement has been termed by Lipietz (1992) the 'Fordist class compromise'. In this context it has been claimed that the 'full employment capitalism' which this model sought to create needed to 'develop new social and political institutions which [reflected] the increased power of the working class. If capitalism can adjust to full employment a fundamental reform will have to be incorporated in it' (Kalecki, cited in Glyn 2001:4).

Because capitalist classes were largely tied to national territories, they developed national identities which helped strengthen their legitimacy and hence their hegemony over the rest of society. Slogans like 'Buy British' and 'Uncle Sam Wants You' helped to promote the myth that Britain and the US were 'classless' unified nations, in which individual interests were indivisible from national interests. This view was reinforced as ruling elites in many countries were seen to be competing with each other in the international arena.

In retrospect this period appears to have been a less aggressive phase of capitalism than the earlier laissez-faire era or the globalisation that we are experiencing today. However, it must not be forgotten that the post-war period was one of US hegemony – giving rise to the notion of the 'American Century' – and while this power was in some respects benign, it was also exercised in the pursuit of geo-political ambitions (Chomsky 2003). Many ordinary people in developing countries who were caught up in a US invasion or a US-inspired war, or lived under a US-backed dictatorship, would probably have regarded it as an imperialist state. This perception was shared by most inhabitants of the socialist world.

It may also be argued, from a broadly Marxist view, that the post-war period was less about the containment and regulation of capitalism, and more a response to the crisis of profitability during the interwar years. From this perspective, the post-Second World War period represented not so much a compromise by capital, but its reconstitution into a new model of accumulation. Although during the Second World War workers, particularly in Britain, enjoyed their first real taste of state-led management and protection, and experienced a growing sense of solidarity and national purpose, the discipline and sacrifice of the war period also prepared them for the conformity that would be demanded by the social democratic 'Fordist' production system that emerged after the victory. Braverman (1974) in particular has shown that advanced technology, mass production, adoption of the capitalist work ethic, and modern management techniques deepened workers' alienation and exploitation instead of liberating them.

A further factor contributing to capitalist renewal after the Second World War was the international regime of unequal exchange between the developed Western powers and the new Third World nations. Decolonialisation had led to independence but, as Fanon (1967) and others pointed out, many of the former colonies had been so deeply integrated with the imperial nations that even after achieving self-determination they continued to be dependent not just for trade and know-how, but also culturally and intellectually. Moreover, the mainstream development debate revolved around Rostow's (1960) notion of 'stages of economic growth', which underpinned modernisation theory and the belief that the Third World could catch up with the West if it followed the latter's 'model' of development. Such a view conveniently ignored the massive distortions caused by colonialisation and the disadvantages faced by producers of raw materials in their relationship with the diversified industrial economies. Despite his 'scientific' approach to development, Rostow was a hawkish Cold Warrior and staunch anti-Communist and, as an adviser to Presidents Kennedy and Johnson, pressed for US intervention in Vietnam (Milne 2007). Although after the Second World War the price of raw materials rose with increasing demand from rapidly expanding industrial economies, this did not always translate into resources for development, as old colonial and post-colonial ties continued to disadvantage the Third World. This tendency was exacerbated by the operations of emerging US multinationals which, through the establishment of economic enclaves and the use of political manipulation, were able to retain most of the wealth they extracted from developing countries.

Finally, labour migration provided a vital contribution to sustained economic growth in the advanced capitalist countries, with 37 million people arriving in the US and 15 million in Europe between 1945 and 1975 (Coates 1991:25–26). These immigrants to the US came from many regions, but mainly Latin America and the Middle East, while those arriving in Europe tended to come from the former colonies. Immigration was often encouraged by the receiving countries, as in the case of British policy towards Jamaica. This massive influx of cheap, unskilled labour was vital in a period of rapid economic development, and helped to limit the demands of indigenous workers. For Marxists like Coates (1980:180), therefore, the reconstituted Western system of the post-war period does not represent much of a compromise for capitalism, as is maintained by the social democratic Left. He argues that if one takes into account the above factors and the tremendous demand that emerged after the war, it is not surprising that 'the 1950s was characterised by a high level of profitability and rapid capital accumulation'. According to Yaffe (1973:48), the productivity of labour in the industrial powers grew significantly during the 1950s and 1960s. Marxists understood that the post-war system was not designed for disciplining capitalism, but for creating a new environment in which it could flourish; still, it was not long after the post-war recovery, when labour's power began to increase, that problems set in for capital. As the Regulation theorist Aglietta (1979:117) contends, the co-ordination between national-level production and consumption helped to delay capitalism's cyclical economic crises, but did not resolve the underlying problem.

Despite the dominance of the Keynesian, nation-state led, post-war system, private capital remained restless. Even in the first years after Bretton Woods, US multinationals were able to take advantage of massive dollar flows to Western Europe and other parts of the world, where America was financing the reconstruction of war-torn economies. Some private international banking activities developed around the financial servicing of these MNCs, but due to national and international regulatory frameworks most areas of private finance faced restrictions on the use and movement of capital. International banking, including credits, loans, and other financial transactions, was conducted principally by national banks and the World Bank.

By the early 1960s, however, once the US had fulfilled its role as the agent of capitalist economic recovery, problems began to arise which threatened the Bretton Woods system. Years of boom in the US and the privileges it enjoyed as issuer of the world's 'fiat' currency were partly to blame for an over-valued dollar, high labour costs, complacency in research and development, a failure to keep up with improvements in production technology, and a resulting fall in the rate of profit for investors in the US. Meanwhile, countries that US capital helped to rebuild, like Germany, France and Japan, had become more efficient economically. Labour productivity in western continental Europe, for instance, grew more rapidly than in the US from the late 1950s onwards, and by 1960 the Common Market's combined exports exceeded those of the US (Engdahl 2004:106).

These changes encouraged American business, and especially MNCs, to extend more of their activities abroad, and from 1950 to 1970 the book value of Foreign Direct Investment (FDI) by US MNCs grew from $11.8 billion to $78.1 billion (cited in Ajami et al. 2006:7). As noted earlier, part of this expansion was based on post-war dollar flows into Europe, but it was accelerated in the mid 1960s through the private capital that became available in the mainly London-based Eurodollar market. This market took the form of an arrangement in which dollars were held by private banks on a special account, outside the jurisdiction of the issuing and host countries. After sterling was made convertible in 1958, that currency came under attack from speculators. This bolstered government support for the Eurodollar market because it attracted dollars into London, easing pressure on the balance of payments. In 1962, the Conservative government of Harold Macmillan authorised the Bank of England to open a facility which allowed non-UK residents to hold dollar deposits in a British account. This legitimised and consolidated the Eurodollar market in London and gave a significant boost to City banks, which could now act as the key brokers for expatriate dollar activities. In the same year, the government approved the formation of the Eurobond market which permitted the issue of foreign securities in London, denominated in currencies other than sterling. These developments provided the impetus for London to replace New York as the world's leading capital market, especially after 1963 when the US increased restrictions on its own financial markets (Helleiner 1996:14, 84). By the mid 1960s the Eurodollar market had become the world's principal arena for raising private funds and servicing new borrowers. The French analyst Servan-Schreiber (1968:11) estimated that as early as 1965, of the $4 billion of new investment in Europe by US multinationals, 55 per cent came from this source.

A significant boost to the market came in 1968 when, partly because of large dollar outflows from the US and the increasing cost of the Vietnam War, legislation was passed that put limits on the issue of foreign loans by US banks (Moffitt 1983:48). To avoid the constraints of domestic legislation, these banks sought to establish branches abroad, particularly in the London Eurodollar market. In 1968, 26 US banks had 375 foreign branches in London with $23 billion in assets. Two years later, 79 banks had 536 branches with over $52 billion in assets (ibid.). The migration of American banks to London led to an expansion of US commercial banking and the growth of independent capital flows. The Bank of International Settlements, or BIS (cited in Callao 1982:208), estimates that the expansion of the Eurodollar market was as follows: it was valued at $9 billion in 1964; $17.5 billion in 1967; $57 billion in 1970; and $475 billion in 1979. In comparison, US reserves averaged just under $16 billion during this period (ibid.). These developments marked the change from a nation-state dominated system of international finance, to one in which private banks became the repositories and distributors of global capital. One observer has described Eurodollars as 'the most dramatic financial innovation in the post-war period' (Schenk 1998).

It is interesting that the UK, which had pursued a strongly Keynesian economic and welfare strategy after the war, should have allowed commercial banks in London to engage in unrestricted capital operations (Strange 1996:47). However, post-war British governments realised that if the UK was to keep any advantages deriving from its former hegemonic status and compete with the US, then the financial power of the City, with its vast international networks, had to be given space to breathe. As noted earlier, the influx of capital into London also helped to offset British balance-of-payments problems.

THE BREAKDOWN OF KEYNESIANISM AND THE RISE OF NEO-LIBERALISM

By 1971 the accumulated problems in the US economy, including an over-extended and overvalued dollar, inadequate gold reserves, demands for greater financial freedoms from US banking and multinational corporate interests, and the repercussions of the Vietnam War, resulted in the Nixon administration taking the momentous decision to abandon the gold parity pledge (Callao 1982). This allowed for a devaluation of the dollar, marking the end of the fixed exchange rates that had underpinned the Bretton Woods system, and took pressure off the US gold reserves, which had fallen to a post-war low, and by 1971 covered only one quarter of official liabilities. It has been argued that the floating of the dollar, which lost about 23 per cent of its value between 1971 and 1973, provided a means by which the US could force some of its international creditors to share the burden of its own economic difficulties (Branford & Kucinski 1990). In effect, with the stroke of a pen, US exports became more competitive in the international system, sparing America from making painful internal adjustments in order to achieve greater efficiencies.

With the dollar anchor no longer in place, there was a move to floating exchange rates that allowed for the internationalisation of capital markets, opening up a completely new set of opportunities for financial speculation and private investment. Currency futures were initially launched in 1972, and by mid decade foreign exchange, in its various forms, grew into the world's largest financial market. As one analyst (Engdahl 2004:129) colourfully states, 'When Nixon decided no longer to honor U.S. currency obligations in gold, he opened the floodgates to a worldwide Las Vegas speculation binge of dimensions never before experienced in history.' It also served to shift power from a system of production, trade and finance that generally served the logical manufacturing and movement of goods, to one in which finance began to play a disproportionately important role. By destroying the central financial control of the Bretton Woods system, Nixon ultimately jeopardised the future of American manufacturing and New Deal-style social development. While the US needed a massive internal injection of capital to modernise its economic and social base, a small and powerful group of New York bankers were looking abroad for more lucrative investment opportunities than those which could be found at home. The growing demands of US MNCs for capital, the unrestricted Eurodollar market, and increasing opportunities for currency speculation were all more attractive than the restrictive environment of domestic investment.

The second stimulus to the expansion of international private capital markets came with the OPEC (Organization of the Petroleum Exporting Countries) oil price rises of the 1970s, which were precipitated by the falling value of the dollar and US support for Israel during the Arab–Israeli war of 1973. During that decade the price of oil rose sevenfold, leading to a massive increase in dollar receipts to oil-producing countries, especially in the Middle East. Those countries sought to invest much of this new wealth because it could not be absorbed by their small economies. It is generally assumed that the US was incensed by the actions of OPEC, and that due to fear of retaliation by Washington, billions of 'petro-dollars' found their way into the private banks that were active in the Eurodollar and currency markets. However, Engdahl (2004:130–141) argues that the 'oil shock' was manufactured by key players in the Nixon administration, including Secretary of State Henry Kissinger. Behind this strategy were international banking interests in New York and London and major American and British oil corporations. These groups were supported by the elite Bilderberg organisation, initially established in the 1950s to counteract anti-American sentiments in Europe, but which by the 1970s had become a key agency in facilitating the ambitions of the emerging transnational elites. The effect of the 'shock' was devastating for world economic growth, but it served to restore the power of the US dollar and provide huge profits for private banks and major multinational oil companies. The US ceased to be world creditor and became the world debtor, and the dollar's underpinning shifted from the official role that had been played by gold, to an unofficial role played by oil.

Despite the manipulative actions of an emerging global power elite, underlying these developments were deep structural and social problems within the Bretton Woods order, especially in the industrial powers. What had been an effective post-war system for reconstructing capitalism, securing social peace, combating the perceived threat of Communism, supporting the consolidation of US hegemony and sustaining a satisfactory rate of profit for capital was by the 1960s losing its viability (Piore & Sabel 1984:165–187; Harvey 1990:141; Reich 1991:75–76; Brenner 2009). Central to this change was an overaccumulation crisis, in which the Keynesian-style capitalist form had reached its limits of expansion within existing national-level institutional and social structures (Clarke 1988; Brenner 2009). This coincided with a falling rate of profit caused principally by the end of post-war reconstruction, the saturation of national markets by standardised goods, growing international competition, and the increasing costs imposed on capital by labour and the welfare-orientated public sector. As international financiers, private speculators and MNCs, with the support of sympathetic state actors, attempted to combat these problems by evading national-level constraints on their activities, the mechanisms of Keynesian control began to break down. This led to 'stagflation' (price inflation combined with economic recession), failing economic policies, labour militancy and the rise of neo-liberal economic thinking.

In Britain and many other developed nations, big business and the emergent neo-liberal Right attributed problems such as falling productivity and inflation to a militant and greedy workforce. This view was increasingly accepted by reformist groups on the social democratic Left, such as some members of Britain's 1970s Labour government including Prime Minister James Callaghan. This perception of British workers was challenged by Marxists (Coates

1980), and intellectuals and politicians on the Labour Left like Stuart Holland and Tony Benn, who respectively championed Labour's Programme 1973 and the Alternative Economic Strategy (AES). These initiatives sought, among their objectives, to reassert state control over the activities of MNCs and private capital, especially in the Eurodollar market. They believed that the problem in Britain, and in other advanced capitalist nations, lay not with labour but with emerging multinational capital, which refused to invest once its rate of profit began to fall due to social demands supported by national-level regulations. Big business was therefore seen to be 'failing the nation on a massive scale and represents a dead weight on the backs of working people who, through taxation, subsidize distributed private profits' (Holland 1975:69). This trend led to a situation where 'financial markets [had become] almost totally divorced from the needs of industrial development' (ibid.:14). The British Trades Union Congress of 1972 was even more forthright, and accused MNCs of 'undermining the national sovereignty of democratically elected governments' (cited in Wickham-Jones 1996:56). In conclusion, Holland (1975:9) claimed:

> The current crisis of Capitalism is not simply a matter of inflation. It reflects fundamental changes in the structure of power that have undermined conventional post-war orthodoxies on society, the State and economic management. Recent acceleration in the trend to monopoly and multinational capital has eroded Keynesian economic policies and undermined the sovereignty of the capitalist nation-state.

This kind of thinking, along with the progressive social democratic policies that formed the substance of Labour's Programme 1973 and, from 1974, the AES, was logical and theoretically persuasive to the Labour Left and socialists, but was anathema to the emerging political Right and its supporters. In the 1970s, businesses and investors could argue, with some justification, that increasing social spending by government, inflation, militant labour, and high taxes and death duties on the rich had all compounded to make unattractive the active use of their capital and skills. Such contradictions were also found in other developed countries, leading to an inevitable systemic crisis and the rise of forces opposed to Keynesianism.

In this battle, the City of London financial markets, and especially the Eurodollar market, played a central role in facilitating the ambitions of the globalising elites. This was revealed at the time of the IMF crisis in the UK in 1976, when the Fund sought to impose 'conditionality' before granting a further loan to the British government. Faced with the prospect of the AES finding favour with moderates in the Labour Party as a reaction to the IMF's demands, US Secretary of State William Rogers (cited in Glyn & Harrison 1980:97) stated:

> We all had the feeling it [the initial attempts to deregulate finance] could come apart in quite a serious way. As I saw it, it was a choice between Britain remaining in the liberal financial system of the West as opposed to a radical change of course because we were concerned about Tony Benn precipitating a policy decision by Britain to turn its back on the IMF. I think if that had happened the whole system would have begun to come apart. God knows what Italy might have done; then France might have taken a radical change in the same direction. It would not only have had consequences for the economic recovery, it would have had great political consequences. So we tended to see it in cosmic terms.

In contrast, Tony Benn (1976) summed up the situation as follows: 'The only question is whether in the siege, you have got the TUC [Trades Union Congress] in the citadel you are defending against the bankers or the bankers with you inside the citadel you are defending against the TUC. I am sure the right thing is to have a much tougher fight on behalf of the British people.'

Further to this point, Helleiner (1994:128) notes: 'Britain had played a vital role in the 1950s and 1960s in promoting a liberal international financial order, and it would continue to do so in the 1980s. Had Britain chosen to introduce tight exchange controls [in the event of a rejection of the IMF conditions], the globalisation trend would have suffered a serious setback.'

The inability of the Labour Left to persuade the rest of the party to accept the AES helped to clear the way for the rise of neo-liberal forces. By the late 1970s and early 1980s, deregulation of international finance and the erosion of the Bretton Woods system was complemented by the rise of New Right political leaders, especially Margaret Thatcher in the UK and Ronald Reagan in the US. Convinced by the theories of free-market economists like Milton Friedman and Friedrich Hayek, and with the support of domestic and international business elites who wanted even more financial deregulation, they embarked on a series of pro-business and anti-labour initiatives. This process would finally destroy the semi-Keynesian model of world development that had been in place since the end of the Second World War. Immediately after taking power in 1979, the Thatcher government abandoned exchange controls, opening up an Aladdin's cave of possibilities for the financial institutions and MNCs.

Deregulation and the emergence of private international banking and credit markets in the 1970s and early 1980s in turn paved the way for the growth of securities markets. Securitisation led to the relative decline in conventional loan business conducted by banks, and an explosion in the issue of marketable bonds. Further financial deregulation such as the 1986 'Big Bang' in the London Stock Exchange, which opened up the Exchange to foreign securities, helped to consolidate this process and facilitate the emergence of a truly global financial system.

Another feature of financial deregulation has been the growth of 'uncommitted facilities', also known as 'derivatives', which provide borrowers and lenders with options to 'hedge' against interest and exchange rate fluctuations, commodities, and virtually anything else that invites speculation. Derivatives can take the form of exchange-traded instruments (including futures and options on interest rates and currencies), stock market index futures, interest rate swaps, etc. But many are traded as 'over-the-counter' instruments which allow financial intermediaries to deal between themselves, shifting huge monetary volumes outside of established exchanges. By avoiding official circuits, players in this forum can engage in risk arbitrage at reduced cost. Such activities are difficult to control, and as one author (Thomson 1998:ix) has suggested, 'Regulatory and legal systems have been left so far behind that the new world of derivatives is a kind of financial Wild West with few rules or codes of behaviour.' In 2002 the respected American market speculator Warren Buffet referred to derivatives as 'financial instruments of mass destruction ... time bombs, for both parties that deal in them and the economic system' (cited in Pratley 2008). By the 1990s, this highly competitive financial services industry was dominated by a few heavily capitalised securities and banking houses, operating in an environment that is perhaps the closest thing to a globally integrated market. According to *The Economist*, five investment banks (Morgan Stanley, Goldman Sachs, Salomon Smith Barney, Merrill Lynch and J.P. Morgan) controlled 50 per cent of global investment banking in 1997. By the mid 1990s the 'usurious money lenders' against which Morgenthau and Keynes had warned had not only returned, but had assumed a level of power that could not have been dreamed of in previous eras. But as Elliot and Atkinson (2008:126) note, they soon realised 'that the unshackling of finance had sent a Frankenstein's monster rampaging around the globe' – one that even they would be unable to control, as we are finding out today.

By the end of the twentieth century, the global capital markets were so huge that they became difficult to conceptualise. In the nineteenth century, and for much of the twentieth century, the amount of money in international circulation approximated investment in real assets plus the trade that it was financing. But by the late 1990s, after deregulation, exchange transactions were 60 times greater than trade values (Harris 1998/99:23). From 1976 to 1980, average world borrowing in the form of security issues was $36.2 billion dollars per annum, but by 1993 this had increased to over $520 billion (OECD 1996). Even more spectacular was the growth of the derivatives market, which from a standing start in the early 1970s had expanded to a $64 trillion ($64,000 billion) market by 1996. This was roughly six times as large as the value of the US and Japanese economies combined (Thomson 1998:x). The daily market in derivatives was recently valued at $6 trillion, which was equivalent to half the annual GDP of the United States (Elliot & Atkinson 2007:229). Institutions and individuals were now free to invest around the globe in search of the best returns, many of which came from short-term speculative ventures or simply moving funds around in the international currency markets. These developments were facilitated politically and economically by the deregulatory legislation of governments, and enabled by advances in information technology. Harris (1998/99) has referred to the actors in global finance as 'electronic capitalists', and, concerning the interconnectivity of the system they inhabit, Castells (1996) writes of the 'network society'.

The deregulation of finance, though presented by its advocates as simply the expression of market 'logic' leading to a more efficient distribution of resources, was, in fact, a highly partial and ideological move that would surreptitiously alter the balance of world power in capital's favour. The result was a system which, rather than producing the transparency and openness so cherished by market purists, instead concocted an invisible spider's web woven with mystique, complexity and deception. The largely faceless champions of this new order came to be seen by a beguiled public as masters of occult financial knowledge, wizards with a Midas touch who conjure fortunes out of thin air. With this mythology in mind, Elliot and Atkinson (2008) refer to this group, and its allies in business and the state, as the 'New Olympians'; like the gods of ancient Greece, they are capricious and distant in their relationship with ordinary mortals who have no say over this self-anointed 'higher order'. Although this is how the 'New Olympians' may wish to be seen, they are not in fact disconnected from the everyday life of common people; they are hard-wired into its very core, because it is the surge of unfettered private capital, which they control, that is the prime mover of globalisation with all its economic, social and class implications. Today we are all beginning to experience the consequences of their financial system's failure (Lambie 2009a).

Financial deregulation was complemented by worldwide market liberalisation, which increased significantly after the Uruguay Round of the General Agreement on Tariffs and Trade (GATT) negotiations in the 1980s. This established a new set of global trade rules including a dismantling of some trade barriers, intellectual property rights, along with freedom of investment and capital movements and liberalisation of services such as banks, and many other measures to free up the movement of goods and services. The GATT was replaced by the World Trade Organization (WTO) in 1995, which assumed new supranational powers to enforce the provisions of global liberalisation. Although the WTO invites national-level representation, it has increasingly become a command centre for global transnational elites, and especially MNCs which now under globalisation have effectively become transnational corporations (TNCs).

THE GLOBAL ERA

From Global Finance to Global Production

The rise of a global financial system and the liberalisation of trade have helped to facilitate the transnationalisation of production. In the Bretton Woods era MNCs, especially those of US origin, benefited from the dollar's status as world currency and were able to carry out large business operations abroad. However, as noted earlier, they were restricted by the system of semi-fixed exchange rates and the ability of nations to control currency flows and speculation. The growth of private capital and the rise of international financial markets and multinational banks (MNBs) opened up this formerly limiting system to new opportunities to raise finance and make investments, allowing production to shadow globally footloose capital movements. MNBs in particular play an important role in providing TNCs with financial arrangements in their host countries while providing the security and flexibility of home branches, often to the detriment of local banking and investment.

The spread of MNBs and increasing capital movements have led to a surge in foreign direct investment (FDI), whereby TNCs locate abroad to start a business, open up subsidiaries, and build production facilities, offices, distribution centres, etc. For example, Toyota and Honda invest in factories in the US, while General Motors (GM) and Ford are investing in factories in Russia, Mexico, and Canada. The main advantages of multiple foreign operations for TNCs are: easier access to flexible and cheaper capital; global purchasing power over suppliers (GM buys steel from 50 countries); spreading fixed costs (like those of research and development) across global sales; transfer pricing (where profits are declared in low- or no-tax zones); and lower labour costs. Between 1945 and 1973 the main economic force driving the world economy was export-based international trade, but since 1980 this tendency has been overtaken by a surge of FDI emanating mainly from TNCs. Between 1983 and 1990, FDI expanded at an average annual rate of 34 per cent, compared with an annual rate of 9 per cent for global merchandise trade (OECD 1992:12). Most FDI flows are still between developed countries, and especially among the so-called Triad bloc: the US, the European Union and Japan/East Asia. But during the past two decades, TNCs have increasingly targeted less-developed countries as their economies become more open, providing easy access and exit routes for foreign investments as well as cheap labour and lax environmental laws.

The key distinction between the 'world economy' and a 'global economy' (the words may be used interchangeably but they mean different things) is the globalisation of the production process itself. The rise since the 1970s of mobile transnational capital has allowed for the decentralisation and functional integration around the world of vast chains of production and distribution, and the instantaneous movement of values. In the previous era based on the 'international' system, composed of independent and semi-independent nation-states, goods were produced mainly in one country using national finance. Some of these goods were sold on the international market, but profits mostly returned home and the cycle was then repeated. Although corporations competed for international markets, the 'locus of economic activity' was the nation-state (Webster 1995:140). Now, under globalisation, not only has production become decentralised and dispersed, but so have finance and the apportioning of profits, which now feed into the global circuits of accumulation rather than returning to a specific nation or nationally based company. Global capitalism is not based on a collection of national economies, related to each other through external exchanges, but on transnational integration. According to Dicken (1998:2), 'in terms of production, plan, firm and industry were essentially national phenomena' until the 1970s, but, during the past few decades, 'trade flows have become far more complex ... transformed into a highly complex, kaleidoscope structure involving the fragmentation of many production processes and their geographic relocation on a global scale in ways which slice through national boundaries'. Based on the experience of their respective companies, corporate executives tend to share this perception and see their businesses no longer as multinational companies, but as transnational 'globally integrated enterprises' (Palmisano 2006). As Robert Reich (1991:124), President Clinton's Secretary of Labour, pointed out, 'The emerging American company knows no national boundaries, feels no geographical constraint'.

As noted previously, in the words of Castells (1996), what we are experiencing is the formation of a global 'network society'. These networks are formed principally around the ways in which production and finance are facilitated by advances in communications, information technologies, transport, etc. But they are also the result of the new methods of organizing production, through such innovations as computer-aided design and manufacturing (CAD/CAM), 'just-in-time' production, small batch production, subcontracting, and outsourcing. These innovations make possible new subdivisions and specialisations in production, so that more and smaller stages of the process can be developed based on measures of efficiency, calculated according to factor costs that come together in ever-lengthening and fragmented production chains.

Globally mobile finance, integrated production, and supporting service networks, have led neo-liberal analysts like Ohmae (1990), Wolf (2004), Barnevik (2001) and others to imagine a global market based on competition and the classical laws of supply and demand, which they predict will eventually benefit everyone. But what we are increasingly seeing is a concentration of decision-making power and economic management in the hands of transnational capital and its agents. Particularly through mergers and acquisitions, core capitalist groups are in the process of forming oligopolistic structures which, rather than leading to a perfect market, are creating a centralised global command economy based on a single mode of production and a single worldwide system.

Labour and Globalisation

Before globalisation, the international division of labour was based, with some exceptions, on the production of manufactured goods in the core industrial powers and of primary goods in the periphery, often, in the latter, using semi- or pre-capitalist forms of labour. This arrangement, which was largely a remnant of colonialisation, started to transform with the expansion of the MNC, especially after the Second World War when such enterprises began to increase their control of world economic activity. Now, under globalisation, with borders becoming more porous and capital seeking lower production costs, the whole international division of labour is being restructured. As Munck (2002:111) notes, 'Massive proletarianisation is at least as much a feature of globalization as the increased mobility of capital.' The point is further substantiated by Freeman (2005) when he states:

> [T]he most fundamental economic development in the era of globalisation [is] the doubling of the global labour force. The entry of China, India and the former Soviet bloc into the global capitalist economy is a turning point in history. For the first time, the vast majority of humans will operate under market capitalism.

While cheap labour in the periphery is important for the new dispersed mode of capitalism, it is by no means the only component in the global restructuring process. Also significant when choosing the location of production is the need to find environments rich in such factors as research and development, specialised technical skills, supplier know-how, and access to key markets. Therefore industry in the core was not abandoned, but rather rationalised and downsized, and the companies' operations distributed according to a matrix of cost factor, knowledge, and strategic considerations. Moreover, cheap and deregulated labour is not only sourced abroad but also drawn into the developed countries. This is stimulated by a combination of increasing poverty in the periphery and an unstated acceptance on the part of core country governments that this human contraband is necessary, both to reduce the strength of organised domestic labour and to provide a readily accessible source of unprotected flexible workers. Consequently, in a US state like California, a labour elite associated with the Silicon Valley high technology industries exists alongside a largely unregulated workforce of which some are illegal immigrants concentrated in agribusiness and other forms of low-level employment. Many traditional and secure American jobs are being exported abroad to cheap labour environments, and often replaced with new ones (Hutton 2007:280–281). However, these tend to be less secure, often with lower wages, and are increasingly located in the service sector, which, unlike manufacturing, lends itself more readily to flexible deregulated employment practices. It is important to understand that it is not so much the geographical distribution of labour that is the problem for workers, but the global restructuring of the relationship between capital and labour.

This process has led to the breakdown of country-centred regimes of accumulation, as domestic circuits of production are being fragmented and integrated into a global network. Consequently, Fordist-style labour organisation and its 'social compromise' are no longer viable, as production now requires (post-Fordist) flexible labour regimes (Cox 1987; Lipietz 1992; Amin 1996; Hoogvelt 1997; Dicken 1998). Labour is no longer treated as (junior) partner in a national-level industrial and political process for deciding the organisation and reproduction of society. It is now considered instead as a factor of production that, like all others, must be utilised in a manner that maximises profits. If the post-war Keynesian consensus produced the Fordist worker, globalisation has resulted in a 'Walmart-isation' of labour, typified by part-time, non-unionised, depoliticised, disempowered and quiescent employees with few benefits, rights, or opportunities to influence the conditions dictated by capital. But as Munck (2002:185) suggests, 'It is an apparent paradox of the era of globalisation that while the labour movement has never been weaker, workers have never been more important to capitalism.'

Seeking to diversify in order to extract benefits on a global scale, this new mode of labour–capital relations forces an integration of national economies and a uniformity not just in conditions of production, as nations deregulate to compete, but also in the civil and political superstructures where social relations of production take shape. As Robinson (1996:16) notes, 'A new "social structure of accumulation" is emerging', one which abandons national contexts and is 'for the first time global'. He continues:

The agent of the global economy is transnational capital, organised institutionally in global corporations, in supranational economic planning agencies and political forums, such as the International Monetary Fund (IMF), the Trilateral Commission and the G7 forum, and managed by a class-conscious transnational elite based in the centers of world capitalism.

In the post-war, pre-globalisation era, states, and especially developed ones, largely contained productive forces within their geographical boundaries, and social classes were obliged to negotiate with each other over 'who gets what' through limited democracy and a general consensus regarding the functional logic of a mixed economy. Once the nation-state began to lose control of finance and production, these ties and mutual responsibilities were broken, allowing ruling elites to shift the process of accumulation into transnational space, diminishing the role of politics and weakening democracy at the national level. This issue will be taken up in subsequent chapters.

Linking the Global and the Local

If, as Robinson suggests, globalisation is producing a new 'social structure of accumulation', then it is important to demonstrate how the local is affected by the global. As we have seen, the TNCs that drive the global economy operate through an infinite range of networks, which on face value are visible organisations spread across the world: a global HQ, transnational production sites, a product image and the distribution of goods in worldwide retail outlets. However, globally distributed production penetrates further than these superficial manifestations indicate, and even the leading brands (Nike, Coca-Cola, Gap, etc.) are deeply integrated into national, regional and local productive and social arenas. The vast multilayered networks of subcontracting, outsourcing and collaboration are shaping the structure of production and social life, and even entering the informal sectors of many countries.

Subcontracting and outsourcing proliferated from the 1970s onwards, first in low-skill labour-intensive industries like textiles, clothes and toys. By the late 1980s, however, 'offshore production' had moved to more high-tech sectors such as semi-conductors, aerospace manufacturing and network computing. This was followed by the worldwide relocation of jobs connected to call centres, graphic design, computer programming, and so on. Decentralised subcontracting is not restricted to manufacturing, but also applies to bureaucratic structures such as government departments and public-sector institutions. Many state agencies, universities and local governments subcontract out services such as food provision, accounting, personnel, payroll, training and security. In the UK, compulsory competitive tendering (CCT) by local governments effected a major shift of functions from the public to the private sector. The US undertook a similar process that even included the privatising and subcontracting out of some aspects of military operations. Private companies like Blackwater are, for example, providing mercenaries for drug control policing in South America, and have virtually taken over external input into security and policing operations in Iraq (Klein 2007). In general, many of the non-direct combat operations in the West's war zones that were previously run by the military are being taken over by private firms (Traynor 2003).

Global production and service chains, or what have been referred to as 'global commodity chains' (Gereffi & Korzeniewicz 1994), are managed by the TNCs which co-ordinate these vast networks, incorporating numerous agents and social groups. This represents the penetration of capital on multiple levels into all parts of the world; it is difficult to separate local circuits of production and distribution from globalised circuits, even when surface appearance gives the impression that local capitalists are retaining their autonomy. The problem is that territorially restricted capital is less able to compete with its transnationally mobile counterpart. As the global circuits subsume local economies, domestic capitalists become incorporated, or are swept aside, by the global orientation of production. Transnational capital drives a shift away from inward development and accumulation around national markets, such as import substitution industrialisation (ISI), towards outward 'development' linked to new products for export and strategies that lead to the deeper integration of domestic economies into the global economy.

After centuries of formation and reformation of the capitalist mode of production, with globalisation all remaining pre-capitalist relations are finally being displaced and absorbed. This fact gives some credence to Fukuyama's sweeping 'End of History' notion.

Transnational Class Formation

While there exist a multitude of studies of material globalisation and its effects on culture and society, there is very little debate on changes in class formation. This is partly due to the dominance of pluralist and structuralist social science perspectives in the analysis of globalisation, which do not recognise class formation as significant or even real. Indeed, Fukuyama has gone so far as to state that 'the class issue has actually been successfully resolved in the West' (1989:9). A further problem with reconstructing a class analysis in a post-Marxist era is that the Left is fragmented and facing internal challenges from such groups as postmodernists, feminists and left-leaning political parties seeking an accommodation with neo-liberal policies, such as New Labour in the UK, who do not see class as a central issue. This tendency to marginalise or abandon class combines with a concept of globalisation based on an inter-state system, which keeps notions of transnational class formation remote from most academic minds.

A few authors such as Goldfrank (1977), Hymer (1979), Van der Pijl (1999), Sklair (1995, 2001), and international political economists of the New Italian School, including Gill and Law (1988), Cox (1987), and Robinson and Harris (2000), have argued that material globalisation has generated its counterpart in the emergence of a supra-national class. This position accords with Marx's approach to the interface between productive processes and political development, which maintains that classes are tied to particular configurations of production relations. A global system of production operating in transnational space therefore gives rise to a concomitant class formation. Among these contemporary theorists, Robinson and Harris (2000) place particular emphasis on the emergence from within national bourgeoisies of a distinct, hegemonic, transnational bourgeois class.

In the nineteenth century, sections of the productive process shifted from regional bases to the creation of joint-stock companies and large corporations, allowing markets to consolidate at the national level. This change in economic activity led to the rise of national capitalist classes. With productive processes now transna-tionalised, Robinson and Harris argue that fractions of these classes have broken away and begun to exercise a new hegemony at the global level, becoming what they call a Transnational Capitalist Class (TCC). As noted earlier, Elliot and Atkinson (2008:4) have observed a similar phenomenon and refer to the 'New Olympians' of business and finance. The American billionaire Warren Buffet, when asked if inequality might lead to possible class warfare stated, 'There's class warfare, all right ... but it's my class, the rich class, that's making war, and we're winning' (Stein 2006). Complementing such observations by academics, journalists and a member of the TCC, an insider from the US political power structure – David Rothkopf (2008), former Deputy Undersecretary of Commerce for

International Trade in the Clinton administration – has recently published a book with the uncompromising title *Superclass: The Global Power Elite and the World They Are Making*. The dust jacket blurb states of this elite:

> Each of them is one in a million. They number six thousand on a planet of six billion. They run our governments, our largest corporations, the powerhouses of international finance, the media, world religions, and, from the shadows, the world's most dangerous criminal and terrorist organizations. They are the global superclass, and they are shaping the history of our time.

In the main text the author writes that 'they see national governments as residues from the past whose only useful function is to facilitate the elite's global operations. Their connections to each other have become more significant than their ties to their home nations and governments'. This development has profound implications for the whole class structure of nation-states, as the historic bloc that was previously contained within state boundaries, and sought to resolve its conflicts and crises principally within those territories, is now being dispersed into global space.

Globalisation and the State

The political organisation of world capitalism has not kept pace with the economic transformations that are taking place under globalisation, and there is a tendency among analysts to see political actors and states as interacting with a series of autonomous global forces over which they have varying levels of control. It is therefore generally accepted that the transnationalisation of economic activity is having some effect on the role of the state, but the nature and extent of this process is one of the most contested topics in the globalisation debate. On the one side, authors like Ohmae (1990), Soros (1998), Cerny (1996) and Guehenno (1996), although approaching the subject from different viewpoints, demonstrate convincingly that where the nation-state meets with the globalisation process, state powers have been substantially modified and restricted. Ohmae, strongly in favour of the expansion of global markets, even suggests that the state is redundant under globalisation and will wither away, and Guehenno talks of 'the twilight of the nation-state'. On the other side, Hirst and Thompson (1996) and Weiss (1998) argue that while the state may be less influential in specific areas under globalisation, this is more to do with shifting roles, functions and priorities, rather than any real loss of power. They also claim that many developments, often believed to be caused by globalisation, do in fact have national origins. Advocates of this view, who see globalisation essentially in quantitative terms, and concentrate on economic trends and statistics giving little attention to social and political factors, suggest that it has been overstated.

It is difficult to generalise about the politics behind different positions on the state and globalisation, but there is a tendency for those with a neo-liberal perspective to see the state as less relevant in the context of globalising market forces; those who still hold Keynesian or leftist views tend to emphasise the continuing importance of state functions. Meanwhile, 'revisionists' like Soros and Stiglitz, while supporting globalisation, also argue that states and transnational agencies must have the discretion to impose controls in order to tame the more ideologically driven and destabilising aspects of neo-liberal policies and practices. Despite the divergence of opinions concerning the relationship between the state and globalisation, they are mostly based on the underlying assumption that the nation-state and the international inter-state system are independent entities that interact with the phenomenon of globalisation, but exist separately from it and behave according to their own logic. This position has been challenged from the discipline of International Political Economy by authors such as Underhill (2001), who argues that states and markets are linked in a mutually dependent 'condominium' and the failure to understand this has led to some theoretically weak reasoning in the globalisation debate. Helleiner (1994) adds to this discourse, showing that fractions within states played a fundamental role in supporting the expansion of globalising forces by facilitating the deregulation of capital markets, and legislating in favour of the interests of private capital.

Robinson (1999) takes the debate further, arguing that the nation-state is neither retaining its primacy nor disappearing, but rather becoming transformed and absorbed into the 'Transnational State' (TNS). This view poses serious questions for international relations theorists, especially those who subscribe to the notion of hegemonic stability. It also causes difficulties for sections of the Left who still see globalisation as being driven by imperialist powers.

Governments are in some ways powerless to resist globalising influences and processes, but just as fractions of capitalist classes once tied to national-level development have broken free to operate transnationally, they have their counterparts among national political, bureaucratic and academic elites who see themselves as adjuncts. As Elliot and Atkinson (2008:4) note, 'Democratically elected governments have, over the past three decades, willingly ceded control of the world economy to a new elite of freebooting, super-rich free-market operatives and their colleagues in national and international institutions.' These authors, making specific reference to the UK, also point to another dimension of the state which accords with Robinson's concept of TNS: 'the new quangocracy: bodies of public sector "heroes" who [can] be relied upon to put New Olympian thinking into practice at the local level' (116). Therefore these 'new [state] functionaries' have the task of dissolving the Keynesian-style welfare state from within, and jettisoning the concept of 'public service'; they act instead as enforcers of the rules of capital, in preparation for its eventual total takeover. The same authors (2008:147–149) note the large increases in UK state spending, especially under the Labour government, which has swelled this ideologically motivated and largely non-productive bureaucracy.

In the 1970s and early 1980s, embryonic transnationalised fractions among national political and intellectual elites in the developed countries set out to take power from embedded national elites and capture policy-making processes. From the mid 1980s to the present, some elites in developing nations have taken the same route. They were supported by their Western counterparts through private development agencies, multilateral organisations like the IMF and World Bank, regional bodies such as NAFTA and the European Union, private non-governmental organisations (NGOs), and a whole network of pro-transnational university departments and academics.

Globalisation and Developing Countries

The effect of globalisation on developing countries is the subject of an extensive debate (Kiely & Marfleet 1998; Leys 1996). As pointed out earlier, in the post-war period the loosely Keynesian Bretton Woods system adopted by the industrial nations was reflected in the developing world by modernisation theory, which accepted a degree of state intervention in the economy. This was put into practice by indigenous semi-Keynesian models of development, which emphasised national-level trade protection and ISI. However, by the 1970s, with worsening terms of trade for raw-material producers, the growing power of MNCs, and a dramatic increase in the price of oil due to the OPEC crisis, such models began to prove unsustainable. One way to confront these problems was to borrow money, not just through traditional multilateral and bilateral arrangements between governments, but also from the private banks in the Eurodollar market. These banks were awash with petro-dollars and aggressively sought to lend to national governments, in the belief that countries, unlike individuals or firms, presented little risk to creditors. The developing countries for their part hoped that with such loans they could pursue debt-led growth, which would eventually result in reduced import dependency. This scenario encouraged irresponsible lending and borrowing, based on a far too sanguine view of countries' capacity to channel these loans into viable development programmes. Indeed, capital became so freely available that even Cuba was able to secure private dollar loans during this period (Hennessy & Lambie 1993:299–301). Between 1973 and 1979, the flow of capital from commercial banks to developing countries grew from $100 billion to $600 billion (Singh 1998:10).

Access to cheap and available credit ceased in the late 1970s, towards the end of the Carter administration in the US. At that time there was a national 'crisis of confidence' in America, generated by recession, an energy crisis, inflation, and the Iran hostage fiasco. These problems seemed to confirm the view that the long post-war boom in the US had come to an end; the malaise that was also felt by many in the wider world. One consequence was that foreign governments began to dispose of their US Treasury holdings, thereby putting downward pressure on the dollar. President Carter responded by appointing Paul Volker, a 'hard money man' closely linked to the Wall Street banks and particularly Rockefeller interests such as Chase Manhattan Bank, to the post of Chairman of the Federal Reserve. His brief was to save the dollar. Volker's 'shock therapy' included dramatically raising interest rates in October 1979, precipitating an even deeper recession that hit American workers hard but restored confidence in the dollar. Volker's move was preceded by similar increases in the UK, which boosted rates on the Eurodollar market from an average of 7 per cent in 1978 to almost 20 per cent by 1980. Third World nations, which had taken out dollar loans from the major international banks at variable rates, suddenly faced increasing interest commitments to the private Western lenders. This was particularly true of Latin American countries, which had contracted the largest proportion of loans, of which 70 per cent were at floating interest rates. Dollar interest rates rose even further during the Reagan administration, when the US sought capital from the international market to fund its growing national deficit, which expanded from $9 billion in 1981 to $207 billion in 1983 due to a combination of increased military expenditure and neo-liberal tax cuts (Helleiner 1994:147).

Increasingly burdensome repayments to the banks, combined with falling export commodity prices and expensive oil imports, led to a series of defaults by developing countries which threatened the world banking system. In this state of crisis, the multilateral agencies such as the World Bank and the IMF did not hesitate to support the creditor banks in the developed economies, and, with support from Western governments, helped to avert catastrophe and re-establish confidence in the international financial system. Once the immediate problem had been contained, these agencies, in their new role as debt collectors, set out to restructure the debtor economies to raise more hard currency for the repayment of the creditor banks. This was achieved through IMF-imposed Stabilisation and Structural Adjustment Programmes (SAPs), based on the implementation of hard-line free-market principles, including the selling of state assets to private investors and the dismantling of state-supported welfare programmes. These internal reforms were complemented by currency devaluations and changes in external trade policy to emphasise exports over imports, thereby generating the funds to pay off debts. Between 1978 and 1992, around 70 countries undertook 566 SAPs (George 1992:xvi). Through the SAPs, more liquid assets were pumped into the circuits of private international finance as debtor nations became net exporters of capital. Most importantly, these programmes served as draconian mechanisms for restructuring the productive, social and state sectors of these countries. By this process, structuralist and developmentalist approaches to state intervention, which had afforded a degree of protection against foreign penetration, were dismantled, allowing for the integration of a large portion of the world into the global market on terms set by transnational capital.

While MNCs were expanding their activities in developing countries in the 1970s, at the same time as OPEC dollars were flooding into the Eurodollar market, their demand for this sort of unrestricted capital was still limited because most of the Third World continued to be protected by tariffs and state financial controls. It was only after the implementation of SAPs in the 1980s and 1990s that these economies were opened up to make them more attractive to TNCs. This is reflected in the massive increases in FDI to developing countries from the mid 1980s onwards. One of the main arguments of the supporters of globalisation is that FDI, which is mainly generated by TNCs, brings employment to developing countries. On face value this might be true, but one has also to consider that it is often the restructuring demanded by SAPs that caused the unemployment in the first place. Moreover, while some of these new jobs may be better paid than previous forms of employment, they are often less secure, highly exploitative and detached from local circuits of subsistence. TNC production, despite relying heavily on labour from developing countries does not directly create levels of employment proportionate to their economic influence. In 2000 it was calculated that while the sales of the 'Top 200' corporations are the equivalent of 27.5 per cent of world economic activity, they employ only 0.78 per cent of the world's workforce. Furthermore, from 1983 to 1999, while the profits of these same firms grew 362.4 per cent, the number of people they employ expanded by only 14.4 per cent (Anderson & Cavanagh 2000).

Although there remains a continuation of unequal centre–periphery relations, globalisation, as we have seen, is not so much about imperialism but transnationalisation. Therefore, while at a superficial level the developing world has been subjected to shocks generated in the First World, the restructuring of the political economy has produced opportunities for local elites in all countries. At the highest levels of this process in Latin America, for example, the privatisation of Mexican telecommunications helped make the entrepreneur Carlos Slim one of the richest men in the world, with an estimated wealth of $59 billion (Mehta 2007). A few Mexican corporations, such as Cemex and Telmex, have also joined the top 100 global corporations. The Ecuadorian billionaire Alvaro Noboa owns over 120 enterprises, most of which are in Latin America, but also extend into Europe, North America, Japan and other countries. Beneath these uppermost echelons are numerous entrepreneurs who have benefited from the global restructuring of their local economies through privatisations and the entry of transnational producers requiring local resources such as land, labour and even capital.

At the other end of the social spectrum are the poor, the workers, and the lower middle classes in developing countries whose lives are being transformed by globalisation. In Latin America, for instance, the peasantry, although never numerous nor politically strong in the region as a whole, is disappearing, as it is drawn into global production chains or the informal sector through expropriation and deregulation. Formalised and regulated labour is also declining in numbers, as are the middle classes that rose during the Keynesian/ structuralist period. Former members of these groups are now moving into new roles and modes of survival. First, many have been absorbed into globally integrated activities such as agribusiness (particularly non-traditional agricultural exports, or NTAE), *maquiladora* factories, and the growing service sector, especially tourism. Second, large numbers have migrated to the US and other countries, where they often become part of a readily exploitable, unprotected labour force vulnerable to the whims of capital. Third, others have drifted into the informal sector where they still remain linked to the global economy through subcontracting and outsourcing. All these changes in labour patterns feed into flexible accumulation networks, in which capital can take advantage of the diminished power of workers to enforce a commodification of their lives.

A Global Corporate Culture and the End of Politics

The global empowerment of private finance and the transnational control of production by the giant corporations have had profound political and social consequences. In the context of a general analysis of globalisation, and consistent with earlier comments about the formation of a Transnational Capitalist Class and the emergence of a Transnational State, it is clear that global capitalism has a mind, as well as a body. As one author (Roelofs 1992:209) has pointed out, elites work continuously 'to promulgate the relevant myths, including most importantly the myth of their own and their office's importance'. In the pre-globalisation period the nation was the guiding 'myth' of business and political elites within their respective geographical territories. Globalisation has led to the formation of new 'myths': 'the global market'; 'the global village'; a global culture that transcends nationality, race, and gender and which is essentially politically neutral. All of this is presumed to be driven by individual lifestyle choices, catered to by an infinite array of consumer goods. Underlying this is what Strange (1990) has called the 'global business civilisation'. In this new 'neutral' world driven by markets and their interaction with individuals, politics has become a casualty. Not only has the Left's aim to 'socialize the state and politicize society' (Croteau 1995) been undermined and rendered irrelevant and utopian, but even the more modest social democratic objective of seeking citizen support (usually for pre-determined elitist projects), through consultation and democracy, has become redundant.

Mainstream politics today is, in fact, apolitical, reduced to a largely meaningless series of contests between parties that are all highly compromised by their ties to corporate power. Party manifestoes (often written according to agendas set by business and by market surveys of public opinion), and personality-driven debates and clashes, are the main substance of the contemporary political 'game'. These in turn are carefully presented in a form designed to guide voter (consumer) choice, as if they were marketable products.

Under globalisation it seems that the rational ordering of social priorities has been lost in a cacophony of media manipulation and political spin. In general, important social issues are conveniently sidetracked in favour of a popular diet of media-fed 'controversies', often based around the personal lives of the rich and famous, and sensational stories about ordinary individuals that aim to have a wide appeal. When real issues are taken up, such as problems related to health care, education or the environment, these are dealt with in isolation. They are presented as single manageable concerns, without reference to the wider system and the largely unrestrained financial and corporate power which determines their outcome. A tentative departure from this process was seen in the 2008 US election, in which the objective condition of recession produced a subjective reaction from citizens who were beginning to insist on policies that might address their needs. This brought President Barack Obama to office because he claimed to represent such interests. In the first 18 months he faced major political opposition to even modest health care reforms, and it remains to be seen if he will have the determination, and the power, to bring about the substantial structural and ideological changes that will be necessary in order to meet growing public demands.

This manipulation and obfuscation of political power and its consequences for the public sector has been called by Boggs (2000:9) the 'corporate colonization' of the public sphere. He goes on to state, 'Corporate networks dominate the state apparatus, own and control the mass media, profoundly shape education and medicine, and penetrate into even the most intimate realms of social life (e.g., the family, sexuality)' (ibid.:69). Speaking specifically of politics, it has been suggested (Greider 1993:336) that 'corporate politics has become the organizational core of the political process – the main connective tissue linking people to their government'.

At a global level, corporations are the guiding force behind the emerging Transnational State. They have considerable influence over such organisations as the World Bank, the IMF and especially the WTO; bodies that operate largely outside of any recognisable democratic control. A clear example of corporate influence on the

WTO is the issue over Trade-Related Intellectual Property Rights (TRIPS), which corporations use to restrict poor countries' access to low-cost generic versions of patented medicines. Additionally, under TRIPS, farmers must pay annual fees to use seeds that have been patented by corporations, which can be highly detrimental to small and subsistence producers who simply cannot afford such costs (Engdahl 2007).

A further instrument of global corporate power is the General Agreement on Trade in Services (GATS). This includes legislation designed to open up the service sector, much of which is currently held in public ownership, for private profit. The process is already well underway in Britain's health service (Pollack & Price 2006). The Confederation of University Faculty Associations of British Columbia (Clift 1999) petitioned the Canadian government to reject GATS in post-secondary education, stating, 'if GATS were applied to the Canadian education sector, the effects would be profound. Education would no longer be considered a public service; instead it would be categorized as merely another commercial enterprise.' Corporations also have disproportionate influence over regional bodies like the European Union (Balanya et al. 2000).

It seems remarkable, given the immense power of the global corporations and their commitment to unrestrained market liberalisation at any cost, that they are nearly invisible to the general public as agents of control and change. But the reason for this obfuscation becomes clear if one analyses the information generated by the corporate media (Time Warner, Bertelsmann, Viacom, Disney/ABC, Rupert Murdoch's News Corporation, etc.), who decide what the masses should know and not know (Schiller 1996). Only rarely do accessible critical studies of corporate power emerge, of which notable examples are Korton's *When Corporations Rule the World* (1995) and Perkins's *Confessions of an Economic Hit Man* (2005). Interestingly, both these writers worked at high levels in the US corporate and government structures. Another book by Bakan, *The Corporation: The Pathological Pursuit of Profit and Power* (2004), has been made into a successful documentary film. However, such efforts to expose corporate power are no match for the global media, and corporate hegemony in general, and remain isolated voices.

It is not surprising that, in this world of 'suffocating consensus' (Borosage 2000), politics has largely atrophied. In its place there is a corporate-designed mythology that promotes markets, limitless consumption, individualism, and identity with products, in which politics, society, culture and life itself are simply component parts.

Key to fostering this myth is that the hand of the instigators is felt, but not seen. At this juncture in world history, they have reduced the human experience to a product with a price; we have forgotten the past and allowed the imposition of their arrogance on our present and foreseeable future.

The Human Consequences of Globalisation

Besides engaging in the theoretical debate about the nature of globalisation, it is also important to examine its consequences for ordinary people. Again this issue is highly contested, but the main body of opinion seems to accept that globalisation has so far resulted in growing inequality. The case that it has also increased poverty finds less agreement, although the two issues are often taken together. One of the main sources of official information on world poverty is the World Bank's 'World Development Reports', which on close scrutiny provide some rather contradictory information; at times they claim a reduction in world poverty, then indicate that there has been an increase. Its methods of measuring poverty have also been questioned (Reddy and Pogge 2005). The United Nations Development Programme (UNDP) Human Development Reports, published since the mid 1980s, have indicated that there has been a growing disparity in wealth, both on a global scale and within individual countries. The 2000 report, for example, claimed that between 1970 and 1998 the richest 20 per cent of the world's population increased their share of income from 70 to 85 per cent, while the share of the poorest 20 per cent has declined from 2.3 per cent to 1.4 per cent. Out of a total of approximately 6.5 billion human beings, 830 million are reportedly chronically undernourished, 1.1 billion lack access to safe water, and 2.6 billion do not have basic sanitation (UNDP 2006). Nearly half the world, approximately three billion people, live on less than two dollars a day (Ramonet 1998). In contrast, the total wealth of the world's three richest individuals is greater than the combined gross domestic product (GDP) of the 48 poorest countries.

Increasing inequality is found not only in developing countries, but also in the industrialised world (Toynbee 2003; Wilkinson 2005; Hutton 2007). Between 1973 and 1990, real wages in the US fell for 80 per cent of the population and rose for 20 per cent. An estimated 34.2 per cent of Americans are categorised as poor to very poor, while the top 10 per cent own 83.2 per cent of all assets (UNDP 1998). The US is the most unequal of the industrial powers and the problem is getting worse, even before the onset of the current recession, with skewed income distribution returning to levels not seen since the turn of the late nineteenth and early twentieth centuries (Piketty & Saez 2006). But this depressing situation may be even worse than the numbers suggest because, as Williams (2008) has shown in his 'Shadow Government Statistics' research programme, 'official' figures for such areas as unemployment are far too optimistic, suggesting that they have been massaged by the authorities. The same could be said of 'official' UK statistics, and probably those produced by most of the Western powers.

Nevertheless, some analysts still argue that global inequality is a myth. Using Gini coefficients (the proportion of income earned by the top 10 per cent divided by that of the bottom 10 per cent) of worldwide income distribution, Wolf (2000:25) claims that there was a 'modest' reduction in global inequality, as a result of economic growth, over the preceding two decades. Even if such figures do indicate some positive developments on a global scale, increasing inequality in major powers like the US and now China, along with an unfolding global recession, suggest that any improvements may soon be reversed.

An important contribution to the debate on levels of poverty and inequality under globalisation, especially in developing countries, is the International Comparison Programme, first carried out by the World Bank and a number of other organisations in 2005, and updated yearly. This exercise undertook the enormous and complex task of gathering data from 146 economies on the prices of goods and services, permitting a more accurate assessment of the actual Purchasing Power Parities (PPP) in each country. Previous poverty calculations were based on the crude measure of GDP per capita at prevailing currency exchange rates, but once these levels are PPP-adjusted to reflect real prices, a different and more precise image is revealed. As one analyst (Milanovic 2008:3) states, commenting on the release of the December 2007 PPP calculations which are the most comprehensive to date, 'implications for the estimates of global inequality and poverty are enormous. The new numbers show global inequality to be significantly greater than even the most pessimistic authors had thought.'

It may be argued that poverty is a historically variable concept and that the poor today are, at least in material terms, not as poor as those who fell into the same category 50 years ago, and certainly cannot be compared to the poor of 100 years ago. But any gains in material wealth have seemingly only been achieved at a cost to human wellbeing and life chances. Being poor, especially in developed nations, increasingly means lack of opportunity, reduced mobility, limited access to social services, deteriorating working conditions, short-term and insecure employment, along with increasing violence and exposure to drugs, crime and social breakdown. On a wider scale, the erosion of community, a growing sense of powerlessness to influence political processes, and no democratic accountability for leaders all results in apathy and increasing alienation. Most of modern society exists within an atomised world dominated by materialism, pointless consumption, and narcissistic individualism. For the rich, money can buy a certain material freedom, although they are increasingly confined to a world of 'gated communities' (both physically and figuratively) which restricts their human potential. But the poor find themselves in a downward spiral that erodes their humanity and offends human dignity. In this sense, today's poor are perhaps the most destitute and dehumanised people any world system has ever created, except in periods of mass institutional exploitation such as slavery.

We should not romanticise the past because life for many was short and brutish, but one feels that modernity and 'development' could have married some of the positive elements of the past with new possibilities, to satisfy material and social needs with advanced technologies and scientific knowledge. The rise in material and social inequality and the decline in the quality of life are, for many, the key problems of globalised modernity. It is also totally unacceptable, and, more importantly, probably unsustainable, that 'the gap between the poorest fifth of the world's people and the richest fifth has increased from 30:1 in 1906 to 78:1 in 1994' (UNICEF 1997), especially since this trend has accelerated in the globalisation era and particularly in the new millenium. The 2008 United Nations University World Institute for Development Economics Research (WIDER) report argues that half of all global assets belong to the richest 2 per cent of the world's population, with two fifths owned by the top 1 per cent. In contrast, the poorest half hold only 1 per cent of total global wealth. It is claimed (Freeman 2010) that in the US, between 1993 and 2007, half of all economic growth went to the richest 1 per cent; and from 2002 to 2006, three quarters of all the economy's growth was captured by that top percentile. As the global recession deepens, and the populations of debtor nations are forced to pay for the failings of the international banking system, these trends are set to intensify.

The Economic Performance of Globalisation

Most advocates of globalisation accept that, as the world adopts integrationist market principles and deregulation, there are winners and losers. But they argue that economic growth, the ostensible rationale for globalisation, will eventually reduce the number of losers. Analysts like Barnevik (2001) and Wolf (2004) therefore believe that poor countries are not 'victims of globalisation', but are rather 'victims of their refusal to globalise'. Following this logic, globalisation is, in fact, the answer to resolving the inequality problem, and countries should accept the inevitability of a global market and seek to adapt to the new environment. World leaders including former US President George W. Bush and former British Prime Minister Tony Blair were outspoken advocates of this view, as are the heads of development agencies such as the World Bank and national-level aid donors like the UK's Department for International Development. At the 2000 World Economic Forum in Davos, former US President Clinton stated, 'I think we have to reconfirm unambiguously that open markets and rules-based trade are the best engines we know of to lift living standards, reduce environmental destruction and build shared prosperity' (Wolf 2000:25). It is perhaps unsurprising that the globalisers of 'New Labour' in the UK, including Tony Blair, subscribe enthusiastically to such views. But what is surprising is that even what remains of the oppositional Left does not question the economic performance of globalisation, and, with a few exceptions such as Chossudovsky (1998), are reluctant to suggest that the whole global enterprise may be flawed and might never achieve acceptable levels of equality and sustainability. It seems that the visible and material impact of globalisation – new technologies, global communications, the collapse of Soviet-style Communism, massive capital movements, powerful corporate imagery, changing lifestyles and patterns of consumption, and the vertiginous pace of change – has lulled many critics of globalisation into sharing the Right's view of inevitability. In the myth the globalisers have created, they are the masters of economic performance, and all non-market driven options are inefficient and anachronistic by comparison.

However, economic performance is precisely where globalisation is most vulnerable to cricitism, even before the current financial crisis. In a report produced by the Washington-based Center for Economic and Policy Research (CEPR) entitled 'The Emperor Has No Growth: Declining Economic Growth Rates in the Era of

Globalisation' (Weisbrot et al. 2001), a number of simple, widely accepted statistics for measuring growth, including GDP per capita, are drawn upon to prove that the performance of the past 20 years of globalisation and market liberalisation has not matched the rhetoric of its advocates, especially when compared to the preceding 20 years of mixed economy. The authors claim that 'from 1960–1980, output per person grew by an average, among all countries, of 83%. For 1980–2000, the average growth of output per person was 33%'.

> [I]n eighty-nine countries 77% – or more than three-fourths – saw their per capita rate of growth fall by at least five percentage points from the period 1960–1980 to the period 1980–2000 ... In Latin America, GDP per capita grew by 75% from 1960–1980, whereas from 1980–2000 it has only risen 6% ... In the United States, the median real wage is about the same today as it was 27 years ago ... that is drastically different from the previous 27 years, during which the typical wage increased by about 80% in real terms.

This section of the report concludes that 'economic growth has slowed dramatically' during the period of globalisation. Such arguments are echoed and theorised in substantial academic works such as Brenner's *The Economics of Global Turbulence* (2009).

The CEPR report further argues that IMF and World Bank policies in support of globalisation have failed to bring development and growth, yet those institutions are reluctant to question the efficacy of the 'fundamentals' that they have promoted. These 'inappropriate economic policies [have] sharply slowed growth in the less developed countries and interrupted it in East Asia [but] their effect on the transition economies of the former Soviet Union and Eastern Europe has been even more drastic'.

The report reaches a conclusion that is of great value for those who seek to challenge the dominant order: 'Globalisation is no more natural or inevitable than the construction of skyscrapers', and 'it should be understood as a conscious political choice'. One might ask, has this political choice been made in error? Or are the champions of globalisation not really concerned about general economic performance, but rather a redistribution of wealth and power to serve their own class, a goal at odds with the interests and wellbeing of the majority of humanity?

Besides growing inequality, ordinary people are increasingly compromised by a global system that functions through the promotion of 'commodity fetishism'. The demand for an infinite number of goods, stimulated by brand loyalties, advertising, fads, fashion, and occasionally necessity, is only sustained on a mountain of debt created by private banks that are not subject to adequate controls on the issue of credit. This precipitated a surge in property values, which in turn encouraged people to remortgage or take home equity loans and accrue even more debt. As we have seen, at the same time many manufacturing jobs in the industrialised world are being exported abroad to low-wage areas, and remaining industry is often highly mechanised or computerised and requires fewer workers. These rationalised jobs are also generally less secure and have weakened terms of employment. Many developed countries, especially the US and Britain, consequently rely more on service industries, which in turn have been driven by the debt-fuelled consumer boom. Economists have seriously questioned the viability of this model of growth (Elliot & Atkinson 2007). Earning power and productive capacity have ceased to correlate with the level of debt that has been generated, and the latter is spinning out of control. There is also no savings cushion to fall back on as a result of static or declining wages and salaries, and the normalisation in the public mind of increasing debt. The consequences of this problem are now apparent in the current financial crisis and looming worldwide recession (Lambie 2009a).

The nature and problems of globalisation make the possibility of single-nation approaches to development less likely, even in a case like China, which some analysts see as the new great power of the twenty-first century. Such a perspective may be misguided, as it appears that in China, as well as other emerging economic giants such as India and Brazil, groups of domestic elites, in collaboration with their international counterparts, have embraced the transnational agenda, mainly for their own benefit. Among their advantages are vast cheap supplies of labour, and access to political power through which to promote their ambitions. The World Bank and the IMF claim that poverty has been reduced in China because of global integration. But most of this improvement took place in the 1970s due to land reforms and before opening up to the global economy (Bardhan 2005). Indeed, recent poverty calculations based on the World Bank's Parity Purchasing Power criteria would suggest that the majority of Chinese are not enjoying an increase in living standards (Milanovic 2008:1). This can be attributed in part to the loss of millions of jobs as state industry and services are dismantled, while less than 20 per cent of the workforce is being absorbed into construction, mining and the new export industries. In general, urban growth is being prioritised at the expense of rural agriculture, which has been neglected, again leading to skewed income distribution and growing inequality (Wan 2008). This is intensifying the divide between city and countryside and weakening the possibility of replacing export dependency with internal demand, as tens of millions are marginalised. A further problem is China's dependency on Western markets, and especially the US, to which it exports a large proportion of its consumer goods, resulting in vast dollar reserves which it relies on to pay for imports and keep down the value of its own currency. If this fragile arrangement were to end, Chinese exports, already based on narrow margins, would become less competitive. This compromise is now an even greater liability as the US begins generating huge external dollar debts to underwrite its internal crisis. Structural problems in the world economy make the Chinese elite's vision of global capitalist integration over-optimistic (Hutton 2007). In 2009 China's inflation was running at 8.5 per cent, while growth had fallen to 6.5 per cent (from nearly 10 per cent). This could precipitate further social discontent with a model that favours the few and excludes the many.

India, often pointed to by mainstream analysts as another emerging economic superpower, was recording an annual growth rate of 9 per cent by 2006, but behind such superficial 'success' lie some disturbing truths. It has been suggested that this stunning growth is only benefiting 10 per cent of the population, while 350 million people still live in poverty with an income of less than a dollar a day (Hilary 2008). Another 900 million eke out a living on under two dollars a day. One million mothers and children die every year because of poverty and limited access to health care (ibid.); 'a quarter of all maternal and neonatal deaths globally occur in India' (cited in Crisp 2007:35). According to the UNDP (2008), there are 1 billion malnourished people on the planet and 40 per cent of these live in India. The sub-continent's child malnutrition figures are worse than Sub-Saharan Africa, and it is home to half the underfed children in the world. In contrast, the Indian IT 'miracle' which we hear so much about in the media involves at most 1 million workers, or 0.25 of 1 per cent of the country's workforce (Bardhan 2005:2). It would appear that inequality is the star performer in India, as, according to the Merill Lynch World Wealth Report (2007), the country now has 93,000 millionaires and one of the fastest-growing numbers of 'net worth individuals'. While the mass of Indians still exist in rural poverty and shanty towns, often with inadequate water, food and services, a few enjoy a Western lifestyle. But this is an increasingly isolated existence, detached from the real economy and only sustainable by living in gated communities (Sengupta 2008). The Indian journalist and novelist Aravind Adiga recently won the Man Booker Prize for his novel *The White Tiger* (2008), which goes beyond the gloss that dominates Western perceptions of India and raises many of the above issues.

In the former Communist countries, integration into the capitalist world in the era of globalisation has produced variable results. The former Soviet Union has been subject to asset stripping of the erstwhile Communist state and the rise of mafia-style elites (oligarchs). Stiglitz (2002) describes vividly how the Soviet state was dismantled and its assets distributed to the private sector, causing massive damage to the economy because of lack of controls. Under then-President Putin the Russian state regained a degree of control, and began implementing minimal social programmes and curbing the worst excesses of private enterprise. According to a 2006 survey (Eberstadt 2008), despite improvements in some areas,

> overall life expectancy in Russia, at fewer than 67 years, was actually lower than it had been at the end of the 1950s, nearly half a century earlier. For a literate, urbanized society during peacetime, such a monumental public health failure is an extraordinary historical anomaly. Russian life expectancy nowadays is about the same as India's, and life expectancy for Russian men, today barely over 60 years, is lower than for their counterparts in Pakistan.

In sharp contrast, overall life expectancy in Cuba rose from 74 years in 1990 to 78 in 2006, despite 16 years of very difficult economic circumstances (UNICEF 2008). However, for a few Russians things have improved, and *Forbes* magazine (Klebnikov 2004) has calculated that, measured against the economic output of the country ($458 billion), there are more billionaires in Russia (36) than in any other nation in the world. The total assets of these 36 richest 'oligarchs' amount to $110 billion – 24 per cent of the country's economic output.

One of the most successful former Communist countries is Poland, which according to the World Bank (2005a) increased its GDP per capita by 50 per cent from the mid 1990s to 2005. However, the same source also reveals that unemployment (at 28 per cent) and poverty have been growing in recent years. The Bank nevertheless continues to call for more freeing up of the market to help reduce poverty. Today, as crisis hits these 'transition' economies, the economic and political models on which they are based are beginning to show their true weaknesses. Even *The Economist* (2008b), which has vigorously supported neo-liberal prescriptions in the former Communist countries, now comments:

> At best, the region is in for more nasty shocks that will need external support from lenders such as the IMF. At worst, some countries face debt restructuring, currency collapse and depression; that raises the spectre of political upheaval, too.

Although statistics can be used selectively to demonstrate different perspectives (under which lie ideologies), to reveal what is happening in the former Communist countries, China, India, and indeed the developing world in general, one must understand their functional and social integration into a global economy as analysed in this chapter. 'Progress' in this context is not so much about development in the conventional sense, but rather the reordering of economics, politics and social relations along market lines. This is presented as an immutable order, and only its implementation and functioning are open to discussion. Even if this system could be successfully established in these countries, one should not be surprised if such 'success' includes increasing poverty and inequality, growing unemployment and crime, the commodification of social life, and the integration of national elites with transnational capitalist interests.

Having presented an interpretation of globalisation, it must be repeated that this is a highly disputed subject, one which is understood in different ways and through different ideological perspectives. Although the author believes that the explanation in this chapter, based on International Political Economy and aspects of Marxism, provides useful insights and sets a context for the rest of the book, it is important to realise that there is no one 'correct' interpretation of globalisation. Moreover, the contested space and ideologies that it generates are parts of the battle for the way the future will unfold. These disparate views, all drawing on different sources for statistics, performance evaluation, developmental perspectives, and even perceptions of human nature, are intellectual forces that coincide with and influence the really-lived experience of globalisation by different communities and classes. Comfortable professional families in the developed world may see globalisation as a positive process and not seek to question its function, except maybe to raise concerns about environmental issues or consumer problems. The poor in such countries are probably too absorbed into a corporate consumer culture and sanitised media to understand the process that is shaping their lives, and therefore tend not to question it specifically. But both these groups may begin to see globalisation as an elite project rather than a given as structural crises deepen, which will in turn encourage them to seek explanations and solutions.

As we have seen, the standard of living of ordinary people is being eroded. One US analyst (Hacker 2006) claims, based on his view that there are two key pillars of economic security for working people, namely the family and the workplace, that since the 1970s corporations and politicians have weakened the underpinning of both. Income security, health care, retirement pensions, and many other factors have become increasingly unstable and unreliable, leaving working people more vulnerable than they have been since the interwar years. Another American study (Warren 2006), focusing on the middle classes, suggests that increases in basic expenses, including health care, education and the cost of credit, have reduced the discretionary income of the average family from almost 50 per cent of total earnings in the early 1970s to less than 30 per cent in the early years of the new millennium. Recession will exacerbate all these problems, and in the West we face a 10–20 year fall-back in living standards, if we are lucky. To resume real economic growth in most developed countries, it will be necessary to pay back decades of accumulated debt at the national and personal levels. The most significant reversal in the current unfolding recession will be the impoverishment of the middle classes, as the veneer of their prosperity melts away. Well-paid professional jobs, many in the service sector; ownership of finance-related products such as shares which have increased in value; asset inflation, especially in housing; limitless consumer choice and readily available credit; all these have fostered the illusion that the middle classes are partners in the transnational elite's global project. This myth will be shattered as their advantages are eroded and their true class position is revealed. In its Global Strategic Trends Programme 2007–2036, the Development Concepts and Doctrine Centre (DCDC) of the British Ministry of Defence (2007:81) stated:

> The middle classes could become a revolutionary class, taking the role envisaged for the proletariat by Marx. The globalization of labour markets and reducing levels of national welfare provision

and employment could reduce peoples' attachment to particular states. The growing gap between themselves and a small number of highly visible super-rich individuals might fuel disillusion with meritocracy, while the growing urban under-classes are likely to pose an increasing threat to social order and stability, as the burden of acquired debt and the failure of pension provision begins to bite. Faced by these twin challenges, the world's middle classes might unite, using access to knowledge, resources and skills to shape transnational processes in their own class interest.

In the developing world, elites and sections of the middle class have also benefited materially from globalisation, but the majority of the population in most of these countries has not, and their lives are being disrupted and changed, often for the worse. At present the most concerted resistance to the effects of globalisation is forming mainly in sections of the disenchanted poor and middle classes in such countries, particularly in Latin America. It is here where practice, experience and theory are finding the greatest synthesis. In this growing counter-hegemony, the 'battle for ideas' is as important as, and complementary to, the fight for basic necessities and rights. Elliot and Atkinson (2008) encapsulate this immensely important realisation when they state, 'We believe that the days of the New Olympians are drawing to a close [because] ... people simply stop[ped] believing in them'.

SUMMARY AND THE CUBAN CONTEXT

To explain globalisation in the second half of the twentieth century and early twenty-first century is, above all, to give a history of the empowerment of transnational capital and its effects on the organisation of production, and on political and social life; this process is inextricably linked with the ascendance of a self-conscious transnational elite, whose class interests are closely tied to the transnationalisation of market forces. But because globalisation is a process, and not an event, its class formations and reformations are still in flux, as are the new combinations of social forces that it engenders. The future of globalisation will not be shaped by market perfectibility, but through the interplay and conflict of these emergent social forces. Ultimately, any change that takes place can only fully manifest itself as a conscious response from the victims of globalisation: the majority of the world's population. This is the least predictable of the variables, but the one on which the future of humanity depends. What is happening in Latin America today may be the embryo of that process, and might provide the Cuban Revolution with new opportunities not only to export its ideology and practices, but to secure its own survival and continuity.

The Cuban Insurrection of 1959 took place at a time when the Bretton Woods system was still functioning. Governments in all developed countries had state-led policies which sought to manage mixed economies with the objectives of achieving growth and full employment. In their relations with less-developed countries (LDCs), they continued to maintain a highly unequal system of trade regulation that favoured themselves, and they were willing to engage in interventionist political strategies to support or undermine foreign governments according to their own needs and regional interests. Nevertheless, reflecting the Bretton Woods ideology, a large and sophisticated debate emerged after the Second World War concerning the issue of economic development. Although this was fought out within a largely Right–Left political framework, there was a general consensus that state-led modernisation was necessary. This line of thinking even prevailed in a major multilateral agency like the World Bank, which would only offer loans to countries that could produce an acceptable national development strategy. Other sources of development funding came principally as bilateral loans or aid, which was essentially government-to-government. Private capital played only a minor role in this field before the 1970s. But, as explained above, the Eurodollar market was swelled with OPEC funds early in that decade when the price of oil increased, resulting in an explosion of private lending to sovereign nations.

In the pre-1970s environment, Cuba was able to present itself as a radical alternative in the development debate. It had shown through its own experience that the belief in modernisation theory that prevailed from the end of the Second World War until 1959, and which assumed that LDCs would go through stages of economic growth mirroring the experiences of industrialised countries, was deeply flawed. A combination of dependency on the production of primary goods, the lack of a diversified export base, an unfair international trading system, pre-capitalist class relations and roles, and foreign manipulation had all combined to make Cuba a highly unequal society, satisfying few of the criteria for successful development.

Breaking free from this condition with the support of the Soviet Bloc allowed Cuba to embark on an alternative strategy, one which promoted a synchronisation of economic and social development and emphasised equality. By taking this course, Cuba ran against the grain of mainstream prescriptions: it advocated and supported revolutions; it allied with Soviet socialism; it promoted social progress equally with economic progress; and it gave lip service to radical ideas like Dependency Theory. Its aim, which it partly achieved, was to shift the whole development debate from an East–West axis, based on competition between the superpowers, to a North–South struggle between the industrialised nations and the Third World. As noted in the Introduction, radical development economists and sympathetic Cubanologists were eager to show how, by following an alternative path, Cuba had not only achieved better results than its neighbours in Latin America and the Caribbean, but even equalled the star performers of Southeast Asia (Zimbalist & Brundenius 1989). But the rise of free-market economics and neo-liberal politicians, and the collapse of the Soviet Bloc, put an end to Cuba's stance as an alternative and reduced it to a remnant of two failed systems: Soviet-style socialism, and radical developmentalism in the context of a semi-Keynesian capitalist world order.

With the rise of globalisation, Cuba's international role in the context of the Cold War has evaporated, and its continuing tenacity to hang onto socialism in the face of unrelenting pressures from neo-liberalism has left the island isolated; it is seemingly living out an anachronism that will end only with the passing of the Castro brothers and the remaining revolutionary leaders who share their ideals. But, as the world focuses on the Cuban Revolution, predicting its inevitable demise in the face of an all-powerful system of neo-liberal globalisation, Cuba looks to what it sees as a failing New World Order. It is a system that does not address the problems of human need, subsistence and dignity on which its own success and continued existence is founded. To the Cuban leadership, the logic of global capitalism is flawed, and as Fidel Castro (2007:397–400 passim) comments:

> The Third World is being required to pay a debt of $2.5 trillion, which is utterly unpayable under the present conditions. And yet $1 trillion is being spent every year on increasingly more sophisticated and lethal weapons. Why and for what? ... A similar amount is being spent on commercial advertising, which produces in billions of people an urge to consume that is impossible to satisfy. Why and for what? ... consumer society is one of the most frightening, terrifying inventions of developed capitalism today in this phase of neo-liberal globalization ... I try to imagine

1.3 billion Chinese with the per capita number of cars that the United States has ... I can't imagine India, with its more than a billion inhabitants, living in a consumer society; I can't imagine the 600 million people who live in sub-Saharan Africa, who don't even have electricity and in some places more than 80 per cent of whom don't know how to read and write, in a consumer society ... Our species, for the first time, is in real danger of extinction – self extinction, due to the madness of human beings themselves, who are the victims of this so-called 'civilization' ... From my point of view, no task is more urgent than creating universal awareness, taking the problem to the masses, to the billions of men and women of every age, including children, who inhabit the planet. The objective conditions, the suffering of the immense majority of those people create the subjective conditions for the task of awareness building ... the battle of ideas is what we are doing.

Castro's argument, with its focus on the developing world, has even greater relevance if one considers that the global financial crisis is draining resources – investment, capital, trade, etc. – from the periphery, as international investors and businesses seek sanctuaries and bailouts in the core.

Globalisation, as argued here, is not some ideal system, supreme and unchallengeable in its destiny, but a historical period that is now facing growing contradictions, challenges and crises. From Cuba's point of view, it is globalisation's social failure that makes its modification or demise most urgent, and also provides the raw material of resistance to which the Revolution can bond – both to extend its socialist experience to other countries, and as a means to chart its own future.

2
Western Liberal Democracy: Definitions, Ideology and Alternatives

The previous chapter sought to explain the process of globalisation, principally in its macro-level political economy manifestation. It argued that although globalisation is presented by its advocates as an 'End of History' scenario in which socialism is dead and market liberalism is the inevitable future for all, the global era is in fact a specific stage in capitalism's trajectory, and one that is becoming increasingly uncertain. The illusion of inevitability that shrouds the political and economic aspects of globalisation, supported by a matrix of financial and business interests, politicians, academics and the media, would be unsustainable if this transitional process did not have deeper roots in societal formation. To fully understand the current world order, it is therefore essential to examine these less visible and more subtle contexts of globalisation's hegemony. Beginning with an analysis of 'democracy' and its historical development under capitalism, this chapter will consider how an evolving and changing economic system has generated different theoretical conceptions of citizen involvement. It also considers the ways in which alternative and radical perceptions of democracy have emerged to challenge the dominant ideology.

The radical political economy approach to globalisation, as argued in Chapter 1, allows us to question the mainstream views that presume the inevitability of Cuban socialism's demise. But to see how Cuba's Revolution might evolve, and not merely survive, it is necessary to delve deeper into the ideological formation of capitalism to reveal its weaknesses and contradictions.

To explore ideology, one has to be aware that there are no immutable or 'correct' positions, but only sets of ideas and theories which are historically and socially variable. Ideas, and their presentation in formalised modes such as theory, are the ways in which humans make sense of the environment they inhabit – 'reality'. But in a world of competitive social relations, there is always an ideological struggle: one which reflects the economic and social conflict that decides 'who gets what', and how the present and future should be organised. The ruling groups that control economic and productive power always seek to present an ideology that favours and supports their material advantage and worldview. The creation and control of this ideological vision, and its presentation as 'normal' and for the general good, is what Gramsci termed hegemony. This concept was referred to in Chapter 1 and will be explored in more detail later in this chapter.

According to Cox (1981:168), 'Theory is always for someone and for some purpose'. Although theory is constructed in 'reality', it also constructs 'reality': the human mind, and the way it interprets and acts upon the world, set the parameters of our existence. Theory, therefore, can serve different purposes and takes two principal forms. The first is what Cox terms 'problem solving' theory, which aims to support, interact with, or adjust the dominant order. The second is 'critical' theory, which examines why the dominant order came into being and the contradictions that manifest themselves as that order evolves. It then employs such knowledge to consider how change can take place, and, in its more activist forms, how strategies may be devised to precipitate such change.

Most of contemporary academia is locked into the mode of 'problem solving' theory, supported by grants and scholarships from government and business in order to provide theoretical and ideological legitimacy for their actions. This process is further confirmed by publications in 'approved' journals as well as academic competitions such as the Research Excellence Framework (REF) in Britain, which rates academic performance according to mainstream criteria. The classification of academic subjects themselves also contributes to this model of knowledge production, because specialisation and insularity of the various 'disciplines' encourages seeking narrowly defined solutions to problems. This detracts from, and obscures, the roots of such problems, which lie in a much wider social and economic matrix. While history evolves as an interactive process, a totality that cannot be understood through its component parts alone, academia is heading in the opposite direction towards greater fragmentation. Such artificial organisation of knowledge obfuscates rather than reveals the workings of society, but it serves an ideological purpose by depoliticising problems and avoiding difficult questions.

Political economy, which seeks a more interdisciplinary interpretation of the world, may be seen, especially in its more radical manifestations, as an example of the application of 'critical' theory. The degrees of 'critical' theory may, perhaps, best be understood by how deep it explores into the dominant order, and the extent of the change it wishes to support. For example, the various epochs of capitalism over the past 500 years have generated different ideological and theoretical perspectives on the world, such as the opposed views of Keynesians and neo-liberals that were examined in Chapter 1. This is a battle in which orthodoxies were challenged and overthrown, and new theoretical concepts were erected on the remains of the old. But despite these dramatic changes, there has been a consistency in the 'worldview' that has complemented capitalism's material manifestations, emphasising, to varying degrees, the 'individual', 'competition', 'markets' and the way society should be organised, based principally on private property. This 'worldview' may also be understood as an 'ontology', which is essentially the core intellectual framework of an age. Ontology, however, does not denote a static belief system, but rather a process that is constantly in flux depending on the way humans experience the world, and the extent to which they accept the elite's interpretive myths – hegemony. Nevertheless, there has been a tendency during most of the period of industrial capitalism for the dominant ontology to be contained within acceptable parameters that do not contradict the workings of capitalism in general.

It is possible to critically analyse theoretical perceptions and ideologies within the 'ontology', and this can lead to change. As noted in Chapter 1, in this context Drucker (1983) regards Keynes as a 'heretic', not an 'infidel'. But to question the ontological foundations of the dominant system is an irreconcilable act (of an 'infidel'), one that is either not understood because it contradicts the established ideological and intellectual order, or profoundly rejected because it threatens the whole structure of reason on which the system builds its legitimacy. In this sense Fidel Castro has the honour of being an 'infidel'. This chapter questions the capitalist ontological framework, because only by doing so can one break free from the restrictive parameters within which democracy has been contained and imagine how things could be different. It is also the author's view, as will be expressed more fully in the final chapter, that the current challenges to neo-liberal globalisation, especially in Latin America, are in fact more than attempts to make 'who gets what' more equal. They are instead the beginnings of a conscious social transformation, one which renders the dominant ontology anachronistic, and not the forces that oppose it.

To analyse ideology, hegemony and ontology, it has to be accepted that objectivity is an illusion, and inevitably one interpretation will be favoured over another. As Gould (1996:36) notes, 'It is dangerous for a scholar even to imagine that he might attain complete neutrality, for then one stops being vigilant about personal [ontological] preferences and their influences – and then one truly falls victim to the dictates of prejudice.' Critical theory is a self-conscious political act which rejects the pseudo-scientific legitimacy that the empiricists seek to attain.

DEMOCRACY: THE CUBAN CONTEXT

In a 1996 article entitled 'Democracy in Cuba: What is a desirable model?', Domínguez, a leading North American Cuba specialist, suggests a number of changes to the Cuban governmental system that would make it more 'democratic' and presumably more effective in the implementation of reform. Among these he includes: greater tolerance of opposition political groups and freedom for them to compete against the ruling Communist party in open elections; fewer restrictions on the emerging private sector; and improved responsiveness by national-level government to the demands of the electorate. Domínguez is a moderate who rejects the extremist politics found in sections of the Cuban exile community, mainly resident in Florida, who seek the downfall of the Castro government and a return to the American-controlled system that existed before the Revolution. He offers sound advice on the measures that will have to be taken if Cuba is to establish a representative democracy and move towards a market economy.

Domínguez's argument is based on the assumption that Cuba is run by an authoritarian regime which permits few democratic openings for the population, and that any future the island might have in the modern world is dependent on its ability to fully embrace democratic and market reforms. Given the current political, economic and ideological climate, dominated by neo-liberal thinking and the belief that global markets are synonymous with democracy and progress, he presents a mainstream view that finds few detractors. This position is shared by other moderate Cubanologists such as Mesa Lago (1993), Eckstein (2003) and López (2002). It is also consistent with the literature on democratisation and 'transitology', as clearly expressed in Linz and Stepan's *Problems of Democratic Transition and Consolidation* (1996:7), in which basic rules are set out for the establishment of liberal parliamentary democracy.

If this kind of thinking is taken at face value, it is bad news for the Cuban Revolution, negating everything it has represented for half a century. However, for those like Domínguez, it is good news for the Cuban people, because it is presumed that if they can break free from their anachronistic Revolution they will benefit from the freedoms that are supposedly being enjoyed by those who have accepted the way of the market. If one subscribes to this view, it would seem illogical and counterproductive for Cubans not to take this opportunity. And if they are not doing so, then the finger of blame must point at the 'authoritarian regime' that is controlling their lives.

Since the collapse of Communism, liberal democracy based on representation and markets has become a *fait accompli* among many theorists and academics. Linz and Stepan (1996:5) argue that (liberal) democracy has become 'the only game in town'. As we saw in Chapter 1, such thinking has been reinforced by Fukuyama, who sees 'the universalization of Western liberal democracy as the final form of human government' (1989:4). He qualified this momentous statement by adding, 'the victory of liberalism has occurred primarily in the realm of ideas or consciousness and is as yet incomplete in the real or material world', but remained firm in the belief that 'the ideal will govern the material world in the long run'. Clearly the idea of the 'End of History' is an evolutionary notion, but this did not prevent the author claiming, 'liberal democracy in reality constitutes the best possible solution to the human problem'.

These views have been criticised from many perspectives, but one cannot deny that over the past 25 years we have entered a world in which liberal democracy and its functioning principle, the market, reign supreme. Indeed, democracy and markets have become inseparable entities in the neo-liberal consciousness, putting an end not only to history, but also to ideology, and therefore removing a principal source of human conflict.

The consolidation of the post-Communist New World Order inspired Diamond and Platter (1993:ix) to proclaim a 'global resurgence of democracy', which they believe constitutes the 'greatest period of democratic ferment'. They argue that this resurgence was made possible by the failure of the anti-democratic forces of the Left, in contrast to the success of the model developed in the West based on the free market and agreement on 'fundamental democratic principles' (30). These changes, they claim, have cleared the way for the citizens of former Communist countries to 'rejoin world civilisation' and to again embrace 'normal society'. This view of contemporary representative democracy in a market environment as a logical, positive, and 'normal' form of human organisation is shared by many other authors. For Axworthy (1992:117), 'The world is in a democratic upsurge unprecedented in history. This upsurge not only conforms to the highest ideals of Western philosophy, but is also our best guarantee of a peaceful world'.

However, some critics do not see such a positive relationship between neo-liberal capitalism and democracy, and point to the growing inequality and economic instability that have been generated by the free rein of capital. This leads them to doubt the viability and long-term sustainability of modern democracy. Therefore, while neo-liberal authors see the 'resurgence' of democracy in a positive light, for Gills and Rocamora (1993) it is associated with a new set of problems:

As the 1990s dawn the global system is descending deeper into an economic and political crisis, indeed a global crisis of democracy ... Instead of a bright New World Order of global democracy, we see the very real and dangerous prospect of a dark period of deepening economic chaos, deprivation, and neo-authoritarianism in much of the world.

Bauzon (1992:10) shares a similar view, and suggests that the well-established Western democratic system is

gradually being eroded even in a place where it is believed to have matured the most [the US], where much of society is racked by drug abuse, crime and social injustice. This is accompanied by a general loss of faith in 'democracy', characterised by declining voting rates and attempts to seek radical and often violent solutions to social and economic problems.

Despite the confidence of the champions of liberal democracy, it is clear, as Bauzon suggests, that even in modern industrial nations democracy is losing its relevance for the population. In the May 1997 general election in Britain, only 72 per cent of registered voters went to the polls in the lowest turnout since 1935, and in the 2001 election it fell to an unprecedented 59 per cent (Walden 2006). In 2005 it rose slightly to 61 per cent and in May 2010, despite a deepening recession and growing public concern about the future of the country, was still only 65 per cent (ukpolitical.info 2010). With democratic influence declining at the level of local government, as more powers are transferred to the centre, voter turnout in local elections is even lower (Wilson 1999:1). One explanation for this apathy is that people in modern consumer society are too distracted to engage in politics. However, it seems from a survey conducted in the UK, the Power Inquiry (2006), that the problem is not a lack of interest in politics but rather frustration with the inability to exercise effective democratic control over government. As the Inquiry's chairperson noted, 'The iPod generation wants more power over its politicians. Doing the business once every four years – and your vote not counting very much – now feels very arid to most people' (Walden 2006). The frustration that is felt by voters has prompted authors to talk of a 'democratic deficit' (Nye 2001) and 'democratic disenchantment' (Hartlyn 2003). As noted previously, it is interesting how in late 2008 objective conditions in the form of the current financial crisis prompted citizens in the US to adopt a more political stance, especially in their successful support of the Democrats' presidential candidate Barack Obama, whose message was 'change'. These objective forces may also produce subjective reactions elsewhere as the crisis unfolds.

Although the representative democracy and free-market solution is by far the most common framework for speculation about Cuba's future, there are still a number of traditional Left academics who see the Cuban 'sovietised' model as continuing to provide a solid economic and social foundation for development. For example, Méndez-Tovar, in his book *Democracy in Cuba?* (1995), sees the Revolution's social achievements as the foundation for the construction of a viable democracy. To support his argument, he gives a general description of democracy elaborated from a selection of definitions and criteria emanating mainly from US sources. He then goes on to argue that revolutionary Cuba, with its emphasis on equality and its successes in such areas as education, health care, social welfare and culture, has been more effective in achieving North American democratic ideals than the US itself. This radical structuralist view is based on the belief that egalitarian social and economic growth is a necessary prerequisite of democracy, and therefore part of the democratic process. Such a view is in sharp contrast to Domínguez, and those sharing the market-led perspectives, who see political democracy as a prerequisite to economic progress. These ideological positions will be explored later in this chapter.

The argument that prioritises economic over political democracy was sometimes used to defend the 'democratic centralism' practised in the former Soviet Bloc. Méndez-Tovar is able to present a convincing case for Cuba because its semi-sovietised system was, and still is, perhaps the most successful of all developing countries in terms of human development indices. Although he is more sympathetic to Cuban 'democracy' than Domínguez, by simply selecting a different set of democratic principles against which to measure the Cuban case, he does not advance our understanding of the Cuban situation. Moreover, now that Cuba has lost its main trading partner and benefactor, the Soviet Union, it is no longer able to sustain such high levels of 'democratic' development, and Méndez-Tovar does not offer any indication of how the Revolution can adapt to confront the new circumstances it faces in the post-Cold War environment.

It would seem that neither the representative democratic model proposed by Domínguez nor the continuing structuralist strategy advocated by Méndez-Tovar offer ready-made solutions to the Cuban problem. One of the difficulties with these system-based views is that they are fixed in their understanding of Cuba; for Domínguez, it is an authoritarian socialist regime that must adapt to the prevailing democratic and market trends, while for Méndez-Tovar, it represents one of the last countries in the world that could potentially continue to promote the state socialist ideal.

The limitation of these perspectives is that although Cuba exhibits both tendencies, it is neither a typical authoritarian dictatorship nor a typical socialist state, at least as represented by the command economy model of the twentieth century. Instead, it presents a complex mix of nationalism and socialism that can be distinguished by significant levels of interaction between the leaders and the masses, and a popular commitment to participation. The Cuban Revolution should not simply be seen either as a defunct system or a champion of a specific set of structuralist, Soviet-style socialist achievements, but can perhaps be more accurately understood as a unique political and economic process that is still in flux. Although the pull of the market is strong, the continuing influence of the island's anti-capitalist Revolution, with its emphasis on equality and participation, is still an important factor in shaping its future. Cuba may eventually take the market route, but at present there is a wide spectrum of ideas within the island about how change should evolve. These include: a market-led preference; a mixed economy with a strong state; or a strengthening and broadening of socialism through increased economic self-sufficiency and greater popular participation in the running of local and national affairs.

Domínguez's prescription for Cuba, based on the dominant model of representative multi-party democracy, and Méndez-Tovar's hopes for the preservation of 'socialist' development, are only valid for certain parts of this spectrum and do not offer ready-made solutions. The problem is not one of analytical accuracy, but of distorted communication; their arguments are only fully relevant within the respective ideological environments out of which they emerge. It is therefore impossible to see democracy as a single definable system, something that can be tested, measured and analysed according to a given set of standards or rules. To explore the possibilities and prospects for democracy in Cuba, one has to go beyond the simple statements of preference chosen by the above authors, which cover the main range of prescriptions for the island, and seek to identify a conceptual framework for democracy that reflects Cuban specificities and potentials. This task must necessarily include a comparative analysis of the historical, political and ideological environments in which various perceptions of democracy have developed.

THE HISTORICAL ROOTS OF DEMOCRACY

The roots of modern democracy are often traced back to the Greeks, who held, as an ideal, 'civic' and 'popular' forms of human interaction, through which they believed it was possible to build community and citizenship and a continuous shared involvement in society's development. Although this ideal provides a kind of touchstone for Western democracy, it is impractical, and perhaps contrived, to seek a democratic continuum from antiquity to the present day; European democracy, unlike literature, cannot claim a coherent 'Great Tradition'. However, classical ideas have retained a general influence on modern views of democracy. Greek thinking and practice, which is encapsulated in Aristotle's (1958:1275) view that citizens are 'those who share in the holding of office', has tended to inform republican and radical currents. Roman law and especially its application in the Empire, where citizens were protected by the law but did not participate in its formulation, have mainly influenced the liberal current (Walzer 1989:211). Between classical times and the twentieth century there were long periods when no recognisable form of democracy existed, such as during the era of European feudalism. It was with the Enlightenment and bourgeois ascendancy that democratic ideals were resurrected, at least in theory. Enlightenment philosophers and social thinkers were inspired by the revolution in science, such as Newton's 'natural philosophy', which combined the logic of mathematics with the mechanics of physical observation and brought order and reason to the understanding of the natural world. They sought to do the same for human organisation, which they wanted to liberate from the Dark Ages that were dominated by irrationality, superstition and tyranny.

Two main philosophical foundations emerged to explain the human condition during the Enlightenment; divine right and natural law. Although competing ideas, both emphasised order and reason, especially in the functioning of government. It was the arguments based on 'natural law', whose main proponents were Hobbes [1588–1679] and Locke [1632–1704], that theoretically opened the space for democracy; if such a law existed, then rights must apply not just to monarchs but also to the people. Power in this sense is seen not as a divine or royal prerogative but an abstract concept, which in practice can be vested in some form of institution. By taking this stance one could not appeal unquestioningly to a higher order as the guiding principle, but had to open up a debate on the nature of humans themselves. In his major work *Leviathan* (1991 [1651]), Hobbes explored this 'nature' and argued that humans were conflictual, ruthlessly competitive, individualistic and engaged constantly in a 'war of all against all'. This pessimistic view was probably influenced by his experience of the English Civil War [1642–51], which also stimulated his desire to find a mechanism, based on reason and political science, that would ensure peace and security for the population. His proposed solution to the human chaos he perceived was the establishment of a strong government which would engage with society by imposing 'contracts', so that the conflictive 'nature' of humans could be ordered, contained and directed towards a more civilised purpose. Ultimately, however, Hobbes felt that human 'nature' was so aggressive that the body in which power was vested, the 'Leviathan', may need, in certain circumstances, to rule by the 'sword'. The prime responsibility of such an organisation was therefore to protect the people from themselves.

Locke, in his *Two Treatises of Government* (1987 [1689]), was more positive about the state of nature that applied to humans. He believed that in their early condition they were co-operative, organised and individually aware of certain rights, such as owning property and having personal liberty. However, this idyllic state later degenerated in more advanced society. It therefore became necessary to organise a 'political society', under which these original principles could be restored and maintained in a workable form. Unlike Hobbes, he envisaged more interaction between people and the body in which power was entrusted. Consequently, while the population would be obliged to delegate their representation to authority, this did not confer on the ruling body virtually unlimited power. This view gave rise to early concepts of civil society as a separate entity, capable of demanding of authority certain responsibilities and obligations. For Locke, power could only be granted through society's consent and should be revocable if the authority in which it was vested did not fulfil its duties. At the time he wrote his *Treatises*, such a system was not feasible, and Hobbes's model was probably more attractive to those in power.

In contrast to Hobbes and Locke, and those thinkers whose ideas have underpinned the liberal tradition in politics and democracy, the French intellectual Rousseau [1712–1778] challenged the validity of a fixed 'natural' law applicable to the human condition. Instead, he sought to re-introduce from the Greek tradition the participatory element in democracy and the notion of civic self-rule. As will be discussed later, this alternative ontological foundation for democracy has tended to influence early republican, Left and radical perspectives.

The ideas of Hobbes and Locke informed the English Revolution of 1688, in which the Catholic King James II was overthrown by a union of parliamentarians and the nobleman William of Orange. This led to the passing of the English Bill of Rights, which increased the power of Parliament over the monarchy. These early political scientists were revolutionary in their time, and continue to provide theoretical reference points and legitimating frameworks for democracy. However, their understanding of the relationship between the governors and the governed based on rationality, reason and natural law, were over time, less tenable as guiding principles. This was particularly true as economies grew and diversified under capitalism, and social relations became more complex.

The Evolution of Liberal Democracy

One of the first thinkers to consider the growing complexity of the modern state and the impracticality of early conceptions of democracy, particularly those that referred back to the Greek model of citizen participation, was the French philosopher Constant [1767–1830] (1988). He argued that in the context of the '*grands Etats modernes*', participatory mechanisms would be difficult to implement. But from his liberal perspective he saw this as a positive development, because he believed it indicated that an independent civil society was forming, providing more opportunity for ordinary citizens to engage in commercial activities and fulfil their individual needs without recourse to authority and the state. In this context, he felt that civil liberties, the rule of law and representation were more important than participation in politics. However, in practice this process would appear not to be driven by citizen choice, as Constant implies, but by systemic necessity. It is precisely the fragmentation and individualisation of social life under capitalism, and the work and consumption patterns that underpin this process, that tend to marginalise the roles of citizenship and participation in politics. A potentially darker force was perceived by the French psychologist Le Bon [1841–1931] (1895), who speculated, 'the age we are about to enter will in truth be the era of crowds', and envisaged a growing need to manipulate the primitive instincts of the masses. His ideas, especially on the subconscious, the collective unconscious and crowd psychology, influenced Freud and his followers, as well as Hitler and Mussolini.

A further contribution to the mass society debate was made by Weber [1864–1920] (1978 vol. 2:1394), who believed that the widening of economic regulation and social citizenship, through the expansion of public services, would narrow the possibilities for the exercise of popular sovereignty and lead to an increase in bureaucratisation. Based on this assumption, he predicted that public administration would increasingly be controlled by technical elites having the levels of expertise required to run modern organisations and systems. Schmitt [1888–1985] extended this argument by claiming that mass politics and the emergence of 'particular interests' (cited in Avritzer 2002:13) had undermined the value of public discussion. Rather than an open debate, politics was reduced to a meaningless façade in parliaments and congresses, manipulated by political representatives behind whom was a struggle between social and economic power groups.

In the nineteenth and early twentieth centuries much of the debate over democracy was mainly academic, because limited franchise kept the masses from interfering with the elite capitalist enterprise, at least through official and legal channels. However, the First World War obliged elites to engage the masses and enlist their support for the conflict, which led to greater democratic compromise. To fight a war of this scale, it was essential to ensure an extensive recruitment of troops. This was facilitated by vigorous campaigns to stimulate a sense of nationalism, both to secure commitment to the war effort and to counter the message of the socialist Second Workers International that had called on the workers of the world to unite against capitalism. Essential to these tasks were new techniques of communication and mass persuasion, including poster art, radio broadcasts and a popular press. The compromise, if it could be seen as such, was that once the masses entered politics, even in a controlled way, there was no turning back.

This move towards populist politics concerned theorists like Mannheim [1893–1947] (1936) and Ortega y Gasset [1883–1955] (1994), who believed that to grant more democratic rights in 'mass society' might allow irresponsible and uneducated elements to undermine liberal elites capable of a higher order of rationality. They also assumed that once the masses became political subjects, opportunities would arise for demagogues to enlist support for the pursuit of their malign ends. This fear was apparently vindicated with the rise of Soviet Communism, with its 'proletarian culture', and of Nazism, with its ruthless manipulation of working-class opinion and prejudices. For the advocates of elitism, the entry of the masses into politics, either as a force acting through democratic structures or as the subjects of extensive propaganda and demagogic control, served to weaken the rationality of democracy.

A somewhat different elitist interpretation was advanced by the twentieth-century Italian social theorists, such as Mosca [1858–1941], Pareto [1848–1923] and Michels [1876–1936], whose ideas did much to reinforce the legitimacy of fascism under Mussolini. Mosca (Albertoni 1987) argued that elite and even dictatorial rule was essential to channel and contain the directionless masses. Pareto (Bottomore 1993) also supported the 'inevitability' and 'necessity' of elite control, and the tendency of all social systems and organisations to produce the perpetual 'circulation of elites'. Michels (Lipset 1968), who was perhaps most influential on Mussolini, proposed the 'Iron Law of Oligarchy', in which he argued that organisational life, even when subjected to new leaders, would always tend towards some form of exclusive control. Such theorists gave substance to the questionable notion that the masses in modern society were amorphous and directionless when it came to politics, and in need of strict guidance. It is easy to deduce from this view that populations require the 'order' of elite democracy and are incapable of coherent independent action. Modern representative democracy, especially in its contemporary functional, procedural and polyarchic forms, is underscored by these elitist notions.

In contrast, a left group of intellectuals represented by the first generation of the Frankfurt School, such as Horkheimer [1895–1973] (1974), Adorno [1903–1969] (1974) and Marcuse [1898–1979]

(1992), argued that the erosion of democracy stemmed not from mass participation in politics, but in the way that elites used the popularisation of politics to exert their influence. In particular, they saw the extension of elitist control from the public to the private sphere, and a tendency for the commodity form to penetrate into the cultural realm.

By the end of the Second World War, all theoretical conceptions of democracy, with the exception of the ideas that had been developed by Gramsci [1891–1937] in the 1920s and 1930s but were not available to mainstream debates, concluded that some form of elitist control was inevitable for better or for worse. Democratic elitism in the second half of the twentieth century adopted two main ideas: one that emphasised limiting the scope of political participation, the other arguing that, to maintain rationality, the role of the masses should be restricted to choosing between groups of elite representatives. Another tendency at that time was for the development of democratic theorising to move away from Europe to the US, partly reflecting the shift in world power from one hegemon (Britain) to another.

An important interwar analyst of 'mass society' and democracy who encapsulated the debates of the period was Schumpeter [1883–1950] (1942). His theories were sceptical of the notion of popular sovereignty and the Enlightenment belief in the rationality of the 'people'. Referring to the witch-hunts of the sixteenth century and the mass movements of the early twentieth century, he claimed that popular forces could not be trusted with the formation of democracy. He further argued, prophetically, that capitalism was in danger of collapsing from within, as democratic majorities pressed for a greater share of economic wealth. In particular, he felt that the creation of an expanded welfare state, and certain tendencies in mass consumption, would limit entrepreneurship and shift income from producers to non-producers. As profits fell, capitalists would be reluctant to invest and governments would be subjected to unbearable inflationary and social pressures. The political solution to this problem, as Schumpeter perceived it, was to use popular participation in politics not as a means to exercise the 'general will', as envisaged by Rousseau, but rather as a mechanism for authorising representative political bodies to take power on behalf of the masses. Assuming that elites would always take positions of control, Schumpeter believed that democratic input in the process of selecting this strata was the only realistic form democracy could take in modern society. This led him to conclude later, 'democracy means only that the people have the opportunity of accepting or refusing the men who are to rule them' (1942:284–285). This abysmal prospect seems completely disconnected from the egalitarian and creative ideals that survived the democratic tradition from Aristotle to Rousseau and have emerged on occasion since, especially when people have sought to push at the limits of their constrained citizenship, from the revolutions of 1848 to the student and worker protests of 1968.

Although Schumpeter and his contemporary Keynes held considerable mutual respect, the latter rejected Schumpeter's economic assumptions. In contrast, Keynes saw in the control of money, credit, spending and taxes, and the large public sector this would generate, a means of achieving economic equilibrium and political peace. Both however, directly and indirectly, subscribed to a view of democracy which posited that the masses should be guided by elites. This concept, which underpinned the structuralist notion that development must take precedence over democracy, was particularly influential in the thinking of modernisation theorists like Rostow (1960). Before the rise of neo-liberal economics in the late 1970s, it was generally thought that, to implement Western-style democracy, less-developed countries would first have to achieve economic growth with equality. The developmentalists, in particular, prescribed a number of state-led macro-economic strategies, such as income redistribution and basic needs policy that would reduce extremes of inequality and lead to a more integrated economy. It was assumed that political democracy would follow economic 'democracy'. The star performers of this model were, in retrospect, the 'Asian Tiger' economies, but many countries in Africa and Latin America also had modest successes with state-led economic growth and limited income redistribution. It is arguable that a radical structuralist model of development, as indicted earlier by Méndez-Tovar in the case of Cuba, was also practised in many socialist countries, particularly those that had abandoned, or significantly reduced, revolutionary and participatory political mechanisms and sought to manage socialism from above. The empirical correlation between economic development and democracy was emphasised by Lipset (1959), who showed that those countries which gave priority to development with equality were more likely to have stable democracies. Conversely, he suggested that nations that did not promote wealth redistribution as part of their development programmes were more susceptible to authoritarian control.

The Keynesian-style structuralist economic strategy, which implied economic development as a precondition of democracy, dominated the international system from the end of the Second World War until the mid 1970s. This model, in both industrialised and Third World nations, emphasised state-led economic management in which private capital was obliged to fall in line with national objectives set by government. In Latin America this period ran approximately from the end of the Great Depression of 1929 until the Debt Crisis of the mid 1980s, and was defined by structuralist and dependency theories, of which the latter had some influence on Cuba. This paradigm of development began to disintegrate after the 'dollar standard' broke down in the early 1970s, which, as we have seen in Chapter 1, caused massive changes in the world's financial system in favour of increased mobility of private capital. With the move from fixed to flexible exchange rates and the redirection of dollar flows through the Eurodollar market after the 1970s oil price rises, the tools of Keynesian economic management were weakened and problems like 'stagflation' began to affect the industrialised economies.

The Schumpeterian proposition that the masses had to be guided and developed by selected elites was modified by the political scientist Downs (1956) who, prefiguring the work of Friedman and Fukuyama and the neo-liberal revolution, moved away from the idea of the irrational masses towards the notion of the rational individual. In the 1920s and 1930s Schumpeter, as well as early public relations specialists like Bernays (1969) and social scientists such as Lippmann (1922), developed his ideas when mass consumption was in its infancy, and much of society was still not fully incorporated into market relations. These thinkers were consequently sceptical about the sustainability of the new culture which they sought to promote, and it is not surprising that they saw the manipulation of primitive irrational forces as the most powerful mode of persuasion. However, by the time Downs was writing, the market came to dominate in all aspects of modern life. Capitalist economic, political and social relations became more deeply entwined, making it possible to construct a more durable and legitimate perception of human nature, one that accorded with a more advanced level of system hegemony.

Downs was particularly influential in applying the economic concept of utility maximisation to the functioning of the political system, whereby it is assumed that individuals will make choices based on their own needs without regard for others. Because the rational person is seen to be motivated by material benefits, the role of elite representatives is reduced to offering and distributing negotiable public goods in an attempt to attract the support of the most individuals. In his work *Capitalism and Freedom*, Friedman (1962:8–9) refines such views and provides a theoretical rationale for neo-liberal economists and policymakers, especially the idea that democracy and markets are symbiotically linked. Friedman claims that there exists 'an intimate connection between economics and politics, [and] that only certain combinations of political and economic arrangements are possible, and that in particular, a society which is socialist cannot also be democratic, in the sense of guaranteeing individual freedom'. He therefore concludes, 'the kind of economic organisation that provides economic freedom directly, namely competitive capitalism, also promotes political freedom because it separates economic power from political power and in this way enables the one to offset the other'. Consequently, the public domain is de-linked from democracy, because there is no incentive to strive for a wider public or developmental good, simply a need to satisfy rational individual consumers. In this context the classical view of popular sovereignty is also a casualty, because public debate, or any kind of public interaction to express the 'general will', is deemed unnecessary, as the individual can theoretically achieve full political expression through the act of choice associated with voting.

The democratic formula proposed by Downs and Friedman negates the structuralist tendency of achieving development before democracy, and promotes democracy as a precondition of economic development. This latter formula assumes a fundamental change in the role of the state, which shifts from agency of development and elite management to facilitator of the market. In Britain and the US, the neo-liberal leaders Thatcher and Reagan sought to expose the state to the primacy of markets and individual choice. Reflecting Downs's speculations, through privatisation and compulsory competitive tendering, public services and goods became ostensibly exposed to consumer choice. These policies, along with tax cuts and other initiatives to promote competition, also set a materialist agenda which obliged elite political groups to compete for approbation and support from voters based on the material benefits they could offer. Such policies, which were complementary to the opening up of national economies to unrestrained market forces and the whims of the financial speculators, were anathema to Keynesians and developmentalists.

The pro-market and deregulatory economic and ideological trend soon influenced policy in the main international development institutions such as the World Bank and the IMF. They demanded that indebted Third World countries should undertake 'structural adjustment', as described in Chapter 1. When living standards fell for the majority of the population because of these policies, the gradual, economic route to democracy could no longer be sustained and was replaced by immediate political democracy, in the form of free elections based on political pluralism and one person one vote. This accorded more closely with neo-liberal thinking which emphasised political democracy before economic development, as clearly set out by Axworthy (1992:117) who states, 'democracy is an essential precondition to economic advance because it is necessary above all to break the traditional equilibrium or acceptance. To thrive democracy requires growth; and to grow, economies need democracy'. However, supporters of the economic route remain equally sure of their position, 'democracy is ... less likely to emerge and evolve in societies in which an impoverished mass confronts a small wealthy elite who control the means of production and distribution' (Pourgerami 1991:9). Both camps can claim large numbers of scholarly advocates.

It would seem that modern Western democracy is not a distillation of all that went before into some form of ideal system that confirms Friedman's (1962) notion that only 'certain combinations of political and economic arrangements' can bring about effective democracy. Rather, in both structuralist and neo-liberal forms, it is a highly compromised and elitist set of arrangements that have produced little more than a democratic shell devoid of substantive content. Although writing before the neo-liberal refinement of the Western democratic model, Schumpeter (1942:42) perhaps best describes this shell in its actual functioning form:

> [D]emocracy is a political method, that is to say, a certain type of institutional arrangement for arriving at political-legislative and administrative decisions and hence incapable of being an end in itself, irrespective of what decisions it will produce under given historical conditions. And this must be the starting point of any attempt at defining it.

Capitalism and Democracy

Despite the powerful assertions from neo-liberal intellectuals concerning the immutable relationship between markets and democracy, and claims that free-market liberalism has in practice given substance to their theorising, neither history nor contemporary developments in the international system would suggest that democracy and capitalism are natural bedfellows. In response to Friedman's argument that economic freedoms brought about political democracy in the West, Macpherson (1962:148) concludes;

> The liberal state which had by the mid-nineteenth century in England established the political freedoms needed to facilitate capitalism was not democratic: that is, it had not extended political freedom to the bulk of the people. When later, it did so, it began to abridge market freedom. The more extensive the political freedom, the less extensive the economic freedom became. At any rate, the historical correlation scarcely suggests that capitalism is a necessary condition for political freedom.

It would also seem that the bourgeois revolutions which complemented the rise of capitalism did not give priority to the establishment of democracy, but were much more concerned with the consolidation of economic and political hegemony over the old feudal order. In this sense, the commodification of the labour force and the means of production, along with the establishment of a liberal state that served capitalist interests, took precedence over democracy. Indeed, any democracy that was established had limited franchise, because the majority of the population probably would have rejected the new bourgeois order. As Boron (1995:10) points out, it was not the emergent bourgeoisie that established democracy but, 'on the contrary, it was the mounting political mobilisation of the subordinate classes, with their demands and struggles, their parties and unions that forced the democratisation of the liberal state'. To which he adds that many of these democratising forces were influenced by socialist ideas. This leads him to suggest, 'capitalist rule is highly flexible and adaptable, and it is always able to mix quite efficiently with alternative forms of political domination, ranging from bourgeois democracy to fascism' (11). For a case tending towards the latter, he points to the Latin American dictatorships of the 1970s.

To advance his argument, Boron cites the research of Bryce, who sought to identify the viable democracies that existed after the First World War, and Dahl, who made a similar survey in the 1970s based on a limited definition of democracy that he termed polyarchy. From the evidence provided by these authors, Boron concludes that very few advances towards democracy were made during this period, and that capitalist development and democracy have had a tenuous relationship at best, with no clear correlation between the two. Although Boron's argument is based on reliable sources, it is clear that his ideological leanings are towards socialism rather than capitalism as a proper foundation for the development of democracy, and he could be accused of bias. However, Silva (1999:35), who balances his argument in favour of capitalist democracy, similarly concludes, 'the functions of the capitalist state apply equally regardless of whether the state is democratic or authoritarian in form'.

The reason for the exclusion of egalitarian content from the notion of Western democracy, and its reduction to procedural form, is well explained by Boron (1995:26–27) who, after questioning the validity of contemporary claims to some form of democratic 'resurgence', states:

> The abstract reasoning that does not call into question 'democracy for which class?' splits the analysis of the social totality into its economic and political components reifying them as isolated 'parts', reducing the political to a procedural question and reproducing the world vision consecrated by bourgeois ideology. Capitalist exploitation is conveniently hidden, thus allowing all kinds of benevolent speculations on the future worlds of 'democracy' – affecting people in their sole capacity as voters, while piously disregarding all the restrictions that originate in the laws of motion of capital and that oppress people in the name of the free market. The entire rationale of this argument is trapped in the ideological universe of bourgeois thought.

On its simplest level, the disagreement over what form democracy should take is suggested by the different stances on the roles of politics and economics, with neo-liberals arguing for the primacy of political democracy, while developmentalists/structuralists argue for the primacy of economics. This debate is highly relevant to contemporary Cuba, which in practice became, in part, an example of the latter view. But with the collapse of Soviet Communism and the rise of neo-liberalism, the island faces unrelenting pressure to establish political democracy as a precondition of economic reform.

Marxists have often been branded utopian for envisaging a dissolution of civil society and its absorption into popular political society, the only foundation for a true democracy in Marx's view.

However, is it not equally or even more utopian to assume the dissolution of political society and its absorption into civil society? But it is not Marx, with his diametrically opposed position, that we should call upon to challenge the current ontology, but one of its founding fathers, Adam Smith. Smith (2007 [1759]) would not have countenanced the level of market hegemony we have today, nor the reduction of humans to calculating automatons with no true feeling for others, as is clear from his statement, 'How selfish soever man may be supposed, there are evidently some principles in his nature, which interest him in the fortune of others, and render their happiness necessary to him, though he derives nothing from it except the pleasure of seeing it.'

Democracy as Participation: A Socialist Perspective

It would be inaccurate and contrived to present a positive and uncomplicated case for 'democracy' under socialism as experienced in most of the Communist and socialist states of the twentieth century. It is in such systems that some of the worst abuses of human rights have taken place, and claims of democracy have often been a sham. Even when it has not been suppressed by authoritarian leaders like Stalin and Mao, democracy in its radical structuralist form, as noted above, is just another elitist model. Nevertheless, socialist theorists such as Rousseau, Marx, Lenin and others have, like their liberal counterparts, also proposed an ideal of how democracy should function. In this respect, despite a poor record in practice, socialist states can claim to:

> have a democratic theory of their own which, in line with Marxist and indeed some earlier theories of democracy, places more emphasis on the content of democracy than upon its form, and upon the socio-economic rights of citizens rather than on their formal independence of state power. (White et al. 1987, cited in Roman 1999:9)

There is not space here to explore this tradition in detail, but some of the main ideas must be identified to make sense of the Cuban democratic process.

Rousseau

When liberal theory in economics and politics was consolidating its hegemony, a voice of dissent emerged in the form of the French intellectual Jean-Jacques Rousseau [1712–1778]. He proposed a series of alternative views of society and democracy, which, as Colletti (1972:170) points out, 'irretrievably isolated Rousseau from his contemporaries, and made his thought appear absurd and paradoxical to them'. Central to the task he set himself was to conceive of an alternative ontology, founded principally on a revised understanding of the human condition. Without this vital root, the arguments of the Left can never be more than a disparate set of disagreements with liberals as the latter's ideas are underpinned by an implicit logic based on a preconceived notion of what it is to be human, which imposes inviolable parameters on any debate. Because Rousseau's work has been paraphrased, his ideas borrowed and his concepts misinterpreted, often without being properly attributed, the following section will draw substantially on his own original words. Particular reference will be made to his *Discourse on the Origin of Inequality* (1993 [1754]), in which he details his disagreement with then-emergent liberalism and outlines his proposal for a new discourse.

Rousseau's starting point in setting out his challenge to the philosophical underpinning of liberal and Enlightenment thought is to question the notion of 'natural law'. This concept, as noted previously, was developed by writers like Hobbes and Locke, and is based on the belief that a higher order, either divinely ordained or occurring in nature, exists to guide humanity (Crowe 1977). Given this immutable extra-human precept, it is for man to obey its principles, which define what is right and what 'must be'. Human access to this order is presumed to be through the use of reason. This is a rather individualistic code of existence with each acting to serve one's own utility, but according to general rules enshrined in legal equality that guide society as a whole. Advocates of 'natural law' believe that, if functioning effectively, it could provide a basis for resolving conflict in society. As a theory, it is deductive because only through a set of given principles can the correct course of action be chosen. As noted earlier, 'natural law' was a reaction against the 'dark ages' and the '*ancien régime*' with its legally enforced privileges and hereditary, God-given rights. Despite its aim to move beyond what it perceives to be an 'unnatural' illegitimate system, 'natural law' establishes a static ontology which like the order it opposes, excludes the possibility of other categories of being or alternative interpretations of existence.

Rousseau begins his *Discourse* by posing the question, 'What is the origin of inequality among men, and is it authorized by natural law?' (1993:31). By taking this stance, he reintroduces the ontological debate into the question of what it means to be human. This also provides the basis on which he can raise an alternative worldview. In his analysis, inequality is divided into two categories: natural and physical on one hand, moral and political on the other. Because he regards the former as largely beyond human control he concentrates on the latter, which he believes is susceptible to human volition. His approach to this question is essential for understanding the different ways in which politics and democracy can be conceptualised: 'Of all human sciences the most useful and most imperfect appears to me to be that of mankind ... for how shall we know the source of inequality between men, if we do not begin by knowing mankind?' (1993:43). No theory of society can exist in isolation and must implicitly or explicitly take a position on what is man. He initiates this debate by considering Aristotle's proposition, 'what is natural has to be investigated not in beings that are depraved, but in those that are good according to nature' (1993:31). Contrary to this advice, he claims that Hobbes (1991 [1651]:89) had identified a state of nature based on 'warre, as is of every man, against every man', producing 'continual fear, and danger of violent death'; 'the life of man is solitary, poore, nasty, brutish and short', hence the need for a strong monarchy or Republic to prevent society descending into chaos (148).

To explore Aristotle's proposition, Rousseau felt it was necessary to examine, even if only through conjecture, the whole human trajectory, rather than taking, as some of his contemporaries had done, some arbitrary stage in that journey, which may be a temporary condition or an anomaly induced by specific conditions. Rousseau starts his analysis at the beginnings of human existence on earth, and presumes a simple being driven by the need to fulfil the requirements of survival. In this state, humans were neither good nor bad, and knew neither vice nor virtue, because they had only very basic dealings with each other. However, as society developed, this primitive being became more complex. First, because of the need to survive in a diverse set of unique natural circumstances, humans acquired characteristics that distinguished them from animals. For the latter, 'nature is the sole agent, whereas man has some share in his own operations, in his character as a free agent' (1993:59). This conscious transcendence of instinct allows for self-improvement and limitless creative possibilities. As self-conscious beings, humans are also able, uniquely in the animal world, to learn from the past and plan for the future. Such possibilities cannot be realised in isolation, but require the co-operation of similar minds, making it necessary for man to develop as a social being. Language, then, becomes the articulation of his social and creative potentials.

From co-operation and shared destiny comes 'compassion [that] is a natural feeling, which, by moderating the violence of love of self in each individual, contributes to the preservation of the whole species' (75–76). This unique set of faculties, however, has equal potential for species perfection or corruption. And in the course of human development there were many 'accidents which may have improved human understanding while depraving the species, and made man wicked while making him sociable' (82). One of the first 'accidents', and in Rousseau's view one of the most pernicious, was the establishment of private property, of which he states:

> The first man who, having enclosed a piece of ground, bethought himself of saying *This is mine*, and found people simple enough to believe him, was the real founder of civil society. From how many crimes, wars and murders, from how many horrors and misfortunes might not any one have saved mankind, by pulling up the stakes, or filling up the ditch, and crying to his fellows, 'Beware of listening to this impostor; you are undone if you once forget that the fruits of the earth belong to us all, and the earth itself to nobody'. (84)

And property led to:

> Insatiable ambition, the thirst of raising their respective fortunes, not so much from real want as from the desire to surpass others, inspired all men with a vile propensity to injure one another, and with a secret jealousy, which is the more dangerous, as it puts on the mask of benevolence, to carry its point with greater security. In a word, there arose rivalry and competition on the one hand, and conflicting interests on the other, together with a secret desire on both of profiting at the expense of others. All these evils were the first effects of property, and the inseparable attendants of growing inequality. (96)

Once this form of inequality became established, and the rich were 'no longer capable of retracing their steps or renouncing the fatal acquisitions they had made' (97),

> it now became the interest of men to appear what they really were not. To be and to seem became two totally different things; and

from this distinction sprang insolent pomp and cheating trickery, with all the numerous vices that go in their train. (95)

As human economic advances took place, and private property became the dominant institution underlying this process, the exploitation of nature itself was tied into this perverse order. This prompted Rousseau to write, 'it was iron and corn, which first civilised men, and ruined humanity' (92).

As avarice and possessive individualism based on private property became more widely established, which in Rousseau's mind led to a 'decrepitude of the species' (91), institutions were formed to consolidate and fraudulently legitimise inequality and the deviant behaviour it produced such as wars and social strife. Therefore, he concludes that humanity's bad habits are the products of civilisation, specifically social hierarchies, property and markets. Although he condemned private property, he accepted in his *Discourse on Political Economy and the Social Contract* (2009 [1755]) that in modern society some form of property regime would exist, but he argued that it should be based on equality, stability and frugality. This was to be partly achieved through a progressive taxation system that took all personal wealth and advantage into account.

Progress based on fundamental inequalities was, for Rousseau, an inauspicious beginning for human development:

> Such was, or may well have been, the origin of society and law, which bound new fetters on the poor, and gave new powers to the rich; which irretrievably destroyed natural liberty, eternally fixed the law of property and inequality, converted clever usurpation into unalterable right, and, for the advantage of a few ambitious individuals, subjected all mankind to perpetual labour, slavery and wretchedness. (1993:99)

In this way, private power gained control over public authority and become accepted as a legitimate form of rule and government, allowing 'politicians [to] indulge in the same sophistry about the love of liberty as philosophers about the state of nature' (102). Eventually, power founded on wealth and ownership became legitimated as a given order, and the avarice, acquisitiveness, and desire for material possessions which it generated regarded as 'natural' human behaviour. In Rousseau's view, this produced a society in which 'we have nothing to show for ourselves but a frivolous and deceitful appearance, honour without virtue, reason without wisdom, and pleasure without happiness' (116). Thus, he not only condemns the rich and those who rule over such a society, but the whole system in which 'usurpations by the rich, robbery by the poor, and the unbridled passions of both, suppressed the cries of natural compassion and the still feeble voice of justice, and filled men with avarice, ambition and vice' (96–97). He concludes, 'it is plainly contrary to the law of nature, however defined, that children should command old men, fools wise men, and that the privileged few should gorge themselves with superfluities, while the starving multitude are in want of the bare necessities of life' (116).

Rousseau believed that the elitist order on which liberal philosophers have founded their analysis was based on a perverted conception of 'human nature'. He therefore takes to task thinkers like Hobbes for presuming that humans are 'naturally' avaricious, warring, and motivated by possessive individualism. This, he argues, is not their 'nature' that is being described, but a construct based on a particular configuration of society which is not immutable, desirable or sustainable. The same applies to such ideas as the liberal notion of equality under the law, independent civil society and democracy defined by political representation, because the perception of human relations on which they are based is fundamentally flawed. As stated earlier, by adopting this position, Rousseau challenges the whole edifice of right-wing thinking and opens space for himself, and the Left, to build a foundation on which to propose an entirely different understanding of the world and man's place in it – an alternative ontology.

On the basis of his refutation of liberal interpretations of human nature and man's state of being in society, Rousseau attempted to raise new possibilities to which humans could aspire and take action to achieve. After all, he believed that one of humanity's greatest potentials was that 'the soul and the passions of men insensibly change their very nature', and this gave at least the chance of the *perfectibilité* of humanity. In general, what he envisaged was a process of change that would seek to produce a new moral and social order in which economic and political equality became the norm, but did not suppress individual creativity (Colletti 1972:151–152). In his popular semi-fictional novel *Émile, ou l'éducation* (1979 [1762]), Rousseau takes on the role of educator of a young man and explains, rather idealistically, how someone could be brought up to become a social individual, able to liberate the self though social responsibility and consciousness. Unlike the liberal individual, Rousseau's citizen is not pre-formed, but must be socialised, educated and psychologically trained to become the ideal type that he envisages. This, he would argue, is not indoctrination, but a process whereby humanity can reconnect with itself.

In describing the forms of social organisation that such a society might adopt, Rousseau sets an agenda for the Left to consider, adopt and revise. Based on his first premise concerning inequality, he believed that in a more equal system it would be possible to dissolve liberalism's sustaining assumption concerning the separation of political and civil society. Instead society should be guided by a 'general will' founded in unity and consensus. He did not, however, envisage a uniform society which reduced the individual to a mere function of the whole. On the contrary, he felt that if ordinary people could achieve a conscious and material transcendence beyond a society based on inequality, human energies could then be concentrated on the pursuit of more social and creative objectives (Colletti 1972:174). Once the values of an antagonistic, materialist and unequal society had been consciously rejected by the majority, then a consensus or 'general will' could be formed on how to develop a new society able to direct human endeavour towards more socially beneficial purposes. Far from repressing the individual, this transition would liberate both the individual and society from 'an assembly of artificial men and factitious passions, which are ... without any real foundation in nature' (Rousseau 1993:114–115).

Central to the argument of Rousseau's *Social Contract* (1978 [1762]), which arises from the philosophical foundation he establishes in his *Discourse on Inequality*, is civic self-rule, in which the co-authoring of laws and certain (social) objectives in society through the exercise of the 'general will' makes citizens free, and renders those laws and objectives legitimate (Bertram 2003). This active participation in the process of deliberation and decision making gives individuals the status of 'citizens' rather than 'subjects', or for that matter simply 'voters'. As Rousseau (1978:195) states, 'obedience to a law which we prescribe to ourselves is liberty'. Again, this concept can be traced back to Aristotle (1958:1275), who defines citizens as 'those who share in the holding of office'. This is in contrast to the liberal view of the individual's relationship with the state or ruling authority, which takes the form of a legal status in which political liberty protects individuals from interference and harm caused by others. However, in this case freedom is not exercised in relation to the political domain, but in the world of private associations. In an environment in which individuals are in a 'warre, as is of every man, against every man' as conceived by

Hobbes, but also share 'a certain propensity in human nature ... to truck, barter, and exchange one thing for another' as envisaged by Adam Smith (1904 vol. 1:21), the sheer demands of existence, need and instinct leave the individual with little time, or inclination, to engage in politics. S/he consequently entrusts law making and necessary administration to professional and distant representatives. Political involvement, therefore, is an 'important but occasional identity, a legal status rather than a fact of everyday life' (Walzer 1989:215). In this context, the reason for the separation of civil and political society in liberal thought becomes clear. Referring to the seventeenth- and eighteenth-century founders of liberalism, Macpherson, in his seminal work the *Political Theory of Possessive Individualism: Hobbes to Locke* (1962), sees this separation as a major impediment to the establishment of democracy. He believed that 'the continued existence of liberal-democratic states in possessive market societies ... has been due to the ability of the possessing class to keep the effective political power in its hands in spite of universal suffrage' (274). With the current neo-liberal emphasis on giving more power to private interests and the market, this statement is even more relevant today.

Returning to Rousseau's argument that active participation in politics and the organisation of society forms part of the individual's sense of self, this does not assume an automatic seamless process, because the accretions of history are seen to have perverted and misguided humans. This gives rise to the need for a guiding force which seeks to promote the participatory ideal. For Rousseau it is the 'legislator', for Marx and Lenin, the Communist/intellectual, and in socialist states such as Cuba, the Vanguard Party. In the purest sense, such an agent does not act from an elitist position for the good of the masses, but rather assumes the role of an instigator, developer and promoter of citizen/socialist consciousness. Therefore, decisions are not taken for the masses, but rather the masses are encouraged to act in the interest of forming a 'general will', socialism and a societal consensus. In the same vein, political representatives are not remote, largely unaccountable individuals who pledge to follow some vague political manifesto and 'have the authority as the representatives of public affairs, whereas in reality they represent particular interests' (Marx, cited in Roman 1999:17). They are 'instructed delegates' who convey the will of the people to the administrative apparatus and political decision makers. For Rousseau and Marx, this process is understood as the intense politicisation of society. This is in contrast to class conflict in capitalist society, in which inequality, privilege, special interests and the general separation of economics and politics creates political tensions. Rather, they propose a situation where economic equality is the objective of society (in Rousseau's terms a 'common destiny'), and therefore all social activity and interests can be brought into the political sphere. In this sense,

> there is nothing that Rousseau insists on more than the active and ceaseless participation of the people and of every citizen in the affairs of the State. The State is near ruin, says Rousseau, when the citizen is too indifferent to attend a public meeting. (Talmon 1970:45)

In this system of *mandat impératif*, it is vital that voters have the right to recall and replace their representatives, as those individuals are not the activists of some particularist political party with partial interests, but are instead citizen participants entrusted with expressing and representing the 'will of the people' and 'popular sovereignty'. Rousseau believed that 'the government should be administered by a few, but the inspection of that government belongs to many' (cited in Roman 1999:16).

It is clear from reading Rousseau's original works that Marx, Lenin and even Gramsci drew on aspects of his thinking, even though they did not always attribute their source. In summary, he not only suggested an ontological foundation for an alternative body of knowledge, but also played a seminal role in initiating such ideas as linking democratic government to economic equality, the merging of civil and political society, political participation and the *mandat impératif*.

Marx

The paradox of legal equality with economic inequality influenced Marx to argue that the separation of civil society and the state in capitalist society made truly representative government unworkable. Once this division of political and civil society ended, enabling society to establish common objectives, then Marx felt that 'politics would become the administration of things, or simply another branch of social production' (Colletti 1972:44). This would represent a depoliticisation of the political sphere. Marx envisaged the transitional form as a 'dictatorship of the proletariat' under which private property would be eliminated, as would the distinction between the state and civil society and the governed and the governors. Although Marx drew many of his ideas from Rousseau, writing almost a century later he had the advantage of historical perspective, and by then capitalism was much more developed and visible. For Marx, therefore, what were seen by Rousseau as historical 'accidents' became more clearly associated with modes of production and the class forces that coalesced around them. Moreover, although inequality was regarded as a problem with a long history, its manifestation under capitalism raised in Marx's mind the possibility of revolutionary transcendence of this specific historical juncture, with a defined class as the agent of potential change. Rousseau's ontology and its foundations in an alternative notion of human nature remained, however, little changed in the thinking of Marx, who saw humans as a 'species being' and history as 'nothing but a continuous transformation of human nature' (1926:124).

Marx did not attempt to develop a theory of socialist society or the democratic structure that would be appropriate to this social formation, mainly because he was involved in analysing the historical movement of capitalism and its intrinsic weaknesses. Besides, in Marx's own terms, it would also be impossible to predict a future society when history was seen by him as an unfolding process based not just on economic laws, but also on the formation and reformation of human consciousness.

Historically, the Paris Commune of 1871, the Russian Soviets of 1905 and 1917, the early part of the Russian Revolution, the revolution within the Spanish Civil War and the evolution of the Soviet Union after Stalin's death are all examples of attempts to follow some form of socialist understanding of democracy.

The Paris Commune

Although Marx (1968a) was not prepared to speculate on the nature of future Communist society, the Paris Commune of 1871 inspired him to consider the practical implications of a shift of power to the workers, and the change in consciousness that this might inspire through revolutionary praxis. The Commune, formed immediately after the defeat of France in the Franco-Prussian War, was in itself only a short episode of proto-socialist rule in Paris (then a city of 2 million) for two months in the spring of 1871. After a four-month siege, in January 1871 the provisional government of Adolphe Thiers sought an armistice with the victorious Prussians, which included a concession allowing the Germans to enter Paris triumphantly for a brief ceremonial occupation. However, the military failings of the government of Napoleon III (which had declared war on the Prussians in the first place), a breakdown in food supplies to the city, growing inequality between rich and poor, and the damage of Prussian shells caused many Parisians to resent such a humiliation. In the face of defeat and occupation, thousands of Parisians joined armed militias, which became known collectively as the National Guard. Each local division of the Guard elected its own officers, many of whom were left-leaning radicals. These radicals and many ordinary working people not only feared the Prussians, but also the reactionary French monarchists who were gaining in strength. In the power vacuum that was created as the Germans entered the city, the National Guard and the workers took the opportunity to increase their military and political control of the situation.

When the provisional government tried to regain control of Paris, its own troops refused to fire on the Guard and the people, and some defected to join ranks with the masses. Faced with a rebellion on that scale, Thiers was forced to withdraw the remains of his government and troops and abandon Paris for Versailles. The effective government of the capital was now the Central Committee of the National Guard, which immediately called for elections to form a Commune (local self-governing council), a right that had been granted to other French towns but denied to Paris because of its radical politics. The 92 members elected to lead the Commune Council were radicals, workers and professionals, from various political groups, designating themselves as delegates rather than representatives. Louis Blanqui, a revolutionary socialist, though in a government prison, was elected as president of the Council.

The Commune was established on 28 March 1871 and adopted the socialist red flag as its banner rather than the republican tricolour. Immediate priorities for the new radical administration of Paris were to restore and improve public services and form a participatory social democracy. Although the Commune was short-lived, it passed a number of progressive laws including the separation of Church and state, suffrage for women and the right of employees to take over and run an enterprise (Tombs 1999). Plans were also drawn up for free education. The local organisations that had been set up during the siege, such as canteens and first aid units, co-operated with the Commune. Indeed, one of the great successes of the Commune was the spontaneous initiatives and voluntary labour provided by workers to run the city administration and social services, which had been abandoned by Thiers. Local assemblies, although supportive of the Commune, continued to work with some autonomy and were often controlled by workers. The key Left groups in the Commune were the Blanquists, who were internationally orientated socialists, the Proudhonists, who had strong anarchist leanings, and the libertarian republicans.

The levels of co-operation between different political groups, the degree of worker control and the insistence on participatory democracy have given the Commune an enduring symbolic status for the Left (Shafer 2005). Crucially, however, the Commune failed to seize the assets of the National Bank of France. These were transferred to the provisional government, which used the money to finance the military retaking of Paris. Marx (1968b) also complained that too much time was spent establishing democratic elections rather than defeating the provisional (Versailles) government. In a similar vein, Lenin (1972:475–478) felt that 'the proletariat stopped half-way: instead of "expropriating the expropriators" it allowed itself to be led astray by dreams of establishing a higher justice'. This led to 'excessive magnanimity on the part of the proletariat: instead of destroying its enemies it sought to exert moral influence over them'. Also, fatally, 'it underestimated the significance of direct military operations in civil war'.

Only a week after it was formed, the Commune came under attack from the provisional government in exile in Versailles, forcing the Commune Council to rely on the National Guard to defend Paris, with the assistance of many foreign political refugees who had settled in the city. Support in other French cities was quashed by Thiers's army, isolating Paris, and gradually the government forces overpowered the National Guard. The most determined resistance came from working-class districts, but the organised and centralised army of Thiers continued its advance, district by district and street by street. By the end of May, only a few pockets of resistance remained. The reprisals by the provisional government were ruthless, and one source estimates that '7,500 were jailed or deported' and 'roughly 20,000 executed' (Anderson 2004). Paris remained under martial law for five years after the Commune collapsed.

Besides the immediate circumstances which led to the defeat of the Commune, its historical timing was also inauspicious. By the 1860s, the 1789–1848 'Age of Revolution' was over. Industrialisation, modernity, technology and a strong state were reshaping much of Europe. The great industrial exhibitions of the time, where numerous new inventions and their applications were demonstrated, further added to the general feeling that a new world was emerging which would bring opportunities for all, including workers. On a practical level, modernist planning had also led to the demolition of many of the narrow streets of old Paris and their replacement with wide boulevards, making it impossible to reproduce the barricades of 1848 and facilitating the army's suppression of revolt (Mason 2007:52). This was the beginning of the era of heavy industrial capitalism, and the new bourgeoisie heading this transformation was confident, and their hegemony plausible. It was not a time for revolution.

Although a radical reformist and social democratic experiment rather than a Communist one, the Commune has become an icon of socialist potential. Marx (1968b) himself acknowledged, 'the majority of the Commune was in no sense socialist, nor could it be', but, like many other writers on the Left, he believed that it was a prototype for a revolutionary government. Despite exasperation on the Marxist Left concerning the inability of the Communards to grasp the moment and attempt to secure state power, the experiences of the Commune strengthened Marx's belief that the working class could organise themselves and seek their own liberation. It also showed that in pursuit of this end, workers would turn towards a political system based on grassroots participatory democracy. These were negations of the elitist myth that the masses were amorphous, incapable of rational decision making and lacking self-identity. The conclusion by Marx (1968a:294–295) on the Commune is important for understanding not only his speculations on the trajectory of working-class power, but also the process of trans-formation of human consciousness:

> The working class did not expect miracles from the Commune. They have no ready-made utopias to introduce *par decret du peuple*. They know that in order to work out their own emancipation ... they will have to pass through long struggles, through a series of historic processes, transforming circumstances and men.

Marx, Engels and later Lenin and Trotsky tried to draw theoretical lessons from the Commune, especially to support Marx's notion of the 'dictatorship of the proletariat' and the 'withering away of the state'. In this respect, an important but perhaps insurmountable problem faced by the Commune was a situation of dual power, in that while the Communards controlled Paris, the official 'bourgeois' French government, constituted in the National Assembly, could still claim to be the legitimate government and used this advantage to sanction its actions against the Commune. From this perspective, a notable distinction can be made between the Marxists and anarchists like Peter Kropotkin [1842–1921] (1989) and Michael Bakunin [1814–1876] (1974). While Marxists saw the need for ruthless military action on the part of the Commune to capture state power and establish a 'dictatorship of the proletariat', anarchists regarded the Commune as an opportunity to dissolve state power, and felt that the Communards should have precipitated a revolutionary general strike and decentralised power to worker's councils.

In retrospect, the Commune represents one of the first attempts to run a current of counter-hegemony against the dominant tide of bourgeois history. It prefigured a classless and stateless society based on the power of the workers, who revealed the potential to bring about a self-transformation from a 'class in itself' to 'a class for itself' (Schulkind 1974:113). It was also seen to be 'the only class capable of social initiative'.

Marx believed that the Commune had, in embryo, overcome the capitalist separation of civil and political society and private and public interests. This was possible because these were not the realities of working-class existence in which life itself was both a political and social experience, and property was not in the hands of workers to any significant degree, but was a bourgeois possession. The separation of economics and the means of subsistence from politics was therefore a construction designed to sustain class inequalities, as it obscured and negated the circumstances of the workers. Bourgeois government had become nothing but the management of an unequal system, and a workers' government had no choice but to dismantle this fraudulent structure that did not serve workers' interests. On a more philosophical level, this also seemed to confirm Marx's belief in human nature, in the sense that the 'individual' and 'society' are not separate social entities as orthodox social science would suggest, but that we are 'social beings'. In his words, 'Above all we must avoid postulating "society" again as an abstraction vis-à-vis the individual. The individual is the social being' (1968c:297).

This leads to a higher plain of Marxist thought which conceives of class beyond the status of a purely economic relationship with ownership and production, to that of loose ensembles of people with different consciousnesses of their environments. In this context, the group that may broadly be seen as the working class is in the best position to transcend dominant conditions; in the process of doing so, however, it abolishes classes, including itself:

The condition for the emancipation of the working class is the abolition of classes [and] the working class in the course of its development, will substitute for the old civil society an association which will exclude classes and their antagonism, and there will be no more political power properly so-called, since political power is precisely the official expression of antagonism in civil society. (Marx 1926:161)

The Russian Soviets

After the Commune, the next real attempt to establish a people's government was the formation of the Russian Soviets between 1905 and 1917, although there were many examples of resistance in which workers gathered together to seek alternative ways to run their lives, involving the creation of councils. The Soviets and their significance have been treated extensively by other authors, including Roman (1999:31–49) in his book on popular power in Cuba, so only the most important points will be made here. The immediate context for the formation of workers' Soviets in Russia in 1905 arose when Czarist government troops fired on peaceful anti-government protesters at a rally in St Petersburg. This act of repression, in which 1000 people were killed and which became known as 'Bloody Sunday', fanned the flames of discontent against the Czarist dictatorship (Anweiler 1974). The St Petersburg rally, and other protests that took place all over Russia, were supported from across a wide spectrum of the population, including sectors of the middle classes and the intelligentsia. For instance, universities closed and lecturers and students took to the streets to demand civil liberties, while lawyers, engineers and doctors, along with other middle-class professions, formed the Union of Unions and demanded a constituent assembly. But it was the workers and peasants that pressed the hardest demands, including economic as well as political reform. To deal with the immediate problems, such as winning strikes and fighting for an eight-hour day, the Russian workers formed themselves into revolutionary councils which were called Soviets. As time passed and the crisis deepened, the Soviets evolved into participatory and democratic organs that co-ordinated and fought for workers' interests. This was clearly demonstrated in the first Soviet that was established in Ivanovna-Voznesensk during the 1905 Textile Strike. At its inception it was an emergency strike committee, but it soon became a workers' council with a wide range of functions and an elected committee from among the town's proletariat. Between September and October, a general strike almost brought the country to a halt, and forced the Czarist government to make concessions to the protesters, including the formation of a token reformist element in the government: the State Duma. Elections to the first Duma (April–June 1906) returned moderate socialists and liberals, who pressed for more reforms. It was consequently closed by Czar Nicholas II, who held discretionary powers over its creation and dissolution. After a further failed attempt at forming a Duma, the Prime Minister Petr Stolypin changed the electoral law to ensure more votes for nobility and landowners.

Two important precedents were set by these events: firstly, the ability of the workers to organise themselves, and secondly, the power of the general strike. This was not lost on revolutionary intellectuals like Trotsky, Lenin, and the Bolsheviks. The Soviets 'served as a starting point for Lenin for the subsequent elaboration of the theory of the Soviets as the form the state would take under the dictatorship of the proletariat' (Koldáiev, cited in Roman 1999:34). The anarchists also drew lessons from these events, particularly about the spontaneity of the workers and the potential for a revolutionary general strike.

The First World War and the disruptions and turmoil it caused in Russia, including the return of disillusioned troops, made the Duma system unworkable, as it did the Russian Provisional Government that was formed after the February 1917 Revolution. The response of workers to the crisis was again to establish their own mechanisms of power in the form of Soviets, the first of which was in Petrograd in March 1917. As the Soviets spread, workers realised the effectiveness of their own power and understood that their interests were no longer served by the Provisional Government. By October, control of the country was effectively in the hands of the Soviets. As during the Paris Commune, workers and their committees took over the functions of the state, but rather than following the procedure of bourgeois government and transferring responsibility to professional representatives, power was kept at the grassroots level (Anweiler 1974:158).

In his work *State and Revolution* (2004 [1917]), Lenin sought to advance Marxist thought beyond, while building upon, the experience of the Commune. He did this by advocating that a socialist government take on the initial form of a 'dictatorship of the proletariat', based on Soviets and with 'intellectual' guidance from the Bolsheviks. This embryonic workers' government would, Lenin argued, provide the first opportunity to implement socialist objectives, including: equality, a symbiotic relationship between governed and governors, the pursuit of consensus and the 'general will', and the merging of civil and political society. It would be the crucible in which socialism and a socialist consciousness could be formed. Hence the call from the Bolsheviks for 'all power to the Soviets', expressing the belief that retaining any vestiges of bourgeois government would corrupt and dilute the purity of a revolution driven by the volition of the workers.

For Lenin, the argument of the Marxist reformists and revisionists of the Second International, such as its leader Bernstein, that the workers should take control of the bourgeois parliamentary state was an illusion, because ultimately it would be corrupting and provide an opportunity for reversion to capitalism. The essential point of *State and Revolution* is that the workers must create a separate structure of state rule informed by their experience of struggle, one that serves their interests and is founded in a form of democracy that represents all, not just a minority. This would be nothing less than a physical and conscious transcendence of bourgeois capitalism. In 1918, Lenin (cited in Roman 1999:41) stated, 'Even in the democratic capitalist republics in the world, the poor never regard the bourgeois parliament as "their" institution. But the Soviets are "their" institution.' With the closure of the Constituent Assembly in January 1918, power was transferred to the Soviets.

Although significant developments took place in theory and practice towards the formation of a workers' state, the realities of the Revolution, including internal struggles between contending political parties, resulted in a disproportionate Bolshevik influence over the Soviets. Consequently, by November 1918 there were only a few delegates in the All-Russian Congress of Soviets who were not Bolsheviks. Although this may be seen as an opportunistic strategy by the Bolsheviks to consolidate their own power, the situation was complex; Russia was struggling through a civil war and faced external aggression from the capitalist powers. Under duress, it was military power and organisation, centralised command and political control that took precedence over democratic and con-stitutional institutions and procedures. The Civil War ended in 1921 with a Bolshevik victory, but with huge loss of life, economic destruction, and social discontent as expressed in the Kronstadt mutiny (Getzler 2002). The establishment of Bolshevik power and a one-party state stands in sad contrast to the Paris Commune, where different parties supporting the workers co-operated with each other and buried their political differences to defend popular democracy.

However, the disappearance of competing political parties vying for power to represent their voters is in accordance with radical theory from Rousseau through to Lenin. In the context of new political arrangements whereby the divisions of bourgeois society are overcome, state and civil society begin to merge and there is consensus based on the 'general will' or 'Communism', in which all society works together to achieve universal goals.

However, when the Bolsheviks leapfrogged the Soviets to establish centralised control, they weakened the mechanism of conscious transformation on which socialism is premised. By the end of the Civil War, they had eradicated the bourgeois state and held supreme power at the expense of not only other parties, but also the Soviets. From this position, they falsely assumed that they had consolidated a workers' state and could proceed directly towards the formation of 'Communism'. This inconsistency seemingly was accepted by Lenin, who stated in the context of discussions in the Soviet Congress in 1920 concerning economic development, 'This marks the beginning of a very happy time when politics will recede into the background ... and engineers and agronomists will do most of the talking ... Henceforth, less politics will be the best politics' (cited in Roman 1999:47). If one goes back to Rousseau and Marx, once the conscious element of change is substituted with didactic instruction and guidance, then the dynamic of true revolutionary progress is lost. Naturally, economic development is important and, undoubtedly, the initial plans of the Bolsheviks were based on the interests of society as a whole. But if this is not carried out in concert with the workers' own understanding and needs concerning the process of change, then, no matter how well-intentioned and benign, it can only lead to a growing separation between party and masses. As the role of the Communist Party became more important, this problem was exacerbated by the New Economic Policy which eventually led to social and economic upheaval and the horrors of the Stalin period.

Besides the sheer physical and psychological terror that Stalin unleashed on his people in the name of Communism, perhaps the greatest travesty of the socialist tradition in the Soviet context was the promotion of a proletarian culture from above. The state agency *Proletkult* had been established by such figures as Trotsky and Lunacharsky in the early years of the Revolution, and was a legitimate attempt to provide a forum for a new cultural orientation; but in Stalin's hands it became another instrument of repression. Stalin's crude methods to enforce socialism from above were repeated by other Communists of the twentieth century including Mao, whose 'Cultural Revolution' led to the deaths of millions of Chinese. This in turn influenced barbarous regimes such as that of Pol Pot in Cambodia, which attempted similar 'purifications' of society in the name of socialism. In the case of the Soviet Union, however, any critical analysis must be tempered by an acknowledgement of the accumulated problems faced by the world's first socialist revolution, not only in the forms of internal civil war and external aggression, but also the vastness of the territories, the diversity of cultures, the backwardness of Russian development and the isolation of the Soviet Union after the failure of the 'world revolution' that was anticipated by Lenin.

After Stalin's death in 1953, many of his methods were renounced. In 1957 the Central Committee of the Communist Party produced a document entitled 'On Improving the Activity of the Soviets and Strengthening their Links with the Masses' (cited in Roman 1999:59), and this was followed by a genuine attempt to increase citizen participation in local government. As shown by authors like Hahn (1988) and White et al. (1987), the stereotypical view resulting from Stalin's legacy and Cold War rhetoric, of the Soviet Union as an inflexible centralised dictatorship, was not accurate. Participatory democratic structures did exist and played a significant role in decision making, especially at the local level. This was also confirmed to the author by a senior Cuban diplomat (interview with Fuentes 1999) who spent many years in the Soviet Union. What emerged was a model of so-called 'democratic centralism', which, in a world that was dominated by capitalism and the impossibility of 'socialism in one country', became a kind of best-case scenario, defining itself under the circumstances as 'really existing socialism'. Many other socialist states, including Cuba, were influenced by this Soviet model, both in terms of state and political organisation, and in developing mechanisms for the fostering of political participation.

The Spanish Civil War

One great but frequently overlooked practical experiment in participatory democracy and workers' power was the revolution that took place during the first few months of the Spanish Civil War (1936–39). The war was the result of accumulated tensions between reactionary traditionalism and progressive republicanism. The democratically elected reformist Popular Front government was a powerful expression of a protracted internal struggle in Spain to establish a durable Republic. The war broke out at a time when the Soviet Union's international strategy under the Third Communist International, the Comintern, was to promote and support anti-fascist forces, including those of traditional European liberal democracy (Thomas 1979). Consequently, when Popular Front governments were elected in France in May 1936 under Leon Blum, and in Spain in February 1936 under Manuel Azaña, they received approbation from Moscow. In response, elements of the anti-Stalinist Left disparagingly voiced the slogan, 'Vote communist to save capitalism'.

The Civil War attracted considerable international attention because it was regarded as a microcosm of wider political conflicts, particularly the rise of fascism and the reaction of the moderate liberal and republican forces that sought to contain its expansion. Although the Popular Front government had been democratically elected, other liberal democracies, including its counterpart in France, were unwilling to come to the Spanish government's aid when it was faced with an illegal and undemocratic nationalist insurrection. Fearful of becoming embroiled in such an explosive and politically volatile conflict, and running the risk of losing the support of their middle-class base who were terrified of Communism, the democracies of Europe and the US abandoned the Spanish Republic to its fate. Only the Soviet Union was willing to come to the Republic's aid. In doing so, it gained enormous prestige among anti-fascist forces throughout the world, and secured control of the war effort including the organisation and direction of foreign non-governmental support for the Republic in the form of the International Brigades.

Besides the official Republican war effort in Spain, which was supported by the Communists, there was also a popular revolution taking place, mainly under the auspices of the anarchists and the semi-Trotskyist *Partido Obrero de Unificación Marxista* (POUM). Both of these had their main power bases in Catalonia, but their influence, combined with that of trade unions, spread throughout Republican Spain. These popular revolutionaries saw in the defence of their towns and villages not only a chance to fight fascism, but also an opportunity to seize political and economic power and begin to transform society along socialist or anarchist lines. The Communists did not recognise the popular uprising because it threatened their power, and any association they had with revolution undermined the moderate image they were trying to project to the European middle classes, who they felt could easily fall prey to fascist propaganda (Fraser 1979). Consequently, in 1937 the Communists attacked and destroyed the leadership of the POUM and isolated the anarchists, putting an end to the main thrust of the popular revolution in Spain.

The few foreign intellectuals, workers and activists who did not sign up to fight with the International Brigades and instead witnessed the Spanish Revolution were mesmerised by its actions and potentials. George Orwell, who joined a POUM battalion in Barcelona in December 1936, wrote in the famous account of his experiences, *Homage to Catalonia* (1979):

> It was the first time that I had been in a town where the working class was in the saddle. Practically every building of any size had been seized by the workers and was draped with red flags or the red and black flags of the anarchists ... the only community of any size in Western Europe where political consciousness and disbelief in capitalism were more normal than their opposites.

Referring to the French intellectual and adventurer André Malraux's response to the popular uprising, the Peruvian poet César Vallejo, who visited Spain during the Civil War, stated, 'Without question the first months of the Spanish Civil War reflected ... an instinctive accent beating hard with pristine popular fervour, which forced Malraux to exclaim: "In this instant, at least, a revolution has been made which is forever pure"' (1937 vol. 2:35, author's translation). The wave of collectivisations that swept over Spain in the summer and autumn of 1936 has also been described as 'the greatest experiment in workers' self-management Western Europe has ever seen' (BBC 1986).

During the few months of the Spanish Revolution, land and industry were collectivised, affecting an estimated 5–7 million people (Leval 1996). Village and sector assemblies were formed to run these collectives, each with elected recallable delegates; rationing was introduced to ensure an equitable distribution of goods; wages were equalised for all workers and most services were made free, including medical care. To defend the Revolution against the nationalist armies and reactionary elements, workers' militias were formed. Democracy and accountability were held to be the cornerstones of anarchist organisation. It has been claimed that in the period of collectivisation there were only six cases of theft from the workplace (ibid.).

A fitting end to this short analysis of socialism and democracy, in some ways bringing us back full-circle to Rousseau and his belief in human potential, is a comment made by the anarchist leader

Buenaventura Durruti. He was asked by a journalist if the masses could win without support from the Republican government, and, even if they could, if the anarchist experiment would not end in disaster. Durruti replied:

> We have always lived in slums and holes in the wall. We will know how to accommodate ourselves for a time. For you must not forget that we can also build. It is we who built these palaces and cities, here in Spain and in America and everywhere. We, the workers. We can build others to take their place. And better ones. We are not in the least afraid of ruins. We are going to inherit the earth. There is not the slightest doubt of that. The bourgeoisie might blast and ruin its own world before it leaves the stage of history. We carry a new world, here in our hearts. That world is growing in this minute. (Paz 1976:229)

In the event, the anarchist experiment was indeed undermined by the lack of support from the Republican government and by the actions of the Communists. However, like in the Paris Commune, errors were also made that contributed to its demise, including the failure to take over the Catalonian banking system, which would have given the revolutionaries greater autonomy.

Throughout the historical current of radical, Left and Marxist approaches to socialism and democracy there are several identifying factors, although not all camps agree on what should be included or how certain issues should be interpreted. Firstly, as indicated by Rousseau, and followed by Marx, Gramsci and some anarchists, radical ideas cannot be supported within a liberal intellectual framework. Consequently, a different ontology has to be identified in which humans can be perceived as social beings able to change their very nature. Secondly, it is principally the oppressed, the masses, the workers who are best placed, because of their subordinate position in bourgeois society, to seek the means to transcend capitalism and hence their own exploitation. Thirdly, in breaking free from the bourgeois/capitalist system, revolutionaries must negate its mechanisms of oppression, not only to secure physical liberty but also conscious liberation from the dominant hegemony. In all of these areas, democracy shifts from representation by elites to participation by the people who, in learning to direct political and economic processes, change themselves, as well as the systems they consciously seek to alter by their volition.

THE IDEOLOGIES OF DEMOCRACY

Problems with Contemporary Definitions

The resurgence of democracy is a fact, but there is disagreement concerning the best path to democratisation, some confusion over the diverse contemporary models, and conflict about the validity of neo-liberal democracy. However, it is important to recognise that theorists who base their views on the 'classical model' share common ground concerning the political principles that democracy must embrace. On this point, Hadenius (1992:6) states:

> I would maintain that it is indeed possible to give the concept of democracy a fairly clear content, at least at its heart. For everything is not in dispute and although opinions differ, it is nevertheless feasible to spell out the main content ... it is based on a core formula concerning the principles of democracy.

Even writers who are critical of aspects of the 'democratic resurgence', such as Rueschemayer (1992) and Hirst (1994), agree on the established principles, which include: one person one vote, free regular multi-party elections, free flow of information, a free press, and elected officials who personify the 'will of the majority'. Essentially, most theorists agree that democracy is founded upon general principles which, when applied, set in motion a series of stages of democratisation that advance towards a preconceived ideal system. It is accepted, nevertheless, that diversity does occur within democratic systems, and this is usually explained by reference to the particular historical circumstances of each society and its distinct cultural and institutional traditions. However, this kind of thinking simply states and restates the rules, formulae and ideology of one general perception of democracy, based on one (liberal) ontological foundation, and does little to open up the debate to consider what other forms democracy might take.

Arblaster (1994:8) takes the debate a step further: 'At the root of all definitions of democracy, however refined and complex, lies the idea of popular power ... an idea of popular sovereignty – the people as the ultimate political authority'. In the US and many other developed Western capitalist states, democracy is understood as empowering individuals, and hence the people, principally through elected officials who represent their interests. However, for social democrats in the post-war years, the most effective measure for giving people power was by structural reform shifting political influence from the centre to local groups. Moving further away from the individualist notion of democracy, Miller (1993:76) argues:

> [T]he deliberative [collectivist democracy as in certain Communist states] view clearly rests on a different conception of 'human nature in politics' from the liberal view. Whereas the latter stresses the importance of giving due weight to each individual's distinct preferences, the former relies on a person's capacity to be swayed by rational arguments and to lay aside particular interests and opinions in deference to overall fairness and the common interest of the collectivity.

Although not referring specifically to democracy, Rose, Kamin and Lewontin (1984:240) clearly identify one of the sources of controversy concerning social theories:

> Every theory of society implies a theory of what it is to be human. Every theorist carries out the same fiction apparently deducing the nature of society from a priori consideration of the innate nature of human beings, whilst inducing the necessary assumptions from the end to be reached.

If various perceptions of democracy are to be analysed, then perhaps the starting point should be the implicit, rarely explicit, assumptions about human nature on which they are founded. Within the elitist liberal tradition, two approaches to democracy have been identified – the political route and the economic route. The former represents liberal and neo-liberal approaches, and the latter represents a Keynesian, developmentalist and social democratic approach.

The Political Route and the Individual

The case for the political (representative) route is well put in its contemporary context by Nwabueze (1993:101): 'Democracy is meaningless without freedom of dissent and respect for the individuality of each person. For man is first and foremost an individual human being, and his individuality must come before the demand of equality with other members of society.' As we have seen, the liberal tradition is premised on the idea of a coherent human subject; the privileged position of individual interests; free association of individuals including the right to contract; the right to acquire and dispose of private property freely; privacy;

the formal equality of individuals; and open public discourse (freedom of speech). Human community in this framework is less about co-operation, and is seen more as an ideal marketplace in which individuals compete. Indeed, many theorists supporting this view fear mass collective action because it is presumed to unleash dangerous irrational tendencies.

Viewing people principally as individuals suggests that humans are essentially independent of their environment and are endowed with a biological or God-given nature that determines their preferences. This implies that our behaviour is innately fixed, and that we have the ability to make choices that will effectively satisfy our individual needs. Avritzer (2002:21) recognises this tendency when he states:

> Downs's theory of democracy does not limit itself to reintroducing individual rationality in the process of political decision-making; it goes further by seeking to connect the principle of utility maximisation with the general functioning of the political system and this view is underpinned by an egoistic definition of human nature [which] leads the author to assume that an individual will opt for his or her own happiness without regard for the happiness of others.

Hinkelammert (1990) argues that neo-liberalism has produced an understanding of democracy that corresponds with its economic theories, in which people respond to democratic choice in the same way as they do to consumer choice. Such a human being will also require a form of democracy in which individual interests are defended by elected representatives who protect him/her from social impositions, mainly in the form of overbearing and interfering government. This point is strongly made by Holden (1988:12), who believes that representative democracy must encourage 'a concern with individual freedoms that centres on the need to limit the power and authority of government'. However, governments can become interventionist when there is an attempt to restrict the free choice of individuals by monopolies, trade unions, criminals, etc.

Within this representative, or neo-liberal, form of democracy, it is essential to have regular free elections with one person one vote, in which the will of the majority (of like-minded individuals) becomes the basis for policy, even if it is a limited majority. The right to impose this will is passed on to an elected representative body which holds power and makes binding decisions on behalf of the electorate. This involves an implicit assumption about humans as independent individuals who make choices that maximise their utility. There are no extensive consultation processes for establishing particular choices, because it is assumed that as long as the policies promote subjective preferences, then the market will adjust, reject or account for diversity through the price mechanism.

This is, in some respects, the application to politics of the economic theory of perfect competition. In practice, the limits of individual freedom are contained within the parameters of the market and the 'rule of money'. The problem with reducing democracy to an act of individual electoral choice, giving power to representatives whose agendas are shaped by non-democratic forces, is that it allows the unequal power structures within the private sphere to be further consolidated. As Gunter Grass (cited in Raby 2006:47) notes, 'parliament is no longer sovereign in its decisions. It depends on powerful pressure groups – the banks and multinationals – which are not subject to any democratic control. Democracy has become a pawn to the dictates of globally volatile capital.'

The Developmentalist View: Constructive/Structuralist Democracy

Those theorists who support the economic/developmentalist route to democracy have a different view of what constitutes human nature:

> Man is innately programmed in such a way that he needs culture to complete him … man is like one of those versatile cake mixes that can be variously prepared to end up as different types of cake … just as a cake has to be baked, so a baby has to be exposed to a specific … culture. (Midgley 1978:286)

Causation is seen here as external, with people presented as *tabulae rasae* (blank slates), and it is their environments that shape their behaviour. Given this view, the function of democracy is to institutionalise political standards and control society to assure equality of rights. Democracy becomes 'constructive' more than 'representative', and the establishment of what is considered to be the best environment takes precedence over individual preferences; therefore, it is the elitist social group, class or representative institution that becomes the focus of attention. The population is perceived as a mass of culturally conditioned beings that require external guidance, principally through education, organisation and explanation. The aim is to bring about a consensus of the majority, based on what is assumed to be in their best interests. Underlying this belief is the idea that humans are susceptible to manipulation and irrational prejudice, and therefore, for Schumpeter, 'Human nature in politics being what it is [allows groups] to create the will of the people' (1942:263). This view could be applied to both liberal and structuralist democracy, but he envisages it mainly in the second context. By selecting 'responsible' elites to act on behalf of the population, he believed that negative behaviour could be avoided, curbing the irrational tendencies of the masses and containing the excesses of demagogic leaders and groups. The notion of the twentieth-century individual as both an irrational consumer and irrational citizen, open to external manipulation, is consistent with the notion of constructive democracy in which the masses are seen to need corrective guidance.

This approach to democracy requires an interventionist state which is not necessarily anti-market or against private enterprise, but ensures that these sectors work to support the objectives of industrial, financial, social and cultural policy. The state empowers itself with political, legal and organisational means by which it can place restrictions on those whose self-interest, or failed training, leads them to step beyond the established social norms. Such assumptions are the foundation for models of democracy with a social democratic, developmentalist and collectivist perspective. In capitalist countries, 'constructive' democracy seeks to maintain the basic structural mechanisms of representative democracy: one person one vote, free elections, etc. But the way it defines and represents the interests of the majority is different from liberal democracy, as it concentrates on structures rather than individuals. However, it is now extremely difficult for governments to promote this kind of democracy, because the controls needed for protecting and shaping society have been undermined by the globalisation of market forces and finance capital. Cerny (1997:1) describes this contest between state and free-market individualism as follows:

Globalisation is leading to a world in which cross cutting and overlapping governance structures and processes increasingly take private, oligarchic forms, where hegemonic neoliberal norms of economic freedom and personal autonomy are deligitimising both democratic governance in general and the credibility of those who try to make democracy work, and in which democratic states are losing the policy autonomy and capacity necessary for transforming what the people want into concrete outputs.

As previously discussed in Chapter 1, in the post-war, pre-globalisation era, nations, and especially developed ones, largely contained productive forces within their geographical boundaries, and social classes were obliged to negotiate over 'who gets what' through democracy articulated via a state having significant power over a mixed economy. Once the nation-state began to lose its influence over finance and production, these ties and responsibilities were broken, as ruling elites were able to shift the process of accumulation into transnational space, diminishing the role of politics and weakening the effectiveness of democracy at the national level. This is not a problem for neo-liberals, however, because consumers' individual interests can be represented just as well, if not better, in a global market which implies more choice (Redwood 1994).

However, it is not only 'structuralist' democracies that are facing problems. 'Representative democratic government is failing badly by the standards of liberal democratic theory' (Hirst 1994:3). In Latin America, in particular, where there has been a dramatic shift from military dictatorships to representative elected civilian government, the new regimes are seen to be democratically weak. Castañeda (1993:245), for example, argues that sudden political democracy has heightened expectations among the poor majorities, and failure to complement political freedom with economic improvements will lead to the return of dictatorships as the poor seek economic justice by non-electoral means. Even in the multilateral institutions such as the World Bank, which promoted neo-liberal structural adjustment, there is concern that if economic growth is not given priority these democracies might fail. The prescribed model, however, would not be based on planning and management, but on increased liberalisation favouring capital and markets.

The democratic perspectives selected above represent the two main ideological and practical paradigms that have influenced the understanding of democracy over the last half-century, but there are many intermediate shades of opinion. Although no one doubts that there has been a recent resurgence of democracy, its outcome and form are contested and the neo-liberal model is increasingly being challenged by those who have different perceptions. While few would disagree that a return to democracy is preferable to authoritarianism (even authors such as Castañeda and Munck (1989), who are critical of the new democracies in Latin America, emphasise the immense relief and sense of freedom felt by most of the citizens who have rid themselves of dictatorship), the issue is far from resolved concerning the form that democracy should take.

These uncertainties about democracy in its current guises have led to much theorising about alternative models, comprised of different mixes of elements from the representative and structuralist formulations. Mainly within the parameters of these two general perceptions of how democracy should be developed, Pinkney (1993) identifies five different democratic systems: 'socialist', 'radical', 'liberal', 'guided' and 'consociational'. Other writers such as Held (1993) have catalogued five further variants based on the 'classical model'. Collier and Levitsky (1997) consider a further 550 sub-types of democracy. Based on this broad yet ideologically restricted view of democracy, Hirst (1994:12), like Dahl before him, seeks to identify the best possible model and suggests a reformation of democracy along 'associative' lines, while retaining the essential structural features of Western practice:

> Associationalism makes accountable representative democracy possible again by limiting the scope of state administration, without diminishing social provision. It enables market-based societies to deliver the substantive goals desired by the citizens, by embedding the market system in a social network of co-ordinate and regulatory institutions.

This view is linked loosely with 'market socialist' ideas in economics. The market and socialism are, however, two irreconcilable entities and claims along these lines are very easy to demolish theoretically (McNally 1993).

The difficulty with this kind of 'pick and mix' approach is that it continues to see democracy as a definable system constructed out of component parts, and does not consider that the source of the problem may lie with the philosophical foundations on which the two main democratic models are based. Fukuyama (1992:338) goes to the heart of the problem, but dismisses it too glibly:

> [W]hile modern societies have evolved towards democracy, modern thought has arrived at an impasse, unable to come to a consensus on what constitutes man ... This confusion in thought can occur despite ... the fact that liberal democracy in reality constitutes the best possible solution to the human problem.

He develops this idea in his later work *The Great Disruption: Human Nature and the Reconstitution of Social Order* (1999).

The issue of democracy goes far beyond the need to establish an identifiable system, and the extent of its relationship with capitalism or some other form of economic and political organisation. It also raises the question: What kind of democracy? Neither the representative nor structuralist approaches are particularly clear about the actual functioning of democracy, and any notion of giving direct power to citizens remains an alien concept. Issues such as equality, popular sovereignty, effective participation and direct democracy have been shelved because they simply cannot be contained within the dominant democratic models. The latter either maintain class inequalities through illusory guiding concepts such as the market or, alternatively, a regime that sets out to design and put into operation a system presumed to be good for its citizens. According to Boron (1995:5), when considering the demise of the most substantive elements of democracy:

> Equality became 'equality of opportunities' with a complete disregard of initial conditions and minimum necessary endowments; and direct democracy and popular sovereignty quietly withered away, their place occupied by a 'representative democracy' in which lobbies and interest groups are far more important than the common people, while a complex set of legal and bureaucratic procedures effectively tended to discourage popular participation in public affairs.

Under the structuralist model, that gave primacy to economic development over political democracy, it could be argued that egalitarianism was brought back into the equation, albeit under the auspices of a technocratic elite who acted in the presumed best interests of the people. However, this combination of politics and economics was eventually subverted by its failure to control the capitalist system and its disaffected ruling classes, who successfully re-established their liberty through the globalisation of markets. It is difficult to accept that democracy can flourish today when the total wealth of the top 8.3 million people (about 0.13 per cent of the world's population) 'rose 8.2 per cent to $30.8 trillion in 2004, giving them control of nearly one quarter of the world's financial assets' (Merrill Lynch – Capgemini 2005). This situation suggests that the contemporary understanding of democracy has made a significant departure from the definition that was proposed by one of the concept's founders, Aristotle, who stated that democracy was 'the rule of the many for the good of the poor' (Boron 1995:7).

Democracy Promotion – Polyarchy

While many of the intellectual concepts and theories which support capitalist-style democracy are conceived and developed in good faith that its application would benefit society as a whole, there is another less explicit dimension to fostering this kind of democracy. As we have seen in Chapter 1, the political economy of the neo-liberal project is more than simply a model of development, but also an attempt by elites to order the world to their advantage. In this context, 'democracy promotion' becomes part of the ideological armoury which enforces this project. When analysts like Domínguez (1996) argue that it is illogical for Cuba to resist the forces of markets and democracy, they believe that this model will eventually benefit the Cuban people. However, when one reveals the more Machiavellian intent of neo-liberalism's elite managers, such a view is untenable.

It should be remembered that elitist manipulation for economic and political ends also took place in those socialist countries that followed so-called 'democratic centralism', but, as will be argued in the two final chapters, this model was never fully adopted by Cuba and is now no longer an option. Moreover, the true test of the Cuban Revolution is not the hope of hanging on to a defunct socialist system, but whether it will act as a guiding influence for the growing counter-hegemony against neo-liberalism.

To understand the propensity of elites to construct and promote an ideological environment that complements their material power, it is important to be aware of the Gramscian theory of hegemony. This form of hegemony should be distinguished from the notion of hegemony used in International Relations (IR) theory. In IR this concept is employed to explain the domination of one state over others, and more precisely to refer to the supreme power of Britain in the nineteenth century and the US in the twentieth. Superficially, domination takes the form of various coercive controls exercised through military, diplomatic, economic and financial power, but in more refined definitions it can imply a synchronised constellation of power which also includes cultural, social and ideological influences. Gramsci's notion of hegemony has more in common with this second definition, but instead of referring to relations between nations he directs his analysis towards the relationship between classes within a nation or social system. Gramsci believed that to achieve sustainable domination, a social class or classes must complement its (visible) physical, material and political power with ideological power.

In advanced capitalism, with its complex state interwoven with society, Gramsci argued that social control takes place on two levels: firstly through 'political society' in the form of the state itself, and secondly, but of equal importance, through 'civil society' in the form of education, religion, media, the family, language, cultural formation, and even myths and superstitions. Whereas the former is the traditional arena for coercion, the latter represents a melange of activity which directly influences popular consciousness, promoting ideas and beliefs which shape the population's view of the world in which it lives.

Once a set of ideas, beliefs or popular notions have been successfully promoted by 'intellectuals' in civil society, through a 'scholastic programme', to the level where they become accepted as 'a general conception of life', hegemony can provide a means of coercion which is managed and sustained for the exploiters by the exploited themselves (Gramsci 1971:103–104). In this way, one class, or fraction of a class, can secure leadership over other classes or strata by gaining, through ideological manipulation, the latter's consent to the former's project of domination. This is especially so in modern capitalist society, where control over mass communications opens up the possibility of distributing and propagating certain sets of favoured ideas. Robinson (1996:21) writes:

> A Gramscian hegemony involves the internalisation on the part of subordinate classes of the moral and cultural values, the codes of practical conduct, and the worldview of the dominant classes or groups – in sum, internalisation of the social logic of the system of domination itself. This logic is imbedded in ideology, which acts as a cohesive force in the social unification (in Gramsci's phrase, 'cement').

But, as Robinson further points out, hegemony is more than just ideology. It is also a social relationship that binds together a 'bloc' of different classes, often against the logic of their (unequal) material relations, in a condition of consensual domination such that subordinate groups give their 'spontaneous consent' to the 'direction imposed on social life' by the ruling factions (22). This is a point that was also made by Schumpeter (1975:263) who states, 'the will of the people is the product and not the motive power of the political process ... Issues and popular will on any issue are manufactured.'

Since Gramsci's theory was rediscovered in the 1960s, it has been associated principally with the control of 'superstructural' elements in civil society (culture, gender, race, religion, etc.), perhaps as a reaction to the crude 'economism' of the Stalinist and Soviet period of Left thinking. However, he believed in an 'ensemble of relations', which did not seek to replace economics and the prevailing mode of production as prime forces behind class and social formation, but rather suggested that those alone were insufficient to explain the complex composition of modern society. Gramsci accepted the base (principally economic factors)–superstructure relationship, yet understood it not in a linear and determinant mode, but rather as the interplay of forces which in distinct historical 'moments' could take on different configurations. Indeed, it is the reciprocity between base and superstructure, and state and civil society, where hegemony is played out. What mattered above all for Gramsci, without undervaluing material forces, was human consciousness. With this in mind, he saw that a simple reaction by the masses against material exploitation would be insufficient to create a successful revolution. What was needed first was the formation of 'counter-hegemony' in civil society, in which the subordinate classes begin to challenge dominant ideological codes and develop an alternative mode of thinking (consciousness). Revolution, for Gramsci, should be constructed in the mind before it is brought to the barricades.

Although Gramsci's concept of hegemony was originally applied to the formation of classes and social groups within the nation-state, it can also be extended into the international arena (Burnham 1991; Cox 1981, 1983; Gill & Law 1988). In this sense, hegemony is not the power of one nation or group of nations over others, but rather 'coercion by consent' in national-level political and civil society, spilling over into international space. This is entirely consistent with the analysis of the transnationalisation of capital and productive forces, because these processes lead to the formation of political and class structures at the level where production itself operates, as can be seen by an extension of Marx's method. As the transnational elite extend their economic and productive power into global space, they also carry their domination over political, social and class relations into the same arena. In this context Gramsci's notion of hegemony, as the exercise of elite power over national civil society in the form of consensual domination, can be extended to refer to a global configuration.

By the early 1990s, the structural changes in world capitalism, and their promotion and enhancement through the deregulatory processes in finance, political economy and national-level legislation, were complemented by the collapse of the Soviet Union, which had stood as the last true ideological and geographical barrier to capitalist expansion. It is from these structural changes within capitalism that the necessity arises for new means of coercion at the level of ideology. Fundamental to this task is a revised understanding, conceptualisation and application of democracy, one that has been defined as 'polyarchy'.

Polyarchy is a term that was first used by Dahl in his book *Polyarchy: Participation and Opposition* (1971). In this study, Dahl attempted to define, within the elitist tradition, a form of democracy that would be manageable in the modern nation-state. One of his main premises was that 'classical' democracy, as implied by the Greek terms 'demos' (people) and 'cratos' (power/government), was unworkable in advanced capitalism. What he believed to be more feasible was the control by 'poly-' (many) '-archy' (rule), or a similar combination depending on how these words are interpreted. Robinson (1996a), in his pathbreaking work *Promoting Polyarchy: Globalization, US Intervention and Hegemony*, extends the use of the term polyarchy by considering the role of capitalist democracy in the context of globalisation. This forms a central component of his *Theory of Global Capitalism* (2004:81–82) in which he states:

> Polyarchy refers to a system in which a small group actually rules, and participation in decision making by the majority is confined to choosing among competing elites in tightly controlled electoral processes. This 'low intensity democracy' does not involve power (cratos) of the people (demos), much less an end to class domination or to substantive inequality, which is growing exponentially under the global economy. Transitions to polyarchy should be seen in the light of the changing nature of transitional social control under globalization ... polyarchy has been promoted by the transnational elite as the political counterpart to neoliberalism.

According to Robinson, therefore, the contemporary mainstream definition and functional application of democracy are not just about a stated set of political, academic and ideological preferences for a particular model; they are also, and more profoundly, an instrument of US foreign policy and global elite interests that must be promoted, supported and implanted as a political counterpart to transnational economic power.

'Democracy promotion' as it is currently championed by the 'international community', and especially by the United States through such agencies as the National Endowment for Democracy, is therefore more than an effort to support a 'universal good' – it is an instrument of hegemonic control. Whereas dictatorships, especially in Latin America, served the needs of an earlier world system, now more subtle means of control are required, ones that accord with the transnational elite's global project. This is facilitated by the globalisation process, itself driven by a self-conscious transnational elite, that, while presenting the possibility of democracy and openness, at the same time closes many doors through which such new freedoms could be extended. Mobile transnational capital, competition for foreign direct investment, deregulation, erosion of public services and the transfer of swathes of the former public sector into private hands – these all serve to weaken the power of local representatives and their popular constituencies to capture and control resources, and to direct them towards groups with the greatest needs, often the majority of the population. Whereas in the past states ruled markets to some degree, now markets rule states, meaning that democracy can flourish because in theory whoever gains political power will be forced to acquiesce to global capital and its national representations. At the level of hegemony, however, as populations are offered democracy as a 'universal good', they cannot complain because any political or economic outcome is ultimately the result of their 'free' choice. This form of coercion by consent is a more powerful instrument of control than the dictatorships and violence that prevailed in a previous era, which were costly to maintain, and politically destabilising.

'Democracy promotion' is not so much about installing democracy, but rather guiding its outcomes through a series of economic, political and ideological manipulations that restrict its potential. The National Endowment for Democracy and other agencies that support global elite interests have been active in this context in numerous countries over the past 25 years, including Russia, Poland, the Ukraine, Mexico, Iran and many others. In the case of Iran these efforts have not yet been successful, and may be replaced by more interventionist and direct means of 'persuasion' (Hammond 2009; Petras 2009).

If Cuba were to embrace contemporary globalisation in all its aspects including 'democracy', it would not only have to abandon the Revolution, but also would be obliged to surrender its sovereignty and independence to a transnational elite and their national-level collaborators. Therefore democracy, as proposed by some analysts and the international community, is the instrument through which Cuba could be penetrated and manipulated to support the wider objectives of exposing its resources to the whims of transnational capital, and quashing its image as an alternative to the dominant order. The issue for Cuba is not just which model of democracy it should follow, but also the defence of the Revolution against forces seeking to tear it apart, surely leaving most of its population in a parlous state with little control over individual lives or collective future.

Participatory Democracy

There is a third, but lesser-known, approach to democracy that draws heavily on the socialist tradition described in this chapter. The author believes that such a form of democracy is supported, in general, by the Cuban state and most of the population. Among the small academic and theoretical following of this view, writers such as Bengelsdorf (1994) and the Cuban scholar Dilla (1993) do not attempt to measure Cuban 'democracy' against dominant democratic models, but rather seek a different defining framework which emphasises participation. It is this perspective, rather than the representative and structuralist routes and others that see democracy as a system, which may offer the most viable approach through which to understand the dynamic of Cuban 'democracy' and its potential for the future.

Participation, as conceived by these authors, is a process of creative social interaction rather than some form of token involvement in a predetermined system. It is also not restricted in the way that other perceptions of democracy are because of their fixed assumptions about human nature. The concept of democracy as a participatory, creative and changing process is suggested by Moore-Lappé (1994:14–15), a founder of the Living Democracy movement in the US:

> To work democracy ... has to be a way of life ... Citizenship is a lot more than voting ... Democracy is never fully in place. It is always in flux, a work in progress. Democracy is dynamic. It evolves in response to the creative actions of citizens. It is what we make of it.

For her, democracy is not a preconceived system that can be perfected by following a set of established rules; it is a social process that changes constantly in response to the creative activity of people. Human nature in this case would appear to be determined neither by innate inheritance nor material environment, because whether humans are independent (as perceived by neo-liberals) or dependent (as seen by structuralists), they are passive as far as their role within democracy is concerned. Gould (1990:132), one of the few modern analysts who considers the importance of human nature when attempting to understand and define democracy, alludes to an alternative notion of the human condition:

> [N]either individuals or social reality are ... immutable entities whose essence is given once and for all. The only thing given once and for all is the free activity of [those] *social individuals* [author's emphasis] who constitute their world and change it.

Defining humans as 'social individuals' would seem to imply that we are both personally independent and socially dependent, and therefore we can only fulfil individual potentials through social activity. Biological inheritance and social experience do not exist each in isolation, but mutually impact upon each other; they are interdependent. As individuals we are able to imagine differently, thus imagination and creativity are subjective. We are constantly influenced by social environments that shape our thinking (consciousness), leading to new ways of thinking and new forms of creativity. But, since we have unique potentials, we will react to, and learn from, our experiences differently. While humans must adapt their creativity to social constraints to survive, and are influenced in their development by economic, historical and cultural circumstances, they will constantly seek ways to realise their potential, and change can often be effectively achieved through collective organisation and action based on coincidence of interest. Humans are, therefore, not only creative and diverse, but also capable of modifying their environments and ultimately even their own nature. Our history becomes a continuous transformation of our nature, which is never static. If humans are so, then democracy can only function as an evolving process, and the inflexible systems of representative and structuralist democracy are unworkable because they cannot respond to such diversity and change.

As we have seen, this kind of thinking is based on an alternative ontological foundation to the one which underpins liberal and structuralist perceptions of democracy, and in its first manifestation owes much to Rousseau. Rousseau is regarded by liberals as utopian, as are his republican and leftist followers, because liberals see human nature as conflictive and individualistic and cannot accept the possibility of humanity's *perfectibilité*. Indeed, within the parameters of liberal ontology such a state would be impossible, since human behaviour is seen as largely predetermined by biological make-up or immutable nature. However, if one conceives of human nature as 'unfinished, malleable, and educatable' (Ryan 1993:xxxi) in the Rousseauian sense, then the pursuit of 'perfectibility' becomes an ongoing project which may never be entirely achievable, but allows humans to combine their potentials to create a better future both for individuals and for the species as a whole. Put another way, Castro (2007:548) states, 'I am totally convinced, from my own experience, that values can be sown in the souls of men, in their intelligence and in their hearts.'

Democracy as a social process, rather than a predetermined system, would rely upon building counter-hegemonic institutions to challenge the dominant hegemony. The role and function of elected officials would be to organise, but not direct, social activity. Therefore the notion of representative democracy, where elected officials can represent the will of the majority, becomes untenable because there is no sustainable majority common interest to represent, as it is always in flux. Likewise, the idea of structuralist democracy, where a political elite seeks consensus, also becomes unworkable, for there is no sustainable consensus. Under mainstream democratic principles, what individuals cannot achieve is the realisation of power in the form of their own self-development and the ability to change their social conditions; economic and social life are determined by representatives, in collaboration with non-representative entities such as capital or the neo-liberal state, whose interests often conflict with popular aspirations.

The experience of exercising individual power becomes democratic as it manifests through co-operation, and initially local and diverse groups may interact with one another to achieve change. This experience is 'lived' by the participants, and the process becomes part of their own self-development and self-realisation. Nevertheless, in this process, individuals and groups become aware of what changes might imply for others and will have to adapt their demands accordingly. People may also pursue more than one cause because they have various roles in life, and consciousness is constituted in different ways. A person can be a worker, a parent, a woman, and an artist and may seek to influence each aspect of their life by diverse means. The democratic process, therefore, can be carried out at multiple levels and in different circumstances. Such a form of democracy can only be fostered through participation, and requires a government which permits and facilitates a high degree of independence at the local level. This government must also establish channels of communication and organisations through which the population can express their opposing views, represent their various interests and decide democratically on actions to be taken.

The Cuban Revolution has not, by any means, perfected the above form of democracy, and the authoritarian structuralist current is still strong. But, as we will see later, the historical and ideological trajectory of the Revolution has led to an emphasis on participation and social interaction for the development of initiatives and the resolution of problems. Everything in Cuba today is in flux, and there is no guarantee that this participatory process will continue or even survive. Interestingly, the crisis precipitated on the island by the collapse of the Soviet Bloc has created both opportunities and obstacles for this kind of democracy. In the next ten years the democratic direction that Cuba will take must be resolved, and in reality there are only two choices: the way proposed by Domínguez – markets and 'procedural' democracy; or the continuing construction of socialism based on a separate ontological understanding of human nature.

3
The Cuban Revolution: Building a Participatory Democratic Process

The two previous chapters sought to explain the process of globalisation and the development of elitist forms of democracy which have led to the contemporary model of democracy/polyarchy. It was also suggested that there exists a republican/socialist democratic alternative that has surfaced at certain times, and which is founded on a different ontology to the one underpinning the dominant order.

This chapter will attempt to ascertain if the historical and political processes that distinguish Cuba from the mainstream flow of neo-liberal globalisation – its experiments in popular participatory democracy and indeed the whole trajectory of the Revolution – reveal an attempt to work towards developing the alternative ontology described in Chapter 2. If so, then the Cuban experience may have a special relevance, not just concerning its own future, but also for those who seek to change the world today: an embryonic counter-hegemony to globalisation in its current form, pursuing not only social justice but a different context for human development based on collective endeavour rather than competitive individualism.

The chapter is divided into three main sections. The first gives a brief selective background to the Insurrection of 1959 and the setting for the subsequent Revolution, focusing on the problems of democracy. This is followed by a short study of the formation of a separate revolutionary ideology from that of mainstream Communism. An analysis is then made of Cuban approaches to democracy and participation during the period of the Revolution with emphasis on the development since 1976 of Cuba's local government system, *Poder Popular* (People's Power).

BACKGROUND TO THE INSURRECTION AND THE BEGINNINGS OF THE REVOLUTION

It should be noted that for reasons of space it is impossible to provide a detailed analysis of the causes of the Cuban Insurrection and the Revolution that followed, and the author assumes that most readers will be familiar with that history. The Revolution is the result of a long process linked to what Hennessy (1964) has termed 'frustrated nationalism'. This nationalist sentiment has its roots in colonial times and was exacerbated by the 1899 US intervention in the Cuban War of Independence (1895–99). At that time, colonial Spain and the Cuban nationalists were locked in a war of attrition which, in the absence of foreign interference, may have resulted in a victory for the latter (Pérez 1988:175). But the consequence of US actions in the so-called Spanish–American War was that America, which had long coveted Cuba, was able to impose its own imperial order on the island. This was enshrined in the Platt Amendment of 1901 that permitted intervention by Washington if Cubans ventured to act in ways that displeased the great power, and which consequently 'served to transform the substance of Cuban sovereignty into an extension of the US national system' (ibid.:186). Further facilitating US control of Cuba was, ironically, the strategy of the nationalist rebels, which was to destroy the sugar plantocracy as an economic class (Blackburn 1963). In the absence of a ruling oligarchy, which in the rest of Latin America was/is the interface with foreign interests and has a powerful controlling influence over domestic development and politics, the US and other foreign powers were able to take over the main sectors of the Cuban economy, a process which continued into the twentieth century. In 1913, total US investments in Cuba amounted to around $220 million, but by 1929 this had risen to $1.525 billion; from 17.7 per cent of US investments in Latin America to 27.3 per cent (Blackburn 1963:58). From the late 1920s, American interests controlled 70 per cent of sugar production (Hennessy 1963:353). In the mid 1950s, corporations and US citizens owned 75 per cent of arable land in Cuba (Franklin 1997) and 76 per cent of Cuban imports originated in the US. The North American stake in the Cuban economy, as a proportion of total economic activity, was seven times more than in any other Latin American country. This disproportionate foreign influence restricted the formation of an independent Cuban entrepreneurial class.

The island's economy was dominated by sugar production, or perhaps more precisely the price of sugar. In the 1950s, 25 per cent of the national workforce was engaged in the sugar industry. Heavily dependent on the export of one commodity, booms and slumps occurred according to world demand, causing uncertainty, short-termism and unreliable employment prospects. Sugar workers faced the additional problem of the crop's seasonal nature, finding employment for half the year and sometimes less. In periods of recession, such as the years immediately before the Insurrection, more than 40 per cent of the population was unemployed or underemployed. The lack of a significant national business sector, and the economic volatility of Cuba's main crop, drove those from within the middle classes who could not find work with a US company to seek employment in politics and public administration. Inevitably this led to corruption and the development of a spoils system. There is a vast literature on the causes of the Revolution. Among the best general studies on the pre-revolutionary period are Louis Pérez's *Cuba: Between Reform and Revolution* (1988) and Hugh Thomas's monumental work *Cuba: or the Pursuit of Freedom* (1971). The articles cited above by Hennessy (1964 & 1963) and Blackburn (1963) are also essential reading, the latter providing an excellent analysis of Cuba's class structure before the Insurrection.

Several important elements became part of the Cuban consciousness in the decades preceding the 1959 Insurrection, and these must be taken into account by any study of Cuban democracy and participation. Before the Revolution, the old multi-party democracy was ridden with graft and corruption and was irrelevant to the majority of the population except, perhaps, when candidates offered money in exchange for votes. Zeitlin (1969:40) claims that even before Batista's illegal seizure of power in 1952:

> Parties and politicians associated with Cuba's 'Congress' were all but universally held in contempt. Parliamentary democracy as a legitimate form of representative government, and the bounds within which major conflicts ought to be resolved and government policy determined, had lost its legitimacy, if indeed it ever existed.

Since the US intervention in the Cuban War of Independence at the end of the nineteenth century and the virtual annexation of the island, the whole Cuban political and economic structure had been compromised and controlled by outside forces. Although Cuba's 1940 constitution was one of the most progressive in Latin America, without economic power, politics always reverted to a spoils system. From the early 1900s to the Insurrection of 1959 politics became a means to an economic end, and as one observer in the 1920s commented:

We made politics our only industry and administrative fraud the only course open to wealth for our compatriots ... This political industry ... is stronger than our sugar industry, which is no longer ours; more lucrative than the railroads, which are managed by foreigners; safer than the banks, than maritime transportation and commercial trade, which also do not belong to us. It frees many Cubans from poverty, carrying them to the edge of a future middle class. (De Carrión, cited in Pérez 1988:215)

Politics in Cuba became synonymous with illegal material gain rather than democracy: 'Every government activity was milked, the lottery, the school lunch programme, driver's licenses, parking meters, teacher's certificates. The police routinely extorted millions in protection money from Havana merchants' (Padula 1974:38). Castro referred to the corrupt and compromised middle class as a 'lumpen bourgeoisie', and some observers have spoken of the 'parody' of a state that represented its interests (Bengelsdorf 1994:69). One of the clearest examples of the spoils system in action was when Prío Socorrás replaced Grau San Martín as president in 1948. Although both came from the Auténtico Party, 10,000 government jobs changed hands (Hennessy 1963:351).

When Castro and his followers marched into Havana in 1959 after a successful Insurrection against the dictator Batista, it was their identification with the tradition of 'frustrated nationalism' and the inherent weakness and illegitimacy of the existing Cuban political system that permitted their victory, more than force of arms or hatred of US imperialism. The Cuban Insurrection was the first successful socialist rebellion in the Americas. It led to the first anti-capitalist revolution in times of world peace, and the first time a socialist insurrection had been victorious without the leadership of the Communist Party (Blackburn 1963).

The Cuban Revolution ushered in a new era of world politics. It challenged orthodoxies of the left; it extended the Cold War to the Americas; it popularised a new revolutionary strategy of armed struggle in which the rootless would be leaders; it energised the concept of Third World solidarity, displacing the priorities of East-West conflict by the urgencies of the North-South divide and revived faith in socialism, canalising anti-imperialist sentiment by equating it with resistance to US hegemony. (Hennessy 1993:11)

The Revolution had no clear class base, but organised workers may have been more important in supporting the Insurrection than was previously thought (Cushion 2009). Perhaps more than any other revolution in the twentieth century, it started out on an immense wave of popular support and faced comparatively little internal resistance; the traditional Latin American ruling elite, the 'oligarchy', were absent, and the political, legal and military structure of the old order had collapsed under the weight of its own illegitimacy (Domínguez 1978). The middle classes lacked sufficient identity and coherence to launch a counter-offensive; some supported Castro, and others either fled to the US or were quickly neutralised (Chanan 1985:88). In 1961, when the US sponsored an invasion of Cuba by proxy forces at the Bay of Pigs (*Playa Giron*) in the hope of precipitating an internal revolt, it failed because the old order had disintegrated and a new society was being constructed based on popular consent. Even the Cuban Socialist (Moscow-line Communist) Party (PSC) had to stand on the sidelines during the first few months of the Revolution as the island's nationalist destiny unfolded and only became involved later, mainly on Castro's terms.

The Cuban Revolution contrasts starkly with the Russian Revolution, in which Bolshevik Party leadership was fundamental and took years to suppress and transform the old order, and then only at enormous human cost. The Soviet Union was also vast, diverse and lacked a nationalist tradition, and its Revolution faced internal resistance, civil war, massive external aggression and economic chaos. The only factor these two revolutions have in common is that they both broke long periods of socialist theorising with a voluntarist call to action.

It does not really matter whether Castro was a Communist sympathiser or a radical nationalist; it was not the ideology of one person or political group that drove the revolutionary process, but popular consensus on the need for a change that would eradicate the ills of the old system. In Castro's (1975) 'History Will Absolve Me' speech, made in his defence at the trial that followed the storming of the Moncada barracks in 1953, he gave a clear synopsis of the injustices in Cuban society. But he did not have to persuade the majority of the population to shun corruption, vice, inequality, illiteracy and poverty; the desire to do so was already present.

The early years of the Revolution were the first time many Cubans were able to participate in a process by which they could actively seek to improve their lives. Unlike many other socialist revolutions, it was the masses, the grassroots and civil society in general that decided the pace and the nature of change; it was not the leaders, who in the initial stages were reacting to, rather than directing, the processes that were unfolding around them. Of particular significance for this popular seizure of power was the role of the Rebel Army. This was not a conventional army, as it was mainly composed of volunteers and ordinary citizens, many of whom came from the lower classes, and of which a significant number, perhaps 80 per cent, were from rural areas. It was a rag-tag people's civilian army.

All of this was underscored by the legitimacy that the Revolution derived from a coherent nationalist tradition. In such circumstances, the population and leadership interacted to produce a new creative experiment which had no clear parameters; a period of spontaneity, but one that at times seemed chaotic (Díaz Castañón 2001:107). The experience had much in common, although enacted in different circumstances, with the Paris Commune, the Spanish Revolution within the Civil War and with other movements in which people began to realise their own power and potentials in the absence of a dominant ruling order. Essential to this process was the attitude of the leadership. Recalling the period immediately before and after the Insurrection, Castro (2007:102) notes, 'I seized upon ... ethics. Ethics, as a model of behaviour, is essential, a fabulous treasure'. This contrasts sharply to the rather mechanistic 'stages of history' formula of the Communists, and coincides with revolutionary social change in which the common goal is the making of a better world. Pérez (1999:482) argues that the revolutionaries sought to create a 'vision' of an 'alternative moral order'.

Although the struggle which led to the 1959 Insurrection had produced a sense of co-operation and involvement among sectors of the population, there was no real structure or experience of mass social organisation, except in the unions. Under the Revolution, the first attempt to build such organisation was the formation of the National Revolutionary Militia (MNR), set up in early 1960 in response to counter-revolutionary activities. Commenting on this early form of participation, Díaz Castañon (cited in Raby 2006:100) states:

> By bringing together in defence of the homeland everyone from the office worker to the housewife and the combatants of the guerrilla struggle, [the Militia] were the first associative space in which everyone could recognise each other as revolutionaries on the basis of the activity in which they were participating, and not just because of the guerrilla legend.

Clearly the new leadership and the Rebel Army were important in initiating and directing aspects of revolutionary change, but in many cases they lacked experience, structures, and capacity to deal directly and in detail with the vast process of transformation that was taking place. Furthermore, as Castro (2007:250–251) notes:

[I]n the first few months ... the bourgeoisie were still running the economy and they'd export products, under-invoice them, and leave part of the money abroad ... Our inexperience cost us dearly. There were also errors on our part that made it easy for the United States to freeze several million dollars belonging to the Cuban government.

The solution to this and other problems was seen to be nationalisation. During the first two years of the Revolution, sugar mills, land, electricity generating plants, newspapers, oil refineries, food processing plants and a whole economic and administrative infrastructure was taken over by the state. Workers, and in some cases managers, played a decisive role in implementing the reforms and putting in place the new structures. A study of the Revolution's early agrarian reforms shows that peasants and workers not only participated in their implementation, but also put pressure on the leadership to let them expropriate the large estates (Martínez-Alier 1977). As Blackburn (1980) further points out, the initial revolutionary period was successful without advanced forms of proletarian organisation such as workers' councils or Soviets, essentially because the old system was rotten and easily swept away by a popular movement committed to change. He concludes that there was a 'vitally important intervention by the masses in the revolutionary process' (ibid.). It is interesting that the Trotskyist Left share with the oppositional Right the belief that Castro and his followers imposed on Cuba a Stalinist-style dictatorship, and that the masses were manipulated and coerced. Trotskyists like Binns and González (1980:6), while holding this view, do however concede that 'the 1959 revolution [Insurrection] was supported by virtually every section of Cuban society, and was incredibly popular'.

While the initial surge of political will and popular commitment were important in initiating the Revolution, there had to be a learning process in which the masses, by changing the world around them, also changed themselves. This symbiotic development was vital to the consolidation of the Revolution, and over time received support from state structures in education, health care and a whole range of initiatives that promoted the 'general will'. In the beginning, however, huge problems had to be overcome to precipitate a transformation. Cuba's underdevelopment had produced a highly unequal society, and those who constituted the mass support of the Revolution were mainly from the poor, undereducated, disadvantaged sector. In these circumstances, ordinary people with little or no experience in administration, management or technical matters assumed positions for which they were ill-prepared. There was also a tendency to allocate responsible positions to those who could be trusted politically, but who were not always the most talented or educated. People who did excel in their jobs were often moved to more important roles, sometimes with disruptive consequences. The early years of the Revolution were characterised by a shortage of expertise and experience, and a melee of activity which sometimes lacked co-ordination and orientation. As Castro (2007:247) notes, 'there was a good dose of anarchy in those days – don't think it was easy'. But with chaos came creativity, and a material and gradual conscious transformation of the old order.

Initially, the dissolution of the old system opened up possibilities for a dramatic redistribution of wealth, and created new opportunities for a wide range of the population. Programmes were carried out, with popular support and involvement, to nationalise and improve health care, education, housing, employment and agriculture (Benjamin 1986). Democracy, which had been meaningless to most people previously, came to be understood as equality, participation, national unity and meeting society's needs, rather than a concept dealing with competing political parties and remote representation (interview with Fuentes 1999). But once the immediate spoils of victory had been distributed, it became clear to the leadership that they needed to find a developmental model which could sustain those benefits and consolidate the revolutionary achievements of the masses. The objective of the US embargo was precisely to prevent this from taking place. From an economic perspective, trade agreements with the Soviet Bloc, the decision to re-emphasise sugar production for export in 1963, and access to West European technology were the key material factors that allowed the Revolution to survive (Hennessy & Lambie 1993).

By the mid 1960s, the state controlled all of industry and 70 per cent of agriculture, and was in a position to make effective national-level decisions (Espina Prieto 1997:86–87). Interestingly, the Communist Party remained subsumed in the revolutionary process. By the time it took up a vanguard role in the 1970s, it had become an organisation deeply integrated with the Cuban project and no longer aligned to Moscow-line strategy, as it had been before the Revolution.

REVOLUTIONARIES AND COMMUNISTS

To support the claim that the Cuban Revolution has not followed the mainstream model of twentieth-century Communism, it is important to identify the ways in which Cuba was able to chart its own course politically, rather than be controlled by the Party and Moscow. The Cuban Communist Party (PCC) was formed in 1925 and was accepted into the Soviet Comintern in 1928 (Thomas 1971:578). Member parties of the Comintern, or Third International, agreed to a number of rules and received instructions on general political strategy from Moscow. The Comintern was founded in 1919 by the hard-pressed revolutionary government in Moscow after a meeting of 50 delegates, 35 of whom represented newly formed Communist parties or groups from 19 different countries (Carr 1985:I, 119). The aim of the organisation was to provide an international workers' forum to continue the project of the First and Second Workers' Internationals, but with the difference that it could now be headquartered in, and receive guidance from, the world's first Communist revolutionary government. In the heady months that followed the end of the First World War, the Comintern was politically inclusive and responded to radical events in Europe, rather than seeking to guide them. Indeed, it was anticipated by Moscow that revolution in a major industrial power would shift the political impetus away from Russia and lead to a world revolution. But by 1920, when the prospect of further revolutions began to fade, Moscow tightened its grip on the Comintern and played a more proactive role in directing its international strategy. This included condemnation of 'infantile-leftism' and some support for a United Front approach in countries where the Communist Party and/or the organised workers were weak (Carr 1979:16). It also marked the beginning of a policy to marginalise Left political groups that did not follow prescriptions from Moscow and promote what Carr (1982:5) has termed the 'Bolshevisation' of foreign Communist parties.

In 1923 political events in Germany again raised the possibility of an international anti-capitalist upsurge, and the Comintern returned briefly to its role of promoter of world revolution. But the failure of the uprising in Germany, the death of Lenin in 1924 and the rise of Stalin led to the further consolidation of Soviet influence over the Comintern, with emphasis on organising satellite parties to defend the Soviet Union's unique status as the first socialist nation. This was underscored by Stalin's notion of 'socialism in one country' (Deutscher 1963:34). In line with this objective, the Comintern's Second Period, which was initiated in 1924, was a time of caution and member parties were encouraged to co-operate with 'progressive' bourgeois movements. The position lasted until the Sixth Comintern Congress of 1928, when Stalin decided that the USSR should re-engage with an international revolutionary strategy and launched the ultra-left Third Period. This was partly a response to the failure of the United Front, especially in China, and the fear of war with the Western powers. It was also rationalised by the growing strength of the Soviet Union itself, and by the perceived crisis in world capitalism, which was later confirmed by the Crash of 1929 and the subsequent economic slump. But, unlike the genuine revolutionary fervour and optimism about Communism's future that had inspired the First Period of the Comintern, this was more of an opportunistic strategy. It served as a pretext to purge and discredit the non-Communist Left abroad, as well as intellectuals in the Soviet Union like Trotsky, Bukharin and Victor Serge, all of whom were independent Marxist thinkers whose ideas had enriched the Communist debate. From that time onwards, foreign Communist parties were obliged to operate under the strict directives of Moscow. Ultimately, the Third Period served to reduce support for the Communists abroad; it undermined alliances with leftist parties who were now branded 'social fascists', further antagonised the Western powers and probably contributed to the rise of fascism.

Stalin's opportunism was further confirmed in the mid 1930s when he launched the Fourth Period, which represented a political *volte-face* in which the Comintern renounced revolution and set out to support electoral politics and progressive bourgeois parties (Carr 1982:123–155). This move was made principally to buy time for the Soviet Union to build up its industrial and military capacity in preparation for war against fascism and particularly Hitler's Germany. By supporting moderate politics, Stalin hoped to change Russia's image from promoter of revolution to defender of civilisation against barbarism, and diminish the appeal of fascist politics for the middle classes, who had suffered the effects of the economic slump and were terrified of Communism. Satellite parties were, therefore, instructed to support a United Front with moderate political forces opposed to fascism. Most notably, this led to the election of Popular Front governments in France and Spain in 1935 and 1936 respectively. As seen in Chapter 2, the Soviet Union's efforts to support the Spanish Republic in the Civil War also served to strengthen its anti-fascist credentials, and secured some respect from the democratic Left and centre parties in Europe and the Americas.

Stalin's ultimate opportunistic policy was the signing of the Molotov–Ribbentrop Pact in 1939, which established a non-aggression treaty with Nazi Germany (Tucker 1992:592–607). By then, however, the writing was on the wall. Two years later, in 1941, Hitler launched Operation Barbarrosa, the world's largest military campaign, with the specific purpose of destroying Communism. In retrospect, the Soviet Union did indeed save the world from Nazi barbarism by defeating Hitler first on the Eastern Front. However, Stalin's obsessive and sometimes psychopathic policies also succeeded in destroying the diversity of Communist and socialist thinking, which had produced some of the most exciting political, economic and cultural debates and experiments of the early twentieth century. Although the Comintern was dissolved in 1943, its reformism survived in the post-war settlements, and in Moscow's Cold War strategy of building socialist hegemony against capitalism rather than seeking direct confrontation.

It has been claimed that, despite joining the Comintern in 1928, the Cuban Communist Party had 'the extraordinary opportunity ... of being perceived not as an "international" movement but rather as an off-spring of the revolutionary traditions of Cuba, and of inserting itself into the real social and political processes of the country' (Caballero 1986:49). Latin America, in general, was seen as peripheral by the Comintern in the 1920s and, even in that context, the Cuban party was regarded as a 'backwater organisation' (Carr 1998:238). It therefore had space to establish its independence. In the 1920s, the Cuban Communists loosely followed the Moscow line by seeking to co-operate with 'progressive' bourgeois parties. Given Cuba's specific historical conditions, it was able to build considerable popular support, and by 1928 was perhaps the most successful Communist Party in Latin America. By 1930, consistent with the Comintern's Third Period, an effort was made by Moscow to bring Latin American parties under greater control. The PCC responded to Soviet directives with an abrupt change of policy, rejecting its former allies in the non-Communist nationalist-reformist camp. However, this did not seem to undermine its influence and, by the time of the 1933 Revolution, the Party had over 10,000 members and led a trade union federation which represented 300,000 workers (Blackburn 1980:85). But Comintern strategy proved to be a liability when the Party had to make major political decisions, as, for example, in August 1933 when it used its influence in the unions to attempt to call off a general strike against the dictator Machado. This move was based on the dogmatic rationale that even if the strike was victorious, it would only lead to bourgeois reformism and not the worker/peasant government envisaged by Moscow (Carr 1998:249). The subsequent refusal of the workers to respond to this misguided directive, and the expulsion of Machado by the popular movement, weakened the authority of the PCC.

When Machado fell there was a power vacuum, and armed workers took over their workplaces and factories and, in some exceptional cases, Soviets were established in sugar *centrales* (Carr 1998:140). This was generally in line with Communist strategy, but was the result of spontaneous actions that were not always instigated by the Party. After Batista's Sergeants' Revolt in September 1933, and the installation of Grau San Martín's radical nationalist government with its programme of 'Cuba for the Cubans', most workers were pacified and those who continued to resist were confronted by the army. But with the fall of Grau's progressive *Auténtico* administration in January 1934, US recognition of the Mendieta government and the rising power of Batista, workers and students again took to the streets. A particularly important action-orientated radical group at that time was *Joven Cuba*, under the leadership of Antonio Guiteras. Guiteras was a socialist who emerged from the radical student generation of 1927. He became Minister of War and the Interior in the Grau government and was one of the key architects of its programme of reforms (Thomas 1971:650). Among the legislation enacted during his short period in office was the nationalisation of various US-owned services, including the telephone company, and laws legalising syndicates and unions. He proposed an eight-hour working day, and established the Nationalisation of Labour Act that led to the expulsion of thousands of workers from other Caribbean islands, especially Haiti, who had provided cheap labour in place of native Cubans. Spaniards were also forbidden by the Act to employ immigrant family members. Politically, Guiteras was influenced by the voluntarist traditions of the Cuban worker's struggle, which highlighted the subjective factor in the revolutionary process. He may also have been aware of Trotskyism (Hansen 1962). When the Grau administration fell, Guiteras and his followers engaged in violent actions which led to increasing clampdowns by the new government, and his movement was forced underground, but its actions and ideas helped perpetuate the Cuban radical nationalist tradition. This was in sharp contrast to the PCC, which had discredited itself in the eyes of workers, nationalists, radical students and intellectuals. Guiteras was assassinated in 1935, before he was able to leave for Mexico where, prefiguring Castro twenty years later, he had planned to prepare for re-engagement in the anti-Batista struggle.

The attempt at revolution in 1933 was based on deeply nationalist and radical currents in Cuban history, which, as far as most Cubans were concerned, were the legitimate forces for change on the island. Crucially, the Grau administration abrogated the Platt Amendment, which was regarded by most Cubans as a humiliation and a travesty of national sovereignty. The PCC, however, saw this popular movement as its principal enemy, more dangerous even than the reactionary forces which it sought to overthrow. The revolutionaries were therefore identified in typical Moscow parlance as 'social fascists' who simply served to divert the worker/peasant revolution (Roca 1935).

From claiming that the main threat to workers were the nationalist-reformist and anti-imperialist groups that brought to power and participated in the Grau San Martín government, in 1935 (when these groups were significantly weakened by repression) the PCC decided, in accordance with the Comintern's Popular Front strategy, to support the formation of a broad 'progressive' alliance with its former enemies (Thomas 1971:697). At that time the Party also changed its name to the United Revolutionary Party (PUR) to reflect its new co-operative spirit. Initially, after adopting this policy, relations with the Cuban government remained tense, but by the late 1930s, as Batista sought office, a marriage of convenience was established with the ex-sergeant. Batista needed a popular political base on which to underpin his power, and the Communists needed legitimacy and a protector to help them rebuild their credibility. After the 1940 election, which brought Batista to power, members of the Party gained access to the Cabinet and took seats in the Senate (Pérez 1988:288). Through its alliance with Batista, and his powerful Ministry of Labour, the Party sought to take full control of the unions and, in turn, prepare workers to accept a set of progressive yet paternalistic reforms that were underwritten by the 1940 Constitution; it was 'the compromise that settled the revolutionary struggles of the 1930s' (Pérez-Stable 1993:36). To reflect this new parliamentary orientation, as well as the Soviet role in the allied war effort and the dissolution of the Comintern in 1944, the Communists changed their name from the United Revolutionary Party (PUR) to the Popular Socialist Party (PSP).

But, when Batista lost power in 1944 to the Auténtico leader Grau, the PSP's fortunes began to wane. Problems continued when Grau was replaced by Carlos Prio Socorras in 1948, and were further compounded as the battle lines of the Cold War took shape. Henceforth, Communists in capitalist nations suffered increasing censure and persecution, especially in Latin America, which lay within the US sphere of influence. With the revolutionary initiatives of 1933 spent, the workers de-politicised, the Communists increasingly ostracised, and the second Grau government incurably corrupt, Cuban radicalism broke down into gang warfare and lost its direction. Commenting on the political apathy of the period, Castro (2007:107) recalls:

> [I]mperialism was simply not discussed ... only within circles of the Communist Party – that is how low the revolutionary spirit of the Cuban people had fallen after the Second World War; it had been crushed under the overwhelming weight of the Yankees' ideological and advertising machine.

The only force that emerged to champion the nationalist radical tradition was the Party of the Cuban Nation (Ortodoxo) that was formed by Eduardo Chíbas in 1947 (Pérez 1988:287). Chíbas had been a student leader in the 1933 Revolution, and rose to the position of Senator in the second Auténtico government of Grau, but became disillusioned with its corruption and decided to form a splinter group. A staunch critic of the Communists because of their political compromises, Chíbas contested the 1948 election and came third due to his ability to rally support from marginalised radicals. Although a mercurial and unpredictable character with no clear ideological stance, his campaign against corruption and his slogan of 'Honour before Money' closely accorded with the ethical roots of Cuban nationalism (Raby 2006:95). He committed suicide with a pistol during a radio broadcast in 1951, creating a vacuum in the nationalist radical movement that was later filled by Castro and his followers. Indeed, Castro and many of the militants of the 26 July Movement (M-26-7) – a name taken from the (failed) storming of the Moncada barracks in Santiago de Cuba in 1953 – had been members of the Ortodoxo's youth wing. These young radicals had supported the revolutionary and action-orientated side of the party's philosophy, and also rejected the opportunist elite leadership, especially after the death of Chibas (Harnecker 1986:26).

Even when Batista returned to office in 1952, the PSP's relations with the government remained tense: firstly, because he gained power through a coup, and secondly, because he needed US support to maintain his illegal regime and therefore any ties to Communists were a liability. Consequently, the PSP entered a difficult period in which it lost control of Cuba's powerful trade union movement, the Confederation of Cuban Workers (CTC), which was taken over by Eusebio Mujal, an ex-Communist turned anti-Communist (Thomas 1971:783). Interestingly, Mujal had been General Secretary of Guiteras's *Joven Cuba* in the mid 1930s (ibid.:700). Politically, the Party found its influence declining, and was trapped between its old protector Batista and the emerging anti-Batista forces. In 1952 the Soviet Union closed its embassy in Havana, believing the country was a lost cause. Although Batista banned the PSP and opposition newspapers, the Party's paper *Hoy* was allowed to remain open, making it difficult for the editors to take an openly anti-dictatorship line.

Mainly because of the strained and, at times, hostile relations between the PSP and radical Cuban nationalists, resulting largely from the Party's tendency to take its instructions from Moscow rather than respond to local circumstances, the insurrectionary activities of Castro and his followers were viewed with disdain by the Communist hierarchy. When the young revolutionary and his followers made their famous attack on the Moncada Barracks, the Party condemned their actions, stating in an article for the US Communist paper the *Daily Worker* (1953) that the task of Communists was to 'combat ... and unmask the putschists and adventurous activities of the bourgeois opposition as being against the interests of the people'. When Castro formed his 26 July Movement, the Communists continued to deride his activities (Castro 2007:576).

Given the stunning success of the revolutionary road to power, it was easy for Castro and his followers to criticise the reformist Communist tradition in Latin America and Cuba with its adherence, since the mid 1930s, to the Soviet Comintern's stages of history thesis. From this perspective most of Latin America was taken to be semi-feudal, and therefore Communists assumed that they should work towards a consolidation of bourgeois power over national elites and foreign imperialism before they could begin to promote a proletarian revolution (Poppino 1964). This strategy was inappropriate for most of Latin America, and in Cuba the prospect of the weak and mainly corrupt bourgeoisie establishing control at a national level and overcoming imperialism must have seemed absurd to Castro, Guevara and others who had been involved in the Insurrection. Foreign intellectuals also joined in the criticism of the Communists on the strength of the revolutionary victory in Cuba. For instance, the French intellectual Regis Debray (1967), who became one of the main advocates of the Cuban 'foco' theory of revolution and joined Guevara in his Bolivia campaign, believed that Latin American Communist parties were subordinated by Moscow 'to a global strategy whose centre of gravity ... lay outside America ... The local CPs, by always acting on the directives of the international, were constantly swimming against the tide of history'.

Despite the Communists' seemingly misguided or perhaps, depending on perspective, pragmatic strategy, based on Stalin's notion of 'socialism in one country', one should not entirely dismiss their role in Latin America and Cuba. When Communist parties were formed in the 1920s and 1930s, they precipitated the first major debate on the significance of Communism and socialism in the region, a discussion taken up by intellectuals like José Carlos Mariátegui in Peru and Julio Antonio Mella, one of the founders of the Cuban Party in 1925. Although with the rise of Stalin the ideology of Comintern-linked parties became ossified, the Communists still promoted radical ideas and were responsible for maintaining an interest in the works of Left thinkers like Marx, Lenin and others. Moreover, among the parties and movements of the Left, the Communists were usually the most organised and, in some cases, won significant gains for workers. Despite deviations in strategy, they also helped to instil a sense of class consciousness in the Latin American proletariat.

Although the Cuban Communists supported the Moscow line of progressive reformism, as the revolutionary initiative of Castro and his followers gained popularity the PSP was obliged to respond. Consequently, in July 1958 Carlos Rafael Rodríguez, a Communist leader who had been a minister without portfolio in Batista's 1940 government, visited the revolutionaries at their base in the Sierra Maestra mountains. According to Scheer and Zeitlin (1964:127–129), from that point the Party decided to support the revolutionaries, but one assumes this was because of their popularity rather than any ideological commitment. When the Insurrection triumphed on 1 January 1959, the part played in the struggle by the leadership of the PSP was notable for its absence (Castro 2007:576).

This was resented by the Rebel Army as was the continuing criticism of the Revolution, and on 22 May 1959 an article appeared in *Revolución*, the daily paper of M-26-7, in which Castro accused the Communists of being 'counter-revolutionaries'. However, this must be understood mainly as a criticism of the Communist leaders, as many rank-and-file Party members, especially young people, participated in the revolutionary struggle. A notable example was Fidel's brother Raúl, who was joined by some of his comrades and ended up controlling the largest 'liberated area', the Sierra Cristal (Oriente province), in the years immediately before the triumph of the Revolution (Blackburn 1980:85). It is also important to acknowledge that the Cuban working class, both in the PSP and the wider CTC, had been politicised by the massive general strike of 1955, and the memories and the experience of that episode no doubt served to prepare workers for the struggle in 1958/59 (Cushion 2008). Some improvement in Party–Insurrectionist relations came about when the PSP indicated approval of the Agrarian Reform Law in May 1959. But even as late as 14 September, nine months after the success of the Insurrection, interactions were strained. An article appeared in *Revolución* condemning the 'disreputable oligarchy of the PSP', in which Carlos Rafael Rodríguez was included by name.

As the Cuban Insurrection became a Revolution and attracted international attention, the Soviet Union began to take an interest in this forgotten Caribbean 'backwater'. Some months into the Revolution, Khrushchev asked the Central Committee's International Division, the KGB and the military to investigate the situation in Cuba. As they knew nothing about Castro, his politics, or the objectives of his movement, it was decided to consult with the Cuban Communists (Khrushchev 2002). The response Khrushchev received from the PSP leadership in Havana was, 'the newcomer [Castro] was a member of the haute bourgeoisie and working for the CIA' (ibid.). Although Castro may not have been aware of this comment, the earlier accusations he had made against the Communists were clearly not far off the mark. As for his own connections with Moscow, he has acknowledged, 'In January 1959 I didn't know a single Soviet, or the leaders' (Castro 2007:288).

CROSSING THE COLD WAR DIVIDE

The Cuban Insurrection must also be set in the context of Cold War superpower relations in the late 1950s and early 1960s. After Stalin's death in 1953 and Khrushchev's accession to power, Soviet policy became more proactive, especially in the Third World. The Insurrection therefore came at a time of rising tensions between Moscow and Washington. At first the US was not fearful of the Castro government and was swift to extend recognition, unsurprising given that American investments in the island were in excess of $900 million. But, as Paterson (1994:242) notes, it soon became clear that Castro 'intended to bury Plattism [the imperialist ideology that had underpinned the Platt Amendment] once and for all, and had long challenged Washington's presumption that its word was fiat in the Western Hemisphere'. Apparently, as early as July and August 1959, the US administration decided to undermine Castro and attempt to remove him from power (Siekmeier 1999:386). When the new Cuban leader proclaimed before the United Nations in September 1960 that US imperialism was the cause of Cuba's plight (Gilderhus 2000:168), the die was cast and he became the '*bête noir*' who stood for everything that the US administration sought to prevent in the region. Cuba's improving relationship with the Soviet Union simply served to consolidate this view. A State Department report issued in 1964 identified Washington's main concern:

> The primary danger we face in Castro is ... in the impact the very existence of his regime has upon the leftist movement in many Latin American countries ... the simple fact is that Castro represents a successful defiance of the US, a negation of our hemispheric policy of almost a century and a half. (Chomsky 2003:90)

Although the 26 July Movement had legitimacy, popularity and the support of large sectors of the population, the revolutionaries were inexperienced in many ways, and the organisational skills and networks of the PSP proved useful in helping to overcome these deficiencies. As the Revolution became more radical, Washington grew more hostile, and the economy deteriorated because of declining sugar production and the American embargo, the PSP also provided a vital link with the Soviet Union, which would gradually replace the US as a sugar market, trading partner and great power protector. In October 1959, a trade accord was signed with the Soviet Union in which the latter agreed to buy 300,000 tons of Cuban sugar. Russia had been ordering similar quantities of sugar since before the Insurrection, but this arrangement was the precursor to wider co-operation and bilateral relations. Perhaps unsatisfied with the response he received from the PSP to his questions about the Revolution and its leader, in February 1960 Khrushchev sent his deputy, Anastas Mikoyen, to further report on the Cuban situation. Not long after he arrived, Mikoyen was won over by the revolutionaries (Khrushchev 2002). His visit resulted in Soviet credits and further purchases of sugar, with the USSR receiving over 400,000 tons in 1960 and 1 million in each of the next four years (Shearman 1987:8). But the most important outcome was that Mikoyen became convinced that the Revolution should be supported politically by Moscow. Partly in response to the strengthening relationship between the USSR and Cuba, in March US President Eisenhower approved a plan to place an embargo on Cuba and step up propaganda and subversion against the Revolution.

Crucially for Cuba's increasingly besieged economy, payment for Cuban sugar was partly in Soviet oil, which started arriving in April. To facilitate the growing co-operation between Havana and Moscow, diplomatic relations were restored in May 1960. Further infuriated by these developments, in June the US prompted Western oil companies in Cuba to refuse to refine the Soviet oil imports. Continuing in the game of reciprocal reprisals, Cuba nationalised the refineries and started to take over US property in the island. The US responded by terminating Cuba's sugar quota of 700,000 tons per annum; the breach was quickly covered by the USSR which agreed to buy the same quantity. In October the US declared a full economic embargo on Cuba, and Havana responded with the nationalisation of all remaining US property, including the banks. Cuba now became a pariah in America's backyard, with only the Soviet Union to turn to.

In January 1961 John Kennedy replaced Dwight Eisenhower in the White House at a time when US-backed activities against Cuba were intensifying and US–Cuban relations were very strained. As the Revolution moved to the Left, more middle-class Cubans departed for the US and remaining dissident elements were given the opportunity to leave the island or face imprisonment. It has been estimated that between 1959 and 1962, 270,000 Cubans migrated to the US, including many professionals who could have been a vital resource for the Revolution (Castro 2007:335). Two months into Kennedy's presidency, the US sponsored an invasion of Cuba by proxy forces who landed at the Bay of Pigs on 17 April. Despite the famous rout of these mercenaries by the Cubans, which delighted the Russians, Khrushchev rightly surmised that the US would simply step up the pressure. As his son notes, at that time 'the defence of

Cuba became a matter of prestige for the Soviet Union, something like West Berlin was for the United States' (Khrushchev 2002). But despite the growing political and economic commitment of the Soviet Union to the Cuban Revolution, Moscow felt uneasy when Castro declared, in a televised interview on 2 December 1961, that he was a Marxist-Leninist and would remain so until the end of his life (Thomas 1971:1373).

Spurred by the victory at the Bay of Pigs, the Cuban leadership felt it could accelerate the revolutionary process, and adopt a radical ideological position. The Russians could tolerate the structural changes that were taking place in Cuba, but viewed Castro's statement as provocative and unnecessary, serving only to further enrage the US. Within Cuba, however, this statement, along with Castro's announcement in April of the same year that Cuba was following a socialist course, were not matters of his personal choice. They accorded with the mood of the population, which by that time was deeply involved in, and committed to, building a different society, one that rejected US domination and sought national dignity and social equality. According to Blackburn (1980:91), as Cuban nationalism began to identify itself with socialism in 1961, there was an 'insatiable popular appetite for the works of Marx and Lenin', which became bestsellers.

Despite conclusively leaving the Western camp to join ranks with its Cold War enemy, relations between 'romantic' revolutionaries and 'dogmatic' Communists remained difficult. In an attempt to bring together the organisations and parties that supported the Revolution, in June 1961 Castro's M-26-7, the PSP led by Blas Roca, and the Revolutionary Directorate (which formed in 1955 by students to fight Batista and supported M-26-7, but had poor relations with the Communists) led by Faure Chomón, formed a single body: the Integrated Revolutionary Organisations (ORI) (Thomas 1971:926). A PSP leader, Aníbal Escalante, became Secretary General, mainly because he had good links with Moscow. It was not long, however, before he began to promote the Party faithful to positions of power within the ORI. This was against the spirit in which the organisation had been conceived and indicated that the PSP might be seeking to use its connections with the Soviet Union to gain more influence in Cuba. Castro (2007:218–219) makes a succinct description of Escalante and his party at that time:

> [Escalante was] a capable, intelligent and good organiser, but he had the deeply rooted sectarian habit of filtering and controlling

everything in favour of his Party. Those were the old tactics, the old obsessions, of a stage in the history of Communism – a ghetto mentality born of the discrimination, exclusion and anti-Communist feelings that people were subjected to for too long.

During the early years of the Revolution, once the war was over, they even did this with the 26th July Movement, despite our excellent relations. They were misguided, mistaken methods, though used by unquestionably honourable, self-sacrificing people who were true revolutionaries and true anti-imperialists.

Arguably, since his declaration that he was a Marxist-Leninist, Castro had been aware of Escalante's manoeuvres, and on 27 March 1962 he finally gave a dramatic speech on television denouncing Escalante and his so-called 'micro-faction' (Thomas 1971:1379). Escalante was forced into exile, and the ORI was reorganised into the United Party of the Cuban Socialist Revolution (PURSC), which would become the re-formed Communist Party of Cuba (PCC) on 3 October 1965 (Azicri 1988:28). The Escalante affair must be seen not just as an internal political squabble, but also in the context of growing US aggression towards Cuba. Partly in response to the defeat of US proxy forces at the Bay of Pigs in April 1961, in November of that year Kennedy sanctioned the preparation of a new invasion plan code-named Operation Mongoose (Chang & Kornbluh 1992:57–60), conducted a mock invasion of a Caribbean island named Ortsac (Castro spelt backwards), and approved extensive destabilisation tactics by the CIA. While the recently victorious revolutionary army at the Bay of Pigs could claim the 'first defeat of imperialism in the Americas', the US was now determined to overthrow Castro and his followers, as Khrushchev feared. In this environment, pro-Moscow factions in the PSP probably felt Cuba should move closer to the Soviet Union for protection.

However, the PSP had, to some extent, discredited itself with Moscow, and its fate was now inconsequential as Cuba was caught up in a wider geo-political game that was drawing in the superpowers. The USSR could not, at this stage, squander the strategic opportunity which the Revolution offered. Consequently, in April 1962 Khrushchev conceived a plan to place medium-range nuclear missiles in Cuba, primarily to approach a strategic balance of nuclear capacity with the US (the ratio was then 9–1 in favour of America), and secondly to defend Cuba (Shearman 1987:12). Castro did not initially believe that such a plan would serve to protect the island, but was persuaded of its viability and the missiles were installed in September. As is well known, when the nuclear sites were discovered by the US it led to the October Missile Crisis. Before the end of the month, the superpowers came to an agreement in which the missiles would be withdrawn if the US would remove its missiles from Turkey and pledge not to invade Cuba. During these negotiations the Cubans were not fully consulted, which angered the leadership and dashed any hope that Russia might support a wider world revolution (Blight & Brenner 2002:84). Although Cuban–Soviet relations were soured by the crisis, Cuba now had little choice but to move closer to the USSR. Consequently, in April 1963, Castro arrived in Moscow to a warm welcome, and was invited to sign a favourable trade agreement which was principally a consolidation and expansion of the exchange of sugar for Russian oil. This period also marked a shift in Cuban economic policy, away from Guevara's optimistic industrialisation strategy and towards a return to large-scale sugar production.

Interestingly, Escalante returned to Cuba in 1964 and took up a minor administrative post, but it was not long before he re-engaged in pro-Moscow activities. He was again taken to task in 1967 when it came to light that he had been conspiring with Cuban Party officials and agents from Moscow to enhance the power of pro-Soviet factions in the country. It was later revealed by Raúl Castro, at a meeting of the Central Committee of the Party in January 1968, that Escalante had produced documents condemning members of the Cuban leadership for pursuing a closer alliance with De Gaulle's France, in preference to improving relations with the USSR (Lambie 1993a:219). This development must have been seen by Escalante and his sympathisers as further evidence of what they regarded as the bourgeois opportunism of Castro and his followers. This time Escalante was sent to prison for 15 years for his subversive activities. Although Cuba had become very dependent economically on the Soviet Union, by the mid 1960s Escalante's failure was a clear signal to Moscow that the revolutionary leadership and a reconstituted Communist party (Cuban Communist Party – PCC) were in control in Havana, and the old days of unquestioningly following the Moscow line were over. It is also significant that the discovery of Escalante's plot was attributed to Manuel Pineiro Losada, the Deputy Interior Minister in charge of State Security. From that time onwards Cuba began building a highly trained, loyal and motivated intelligence service to defend the Revolution.

Ultimately the Revolution consolidated its power, popularity and legitimacy based on co-operation and trust between committed leaders and a motivated and supportive population, all dedicated to the pursuit of national self-determination. During the first ten years of the Revolution the Communist Party was virtually inactive, apart from the work of the Politburo, and the 100-member Central Committee was rarely convened. By 1969 party membership numbered only 55,000, which was around 0.7 per cent of the population (Fuller 1992). In the 1970s, with revolutionary power secured and a closer relationship established between Cuba and the USSR, the PCC's apparatus began to grow and by the end of the 1970s the Party had over 200,000 members and took on a vanguard role. In contrast, the Committees for the Defence of the Revolution (CDRs), one of the main organs of popular participation since the beginning of the Revolution, had 4.8 million members (Blackburn 1980:9).

Given the independent trajectory of the Revolution, Cuba followed a dual-track strategy in its relations with the Soviet Union. On the one hand, to survive and develop, the Revolution needed the support of the Soviet Union, and this became particularly clear in the 1970s when Cuba joined the Soviet common market, the Council for Mutual Economic Assistance (CMEA). But on the other hand, Castro and his followers realised that Moscow did not wish to encourage Cuba's revolutionary ambitions at home or abroad, and in this objective they were alone. Havana believed that international socialism should be concerned with confronting Third World problems, such as underdevelopment, imperialist domination and economic dependency. This North–South perspective clashed with the Soviet Union's East–West orientation, in which the priorities were: limited co-operation with the 'imperialists' to avoid nuclear escalation and possible war; reduction in the disparity of nuclear weapons capabilities; and the use of international diplomacy to gain support for, or neutrality towards, the USSR. This included winning favour in the Third World by providing assistance, aid, markets and technology. Indeed, in its foreign policy Cuba was sometimes a liability to the wider international strategy of the USSR, especially in Latin America where Moscow wanted to keep the peace with the US. Cuba's practical experiments in participation, consciousness-building and moral incentives were simply incomprehensible and irritating to the Soviets. Clearly, neither the original Communist Party of Cuba, nor the Soviet Union, can be credited with giving the Revolution its ideology or its identity.

CHARTING A SEPARATE SOCIALIST PATH

While Cuba needed the Soviet Union's technical expertise, economic support and reciprocal trade, the idealistic Cuban leadership aimed at more than material development, and sought to channel the popular energies of the Revolution into a process of socialist transformation. The concept of democracy played an important part in guiding this effort, and on 26 July 1959, on the anniversary of the storming of the Moncada Barracks, Castro proclaimed at a mass rally of over 1 million people, 'Cuba's revolutionary government was like that of ancient Athens ... except better, because [it] was not for the privileged classes or the oligarchy. This is a true democracy' (cited by American Experience 2009). Only a few months into the Revolution, this was received by those in attendance not as mere idealism as they were already involved in numerous ways in the transformation of Cuban society. But, as the Revolution unfolded, more sophisticated ideas began to emerge as to how social and economic change might take place. Some claimed that socialism and Communism could be created simultaneously. Ernesto (Che) Guevara was the principal advocate of this ideal, arguing that through the restructuring of production and the work ethic it would be possible to produce a 'new [socialist] man', motivated by moral rather than material incentives. From this perspective, he believed, 'Our task is to enlarge democracy within the revolution as much as possible. ... We feel that the government's chief function is to assure channels for the expression of the popular will' (cited in Zeitlin 1970:78). Guevara realised that it was not enough to demystify the old consciousness, and that the Revolution needed to establish its own hegemony. In practice, however, many democratic possibilities were overlooked or dismissed in the drive to achieve the ideal, and some of the functions that might have been undertaken democratically were gradually taken over by the central plan, the bureaucracy and later the Communist Party.

At a theoretical level, Cuba's post-Insurrection socialist development strategy was the subject of the so-called 'Great Debate' between Guevara and the French economist Charles Bettelheim (Pérez-Stable 1993:95–96). While both accepted that central planning was necessary for the building of a socialist society, Bettelheim, who had studied Soviet and Chinese economic planning, favoured material incentives for workers, decentralised decision making, the use of market mechanisms and acceptance of the law of value. He also advocated the development of a diversified economy based on agriculture, selective industrialisation and mixed forms of property ownership, a strategy which resembled the New Economic Policy initiated by Lenin in 1922. Guevara argued, in such journals as *Nuestra Industria, Cuba Socialista* and *Comercio Exterior*, that while capitalist mechanisms might be manipulated through central planning to create a more equal society, they would not produce a socialist consciousness, and his 'Budgetary System of Finance' was designed to de-monetise the economy and base prices on alternative criteria. As Silverman (1971:15) notes, Guevara's 'ultimate aim [was] to consciously use the process of socialist development as a force to create a new morality'. In practice this required the abolition of the market, and rapid centralised industrialistion linked to deeply integrated social involvement. Although he accepted that planning methods, technologies of production and organisational techniques originating in capitalism would still have to be employed, this should not prevent the construction of a socialist consciousness through action such as voluntary work and participation in mass organisations like the CDRs. It was in this 'crucible of action' that Guevara believed an alternative consciousness would be created (Fagen 1969:7). He realised that under capitalism the workers were separated not only from control over the material fruits of production, but also from the power to direct production towards social ends and as a means of creative personal development. As Marx (1972:243–244) had stated, 'It must never be forgotten that the production of ... surplus value ... is the immediate and compelling motive of capitalist production'. Subjugation to this process is possible because the mode of production is based on private property with which workers engage not as humans but as commodities; they sell their labour power. Their lives are thus largely outside of their individual and collective control, and are ruled by the anarchy of competitive commodity exchange and the forces of supply and demand.

> In capitalist society individuals are controlled by a pitiless law usually beyond their comprehension. The alienated human specimen is tied to society as a whole by an invisible umbilical cord: the law of value. This law acts on all aspects of one's life, shaping its course and destiny .... The commodity is the economic cell of capitalist society ... the economic foundation ... of consciousness. (Guevara, cited in Cole forthcoming)

Socialism for Guevara was, therefore, more than simply capturing the means of production and reorganising them under a benign state to achieve a re-ordering of 'who gets what'; it was the incorporation of productive activity into the process of human self-creation. To achieve this end, it was essential to eliminate capitalism and the law of value, not just because it is exploitative, but because it is the material base of alienation. While such a system exists, humans will be tied to a 'mythical' order in which the market, money value, selfish individualism, inequality and so on are seen as given, and are accepted as the parameters of existence. For this reason, 'the ultimate and most important revolutionary aspiration [is] to see human beings liberated from their alienation' (ibid.). In this respect, Bettelheim's formula for a transition to socialism was regarded by Guevara as inadequate, because it failed to stimulate the fusion of production with an evolving social process. Instead, it offered 'material incentives' which perpetuated an individualised and separated relationship between productive activity and human development. Socialism required more than this: it demanded an ethical commitment and moral duty to social progress. A level of involvement that was not just individual, nor just social, but corresponded to the dialectic between the two. It is only by grasping this link between production and human consciousness that one can understand the meaning of Guevara's concepts of the 'new man' and a 'moral economy'.

For Bettelheim (1975:113), like most economists who had been influenced by the Soviet and Chinese models, human development was shaped by external circumstances, and socialist transformation must therefore be based on such factors: 'the decisive lever in the modification of human behaviour is the contribution of technical changes to the organisation of production ... and acquiring business knowledge for the development of the forces of production'. As we have seen, Guevara dissented from this view, believing that, through the encouragement of socially co-operative work and self-sacrifice, a socialist consciousness could be formed in parallel with the creation of a socialist economy. In terms of implementation, Guevara's initiative, underpinned by the Budgetary Finance System for State Enterprises, was developed from 1961 until 1964 out of the Ministry of Industries (MININD) in which he was minister, while Bettelheim's Economic Calculation System influenced the work of the National Institute for Agrarian Reform (INRA).

One problem with Guevara's 'Cuban heresy' was not its deviation from 'scientific socialism', which was welcomed by some, but its limited view of participation (Karol 1971). Essentially, the leadership set the criteria of production for social need, and the Revolution acted as the paternalistic organiser of society in the form of bureaucracy, technicians and committees of mass organisations. Individual participation was restricted to economic contributions, some of which were voluntary, and there was no parallel participatory process in which the individual could exercise pluralist political development or channel their ideas into the decision-making process. In 1962, MININD set up Committees for the Local Organisation of Industry (CILOs), which sought to strengthen the process of decision making at the factory level and stimulate a politicisation of local productive activities (Cole forthcoming). Such initiatives, however, lost their momentum when Guevara left Cuba in December 1964 to help foment revolution in Africa and later Bolivia, from which he never returned for any significant time. Despite the wane of Guevara's influence, in 1965 Workers' Councils (*Consejos de Trabajo*) were set up, offering the possibility of greater worker involvement in decision making; but in practice their functions were limited to dealing with issues of discipline and violations of labour law (Habel 1989:81). Trade unions were virtually non-existent at this stage of the Revolution.

Despite these constraints on democratic possibilities, the leaders of the Revolution continued to maintain intellectual and moral legitimacy. Their power was real, but was seen by many Cubans as a grant of trust, requiring the leadership to accept failure and mistakes, and demanding honesty, openness and commitment. As Castro stated in his 1968 speech against the bureaucracy, 'All we ask of the people is to trust their leaders and their revolutionary government' (cited in Bengelsdorf 1994:95) on the basis that those in charge were acting for 'a people's state' (Fagen 1969:86). The leadership has always understood its symbiotic relationship with the population, and has rarely attempted to exceed its generally accepted rights and responsibilities. Consequently, Cuban civil society has never been absorbed by the state, as happened in many other socialist countries, but interacts with it in a creative, if not always equal, dynamic. This continuous partnership also contrasts starkly with representative democracy, in which power is conferred for several years by voting for a party platform, which may or may not be implemented, and civil society and the state are seen to be separate entities. Dilla (1999:31) suggests that 'civil society in Cuba has emerged from the bosom of the socialist project and numerous participation spaces characterized by solidarity and collective action on behalf of the common good'. This process has produced a deep interaction between the state and civil society that blurs the distinction between the two, creating a dynamic linkage in which citizens share with the government a general support for socialism, social equality, and a rejection of US policy towards Cuba, Latin America and the rest of the world. In a sense, this is the beginning of a live experiment to create an environment in which to express the 'general will' as envisaged by Rousseau.

There has been much speculation concerning the actual intellectual influences on Guevara's thinking, and the concept of revolutionary praxis which he seems to have stimulated. However, it is safe to suggest that he was aware of an independent Marxist tradition in Latin America that questioned the strategies of the Moscow-line Communist parties and their concept of 'stages of history'. On the prospect of a bourgeois revolution in Latin America, Guevara said:

> [T]he indigenous bourgeoisies have lost all capacity to oppose imperialism – if they ever had any – and are only dragged along behind it like a caboose. There are no other alternatives. Either a socialist revolution or a caricature of revolution. (Deutschmann 1987:351–352)

This position had previously been adopted in the late 1920s by the Peruvian intellectual José Carlos Mariátegui (Lambie 1992), one of the first, and perhaps the most important, Marxists in the Americas.

A crucial intellectual influence on Castro, and perhaps also on Guevara to some extent, was Cuba's own indigenous intellectual José Martí. In his 1953 'History Will Absolve Me' speech, Castro said, speaking of Martí, 'I carry in my heart the teachings of the master' (1975:8) and referred to Martí as the 'instigator of the 26th July' attack on the Moncada Barracks and all that transpired from that event. During the address he mentioned him 17 times and cited him verbatim, without notes. Martí was born in 1853, and at the age of 18 was exiled to Spain because of his opposition to colonial rule in Cuba. He only returned to Cuba for a few short visits, the last of which was in 1895 during which he was killed fighting against the Spanish. Rather like Mariátegui (1959 vol. 11:146), his years abroad, including stays in Spain, Guatemala, Mexico and Venezuela before settling in the US, led to his 'rediscovery' of Latin America and Cuba. Along with Mariátegui, he also became one of Latin America's greatest radical intellectuals. However, unlike his Peruvian counterpart, he was a populist and humanist and not a

Marxist. Typical of the Latin American '*pensador*', his thinking was eclectic and wide-ranging, which has allowed diverse ideologues to consider him their mentor. As Blackburn (1980:84) points out, the leaders of the Cuban liberation movement, Martí, Antonio Maceo and Máximo Gómez, were not socialists but 'passionate adherents of the ideal of the Social Republic, as represented by the Paris Commune of 1871 or the Spanish Federal Republic of 1874–5'.

Besides being an intellectual, Martí was a man of action. This endeared him to many, especially Castro, Castro's followers, and all those acting within the Cuban nationalist tradition. In forming the Cuban Revolutionary Party (PRC), he set out an agenda for Cuban self-determination that would include: racial harmony (as he had stated, 'the souls of white men and negroes have risen together from the battlefield where they have fought and died for Cuba'); an end to the sugar plantocracy and the latifundia system of land ownership, which was to be replaced by a small peasantry and a diversified economy; and government and administration regulated by popular democracy (Kirk 1984). He envisaged a rejuvenated Cuban republic that would seek to be 'with all and for all', and in this newly constituted form would be better equipped to resist imperialist influence from the US (of which he wrote: 'I have lived inside the monster and know its entrails'). Martí's death, and US intervention in the War of Independence, produced precisely the reverse of his dream; but his heroic failure would inspire those who sought change in the future.

The 'cult' of Martí gathered momentum in the 1930s and 1940s, especially after the failed 1933 Revolution: 'It provided a flight into a world of fantasy where, in the style of Rodo's Ariel, Cuban spirituality was contrasted with United States materialism and greed' (Hennessy 1963:354). For Castro in particular, aspects of Martí's eclectic thinking provided legitimacy, rather than ideology and guidance. Martí's belief in the 'hero', as saviour, guide and symbiotic link with the people, was the perfect defining role for the leaders of the Revolution, and set their task apart from the formulistic strategies of the Communists. Since his imprisonment after the attack on the Moncada Barracks, and perhaps before, Castro had been reading the works of Marx and Lenin and gradually forming an understanding of historical materialism. However, the specific conditions of Cuba, with its weak middle class, under-educated and dispossessed peasantry, opportunist trade unions and culture dominated by American individualism and materialism, made the classical theory of revolution inoperable. Such circumstances needed a unifying myth, one to which Martí had given form, substance and historical durability. By marrying European revolutionary theory with specific Cuban conditions and the way they were interpreted in the national consciousness, Castro and Guevara gave primacy to hegemony, rather than material circumstances, in the making of the Revolution. This idea was first developed in Latin America by Mariátegui, whose work on the power of myth, and its application in specific circumstances and social conditions which lacked political maturity, was taken from his reading of Georges Sorel and Antonio Gramsci (Lambie 1992).

There is evidence that the ideas of Gramsci had some influence on the intellectual debate in Cuba in the 1960s. Gramsci's thinking was first introduced into Latin America by Mariátegui in the 1920s, but the latter's death in 1930, and the pressures for conformity imposed on the Left by the Soviet Comintern, extinguished this current of thought for another 30 years. Gramsci's *Historical Materialism and the Philosophy of Benedetto Croce* was first translated into Spanish in Argentina in 1958, and soon found its way to Cuba. In the early 1960s many of his other works came out in Spanish under the same publisher. Although his writings were tolerated in Cuba, those who took up his ideas were regarded as 'heretics'; however, for some his views were 'oxygen for thought' (Martínez Puentes 2003:80–81).

Although Guevara may not have read Gramsci, or Mariátegui, it has been claimed that he shared with them a belief in the philosophy of praxis; a revolution in action and consciousness based in evolving social and individual experience, rather than some sterile structural and formulistic notion of change (Kohan 1997; Massardo 1999). Again, we are reminded of Rousseau's belief that the precept of natural law, which assumed a fixed human nature, must be challenged and replaced with a more dynamic understanding of human development, one which reflects the importance of the individual's interaction with society. In this context, personal potentials, rather than being established through aggressive competition, are realised in an environment of co-operation. Social consensus on key issues provides the foundation on which individuals can form their subjective creativity and difference. According to Colletti (1972), Castro said that he carried a copy of Rousseau's *Social Contract* with him during the period of the struggle against Batista (cited in Roman 1999:10). Castro also claims to have read Rousseau while he was in prison after the storming of the Moncada Barracks, and he mentions him in his 'History Will Absolve Me' speech in the context of supporting revolutionary change.

It is useful, and sometimes revealing, to trace the influences on key individuals. But the important point, especially with regard to Rousseau's, and later Marx's, separate ontological perspectives, is that the experience of the historical situation is what changes consciousness, not simply the guiding hand of intellectuals. In practice, these two forces act together, but – as in the Paris Commune, the Russian Soviets, the Revolution in the Spanish Civil War and the Cuban Revolution – it is ordinary people, learning from direct experience, who begin and continue the process of praxis and transformation. This point is superbly expressed by Martí:

> To be able to understand we have to examine reality; the most credible source of truth comes from our own existence; that is our experience; we have to learn to observe in order to create; we have to think about our experience; that is we have to reflect. (Cole forthcoming)

While emphasising the important role of the Communist/intellectual in the revolutionary process, Marx stressed 'the emancipation of the workers must be the task of the workers themselves' (1970:28). In a Hispanic context, this concept is clearly expressed by the Peruvian poet, César Vallejo (1984 [1937]:36–37), who wrote as witness to the revolution that was taking place during the Spanish Civil War:

> [T]he popular Spanish epic is unique in history. It reveals what a people are capable of when pushed by an undivided force and by their own means and civic inspirations to defend their rights. The Spanish people laid bare a vast military insurrection within a few months, stopped two powerful foreign invaders, and created a strict, revolutionary order; they built their economy on a new foundation, established from head to foot a great popular army and, to sum up, placed themselves in the vanguard of civilization, defending the endangered universal democracy with blood never equalled in purity and generous passion. And this entire miracle – it must be insisted – was carried out by the sovereign masses, which are sufficient by themselves for their invincible future. [author's translation]

This idea is then brilliantly incorporated by Vallejo (1978 [1938]) into his volume of poetry on the Spanish Civil War, *España, aparta de mi este cáliz* ('Spain, take this cup away from me'). For example, in the poem '*Pequeño responso a un héroe de la República*' ('Brief response to a hero of the Republic'), the poet (intellectual) is observing the corpse of a volunteer who had died in the struggle against Franco's Nationalists, and he considers the significance of this death (Lambie 1999a:382). In his view, although the leaders of the Republican government were directing the struggle, and poets and intellectuals like himself were making their literary skills and wider influence available to the Republican cause, it was the ordinary volunteers who were the embodiment of resistance to the old order; they were the creators of the future. The true revolutionary process was the self-realisation of their power to change the circumstances that had oppressed them. Observing the dead volunteer, Vallejo therefore envisages that '*un libro retornaba de su cádaver muerto*' ('a book sprouted from his dead corpse') (254); and that even in death he had created '*poesía en la carta moral que acompañara / a su corazón*' ('poetry in the moral text that accords with / his heart') (254). This perspective, as we saw in Chapter 2, coincided with the anarchist leader Durruti, who also saw the masses as the true 'authors' of the Revolution.

It is interesting that when most academics analyse revolutions and transformative processes, they focus almost exclusively on leaders. In turn, they seek to interpret the ideas and actions of these prominent figures based on the influence of other elites. These factors are important, but must be recognised as only partial explanations for most instances of significant socio-economic change. The issue of the role of intellectuals in society, and exactly what constitutes intellectual formation, is a complex debate (Lambie 2000). However, on the specific issue of academic approaches to leaders, the difficulty lies ultimately in the ideological composition of the academics themselves, which is rooted in the dominant ontology, one that emphasises individualism, elite leadership and an immutable order of human nature. Given this perspective, it is difficult to imagine a set of ideas or a consciousness emerging out of what seems to be thin air. From the ridicule of Marx's observations on the autonomy of workers in the Paris Commune, to contemporary views that see socialism as utopian, there is an ideological intolerance of any idea that defies the implicit ontological parameters of liberalism.

When the dominant liberal interpretive framework does encounter what appears to be spontaneous action and organisation at the grassroots level, it sees this in terms of civil society freeing itself from the state, and as an expression of self-help. This view is theorised in Hernando de Soto's work *The Other Path* (1989), which interprets the survival strategies of the poor in developing countries as a blossoming of individual initiative. A similar ideological perspective permeates much of the NGO philosophy, with its emphasis on micro-credit and market-orientated initiatives to resolve problems in civil society without the involvement of the state. This kind of thinking also informs much of the policy-driven theory that dominates sections of academia in Western countries. For instance, as procedural democracies such as the UK struggle to deal with the 'democratic deficit', and governments become concerned about political legitimacy, policies are devised to enhance 'participation' and 'citizenship' in an attempt to give substance to liberal hegemony. Lack of 'participation' or understanding of 'citizenship' is seen as an educational issue, and citizens have to be instructed and 'enabled' by policy makers and academics to realise their 'democratic' rights. At its core, this is nothing more than a thinly concealed indoctrination exercise to impose the rule of the market onto the organisation of local structures. Commenting on the role of academics and intellectuals in general, Wayne (2003:23–24) points out:

> One way in which intellectuals have attempted to explain their social role has been to depoliticise what it means to be elaborators and disseminators of ideas. This involves uncoupling knowledge production from vested social interests, defining professionalism as rising above the social conflict between capital and labour, and instead promoting 'objectivity' and 'rationality' as the very essence of what it is that intellectuals do ... the ideology of 'objectivity' has, under the guise of working for all humanity, justified their role to capitalists ...

This attitude concerning the role of academics and intellectuals was famously defended by the French writer Romain Roland after the First World War, in his work *Au-dessus de la mêlée* ('Above the Battle') (1915). Roland's position may be justified if one argues that the shock and horror of war temporarily divested life of meaning in the minds of rational people, and retreat into the ivory tower became a mode of defence against this malaise. However, modern intellectuals have no such excuse, and have increasingly become *apparatchiks* of a knowledge-production system that is driven by money, career climbing and prestige, all of which can be attained through conformity.

Ultimately, only by grasping the idea that human nature is not immutable can one transcend these intellectual limitations and imagine the unimaginable. Martí, Guevara, Castro and other

Cuban leaders understood this intellectually and intuitively, both by participating in the historical process themselves, and by not losing touch with the masses. Of course, the Cuban political process has fluctuated in the emphasis it has given to leadership or to participation, but the two have interacted more fully and more continuously than has been seen in any other country.

EXPERIMENTS IN PARTICIPATORY DEMOCRACY

In the 1960s Cubans did, in general, accept demands for voluntary work, but were perhaps motivated more by the benefits brought by the Revolution, its historical legitimacy and the popularity of the leadership, than by any notion of creating a socialist transformation. The mutually reinforcing relationship between the people and the revolutionary leaders was strengthened by the mass organisations such as the Confederation of Cuban Workers (CTC), the National Association of Small Farmers (ANAP), the Federation of Cuban Women (FMC), the Young Communist League (UJC), the Federation of University Students (FEU), the Committees for the Defence of the Revolution (CDRs) and later the Communist Party.

In addition to these large organisations, there are a number of smaller professional and interest-specific associations that represent other sectors of society: economists, lawyers, journalists, artists, writers, and many other groups. 'These associations and organizations embrace practically the entire universe of activities, interests and problems of all Cubans ... no decision on matters that concern these organizations is made without their consent' (Alarcón 1999:8). For Saney (2004:66), the mass organisations are the mechanisms which articulate Cuba's participatory culture and are seen to be 'national and inclusive, augmenting the representative governmental structures by providing organizational and institutional means by which civil society both expresses itself and intervenes in the decision-making process'. While the above authors see these organisations as a means by which the ideas, problems, concerns and interests of ordinary people are expressed and communicated upwards to the decision makers, others regard them as vertical, downward 'transmission belts' (Aguirre 1998; Amaro 1996). Again the difference may lie in the distinct intellectual environments that inform these views. Both are correct, but only within the ideological structures in which the analyses are based.

The CDRs were set up initially by Castro in September 1960 as local popular organisations which could respond to anti-revolutionary forces, 'the enemy within', at street level (Fagen 1969:71), and drew inspiration from the experiences of the militias that had been established earlier in the year. Their formation coincided with the Revolution's move to the Left and towards socialism. In the climate of the times, the CDRs soon began to go beyond their role of counteracting anti-revolutionary activity, and started to act as the main bodies for organising voluntary labour. They played a particularly important role in promoting mass participation, political awareness, and the notion that local power was an effective force. CDRs were open to all over the age of 14, were inclusive rather than exclusive, and within twelve months had 800,000 members. This horizontal form of participation served to balance against vertical centralised control, but rather than provide an arena for independent grassroots action, became tightly interwoven with wider state objectives (ibid.:91). In this context it has been claimed (Aguirre 1998) that today the main role of the CDRs is to ensure conformity at the local level while the leadership sets the revolutionary objectives. They are also believed to encourage 'spying' and denunciations of those who do not conform. From a more positive perspective, Saney (2004) argues that the CDRs cover a wide range of social and community functions and are particularly effective in mobilisations and organisation at the street level.

After the Insurrection, commissions were set up temporarily to oversee municipal government. These were superseded in 1961 by a more formal local structure, the *Juntas de Coordinación, Ejecución e Inspección* (JUCEI) – Co-ordination, Delivery and Inspection Committees (Dilla et al. 1993:28). The responsibility of this new organisation was to co-ordinate and supervise the application of central policies at the local level. The *Juntas* took the form of councils composed of representatives from local organisations. In 1966, the JUCEI was replaced by *Poder Local* (Local Power), which aimed to increase administrative decentralisation and make local government more responsive to grassroots organisations. However, *Poder Local* never established any significant autonomy from central government, and was presided over by the Party. Nevertheless it was important in building and developing the structures of decentralisation, and many of its practices and personnel were carried over into *Poder Popular* (People's Power) when it was formed in 1976 (Roman 1999:65).

From the triumph of the Revolution to the establishment of *Poder Popular*, it was not local government but the CDRs that played the most important co-ordinating role at the municipal level, and provided the best opportunities for participation. In some areas such as distribution of basic goods and implementation of urban reforms, the CDRs functioned as a kind of spontaneous local government, driven in part by popular views on how things should be organised.

Mass participation, although limited, and material improvements based on equality, were the foundations of the Revolution's popular appeal. Trust in the revolutionary leadership was also significant in creating a sense of involvement among the population; especially important were speeches by Fidel Castro in which he would address audiences of tens of thousands with long educative tracts on developments within the Revolution, containing self-criticism and admission of errors. Of course, with large audiences two-way communication was difficult, but listeners were usually satisfied because he would deal, often in detail, with issues that concerned ordinary people. Castro and other leaders also frequently travelled around the island to visit projects and places of work, meeting the population face-to-face to hold frank exchanges. The relationship between the Cuban population and the leadership can be seen either as a kind of 'direct democracy' or, from a more sceptical perspective, a form of paternalism.

Another important example of mass participation was through such initiatives as the Literacy Campaign of 1961, in which educated Cubans taught reading and writing skills to the illiterate. This campaign was a success not only in educative terms, but also because it created an environment for political development for both teachers and students. Essentially, popular involvement during the 1960s took the form of collective action to achieve goals identified by the leadership, described as 'command-mass participation' by one observer (Petras 1973:289). Active participation came at the level of implementing goals, not setting them. Another observer has spoken of a 'subculture of local democracy' in which, in contrast to mass campaigns, democracy is experienced through 'activities that are of small scale, institutions and practices [CDRs, people's courts, etc.] which involve citizens in decisions directly tied to problems of the neighbourhood and workplace' (interview with Dilla 1996). Such activities and policies, seen by the Cuban leadership as necessary experiences for the creation of a 'revolutionary consciousness', irritated analysts like Bettelheim and Dumont (1974) who adhered to the notion of 'scientific socialism', in which socialism is a system that can be realised through efficient economic planning.

Throughout the 1960s, even after Guevara's death in 1967, centralised planning, combined with voluntary work and consciousness building, dominated economic policy. But in 1970, mainly due to shortages of hard currency necessary for importing essential intermediate goods, an attempt was made to produce a record sugar harvest of 10 million tons. This was to be the ultimate test of a system based on mass participation and voluntary work, and, with the export-earning capacity it would generate, could have allowed Cuba to chart an independent route to development. By that time, however, some people were tired of the endless exhortations for voluntary commitment and self-sacrifice, and were discouraged by failures to co-ordinate labour effectively, and the result was growing absenteeism. In the event, while Cuba produced 8.5 million tons of sugar, the largest harvest ever recorded, it failed to meet the official target. However, more damaging than the shortfall was the massive economic dislocation and widespread popular resentment as labour and resources were diverted, often wastefully, towards the campaign. This failure, and the problems it caused, were quickly acknowledged by Castro (1972:296), who recanted in front of the people for the miscalculation: 'we alone are the ones who have lost this battle, the administrative apparatus and the leaders of the revolution'.

The 1970 sugar harvest, and the problems it created, is seen by many analysts as the nemesis of the 'Cuban heresy'. According to Roca (1976:65), 'The harvest failure gave an unequivocal signal to abandon ideological radicalism in favour of more moderate, orthodox economic policies and social goals.' Dumont (1974), Ghai et al. (1988), Mesa-Lago (1981:11) and others agree with Roca that the 1960s had been a failure because Cuba had 'ignore[ed] many basic economic laws'. For these analysts, socialism, or perhaps more precisely Third World development, is about choosing the right economic strategy, and particularly 'getting the prices right'; the implication is that once this has been achieved, other factors, including human behaviour, will fall into place. This view does not recognise or accept the primacy of participation and co-operation in the creation of socialism and a socialist consciousness. For Guevara (1960:113), 'work will [become] man's greatest dignity, a social duty, a pleasure given to man, the most creative activity there is [not the] old fashioned mentality that dates back to the capitalist world, where work [is] a sad duty and necessity'.

Some of Cuba's initiatives in the 1960s were naive, misguided and unco-ordinated, but mistakes as well as successes were shared with and experienced by the population, the majority of whom were still committed to the Revolution and their role in it. The policies of that decade had produced shortages and inconsistencies that annoyed everyone, and such problems were often blamed on the leadership. But through the mass organisations and participation, ordinary people felt they had a stake in the Revolution, which they perceived not as a system imposed from above, but as a process of transformation in which they were deeply involved, for better or for worse. Analysts who saw this period as one of romantic idealism which ran against economic laws are challenged by the Cuban economist Rodríguez (1988:101) who states, 'Because the interrelationships between the political, economic, and social aspects of the Revolution is not examined, Cubanologists fail to sustain the thesis that socialist development in Cuba lacks an appropriate economic base.'

Another, often neglected, factor when considering popular involvement and identification with the Revolution in the 1960s is Cuba's international position. Cuba experienced the first socialist revolution in the Americas, and its reverberations throughout the region were extraordinary. In those years virtually every Latin American country had a guerrilla group attempting to put the Cuban insurrectionary model into practice. Guevara visited Africa and South America to promote revolution along Cuban lines. As we have seen, the 1960s also saw the rout of US proxy forces at the Bay of Pigs in 1961, and the dramatic Cuban Missile Crisis in 1962. In 1966 representatives from developing countries on three continents gathered in Havana for the Tricontinental Congress, seeking a united strategy to promote revolution and change in the Third World. This was a challenge to the Soviet Union's claim to be the natural leader of the underdeveloped nations, and was in direct contravention of their advice to the Cuban leadership to renounce violence and support the political road to socialism. As argued previously, Cuba's aim was to shift the perceived axis of world struggle away from the sterile East–West contest between the Cold War superpowers and their respective spheres of influence, towards a North–South axis which divided rich and poor nations. From this latter perspective Cuba was elevated from Cold War pawn to champion of the Third World – a far more dignified role.

Many Left intellectuals throughout the world saw revolutionary Cuba as a refreshing alternative to Soviet Communism. This once wretched island, better known for the services it provided to the US 'pleasure industry' than for its history, became the socialist superstar of the 1960s. As noted in the Introduction, radicals in the Third World looked to Havana, not Moscow, for inspiration, and students in developed countries who participated in the anti-government protests of 1968 carried banners displaying Guevara, not Lenin. Cuba's unprecedented dignity and importance in the world left a deep impression on the Cuban population. It seemed as though even the most humble sugar-cane cutter was not only contributing to the creation of a more equal society in Cuba, but also to the making of a better world. Guevara's death in Bolivia in October 1967 was a debilitating blow to Cuba's international revolutionary strategy, and Castro (1987) blamed his death in part on the Bolivian Communist Party and by implication the Soviet Union.

FROM IDEALISM TO SOCIALIST ORTHODOXY

For those analysts who perceive the 1960s mainly in terms of economic failures, the course of Cuban development in the 1970s is logical and predictable. Because of internal economic problems, Cuba was obliged to turn increasingly towards the Soviet Bloc for assistance, but one of the conditions set by Moscow for its support was that the island should curb its errant foreign policy. As noted previously, in 1973 Cuba was accepted into the Communist common market – the Council for Mutual Economic Assistance (CMEA) – and structured its economy according to its commitments within this trading area. This included the establishment in 1976 of a new economic model based on five-year plans, the *Sistema de Dirección y Planificación de la Economía* (SDPE – System of Direction and Planning of the Economy), which was influenced by Soviet advisers. With respect to this, Mesa-Lago's (1978) 'Sovietisation of Cuba' thesis is substantially correct. Commenting on the 1960s, he points out:

> The appealing, quixotic attempt to skip the transitional phase of socialism and rapidly create a 'New Man' in an egalitarian communistic society through the device of the development of consciousness, the use of moral incentive and labour mobilisation has been quietly halted.

Authors such as Ibarra (1995) and Miller (2003) also note that in the 1970s emphasis shifted towards 'quantitative' achievements, to the extent that many intellectual freedoms were lost. The Cuban intellectual Dilla (interview 1996) speaks of a 'very grey and monotonous period in Cuban academic life' in the 1970s, which he associates particularly with the official closing down of the activities of the *Pensamiento Crítico* group, who sought to continue the radical debates of the 1960s in their journal of the same name. As official ideology hardened, the works of Guevara and the few copies of Gramsci were also removed from bookshop shelves, and replaced by Soviet manuals and the writings of Nikita Khrushchev, Leonid Brezhnev and other luminaries of 'scientific socialism'. Memories of this period still invite negative reactions, as in January 2007 when 450 Cuban writers and artists called a meeting with Culture Minister Abel Prieto to complain about a television programme which apparently endorsed the censorship of the 1970s (Arreola, 2007).

However, the stabilisation of economic policy, along with preferential trade agreements and generous aid packages from the Soviet Union, allowed Cuba to undertake an impressive programme of reforms. During the 1970s the Revolution made commendable advances in health care, education, welfare provision, women's rights and many other areas that are neglected in most less-developed countries. Health care and education before the Revolution were quite advanced by Latin American standards but very unevenly distributed, favouring the well-off in Havana and in the provincial capitals. Agricultural workers in the countryside fared worst, with virtually no access to health care or even basic schooling. In the early years of the Revolution, health standards deteriorated as many medical professionals fled to the US. But by the mid 1960s significant improvements began to appear as a new group of professionals was trained and expenditure on health infrastructure was increased. A good indicator of health performance is the infant mortality rate, which in 1957 was 32.3 per 1000 babies born, but by 1984 had fallen to 16 per 1000, the average for developed countries (Pérez 1988:362–364). Huge strides were made in most areas of health, and by the late 1980s life expectancy in Cuba was similar to that in the US. Based on this achievement, Cuba became a 'World Medical Power' (Feinsilver 1989) exporting its expertise, especially to developing countries. This not only helped to improve health care, but presented the Revolution as a just and dedicated movement that addressed the real problems faced by the Third World.

These achievements were attained in a society that had shunned market principles and, if one did not pay too much attention to the extent of Soviet aid and subsidies, the Cubans could also claim that this system had produced some of the highest material standards in Latin America. Brundenius (1985) has calculated Cuban economic growth from 1972–81 as 7.8 per cent per annum, which was similar to the 'Asian Tiger' economies. Economists who had criticised Cuba in the 1960s could rest their case. The Castro government had finally reconciled itself to the 'well trodden paths' of Soviet economic planning, a comprehensible model which analysts could criticise or support according to their political preferences. Those sections of the Left who in the 1960s had believed that Cuba offered something different, a new socialist opening, became disillusioned in the 1970s and abandoned the Cuban cause. By the time of the Nicaraguan Revolution in 1979, the vacuum had been filled by apolitical solidarity movements, which knew little of the Cuban Revolution or its political significance.

While Cuba did move closer to the Soviet Union in the 1970s, it did not become a proxy state and its 'Sovietisation' was only partial (Hennessy 1988). The island maintained some autonomy in several key areas. Firstly, in foreign policy, where it sometimes served the interests of Moscow, as in its support of Ethiopia in its war with Somalia in the late 1970s. More often it sought to pursue its own objectives as with its 1975 intervention in Angola (Shearman 1987). Secondly, in foreign trade a high percentage of transactions were with capitalist countries, especially when the market price for sugar was high. In 1974, for example, sugar prices reached a record level allowing Cuba to conduct 45 per cent of its import/export trade in hard currency, which along with the loans it contracted with commercial banks increased its scope to pursue independent economic initiatives (Lambie 1993b:276, 311). Thirdly, participation and the formation of political consciousness continued to be a priority despite the constraints resulting from the closer relationship with the Soviet Union, and the adoption of some of its practices.

PEOPLE'S POWER?

While Azicri (1988:134) and many other Cubanologists claim that 'subjectivism and consciousness were replaced with objective [economic] channels' in the 1970s, the Cuban leadership still gave consideration to 'the human factor'. In a speech made to the Cuban Federation of Women, in response to the problems caused by the 1970 sugar harvest, Castro (Taber 1983:111) did not envisage the future of revolutionary development solely in objective economic terms:

[T]he revolution is entering a new phase ... one in which the revolution will have to tackle ever more complex problems with new methods, with the experience accumulated through the years, and, above all with the energy accumulated through these years in the field we can bring about a change in conditions – that is, in the subjective factor, in the human factor ... the objective factors are there, but they do not enter into our sphere of activity. We can change those objective factors ... such natural problems as drought, and our present low-productivity problems can be remedied by means of new technology, new machines. There are some objective factors that can and should be changed, but only humans can affect such changes; only humans can alter such conditions – which is why our effort can and should be directed toward humanity.

In the 1960s, popular participation in Cuba was introduced in a rather disorganised and *dirigiste* fashion, and the 1970 sugar harvest made it clear to the population and the leadership that the channels for participation would have to be restructured. Directed mass economic engagement did not give individuals an opportunity to express their own subjective thinking, which led to complaints in the late 1960s that central planners had become unresponsive to, and even unaware of, local conditions. These problems prompted Castro (ibid.:142) to state in 1970: 'We are trying to find a way how, starting with our mass organisations, to create other organisations in which the workers, as workers, the Committees for the Defence of the Revolution; the women, the young people – in fact, everybody – will be represented.'

Part of the solution to the problem seemed to be decentralisation of decision making – the participation of the individual in organised bodies where social agreements could be made and majorities would be powerful enough to implement them. To this effect Castro (ibid.:106) made a number of statements:

We have been able to unleash in millions of people the energy, interest, and will to move ahead in spite of the fact that we are a small country. Now we must know how to channel that energy, guiding that formidable and extraordinary mass movement toward the possibility of ever greater participation in the decisions that effect their lives ... if we give our mass organisations ever greater participation in the districts and the cities ... ever greater participation in the decision making process, we shall be following the logical and natural course of events in a revolutionary process ...

In the same year (1970) that Castro was making these statements, thousands of meetings were held all over the island involving mass organisations, factory workers and others to discuss what went wrong in the harvest, and provide suggestions on how popular participation and decision making could be improved in the future. One outcome of these deliberations was the formation in 1976 of a new form of local government called *Organos del Poder Popular* (Organs of People's Power – OPP) – more commonly known as *Poder Popular* (People's Power). The new Constitution of the same year stated, 'all the power belongs to the working people who exercise it directly or through the assemblies of *Poder Popular* and other organs of the state which derive their authority from these assemblies'. But, as Bengelsdorf (1994:113–114) notes, this utopian aspiration was tempered by the directive that the Communist Party 'must guide, promote and control the work of state organs'.

This was linked to a wider process of institutionalisation which included: a restructuring of the work process – which gave more emphasis to performance norms and material incentives; a reformed legal structure; the revival of trade unions; a family code; and more, all of which was consolidated in the 1976 Constitution (Dilla et al. 1993:29). As we have seen, analysts saw increases in Cuban economic output in the 1970s as the product of more rational economic plans and incentivisation. However, it has been argued that the improvement in social relations and greater scope for worker representation, created by the above reforms, also contributed to improved economic productivity (Zimbalist & Eckstein, cited in Habel 1989:83).

The functions and operation of *Poder Popular* have been extensively studied (Harnecker 1979; Benglesdorf 1994; LeoGrande 1989; August 1999; Lambie 1999b), and the work of Roman (1999) is the most comprehensive. His study of this institution goes beyond those of most analysts by considering its intellectual and ideological underpinnings; this approach accords with the one taken by the present author. The following short description and analysis of *Poder Popular* does not seek to introduce new material on how this political process functions. Rather, its inclusion serves to support the ongoing argument that Cuba has attempted to produce an alternative approach to democracy and human progress to the one prescribed by the capitalist West.

In the broadest sense *Poder Popular* was an attempt to balance the structures of the System of Economic Management and Planning (Sistema de Dirección y Planificación de la Economía – SPDE) with the social and participative ethics of the Revolution. Soon after its establishment, Castro proclaimed: 'there are so few places in Latin America or in the world where the local bodies of power have so many attributions, so many things under its control' (Bengelsdorf 1994:105). Decentralisation, however, does not equal democracy; it is necessary to ascertain to what extent *Poder Popular* extended participatory democracy to the Cuban masses.

Participation as popular interaction with the state and other controlling institutions, in which the citizen is able to influence decision making, is not a central component of representative democracy; voting alone is not sufficient to constitute participation. As we saw in Chapter 2, promotion of democracy and participation in the capitalist powers since the 1980s has increasingly attempted to link the concepts with consumerism and market orientation. Equally, 'structuralist' democracy, and especially in its most extreme manifestation of 'democratic centralism', which existed in the former Soviet Bloc, does not usually encourage participation, and decentralised government structures often are just 'conveyor belts' for the extension and delivery of centrally devised policies.

Since the beginning of the Revolution, Cuba has claimed to pursue a different approach to democracy which emphasises participation, not only as a means to carry out the popular will, but also to provide an environment for the development of a socialist consciousness. This aim, and the attempts to put it into practice, distinguish Cuba from its former and existing socialist allies, and sets a course that is diametrically opposed to contemporary Western concepts of participation.

Poder Popular (OPP) was designed as a new organ of citizen involvement and was first established in Matanzas province in 1974, then extended to the whole of the island in 1976 (LeoGrande 1989:195). Its aim was to channel the ad hoc participation of the 1960s into a formal structure in which individuals could register their preferences and problems and influence decision making. *Poder Popular*, which remains the main forum for representing local interests, is similar to what we know in developed capitalist countries as local government, and consists of both a local body of elected representatives and an administrative component. Its structure is based on the geographical divisions of Cuba, which is split into 15 provinces that in turn are divided into 169 municipalities. The National Assembly is the highest level of the OPP structure which constitutes the government of Cuba, and is 'the only organ in the Republic invested with constituent and legislative authority' (Constitution of Cuba 1976, Section 7, Article 68). Directly under the National OPP are the Provincial OPPs, and under them the Municipal OPPs.

Municipalities are further divided into *circumscripciónes*, similar to English 'wards', in which candidates are nominated and elected to represent the local area on the municipal or local council. Municipal elections take place every two and a half years. They are organised by electoral commissions, often headed by a local Party (PCC) leader, which also include representatives from different mass and social organisations such as the CDRs and the Federation of Cuban Women. The general responsibility of the commissions is to ensure a well-organised and fair election.

The electoral process begins with a meeting of the *circumscripción* in which candidates are proposed, usually because they are known locally and personally acquainted with the person proposing them. Nomination is open to members of the PCC and any other organisation; however, electioneering is not permitted. After nomination, the candidates prepare a brief biography, including their photograph, which must be clearly displayed in a designated place. There are usually between four and seven candidates, but never fewer than two. After a secret ballot, the victorious candidate, who must obtain 50 per cent of the vote (which often requires a second round), becomes a delegate to the Municipal Assembly; the task is unpaid, and undertaken in addition to one's regular work. This non-oppositional form of delegate elections in Cuba coincides with the current in socialist thinking that there should be no separation of civil and political society. Marx's view, as explained by Colletti (cited in Roman 1999:18), was that democracy would only operate effectively when 'society is an organism of solidarity and homogenous interests, and the distinct "political" sphere vanishes along with the division between governors and governed. This means that politics becomes the administration of things, or simply another branch of social production.' The task of delegates therefore is not to compete against each other based on political manifestos, but to act as 'instructed' representatives of the people. One is reminded here of Rousseau's *'mandat impératif'*.

Attendance at election meetings is usually high. In San Miguel del Padrón, a municipality of over 150,000 on the outskirts of Havana, attendance was estimated at over 80 per cent even during the very difficult period of the 1990s, and never fell below 50 per cent (interview with Pérez-Vizcano 1997). Two weeks after the election, the Municipal Assembly is formed (the number of delegates can vary between 61 and 200), and in its first session an executive committee and delegates to represent the municipality on the Provincial Assembly are elected. If the municipal election coincides with national elections, which are held every five years, then delegates to the National Assembly (the highest body of *Poder Popular*) are also elected during this first session. According to electoral rules, all of the executive committee members and more than half of the provincial delegates and representatives in the National Assembly must be selected from municipal delegates. Voting for representatives to these non-municipal bodies is based on lists of candidates prepared by a Candidates Commission, which is practically the same body as the Electoral Commission and subject to substantial PCC influence.

Municipal and provincial assemblies are required to meet at least twice a year (although most meet more frequently) and contact between delegates and electorate takes place regularly. Typically, delegates hold *despachos* (consultative meetings) every week to which citizens bring their requests and complaints, and every six months a *circumscripción* meeting is held in which people can air their views and receive responses from the delegate. These meetings are known as *rendiciones de cuenta* (renderings of accounts), because of the 'report back' function which the delegate performs in responding to citizen requests (*plantamientos*) from the previous meeting. Attendance at such meetings is usually higher than 50 per cent of the active population. It is at this point of contact between citizen, delegate, and in turn the government's administrative and delivery systems, that participation in Cuba's formal democracy is most visibly exercised (Dilla, cited in Roman 1999:156). At this level, the people not only present information to their representative and receive responses, but they are also free, in many cases, to act on their own behalf by deciding collectively to tackle problems through voluntary labour. Moreover, in contrast to other local government systems, a delegate can be removed at any time if the electorate are not happy with their performance. Recall is uncommon, but acts as a real sanction, serving to reinforce democracy as a reflection of citizens' wishes (Greenwood & Lambie 1999:64).

Circumscripción meetings are often held in very informal surroundings; citizens sometimes assemble in a street, and bring chairs out of nearby houses. Once the delegate's report has been presented, the floor is thrown open for discussion. In meetings attended by the author in Havana between 1995–96 there seemed to be a high level of spontaneity among participants, who readily aired their views and complaints. Sometimes the atmosphere was quite electric when several citizens took a similar view or a disagreement broke out. Issues discussed such as housing, refuse collection, and the quality of food in state restaurants were treated very seriously, and it was clear that attendees felt they had a right to demand improvements, even though, given the crisis of that period, they knew most demands would remain unfulfilled. Delegates usually had a difficult time, and were often admonished and told to negotiate more forcefully with the municipal authorities.

In practice, much of the work of municipal and provincial government is conducted by an appointed *Consejo de Administración* (Management Council), which has executive powers. The elected assemblies must approve membership of the *Consejo,* but otherwise have little direct control over its activities. However, it is assisted by professional delegates, some with specific service responsibilities, chosen by the assemblies from their own memberships and removable by them as well. The whole process is overlain by the influence of the PCC at every level, ensuring that the state/party system pervades at lower as well as national levels of government.

In Cuba, approximately 90 per cent of formal economic activities are run by the state, and therefore the range of responsibilities afforded to provincial and local government is much greater than sub-central government in capitalist systems. Both Municipal and Provincial Assemblies, for example, administer aspects of economic production and distribution, as well as public services and cultural, educational and recreational activities. Because the municipalities are closest to the population, their responsibilities are the widest, including management of some local factories, distribution outlets, schools, clinics, hospitals, sports facilities, housing construction and maintenance, local transportation, water supply, sewerage, etc. Provincial authorities generally have responsibility for the above functions when their operations cross over municipal boundaries. Examples might include a college or hospital which serves several municipalities or a factory that produces for more than one municipality, and province-wide services such as special schools. National-level industries such as sugar production and extraction, and electricity generation and distribution, are controlled by the respective ministries and their regional branches. Local government usually provides labour for these sectors when a plant falls within its area. Local and provincial government combined are responsible for approximately 45 per cent of all public expenditure, including 83 per cent on education and 92 per cent on health (interview with Hernández 1996).

National policy affecting local services is decided centrally. In extraordinary circumstances, as in the case of the ongoing problem of poor housing, central government has attempted to respond to persistent popular demand for improvements generated through the *Poder Popular* structure. Such decisions at the national level concerning priorities and standards are implemented principally through a hierarchy of financial controls. Municipal budgets are overseen by provincial administration, and provincial budgets by the National Assembly. Budgets are calculated and set by the Ministry of Finance and Prices through complex formulae which reflect previous expenditure plus needs and resources assessed on the basis of national statistical indicators. In this system equality is a priority, but selection of key areas of provision is centrally determined and emphasis is placed on education, health care and social services, while housing and infrastructure maintenance has been relatively neglected. However, according to representatives of the *Consejo de Administración* in Matanzas (interview 1996), before the economic crisis precipitated by the collapse of the Soviet Bloc, there were sufficient financial resources at the municipal level to respond to local initiatives and preferences. Once statutory obligations were fulfilled, there were opportunities for virement of funds to deal with matters reflecting specifically local needs. In this sense, the system was flexible and responsive to local demands as well as providing a uniform standard for key services. Under such conditions, citizens were eager to participate, because they had a role in the running of the municipality, and what it provided.

The issue of the Communist Party's influence on *Poder Popular* is complex (Dilla et al. 1993:61–67). The Party is not directly involved in the selection of candidates and cannot, by law, directly manipulate the democratic process (Roman 1999:118). But because of its vital and co-ordinated role at all levels of Cuban society and polity, it has a close link with the functioning of *Poder Popular*. It is also noticeable that at the higher levels of the system, and especially the National Assembly, the Party has a disproportionate influence (ibid.:91). As we have seen, the Party was re-formed as the Cuban Communist Party (PCC) in 1965, and gradually became a vanguard organisation to lead the population towards socialism. It is perhaps no coincidence that the PCC gained in strength at the same time that the state structure was being reorganised in the early 1970s. The Party's first congress was held in 1975, before the ratification of the new Cuban Constitution. PCC members are bound by the decisions of their Party, which is not a flexible political structure when faced by popular demands that do not accord with predetermined objectives.

The overlap between the PCC and the organs of state power is clearly evident in *Poder Popular*, given that at the municipal level around 75 per cent of delegates are Party members, while at provincial and national levels their representation is nearer to 100 per cent. This dramatic increase from substantial to exclusive representation at the higher levels is mainly because provincial and national deputies, until recently, were not directly elected by the population but by municipal assemblies, which, as noted earlier, select from lists prepared by electoral committees organised by the Party. One should not assume, however, that the position adopted by the Party is always, or even frequently, contrary to the demands of the population. More than any other socialist country, Cuba is dedicated to social equality and high levels of social provision, as illustrated in the island's remarkable performance in health care and education, where it rivals, and in some areas surpasses, standards in developed economies. The Party, therefore, as the Revolution's sole political organ, is dedicated to sustaining these achievements which are valued and demanded by the population. It is also the only institution at the local level that has a structure which extends through the entire economic system up to the national decision-making process. Hence its members are in a good position to play a guiding role in local affairs, especially by indicating which demands may be worth pursuing, and which are futile because of high-level policy decisions or lack of resources. This role has been particularly important during the period of crisis which began with the collapse of the Soviet Bloc.

The Party in Cuba is seen by the population in a different light than were ruling Communist Parties in the former socialist countries. In the latter, the Party was held by many to be an institution which gave its members access to privileges unavailable to the rest of the population, was rife with corruption, insensitive to the needs of the people and in general constituted an elite political class. In Cuba very few people regard the Party in this way, and such a perception would indeed be inaccurate. The PCC may share some of the faults of its counterparts in the former Communist countries, but to a significantly lesser degree, especially regarding corruption which is very dimly regarded by the Cuban leadership. Clearly, the role of the Party in *Poder Popular* is restrictive, and does serve to channel popular demands and discourage the growth of opposition to policy decisions at the higher levels. On the other hand, it does not significantly suppress or render ineffectual the democratic and participatory process at local level.

As Fuller (1992) has argued, in the 1970s and early 1980s Cuba did make democratic advances in both the workplace and in local government; but while this may be true at a functional and organisational level, the creative (and destructive) dynamic of the 1960s had been neglected. Sovietised economic planning, commitments to the CMEA, reliance on Soviet aid and the conformity that this demanded sapped the revolutionary impetus for leadership and population to interact in a way that maintained a conscious engagement with the process of change. Generally, in the 1970s the building of socialism steered disproportionately towards achieving material goals rather than forming consciousness. *Poder Popular* provided a functional mechanism that allowed for continuing subjective action and participation, but at a reduced and more structural level.

Authors who have made studies of the workings of *Poder Popular* (Roman 1999; LeoGrande 1989), Cubans themselves including academics (interview with Dilla 1996), and participants (see Roman 1999:164–166) identify inadequacies in the system. For example, while there are fluid and fairly effective mechanisms for citizen participation concerning local issues, this influence rarely extends to matters of national importance. At this top level, key decisions are usually at the discretion of the high command of the Revolution and the Party. Moreover, while *Poder Popular* is a good mechanism for allowing citizens to place requests and questions (*planteamientos*) and receive explanations through the local delegates, it is not always as effective at the stage of implementation and action. This can be a consequence of bureaucratic inefficiency, diffidence, lack of authority of delegates (Roman 1999:165), or, most commonly, since the collapse of the Soviet Bloc, a shortage of resources. Clearly a case can be made for the shortcomings of *Poder Popular* which would be acknowledged and understood by many Cubans. However the crucial issue is not so much with the functional performance of the system, but rather how effective it is as a mechanism of participation in the context of constructing socialism. That is, socialism understood as the transformation of society through the evolution of consciousness and the formation of social individuals who participate, rather than compete, to build their futures.

This is perhaps best expressed by the Cuban social scientist Martínez-Herédia (1992:64), who believes that participatory democracy is central to the creative dynamic of socialism, and echoes Rousseau's notion of *perfectibilité*:

> Socialism is ... a process of successive upheavals not only in the economy, politics and ideology but in conscious and organised action. It is a process premised on unleashing the power of the people, who learn to change themselves along with their circumstances. Revolutions within the revolution demand creativity and unity with respect to principles and organisation and broad and growing participation. In other words, they must become a gigantic school through which people learn to direct social processes. Socialism is not constructed spontaneously, nor is it something that can be bestowed.

4
The Revolution in Crisis

As argued in the previous chapter, the Insurrection of 1959 and the unique trajectory of the Cuban Revolution during its first twenty years were the outcomes of an internal political process. However, to survive in a hostile world, the Revolution came to depend heavily on the Soviet Union. Consequently, at the time of the collapse of the Soviet Bloc even the most sympathetic observers of Cuba felt it was only a matter of time before it too succumbed to the forces that had undermined Communism. In April 1989 the author flew to Havana on the Russian airline Aeroflot, coincidentally at the same time as a high-level Soviet delegation led by Premier Gorbachev was visiting Cuba. By then changes had begun to take place in the Soviet Union and it was clear that, while Gorbachev would continue to express solidarity with Havana, the true purpose of the mission was to tell Castro that the relationship would be very different in the future. In a discussion with a Soviet journalist on the plane, the author was informed that the Cubans were to have 'their life support machine switched off'. This chapter explains the impact on Cuba of Communism's collapse, and analyses some of the ways in which the Revolution survived the crisis and the problems faced including massive economic dislocation, corruption and youth discontent. There are many studies of Cuba's post-Soviet predicament and some of these will be cited, but because the author was personally involved with the implementation of aspects of reform, reference will also be made to that experience.

THE COLLAPSE OF THE SOVIET BLOC: A LONE STRUGGLE IN A HOSTILE WORLD

Serious problems began to plague the Cuban economy before the collapse of Communism. As noted in the Introduction, relations with the Soviet Union became less predictable in the early 1980s, especially when Moscow seemed unresponsive to the 1983 US invasion of Grenada, leaving Cuba to feel isolated. This concern made the Cuban leadership reconsider their military strategy. Up to that time the army had been highly dependent on advanced Soviet military equipment, which was used both to defend Cuba from external aggression and to engage in international campaigns. But if their Soviet ally was becoming unreliable, then it would be necessary to prepare for a less equipment-based, and more civilian-orientated, form of defence: 'War of all the People' (Klepak 2005:46). The victory of Cuban and Angolan forces over the South African backed UNITA at the 1988 battle of Cuito Cuanavale was the last major Cuban battle that was dependent on Soviet technology.

By 1986, a combination of low market prices for Cuba's principal exports of sugar and surplus Soviet oil, increasing interest rates on accumulated hard currency debt, an inability to negotiate new loans and a resulting cutback in imports of intermediate goods from capitalist countries all led to a significant downturn in the economy. Moreover, Gorbachev's introduction of *perestroika*, *glasnost* and market-orientated policies made the Cubans realise that their superpower protector was embarking on a separate track – one that would become increasingly unacceptable to Havana. The decade ended with a series of corruption scandals that rocked the Revolution, most notably the 1989 trial and execution of the Angolan War hero General Arnaldo Ochoa for involvement in drug smuggling.

In 1986 the Cuban government launched the 'Campaign of Rectification of Errors and Negative Tendencies', which besides being a reaction to the above warning signals, was also a response to the failings of the SPDE (System of Economic Management and Planning) economic system that was deemed to be too bureaucratic and economistic (Cole 1998). It was decided that to survive, Cuba must go back to its revolutionary roots, including a re-emphasis on political consciousness as a means of dealing with change. Reviewing the previous decade and speculating on a future strategy, President Castro (1987:225) stated:

[W]e began to go off course; ... what was happening to us; the blind belief ... that the construction of socialism is basically a question of mechanisms ... I think the construction of socialism and communism is essentially a political task ... it must be fundamentally the fruit of the development of awareness ...

We must appeal to people's consciousness, and the other mechanisms, the economic factors, ...we must use these economic mechanisms in material production, but with this concept, as an auxiliary means or instrument of political and revolutionary work; because believing that these methods will give us the miracle of efficiency and economic and social development is one of the most ridiculous illusions there could ever be.

The economic and political agenda for the 'rectification' process was to eliminate wastefulness, improve participation and reduce bureaucratic planning procedures. The private farmer's markets were also shut down and Castro denounced those who had sought to profit at the expense of the population. But more than a set of economic and political measures, the campaign was an attempt, in part, to return to Guevara's 'moral economy' and the social consciousness building of the 1960s. In practice, resources were concentrated in those areas that had always made the Revolution popular: health care, education and improvements in housing. A *Plan Alimentario* was instigated to make Cuba more self-sufficient in food production and reduce dependence on sugar exports. Emphasis was also placed on new sources of hard currency earnings, such as the emerging biotechnology and tourist industries. Military reform continued with a concentration on the popular defence of the nation, in line with the revolutionary spirit which had led to the successful 1959 Insurrection. These changes of direction dominated debates in the third and fourth Cuban Communist Party Congresses in 1986 and 1991. During this process, a document known as the 'Call to the Fourth Party Congress' was produced, notable for the extent of public participation it invited and the willingness it expressed to open up the direction of the Revolution for debate (Hernández 2003). One of the political decisions that emerged from these consultations was Cuba's rejection of Soviet restructuring in the form of *perestroika* and *glasnost*, policies which were seen to be 'capitalist' and 'counter-revolutionary'. As Castro noted, 'Perestroika is another man's wife. I don't want to get involved' (cited in Keller 1989).

While the 'Rectification Campaign' was being implemented, Communism collapsed. It immediately became clear that nothing could have prepared Cuba for such a tremendous economic and political shock. With the demise of the Soviet Bloc, Cuba lost its main trading partners and a vital source of aid, soft loans and political support. Perhaps no other country in peacetime in the twentieth century has suffered such a dramatic downturn in its economy in such a short period. In a few months Cuba was isolated ideologically and economically.

In 1987–88, 85 per cent of the island's trade was with CMEA countries, of which 70 per cent was with the Soviet Union (Carranza et al. 1995). 63 per cent of sugar, 71 per cent of nickel, 95 per cent of citrus fruits and 100 per cent of electronic goods were exported to socialist countries; while Cuba imported 63 per cent of its foodstuffs, 86 per cent of raw materials, 98 per cent of petroleum or oil, 80 per cent of machinery and technical equipment and 74 per cent of manufactured goods from the same set of countries (ibid.). By 1991, Cuba's trade with Eastern Europe had virtually disappeared, and with the Soviet Union had fallen to 30 per cent of its 1988 level (Zimbalist 1992). But worse was still to come, mainly because of poor sugar harvests in 1992 and 1993, and a tightening of the US embargo in the form of the Cuban Democracy Act (Torrecelli Act), which prohibited foreign subsidiaries of US companies from trading with Cuba and curbed dollar remittances to the island from the US. The island's capacity to import fell from $8 billion in 1989 to $1.7 billion in 1993 (Ministry of Finance and Prices 1997:11). According to a more recent estimate, between 1989 and 1993 there was a 35 per cent decline in Cuban GDP and a 78 per cent decrease in imports (Cabrisas 2005).

During this period the state agricultural system could not supply enough food to meet the basic needs of the population, making Cuba's 60 per cent import dependence on food for internal consumption seem like the most serious error of the Revolution. Furthermore, the transport system was reduced to between 10–20 per cent of normal capacity, and a whole range of import-dependent services were cut. Education and health care, the pillars of revolutionary development, were given priority access to resources. But as supplies dried up, basic materials like pens and paper became unavailable, and imported medicines were cut, forcing many people to turn to herbal and traditional remedies.

Faced with unprecedented economic and social problems, in 1990 the Cuban government launched the 'Special Period in Time of Peace', which included a 'zero option' contingency plan for total isolation of the economy (Bengelsdorf 1994:138). Despite this military-style strategy, in practice the Cuban government lost a measure of control over the economy and society during the next decade. After all, a state that supplied virtually everything to the population was suddenly disconnected from its main sources of provision, and had to let people try to resolve their own shortages.

In the medium term, Cuba had no alternative but to partially reorientate its economy towards the market. This consisted of a drive to attract foreign investment, and increasing emphasis, as mentioned previously, on hard currency transactions such as tourism and biotechnology export products. This trend required the acquisition of market expertise to develop and run these initiatives. As a consequence, the Cuban government approached the European Union in 1993 with a view to developing a co-operation programme to provide training and technical support to the Ministry of Finance and Prices to undertake reforms in taxation, budgeting and accounting. This project, in which the author played a role, provides some useful insights into Cuba's flirtation with capitalism.

In the early 1990s relations between the EU and Cuba were improving, and in September 1993 the European Parliament suggested, for the first time, that a Co-operation Agreement should be signed with Cuba (the only country in Latin America and the Caribbean not to have such an arrangement). In November it also passed a resolution (A3-0243/93) condemning the Torricelli Act (Lambie 1998:25). This was followed by a visit to Havana in April 1994 by European Commission Vice-President Manuel Marín, which resulted in a call to 'normalise' relations and set up a line of humanitarian aid and support for technical and management training. What the US had failed to achieve in three and a half decades of hostility towards Cuba (i.e. Cuba joining the 'international community'), the EU hoped could be accomplished in a few years. As a result of Marín's visit, an EU-funded project was agreed with the Ministry of Finance and the author was appointed co-director, firstly with the Minister Dr José Luis Rodríguez, and later with other senior members of the Ministry. This project, entitled 'Assistance with the Creation of a Fiscal and Budgetary Administration in Cuba' (EU designations CUB/B7-3011/95/044 & CUB/B7-3011/98/095), ran from June 1995 to December 1996, and again for 18 months from January 2000. The European consortium that was formed for its delivery, which included De Montfort University in the UK, the German Economic Research Institute (DIW) in Berlin and the Complutense University in Spain, was called the Cuba Financial Reform Group (CFRG).

During the first months of the project, relations between the EU and Cuba continued to improve, and progress was made towards the establishment of a full Co-operation Agreement. But the shooting down of two US civilian light aircraft by the Cubans in February 1996, followed by the approval of the Helms-Burton Act in the US Congress in March, which further tightened the embargo, put the EU in a difficult position. Subsequently, Commissioner Marín made a second visit to Cuba, but the meeting with President Castro went badly, especially when the EU delegation pressed the need for a move towards multi-party democracy (discussion with EU officials 1996). Castro made it clear to Marín that, in his opinion, although Cuba faced unprecedented difficulties, it was the global capitalist system that had a legitimacy crisis, not the Revolution. A combination of this failed meeting, pressure from the US and the establishment of the 'Common Position' by the EU in November 1996 (the right-wing government of Aznar in Spain stepped up demands on Cuba for multi-party democracy and a reduction in perceived human rights abuses), all led to a deterioration of EU–Cuban relations (Lambie 1998:30). The situation remained virtually unchanged until the recent decision (June 2008) by the European Parliament to lift diplomatic sanctions on Cuba, clearing the way for possible new co-operation agreements. However, at the time of this book's completion in June 2010, this potential opening had not led to a significant improvement in Cuban–EU relations.

During the initial phase of the CFRG project, the author and his colleagues became aware of significant, and perhaps irreconcilable, differences between Cuba's finance and planning system and capitalist models. Despite good will on both sides, initial meetings revealed that this incompatibility in managerial, organisational and political approaches would make it difficult to establish viable co-operation. It also became clear that Cuba was not an economy in transition, in which new methods could be implemented as part of a wider process of change. Rather, Western expertise was to be cautiously introduced to facilitate the functioning of tentative internal market initiatives, and provide the necessary skills to engage with foreign capital. To this effect, Carlos Lage (cited in Pérez-López 1994:191), the then Vice-President, proclaimed:

> Our opening is not an opening toward capitalism, but rather a socialist opening towards a capitalist world. It is based on certain principles that guarantee the preservation of socialist order over our economy and our ability to meet our economic and social objectives.

This served to create a degree of misunderstanding between the EU and the Cuban government. The former saw Cuba's reforms as a gradual transition towards the market while the latter wanted to obtain skills to implement mechanisms of control over emergent capitalist practices. In this context, the author recalls an interesting debate over a *paladar* (small private restaurant restricted to twelve seats and family-only employees) in a prime location in Havana that was doing exceptionally good business, and for which the newly devised fixed licence fee and tax were almost irrelevant. While the CFRG argued for a more advanced taxation system that would require the keeping of accounts by the restaurateur, the Ministry was concerned (without saying as much) that these kinds of developments would incrementally lead to the formation of capitalist social relations. There were also many other technical problems regarding how one controlled such processes in an economy that was not undergoing a transition.

From the mid to late 1990s, some of the most significant reforms in the domestic economy were: controlling inflation by reducing excess liquidity; reduction of the budget deficit; encouraging alternative means of increasing production by allowing wider self-employment; turning state farms into co-operatives and granting greater autonomy to state enterprises; legalisation of possession of the US dollar (1993), and freedom for Cubans to conduct transactions in dollars and buy in hard currency shops; the beginnings of a taxation system on private individuals and corporations; the legalisation of private markets for the selling to the public of surplus agricultural produce (over what was required by the state); price increases of consumer goods; civil service cuts; restructuring of production; and the implementation of new concepts of planning and administration (interview with Toledo 1996).

By the mid 1990s the economy had stabilised, although at a lower level than before the collapse in 1990/91, and there was much debate about the extent to which market-orientated reforms should be permitted to shape the recovery process. Cuban economists (Carranza et al. 1995) published a book suggesting the possibility of Cuba moving towards a mixed economy. Some outside observers (Gordon 1997) concurred with this view and spoke of a transition to some form of 'entrepreneurial socialism'. In meetings with Cuban technocrats in connection with the EU projects mentioned above, the author and his European colleagues often felt market options were being seriously considered in various areas of the economy. Sometimes we were given the impression this attitude was very functionalist, and it seemed that in some people's minds it was simply a matter of replacing Soviet manuals with Western ones. Dilla (1999:231) refers to 'a new technocratic elite', and Burchardt (1995:68) speaks of a 'technocratic-entrepreneurial group' emerging in the mid 1990s – a 'new power elite' that could become the 'avant-garde for a capitalist transformation'.

This was a tendency that the author also witnessed at first hand while working on a British government-funded project to assist democratic transition in Poland. But in Cuba the necessary transitional opening that could have given hegemonic leadership to this faction did not take place. For some Cuban officials and academics, the limited market reforms, visits abroad, and working with foreign consultants and businesses introduced them to a new environment that promised material reward for their efforts comparable with those afforded to their foreign counterparts. And during the second half of the 1990s, their voices were being heard in government. Indirectly, one would learn of disagreements between some senior officials and President Castro, as the latter continued to see the market as the antithesis of 'revolutionary' objectives. Speaking of one aspect of the reforms, Castro (2007:488) stated:

> [W]e had to agree to foreign currency shops [because the Cuban state needed to control goods priced in hard currency to capture taxes], which we hated, because we knew what it meant [providing privileges for those who had dollar income from abroad or were working in the black market at home].

Although EU support was ultimately premised on Cuba moving towards the market, there was a genuine desire among many officials in Brussels to provide a benign alternative to the aggressive stance of the US. However, pressure from Washington and right-wing elements in Europe eventually made the EU an unreliable partner for Cuba: a fair-weather friend. Some of Cuba's own actions also did not help the relationship (Lambie 1998).

President Castro and members of the Cuban leadership believed that Cuba would always be alone, and a pariah, while it pursued its socialist course, and refused to enter a process of transition. However, their sights went beyond national survival to an analysis of prospects for a globalising world system. Seeing the failings of the neo-liberal elites to consolidate their hegemony, especially in Latin America, and the growing inequality created by structural adjustment programmes and global market exposure, it was concluded, as we have seen, that neo-liberalism was unsustainable and would produce new openings for the Cuban Revolution. This becomes clear in many of the speeches Castro made in the 1990s, some of which have been published in collections such as *Capitalism in Crisis* (2000).

As a member of the UK–Cuba Initiative, which in the 1990s was led by the late Baroness Young of the British House of Lords, the author participated in several roundtable meetings with President Castro. During these discussions, though he was always polite and informative, he made it clear that the Cuban leadership did not see socialism and market reform to be compatible. The President himself, then and today in his retirement, has a strong sense of destiny: an unshakable belief that history 'will absolve' him, and the Revolution.

MAINTAINING SOCIALISM AND PARTICIPATION IN THE MIDST OF CAPITALIST ENCROACHMENT

The first market mechanisms introduced into Cuba brought some benefits, but there were also negative effects, especially in socialist terms. By far the greatest problem facing the Cuban leadership was the growing inequality that these reforms engendered, particularly because of the circulation of two currencies, the peso and the US dollar (Ritter 1995). Although it was essential to legalise the dollar to bring it into the open, to reduce the black market and for taxation purposes, one Cuban official concluded, 'the day they legalised the dollar, the Revolution died' (interview, Ministry of Finance 1998). Ironically, by the mid 1990s, because of these reforms, it was those workers who remained faithful to the state-run economic system who were penalised economically; a peso wage or salary no longer covered basic needs, but those who had access to dollars could afford the necessities and acquire the new imported goods on offer in the hard currency shops. Therefore, it was the black marketeers, the money changers, entrepreneurs or workers in tourism, and those who received dollar remittances from the US, who benefited most from these reforms. Who could blame an engineer or university professor for becoming a taxi driver or a tour guide, when such employment offered the potential to earn many times more than in underfunded and underpaid state employment? It is generally accepted in Cuba that all workers should be paid in Cuban pesos, but employment in the black market and in and around tourism offered the possibility of gaining access to hard currency. This bifurcation of the currency and growing inequality weakened social cohesion. As a response, in November 2004 the Cuban authorities stopped the use of dollars as legal tender and issued a national hard currency equivalent, the Cuban Convertible Peso (CUC). Those who hold dollars and other foreign currency have to convert into CUCs at official rates to buy goods in Cuba. This gives the government greater control over inflows of hard currency from abroad and allows for a more equitable distribution of resources. For instance, more Cubans have part of their salaries and/or bonuses paid in CUCs. However, problems of privilege and inequality still exist because of the divisions between the old peso economy and the new hard currency.

Adapting Political and Participatory Institutions to Confront the Crisis

Faced with a crisis which threatened the heart of the Revolution, in the early 1990s the government acted in two synchronised ways: politically, as it sought to expand social responsibility and citizen involvement in the resolution of problems; and economically, to allow the maximum use of local knowledge and resources in conjunction with state support. Politically, after the Party Congress of 1991, *Consejos Populares* (Local Councils), composed of local government delegates and representatives of key enterprises, were formed to give more decision-making power to communities during the 'Special Period' (interview with Ramirez García 1999). A new type of workplace assembly called *Parlementos Obreros* (Workers' Parliaments) was also established, which acted principally as a forum to allow workers to express their opinions on how the crisis had affected them. The creation of such workers' assemblies, in particular, were regarded by many as an extraordinary moment in the development of citizen consultation, and opened an important space in which to register, and sometimes act upon, popular concerns. These two new organisations, along with the trade unions, *Poder Popular* and CDRs, were also consulted on major issues confronting the economy, with some channels of feedback to the leadership. As Castro (2007:619) notes, 'We follow public opinion with a microscope. And we can tell you the state of public opinion in Havana ... and in the rest of the country ... all the opinions. Even the adverse ones.'

With 7.5 million members out of Cuba's total population of around 12 million, the CDRs collectively form the island's largest mass organisation. However, their role has perhaps been reduced, and in some cases corrupted, with the rise of the black market. It became necessary, therefore, to strengthen their functions as a mechanism of social cohesion, and an interface between the population and government. In this respect, they were given the task of explaining to the population the social necessity of the new tax system (interview with González 1996).

In 1993, direct elections of deputies from the base to the National Assembly were allowed for the first time. The Cuban leadership presented this exercise as a referendum on the Revolution itself. Although the voting process made it difficult to establish clearly who was for or against, it is generally accepted that about 80 per cent of the electorate broadly supported the government. Thirty per cent of the candidates elected were also non-Party members, which may suggest the voters felt that independents might better defend local decisions at the national level. In practice, ten new standing committees were formed in the National Assembly to provide continuous communication between the central and local governments. Although Cuba has not made any moves towards multi-party elections and representative government, as understood currently in mainstream political science, it has extended and permitted participatory opportunities deep within civil society.

Critics of Cuba (Gunn 1995; Espinosa 1999) see changes precipitated by the collapse of the Soviet Bloc as the birth pangs of an independent civil society and an opening to capitalism. On the contrary, Dilla (2000) believes that the evolving and creative relationship between the state and civil society has been a safety valve which has allowed the system to survive. In this sense, the state has conceded to greater decentralisation and experimentation, not only to accommodate a discontented population, but also as part of a constantly unfolding process of consultation. To some extent, the state can guide and manipulate this process, but if it exceeds its rights and obligations it could tip the balance and lose the asset on which its legitimacy depends: social consensus. Dilla (2000:41) draws our attention to the nature of the Cuban citizen: 'in Cuba we are dealing with a participative practice that includes highly qualified subjects with broad political experience acquired through decades of local mobilization and participation'. However, he warns, referring to the new openings that have taken place in civil society since the 1990s, 'these embryonic social movements and their citizens suffer from the misunderstanding or the utilitarianism of the bureaucracy trained in the control and vertical allocation of resources'.

Since the mid 1990s, an open debate on civil society has emerged in Cuba. Once shunned as a capitalist construction serving to legitimise the inherent inequalities of market relations, Cuban intellectuals have begun to address this concept and its relevance for Cuba (Acanda 2002; Hart 1996; Dilla 1999, 2000, 2002;

Hernández 1994, 2003). A synopsis of this debate (Recio Silva 1999) was published in the Cuban journal *Temas*, entitled '*Sociedad civil en los 90: el debate cubano*'. The reasons for the willingness to enter into such a discussion are manifold, but perhaps the most significant are: to engage Western mainstream academia on its own territory to challenge its hegemony of ideas; to provide an ideological framework for Cuban notions of participation, democracy and citizen–state relations; and the building of intellectual legitimacy, not just to defend Cuba's political and social processes, but also the newly emerging social movements in Latin America that are seeking separate spaces outside the parameters of neo-liberalism.

At a practical and economic level, the crisis of the 1990s had a negative impact on Cuba's comprehensive system of social provision, some of which is within the jurisdiction of *Poder Popular*. With a catastrophic decline in the resources available to the municipalities, delegates were no longer in a position to resolve even the most basic of problems. Citizens who visited delegate's *despachos* or attended *circumscripción* meetings soon learned that it was a waste of time to mention deficiencies in transport, maintenance, and shortages in household supplies or a whole range of other goods and services, because funds were rarely available. As a matter of necessity, virtually every Cuban citizen had to turn to the rapidly growing black market (fuelled by theft from state enterprises, illegal private sales of agricultural produce, and goods brought in by tourists or obtained from tourist shops by Cubans with access to hard currency) in an attempt to satisfy their basic needs.

Peri-Urban Horticulture: Solving Shortages Through Grassroots Initiative and State Responsiveness

Partly to counter a large-scale desertion from areas of state control into the informal sectors of the economy, the government sought to generate new openings and opportunities which encouraged participation and co-operation. In a practical sense, in some ways, these complemented the market-orientated developments, but on a political level they contradicted them and provided a socialist alternative. Many such initiatives, like their market-style counterparts, emerged independently from within local communities, but also required state acknowledgement and support to bring them out into the open, and to make them part of a coherent economic and political endeavour (interview with Martínez Heredia 2004). In an attempt to strengthen the civil society/state interface, the CDRs were encouraged by government to find ways of solving economic shortages. They were also made responsible for organising contingents to work in the countryside on food production campaigns (interview with Dilla 1996). Due mainly to the cessation of imports of fertilisers, pesticides, agricultural machinery and food from the Soviet Bloc in the early 1990s, agricultural production declined dramatically, halving the caloric intake of Cubans. Manpower became a vital resource as output had to be doubled to meet basic needs, but with substantially less material input. However, because food shortages directly affected everyone, the call to increase production stimulated a spirit of collective responsibility. While the state took direct action to increase agricultural production, there was at the same time a parallel and complementary wave of popular initiatives to produce food.

As noted earlier, in the late 1980s a National Food Programme (*Plan Alimentario*) was launched, as part of the emerging de-Sovietisation trend of the Rectification Campaign. The aim of this plan was to convert to vegetable production areas of land that were traditionally planted with sugar cane. But rather than maintaining state farms, decentralised small-scale units were encouraged, especially in the form of self-provisioning *autoconsumos*. These are principally linked to organisations (factories, schools, ministries, sugar cane complexes, hospitals, etc.). Plots are tended by the employees who produce for the canteen, and sell surpluses to workers at low prices. When the Soviet Bloc collapsed, this programme was extended and expanded in the drive to increase agricultural production. To achieve this end, the success of *autoconsumos* was transferred into a national-level programme to develop peri-urban horticulture. This initiative is an interesting example of the fusion between the state and civil society. In this context, *Poder Popular* provided an interface between the Ministry of Agriculture's newly formed Agricultural Department for the City of Havana and the *Consejos Populares*, mass organisations, the CDRs and local community groups and individuals. Working with the Ministry, *Poder Popular* was able to provide, or facilitate access to, land, material resources, transport, training and advice, outreach workers, local libraries, seed stores and other support services for the new producers (interview with Leon Vega 1995). This endeavour was supported by new planning laws which designated vacant and unused land, as well as some gardens and public spaces, for food production. Havana, the largest city in the Caribbean with a population of 2.2 million, had the most pressing problems concerning food supply and distribution, and was given priority by this programme. However, it was not long before the initiative had spread to all urban centres in the country. Moreover, according to Rosset and Benjamin (1994), this 'new agricultural model' represented the largest conversion from conventional agriculture to organic and semi-organic farming that the world has ever known.

This was more than simply a government initiative and was, above all, a response to intensifying citizen demands that the state provide the means for the population to meet its basic needs, which could no longer be satisfied by traditional centralised structures. As Murphy (2000) notes, 'By 1994 a spontaneous decentralised movement of urban residents joined a planned government strategy to create 8000 city farms in Havana alone'. The production units that make up this 'new agricultural model' can take many forms. These include: *Autoconsumos,* as described above; *Huertas Populares,* an area of land near to a centre of habitation which is divided into plots; *Organopónicos,* which are usually larger units established on reclaimed land and run as co-operatives or by the state; *Clubes de Horticultores,* which take a similar form to British allotment societies, but with higher levels of integration to other local institutions. There is also a programme called *Mi Huerta* to support the individual gardener with a small plot, or even just window boxes (interview with Aguilera 1996). Most of this production is based on organic methods, partly because of the prohibitive cost of imported chemical fertilisers and pesticides, but also as a growing commitment to the organic movement (Rosset & Benjamin 1994; Funes et al. 2002). Since much of the reclaimed land is unsuitable for agricultural use, a raised-bed system of cultivation is often employed, especially in *organopónicos,* for which soil has to be brought from elsewhere. With the support of various agencies, seed stores (*Tiendas consultorio agrícola*) have been established throughout the country which, apart from providing seeds, also supply technical advice and materials such as compost, gardening tools, bio-fertilisers and bio-pest-control agents (interview with Rodríguez Nodals 2005). These stores are largely self-financing and run by self-employed managers, but prices are checked by the state to ensure that they remain affordable. Various government institutions have been created to manage the development of urban horticulture (The Cuban Association for Agriculture and Forestry – ACTAF), and to provide scientific support (National Institute for Basic Research in Tropical Agriculture – INIFAT, and the Plant Protection Research Institute – INISAV). Interestingly, in the case of organic production, some of the scientific institutes work closely with Cuba's biotechnology sector. While regarded as a contradictory relationship in the West, Cuba sees a possibility, through genetic manipulation, to challenge the 'seed imperialism' that has existed since the conquest of the Americas, when European varietals were introduced to replace diverse native species. Transnational corporate biotechnology with its 'terminator genes' and adapted resistance factors, specifically geared to a global system of profit generation, is perhaps the ultimate expression of 'seed imperialism'; but Cuban science seeks to reverse this process to approximate the genetic codes of original varieties that were suitable for local tropical conditions.

In the municipality of Santa Fé, a *Club de Horticultores* was created in 1993 which has its own political structure composed of a president, secretary and committee (Fernández & Ortazo 1996). To develop its interests, the club and its members sought gardening advice from the Ministry of Agriculture, which has hundreds of outreach workers. The local *Consejo Popular* and municipal delegates of *Poder Popular* channelled requests for resources and land to the municipal council and higher, and contacts have been made with scientific institutes to seek advice on pest control and growing techniques. Foreign NGOs have also been invited to contribute expertise and resources which are not available in Cuba. However, this has become a controversial area, as the kind of support offered by these agencies is often associated with market-orientated managerialism (Blaufuss 2005).

While most gardeners only work on plots in their spare time, the members of the club and their families soon became almost self-sufficient in vegetable and meat production, and when they have a surplus it is either distributed to the local schools or sold on the open market. All decisions, including forming links with NGOs, are taken by the club's members and their families. A further example of a popular initiative in horticultural production is a retirement home on the outskirts of Havana, which has established its own *Organopónico*. Its members have also created a broad spectrum of interactive relationships in the local community to assist their project. Now the home is self-sufficient in food, and any surpluses are sent to a local school (interview with Sanchez Naranjo 1999). Some municipal governments encourage 'voluntary' contributions of produce to schools, hospitals, etc., as a form of 'social rent' for access to the free use of state land (Koont 2004). According to one source (Moskow 1995), by 1995 80 per cent of Havana's gardeners were making regular donations to institutions. From the author's own observations, many growers also give their produce to neighbours and friends. As Murphy (2000) points out, '[The] commitment to share the food harvest is a powerful testament to the spirit of collectivity and solidarity of the Cuban people, and has allowed them to survive the worst moments of the economic crisis'.

One initiative that demonstrates another interesting example of popular organisation is the Community Project for the Conservation of Organic Produce. The project is run by two retired scientists who have developed numerous innovative ways to conserve and prepare food (interviews with Figueroa & Lama 1996, 1998, 2000, 2007). Based on this work, they encourage the local community to grow vegetables, fruits and herbs in their gardens and provide classes and support for new participants. In collaboration with local schools, the project places particular emphasis on encouraging children to take an interest in plants and vegetarian food. While the state does not fund or grant special concessions to the project, the founders and organisers have been given airtime on radio and television to teach growing, preparation and preservation techniques. Now their successful weekly food programmes are broadcast throughout Cuba. In this sense, the state is a benign and responsive structure, rather than a directing force, and can react to popular initiatives in an environment in which market relations are largely absent; it is participation and co-operation which give the impetus for action.

Besides the move towards peri-urban horticulture, a second tier of agricultural reform has been initiated which involves the breakup of state farms into self-managed co-operatives known as Basic Units of Co-operative Production (UBPCs). Although these units are still required to sell a large proportion of their produce to the state at set prices, surplus can be taken to the open market. This, along with increased autonomy of the workers to manage themselves, has led to improved motivation and increases in production. This form of structure can overlap with peri-urban horticulture, and a number of *organopónicos* are organised on these lines. Combined, peri-urban and UBPC production, along with farmers on private land, have significantly contributed to a reduction in Cuba's food import dependency from 60.2 per cent in 1989 to 42 per cent in 1997 (interview with Alvarez-Escobar 2004). Although the new initiatives in agriculture have improved food security, it has recently been claimed that private producers, who only control 15 per cent of agricultural land use, supply 60 per cent of food consumed (*Cuba Briefing* 2007, Issue 377). This may be partly explained by the opening up of markets to private farmers in the 1990s, and the drive to increase food production in which, as an incentive, the state is paying more to private producers for the food it buys from them.

It is also difficult to measure the precise output of more informal means of growing, such as neighbourhood gardens, from which often little, if any, of the produce enters the market.

Cuba's country-wide initiative in peri-urban horticulture is not only suitable to the specific circumstances of the 'Special Period', but also relevant in an increasingly urbanised world. According to the UNDP (1996), by 2025 80 per cent of the world's population will live in urban centres (a level Cuba has already reached), but there are questions about the possibility of feeding such high concentrations of people. Of particular concern is globalisation's current tendency to widen the gap between rich and poor, combined with the need for indebted countries to prioritise export agriculture instead of improving national food security (Moore-Lappe et al. 1998). A further problem is that with a large proportion of land privately owned in most countries, and a tendency for this kind of ownership to increase at the expense of public property, it is very difficult for governments to assign land for popular agricultural use. In the urban environment, this is exacerbated by rising land prices and building booms, as can be seen in China today. While privatisation, markets and individual endeavour are being promoted by the major countries as the means of resolving problems of subsistence, the UNDP (1996) has evidence to suggest it is social organisation and collaboration which are the key factors in successful popular agricultural development. But as we have seen in the case of Cuba, these factors must be stimulated with state support, which is unlikely in most countries where the state is retreating and abandoning some of its powers and responsibilities. The emerging global food crisis will make these issues more pressing.

Defending Revolutionary Achievements: Health Care

Besides new initiatives that have been introduced during the 'Special Period', Cuba remains determined to defend standards in its core areas of social provision: health care, education, housing, sports and culture. Without Soviet subsidies, Cuba's detractors believed the Revolution would implode and its social services deteriorate. Concerning health, it is not surprising that during the 1990s shortages of medicines, scarcity of food, the tightening US embargo, and the duress of living through very hard times led to several epidemics and a general decline in the wellbeing of the population (Barry 2000). But by the end of the decade it was clear that the Revolution was not going to collapse, and indices in several areas of social provision, including health care, began to improve. Again one must pose the question: Is Cuba's performance in human development a quantitative and technological achievement, or part of a social process? Given that after the collapse of the Soviet Bloc many material inputs decreased, and it would have been impossible to improve technical skills sufficiently to compensate, one must consider social organisation as a factor. There is not space here to enter into the complex debate about Cuba's panoply of state provision and its functions. But to illustrate the above point, reference will be made to aspects of the Cuban health care system.

Before the Revolution, as indicated previously, Cuban health care was good by Latin American standards and produced a number of famous doctors, including Carlos Finley, whose research on yellow fever led to its eradication in Cuba. Two contributory factors in the development of Cuban health care were the progressive social legislation that was established as part of Batista's 1940 Constitution (some of which was dismantled after his coup in 1952), and the existence of mutualist medical centres which were based on members' monthly contributions. The latter were mainly established by the Spanish and provided adequate, reasonably inexpensive, health care. The main problem with the Cuban health care system before 1959 was unequal access; those living in the main cities, especially Havana which had over 60 per cent of all doctors in Cuba, had good service, while only 8 per cent of the rural population could call upon a doctor if they were ill (Hernández 1969).

In the early years of the Revolution, health care in Cuba deteriorated as investment in American-dominated infrastructure declined. Over half of the country's 6000 physicians left for the US (Claudio 1999:249), some in pursuit of their rich émigré patients. In the short term this presented an enormous problem, but also an opportunity to build a new health care system that accorded with the revolutionary priorities of universality, equitable access and government control (Rodríguez & Carrizo Moreno 1987). From the early 1960s to the 1980s, Cuba developed such a programme, placing emphasis on primary care, preventative activities and delivery through a comprehensive system of holistic care in the community, closely integrated with the neighbourhood and the family (Pietroni 2000). By the late 1970s, Cuban health statistics compared favourably with those of most developed nations, and the country began to produce its own pharmaceuticals and engage in medical research. Today, Cuba has research and development facilities of an international standard in biotechnology, immunology and other medical fields, and in some specialisms, such as the production of vaccines, it is a world leader.

Since 1983, family doctors have been located directly in residential areas, with a home, an equipped clinic (*consultorio*), nursing support and responsibility for around 100 families (Spiegel & Yassi 2004). This works well in the case of emergencies, as medical staff can be on call 24 hours a day. It is also effective for general care, as doctors are considered members of the community, breaking down the barrier between specialised professionals and ordinary people. On one occasion, while visiting a family in Cuba, the author witnessed an impromptu consultation between a doctor and a patient as they walked up the steps together into a block of flats. For the treatment of more serious medical problems the system moves from a horizontal mode to a vertical one, as the local doctor may refer the patient to the neighbourhood polyclinic which, in turn, can arrange for hospital treatment if necessary.

Consistent with Cuba's participatory approach to social and political development, the role of the local doctor goes beyond diagnosis and treatment. This includes a range of activities which help to foster a 'health culture', in synchronisation with social processes and other 'non-medical determinants of health', such as education, nutrition, cultural activities, sport, etc. A community doctor may promote health-related activities and give support with his medical knowledge, but such initiatives are often run by community organisations such as the CDRs and the Federation of Cuban Women. For instance, the author witnessed the workings of a *Circulo de abuelos* (Grandparents' Circle) which met for exercise sessions in a local park. Although aided by local doctors with advice and tests for blood pressure, etc., it was organised by the local CDR and an old people's home, and was linked with other organisations which gave participants further access to assistance and opportunities for socialisation. Again, as with the aforementioned project encouraging the growing and preservation of food, it is the networks of neighbourhood bodies run by ordinary people that provide the commitment, energy and will to advance local interests. This is the interface where the technical and specialised meets the local and participatory, in which the latter realises its own potentials and possibilities on a cascading scale, resulting in community and individual empowerment. A study of health care in Cuba by Western analysts (Spiegel & Yassi 2004) states, 'it is our impression from our work in Cuba over the past 8 years that there is an extremely high level of social capability to undertake collaborative activity at a local level to address collective needs'. Another author (Farag 2000) who has studied Cuban health care notes, 'It was most intriguing to observe a population that was not only determined to find solutions to all obstacles but did so with a great passion for communal welfare.'

The World Bank, the largest international health funding body, promotes the idea that economic growth is the only means to eradicate poverty and improve health (Dollar 2002). The difficulty with the World Bank formula, besides the problem of global recession, is that it does not acknowledge that while globalisation and neo-liberal restructuring may lead to growth in terms of GDP, that growth is marred by rising inequality. Indeed, IMF structural adjustment programmes have largely served to undermine social services, including health. This, along with a wave of privatisa-tions, has left many of the poor with significantly reduced access to medical care. Consequently some analysts question mainstream assumptions about the Bank's growth formula for developing countries (Rodrik 1999) and the effectiveness of globalisation in producing conditions conducive to improving public health (Cornia 2001). In comparison, during the post-war period of Keynesian and structuralist-style development, not only was growth generally stronger, but limited wealth redistribution and state intervention ensured improvements in social provision, including health. But in sharpest contrast is Cuba's state-funded, non-commercial, participatory health care system which has been obliged to operate in an environment of dramatic economic contraction, yet performs better than any country in the region and most of the world, based on generally accepted health indicators. For example, according to the WHO's World Health Chart for 2001, in the category of child mortality rate (up to five years of age per 1000 live births) between 1995 and 1999, Cuba stands out alone as the highest achieving country when its GDP per capita (USD Purchasing Power Parity – PPP) is taken into account. Its PPP of approximately $1800 per capita is similar to those of India, Pakistan, Vietnam, Nicaragua and Honduras, but its child survival rate of 991 per 1000 far exceeds those countries, for which the figure ranges from 900–965. Moreover, Cuban results equal those of the US, which has an individual PPP of $35,000. Similar results can be seen in other major categories of health performance.

During 19 years of crisis, in which Cuba has still not returned to the levels of economic activity of the late 1980s, health standards have, despite setbacks, continued to improve. An analysis of WHO

(2004, 2005) key health statistics, such as life expectancy and infant mortality up to five years of age, suggests Cuba's performance has kept up with, and is approximately equal to, the US. Cuba, however, has twice as many physicians per 1000 people (5.91) compared to the US (2.56). Although impressive, perhaps more relevant to this study is to compare Cuba with the rest of Latin America. In the region, national health systems were drastically overhauled by a series of reforms in the 1990s, in which governments were urged by donors and the international financial bodies to make major institutional changes, including privatisation and the separation of purchaser and provider functions (De Vos et al. 2006). Based on figures supplied by the Pan American Health Organisation (1995–2004) and the World Bank (2005), the following selective comparisons can be made:

Table 4.1

Country	1995–2006 a		1995–2004 b		1995–2004 c		1995–2003/4 d	
Argentina	72.7	75.1	22.8	14.4	20.7	16.7	10,160	11,410
Bolivia	61.2	65.2	70.0	51.6	79.0	67.6	2,020	2,490
Colombia	69.7	73.1	32.0	24.2	35.7	30.9	5,740	6,410
Costa Rica	76.6	78.7	12.9	9.7	12.9	11.9	6,590	9,140
Cuba	*75.5*	*78.3*	*11.9*	*5.6*	*9.6*	*7.1*	*n/a*	*Est 1,800*
Mexico	72.8	76.0	29.9	19.0	28.4	22.9	6,610	8,980
Jamaica	71.6	71.0	16.1	14.6	20.9	20.3	3,360	3,790
USA	76.0	77.8	7.5	6.7	8.7	8.3	27,650	37,750

a) Life expectancy at birth (male and female)
b) Infant mortality per 1000 births (estimated)
c) Infant mortality per 1000 under five years (estimated)
d) Gross national income per capita $US – 'purchasing power parity'

As shown in Table 4.1, it can be seen that from the mid 1990s, even though Latin America was arguably just emerging out of the crisis caused by the depression of the 1980s – the so-called 'Lost Decade' – performance in the region on key indicators of health has, in the main, not been impressive. Cuba, on the other hand, in the depths of economic depression in the early to mid 1990s, has made significant improvements in these areas. For a comparative analysis of Cuba and a country that has followed mainstream prescriptions for health promotion, see De Vos et al. (2006), 'Colombia and Cuba, Contrasting Models in Latin America's Health Sector Reform'.

Although Cuba is now registering economic growth, improvements in public health have not been dependent on this factor alone. Instead, emphasis has been placed on improving the mechanisms of social integration. In 1989, with crisis looming, Cuba launched its 'healthy municipalities strategy', which emphasised strengthening 'non-medical determinants' of health (Spiegel & Yassi 2004). Bringing various areas of social provision into closer co-operation helped to promote participation and community cohesion as mechanisms for dealing with shortages and problems. Once into the 'Special Period', the Ministry of Health sought to deepen the process of community involvement. Consequently, much decision making was decentralised to the new 'Consejos Populares', which in turn encouraged local people to actively intervene in the organisation of their own health care, both linked to state provision, and in the form of new popular initiatives such as the revival of traditional and herbal medicines. When such initiatives began to gain acceptance, communities often sought state support for their further development which, as we have seen in the case of peri-urban horticulture, could take various forms, often guided by the population. In this way health, education, sport, nutrition, etc., combine into a social process in which people increasingly seek to solve their problems, not through self-help, as favoured by the advocates of neo-liberalism, but by a combination of community action, popular involvement, and interaction with the state. Such co-operation and participation has prompted one Cuban academic (Hernández 2008:78) to claim:

> [I]n relative terms, Cuba is further ahead in its democratic civic culture than any other society I've known. Democratic civic culture in Cuba is expressed when people say what they think and stand up for their rights and needs, despite the existence of an administrative structure of control.

A Socialist Route to Economic Recovery?

A combination of pragmatic and experimental reforms, with a continuing reliance on social involvement in maintaining the core achievements of the Revolution and developing aspects of change, has resulted in the survival of Cuban socialism and significant economic recovery. As early as the mid to late 1990s, the feeling among senior Cuban officials was that the economy had 'turned the corner', but a long struggle still lay ahead to return to the levels that existed before the collapse of the Soviet Union. Growth continued into the new millennium, and in 2006 Cuba's Economy Minister claimed an annual rate of 12.5 per cent, and predicted over 10 per cent for 2007 (*Cuba Briefing* 2007, Issue 345). Even allowing for the differences between the UN's standard measures of economic output which exclude social services, and Cuban methods which include them, these figures are impressive. Cuba's economic performance has been traced by external sources, of which perhaps the most consistent and reliable are the Economist Intelligence Unit's country reports on the island. A contributor to these reports (Morris 2002:1) produced an independent paper entitled 'What Economists Might Learn from Cuba, 1990–2000'. Although an 'economist's' view, she noted that there was more to Cuba's 'miracle' than the simple selection of management tools:

> There are three lessons we might learn from this [Cuba's economic and social performance]: first, by prioritising basic needs provision the government ensured that hardship was shared, at least in the formal sector, so that public confidence in the state was not destroyed; second, by allowing public participation in the design of macroeconomic stabilisation policy, consensus was built and distributive effects reflected public preferences; and third, by introducing structural changes gradually, institutional transformations were carried out in line with the development of training, regulatory capacity and social attitudes.

These 'lessons' run completely against the grain of neo-liberal policy making in Latin America and other parts of the world, where the 'social' dimension has been abandoned for the presumed regulatory and distributive order of the market. According to retired president Fidel Castro (2004:4):

> The great hero in this feat [Cuban economic success/survival] has been the people, who have contributed tremendous sacrifices and immense trust. Our survival has been the result of justice and of the ideas planted over 40 years of revolution. This genuine miracle would have been impossible without unity and without socialism.

CUBA'S REVOLUTIONARY MALAISE: SEEKING SOLUTIONS

The Cuban Revolution's ability to survive the collapse of Communism and a continuing US embargo, and then begin to register a level of growth that was one of the highest in Latin America, are remarkable feats that even Cuba's detractors find difficult to diminish. These achievements, however, must be set against the negative effects of the crisis: corruption, poor productivity, underemployment, inefficiency in many areas and bureaucratic inertia. Many outside observers suggest that by prioritising the forces of the market, these problems can be overcome, forgetting perhaps that Cuba's performance so far has principally been based on non-market options. Although most Cubans on the island would reject the market solution they realise that a combination of revolutionary tenacity, socialism and limited market reforms have staved off collapse; they believe that the future must be based on a modified process of socialist construction. This process will be one that draws strongly on the past, but introduces new elements that will allow the Revolution to survive and develop in a changing world.

Socialism, Markets and Corruption

Although there are many aspects of Cuban life that require reform and change, perhaps the core problems which need to be tackled before others can be successfully dealt with are corruption and the deterioration of social cohesion. It should be emphasised, at the outset of this debate, that corruption in Cuba is almost entirely at the functioning sector of the economy, mainly driven by need, while among the Cuban leadership and at the higher levels of the state it is minimal. This is acknowledged even by the representatives of nations that have disagreements with Cuba. For instance, at a briefing given by the then British Ambassador (Dew 2006) in Havana to a group of British businesspeople, he stated that the Cuban government was 'Fantastically incorrupt in comparison to the rest of Latin America'. But, he pointed out, in a society that had faced so many problems and in which the average salary was equivalent to $17 a month, with prices going up all the time, corruption was inevitable at the street level. Despite tensions between Cuba and the UK and European Union at that time, he also added that Cuba had a 'Highly organised and successful government' and that the Cuban population as well as many outsiders had 'Confidence in the way government runs this country'.

Before the debacle of the early 1990s, there may have been certain levels of corruption in Cuban society, but these were limited by economic and social organisation based on need and equality, and the relative absence of markets and opportunities for enrichment. Talking to Cubans about this period, they recall much inefficiency and waste in certain areas of the economy, but they also remember a state-led system that provided not only good basics such as health care and education, but also a variety of opportunities to obtain essential consumer goods, certain luxuries, entertainment and cheap national vacations with reasonable standards. They also recall a level of community co-operation and interaction that was much stronger than today. Now, in many parts of Cuba, and especially the cities, it is important to take security measures to protect one's home, and the days when people rarely locked doors facing into public space are over. For most foreigners the levels of threat to individuals and property in Cuba are still remarkably low, but for Cubans there has been a notable deterioration over the past 20 years.

Once the pre-1990s system, partly upheld by Soviet subsidies, broke down, people were obliged to find ways to survive that were often no longer community orientated or state dependent. In this context, some forms of corruption became inevitable. In contrast, when the old Soviet Bloc collapsed and abandoned socialism, theft and corruption simply became legalised, as state assets, paid for and built by the efforts of workers, were privatised and handed over to favoured elites and foreign investors. Cuba was determined to avoid such a process, but as new forces were released into society as a result of a vast economic contraction, it became impossible to control completely the negative outcomes. As noted earlier in this chapter, Cuba was caught up in a kind of limbo in which markets were introduced, but there was no intention to form a market society with appropriate regulations. Reforms in general were undertaken to open up the economy to new initiatives, but not as a precursor to deeper changes that would lead to the dissolution of socialism. This complex mix was agitated by the introduction of a dual currency after the legalisation of the dollar. Corruption, in this context, cannot simply be blamed solely on the 'market' or the 'evils of capitalism', but is an inevitable consequence of the measures that were taken to deal with the crisis – measures which, in many cases, had no precedent and were unique to the Cuban situation.

The Cuban leadership's desire to retrench revolutionary values began with attempts to roll back the market reforms of the 1990s, which were perceived to have opened up new avenues for corruption and to have caused a decline in socialist values. From another perspective, one could argue that by bringing private commercial activity into the open through licensing, appropriate legislation and taxation, corruption would be reduced as private commercial activity migrated from the informal to the formal sector. However, in socialist terms such market openings threatened to create a two-tier system, which would cause increasing inequality and erode social consensus. By the early years of the new millennium, the foreign press began to note a change in government policy from the experimental years of the 1990s, when market-style reforms were introduced. One journalist (Frank 2004a) claimed that private family restaurants (*paladares*) and bed-and-breakfast-style establishments (*casas particulares*) had declined from around 200,000 in 1995 to fewer than half that number. Visits (in 2005, 2006 and 2007) to Cuba by the author, both for research purposes and with British business groups organised under the auspices of the UK Cuba Initiative, also revealed that the market experiments of the 1990s were being suffocated, and increasing emphasis placed on state and social organisation of the economy. This was felt and experienced in Cuba not just as a policy swing by the leadership, but as part of a 'Battle for Ideas'. As the Head of the Centre for the Study of the Cuban Economy at Havana University, Juan Triana, suggested, '*Cuentapropismo* [self-employment] is the least akin to socialism of all forms of production. It's the mode of production that emphasises most the role of the individual [and therefore] not the option for Cuba' (cited in Boadle 2003).

In a speech delivered at the University of Havana in November 2005, Fidel Castro (2005), always a staunch opponent of the market and all it symbolises, criticised the 'new rich' in Cuba, including the owners of '*paladares*' and other forms of small business, black marketeers and those receiving more than small remittances from family in the US, stating:

> The empire [US] was hoping that Cuba would have many more *paladares*, but it appears that there will be no more of them. What do they think that we have become, neo-liberals? No one here has become a neo-liberal ... the country will have much more, but it will never be a society of consumption ... It will be a society of knowledge, of culture, of the most extraordinary human development that one can imagine.

But despite this period of market reversal and the optimistic statements which accompanied it, problems persisted, of which corruption remains perhaps the most intractable. Corruption has, in fact, now become a kind of necessary tier in the economy, allowing it to function and overcome inefficiencies and inertia caused by shortages and inequalities. Almost everyone in Cuba engages in a corrupt or semi-corrupt activity virtually every day, just in the normal process of fulfilling needs. Although undesirable, this is accepted and understood by most Cubans, including the leadership. Problems arise, however, when such activities become regularised, and provide the preferred means of subsistence for a significant section of society. Among such groups, there is also the opportunity for personal enrichment and the temptation to engage in ever more daring and large-scale corruption.

The range and specific details of these practices are diverse. During the author's recent visits, he observed a number of irregularities. One indication of the extent of low-level corruption was provided by an auditing specialist from the UK, who visited Cuba in 2000 during the second European Commission project mentioned above. While delivering classes at the Ministry of Finance, he was told of several instances of corruption, and claims to have counted over 50 examples in shops and among service providers while he was at leisure in Havana. While visiting in March 2007 it was clear to the author that the system of state-run tourist taxis was riddled with corruption. One also heard of major examples of fraud such as a scam at the international airport, where officials had fixed up a parallel computing system through which they issued and charged for import licences.

Since the emergence of significant corruption, the Cuban government has made considerable effort to bring into force controls and social pressures to deter these practices. However, it is only recently that such initiatives have been co-ordinated through a national-level campaign, one that seeks to tackle corruption not just as a social and technical problem, but also as an ideological issue linked to encroaching liberalism and declining socialist values. Raúl Castro warned senior Communist Party leaders, bureaucrats, and managers at state-owned enterprises that 'liberalism has led to a lack of respect for the party and government within tourism and other economic sectors', and that, if necessary, more areas of the Cuban economy would be brought under the control of the military (cited in Frank 2004b). It is interesting how the Cuban military (*Fuerzas Armadas Revolucionarias* – FAR), through its power within the Cuban system and its deeply integrated relationship with society, has been effectively used to avoid the formation of an embedded capitalist class. Steering a course between small private businesses and traditional state-run enterprises, the military's Enterprise Management Group Inc. (GAESA) has established effective operations in tourism, agriculture, information technology, manufacturing, transport services and many other areas (Focus on Cuba 2003).

In the same speech cited earlier that Fidel Castro made at the University of Havana, he openly spoke of corruption as a mortal threat to the Revolution, stating, 'we can destroy it [the revolution] and it would be our fault ... either we root out the problem or we die'. Shortly after this address, an offensive targeted Cuba's petrol stations where there was evidence of massive theft. Young Communist Party cadres, along with some disenchanted youth who had been retrained, were brought in to replace the old corrupt structure and some of its staff. Suspected 'irregularities' in various sectors of the economy were also reported in the Cuban daily newspaper *Granma* and the Communist youth paper *Juventud Rebelde* in early 2006 (cited in *Cuba Briefing* 2006, Issues 300 & 329). The latter aimed its criticism at enterprises that overcharged the population, calling for a popular response to this economic abuse.

In late July 2006, Fidel Castro underwent major surgery for an intestinal problem, and although Cuban government sources spoke of a rapid recovery, it soon became clear that complications had set in and the president's life was in danger. As a consequence, the interest of the international community shifted to the issue of Cuba's future without Fidel Castro, based on the assumption that without his guiding hand the Revolution would begin to implode. When his brother Raúl stood in as leader in his absence, some observers soon realised that a transition was not imminent, even without Fidel (Sweig 2007), and the focus again turned to internal reforms. Responding to claims that Cuba could not survive without Fidel, Ricardo Alarcón, the president of Cuba's National Assembly, stated to a Russian newspaper, 'decisions [in Cuba] are taken not individually but collegiately, regardless of who heads the State Council' (*Cuba Briefing* 2006, Issue 335). This point was also made by Fidel (2007:572) in an interview in 2006. Continuing calm in Cuba and a general atmosphere of 'business as usual' seemed to confirm this claim.

In September 2006, Raúl Castro indicated that the anti-corruption campaign was a national priority, and he called on the workers and their trade unions to lead the battle against this economic and social ill. Rhetoric was followed by action, as the press stepped up its anti-corruption reporting and those who were suspected of illegal activities were brought before the law, including one Politburo member, Juan Carlos Robinson.

Juventud Rebelde has continued to spearhead the anti-corruption campaign in the media, but *Trabajadores*, the paper of the Cuban Labour Federation (CTC), and *Granma* also identify and openly criticise corrupt practices. In February 2007 all three commented on irregularities in the state-run distribution and retail network (MINCIN), which had been revealed in an official inspection. Citing the inspector's report, *Juventud Rebelde* (23 February) stated that out of 33,843 inspections, 'abnormalities' were revealed in 90 per cent of operations which had resulted in the implementation of 5,742 disciplinary measures. It went on to blame the problem on 'economic chaos and a slackening off in morals and discipline'. *Trabajadores* (27 February) spoke of a 'persistent lack of administrative control, robbery and an inadequate accounting system', and called for action to stop this 'disorder with impunity in its tracks'. *Granma* (19 February) reported on the alarming audacity of thieves who had removed galvanised steel and cables from electrical pylons. On 19 May, *Juventud Rebelde* concluded that the 'Special Period' (1991 until today) has resulted in '17 years of labour indiscipline'. State television and radio have also joined the debate about corruption and declining work ethics. The Cuban radio programme 'Straight Talk' (*Cuba Briefing* 2007, Issue 357) has been particularly frank in identifying Cuba's problems; many of which it claims have conveniently been blamed on the US blockade, though this is not always justified.

By the end of 2006, statements emerged from Cuba suggesting that the anti-corruption campaign was part of a wider strategy to find a renewed direction for aspects of the Revolution and instil it with more vigour. In an interview with the *Scotsman* newspaper (Fawthrop 2006), Mariela Castro, a daughter of Raúl who is noted for her outspokenness, indicated that a period of self-analysis was beginning that would address the country's problems; but this process rejected a market route and emphasised the strength of 'collective capacities' and consultations with the population. She also pointed out, however, that there were some officials at high levels who favoured market solutions. Shortly after these statements by his daughter, in an address to the Seventh Congress of the Cuban Federation of University Students held at Havana University on 20 December, Raúl called on the younger generation to 'fearlessly engage in public debate and analysis' (Snow 2006a). On 22 December, he followed this up in an address to the National Assembly in which he complained about inefficiencies in the Cuban economy, especially in such areas as food production and distribution and the transport system in general (Snow 2006b). He exhorted his colleagues to 'Tell the truth, without justifications, because we are tired of justifications in this Revolution ... the Revolution cannot lie ... this isn't to say that there have been comrades who have lied, but the imprecision, inexact data, consciously or unconsciously masked, can no longer continue' (ibid.). He also called for more self-criticism and open discussion in the state-run media. The message was repeated by Rolando Alfonso Borges, the Head of the Ideology Department of the Communist Party (*Cuba Briefing* 2007, Issue 341). In response, *Granma* advised journalists to be ready to engage with 'the great transformations and needs of the Revolution', warning that, 'The people must have its problems reflected in our media with greater frequency' (ibid.).

Outside observers were unsure how to interpret these general statements, except to acknowledge that something significant was occurring in Cuba (San Martin 2007). Some believed this was an indication that preparations are being made for an opening to the market, which would be the natural ideological perspective of the mainstream analysts. But such assumptions do not correspond to other more specific signals, such as calls in the Cuban media for a reduction of the emerging consumerist behaviour and lifestyles, especially amongst the young (*Juventud Rebelde* 6 January and 31 January 2007). Demands in the press for action against corruption and consumerist values were complemented by comments from Ricardo Alarcón, who bemoaned the return of significant inequalities in Cuban society. In an interview with the Argentine newspaper *Clarín*, he stated, 'one of the most painful things for Cubans to see is how some of the phenomena that we were so proud to have eradicated completely, have returned' (cited in *Cuba Briefing* 2007, Issue 353). He blamed these 'bitter contradictions' and 'deformities' on the dual currency and the introduction of elements of the free market into Cuban society. Cuba's former vice-president Carlos Lage also acknowledged, in a speech commemorating the founding of the Communist Youth Union, that the Cuban system was 'not as ideal as the one we wished for, or achieved years ago', and called upon Cuba's youth to be 'immune to the siren song' of materialism (*Cuba Briefing* 2007, Issue 354). As the anti-corruption campaign gained momentum, it appeared that 'revolutionary values' were to be marshalled to overcome this threat, and not some concession to the market. Indeed, it is the partial opening to capitalism that has been blamed for the social malaise occurring today. For instance, Deputy Attorney General Carlos Rangel linked corruption to 'the economic system of monetary-mercantile social relations [and] the legal framework and state oversight mechanism, which were not prepared to face the consequences of the economic opening' (*Cuba Briefing* 2007, Issue 377). Although all the state's legal, administrative and political power is being employed in the battle against corruption, the key factor remains popular acceptance of the strategy. It will be difficult to make people take on this 'moral' campaign if 'material' improvements and greater equality are not forthcoming as a reward for their efforts. As Rafael Hernández, editor of the Cuban journal *Temas*, has noted, 'The Cuban people can believe that the economy is growing statistically, but it is not growing in their homes' (cited in *Cuba Briefing* 2007, Issue 352).

A further particularly corrosive problem caused by the austerity of the 'Special Period', growing corruption, and now the world-wide recession has been deteriorating physical standards and morale in education and health care: the two beacons of achievement of the Revolution. On 28 October 2007, *Juventud Rebelde* reported that dentistry in Cuba was short of materials and staff, and was not delivering a reliable service to the population. One result of this was the emergence of private informal facilities which were charging for treatment. Based on discussions with a number of Cubans in the Havana district of Vedado during March 2007, the author learned that some medical procedures were very difficult to obtain through official channels, and private payments were often made to medical staff to overcome this problem. Certain drugs were also in short supply and had to be obtained through private sources. Unfortunately, even in Cuba's most prestigious social service, corruption is eroding values and creating inequalities. These problems have been exacerbated by the vast transfer of medical personnel and resources to Venezuela. One senior Cuban health official (Alcides Lorenzo Rodríguez), who defected to the US, claims that around 26,000 of the 31,000 doctors who previously staffed Cuba's primary care system have been sent abroad, seriously debilitating domestic health care provision (Cancio Isla 2006). The same source also suggests that in the effort to cover the shortage, medical students are treating patients before they are fully trained.

Education is also facing problems. Following statements by Education Minister Luis Ignacio Gomez to the National Assembly, *Granma* reported on 25 October 2007 that teachers were leaving their profession because of low pay which was not commensurate with the demands and responsibility of their work. They also complained of material shortages, housing and transport problems and lack of recognition for their efforts. It was further reported that many young teachers coming into the profession had not completed their studies, and did not have the required qualifications. The Minister himself has now been fired and blamed for many of these problems (*Granma*, 22 April 2008).

Unquestionably, the majority of Cubans are still struggling in their daily lives and are obliged to find ways to survive outside of official structures – in Cuban parlance, to go 'hunting and gathering', which often includes acting illegally. A minority however have used the Special Period to attempt to establish corrupt practices as a primary mode of existence. The task of the leadership is to win over the first group through consultation, education and incentives to support and implement new policies that are collectively recognised as fair and feasible. If this is successful, the second group will be isolated and marginalised, as their actions will be seen as counterproductive to the agreed 'general will'. In an ideal world the way to achieve this task would be to try to restore revolutionary values and avoid any further encroachment of the market and its concomitant social divisiveness. This clearly has been the preferred option of Fidel, and in his view (2007:596–599) it is through extended participation that this could be achieved:

> We've invited everyone, the entire nation, to take part in a great battle, a battle against any and all offences ... the people themselves are going to fix it, the Revolution is going to fix it. And how? There will greater and greater participation and we will be a nation with a holistic, unified general culture.

The problem remains that corruption, inequality, low productivity and poor material living standards have become deeply embedded in Cuban society, mainly because of external pressures and the consequent need for internal compromises. The Revolution, as understood in this book, can only survive in the long term by following the road to socialism as conscious collective action – a concept central to the thinking of Fidel and many Cubans. However, Cuba has a new leader, Raúl Castro, still a hardened revolutionary, but some feel he is perhaps more pragmatic than his brother. He is a president apparently willing to make some compromises to address immediate problems behind which there is a significant level of popular discontent. This issue will be taken up again in the final chapter.

Cultural and Youth Responses to the 'Special Period'

The combination of difficulties in Cuban society, and a growing willingness to discuss them at official levels, has led to open cultural responses, notably in Cuban filmmaking. In the February 2007 Cuban Film Festival, young filmmakers like Aram Vidal and Alina Rodríguez showed works that seek to reveal everyday life experiences in Cuba that are not reflected in other media. Vidal's documentaries *Calle G* and *De Generación* focus on youth culture and the generation gap, in which the political project of the older revolutionaries is no longer shared by some younger people. Rodríguez's documentary *Buscándote Havana* deals with the life of migrants from the interior who have moved to Havana (Lambie 2009b:72).

Issues of poverty, social decay and a generational gap are real in Cuba; they are core problems that have to be addressed, but they must be set in a comparative international context. It is interesting, and particularly daunting, that many young Cubans have spent all of their conscious lives in a Cuba that is very different to the one experienced by their parents in the period before the collapse of the Soviet Bloc. Contemporary Cuban youth have grown up with shortages, crisis, social flux and the temptations of materialism, exacerbated by tourism and a globalising world with its immense power of information dissemination. *Juventud Rebelde* noted in an investigation of non-institutional entertainment such as house parties that fun among some sectors of the young 'cannot be conceived of without drinking and chain-smoking', and that Hollywood was the favourite cigarette 'because it most resembles foreign brands'. Some young men apparently believe that success with women necessitates wearing 'brand name clothes', having 'deep pockets' and some form of transport (cited in *Cuba Briefing* 2007, Issue 343).

Writers have also taken to describing Cuban 'realities' in their fiction, with such works as Pedro Juan Gutierrez's *Dirty Havana Trilogy* (2001) and *Tropical Animal* (2003) becoming international bestsellers. Gutierrez's so-called '*dirty realism*' concentrates heavily on seedy sexual exploits in low-life Cuba. Comments on the dust jacket of the book *Dirty Havana Trilogy* include: 'a damning portrait of vice and poverty in a third-world country' and 'this Havana is one of the sleaziest cities you are ever likely to explore'.

It cannot be denied that Cuba's massive economic contraction, after the collapse of the Soviet Bloc, and now the effects of the global recession, have left sections of society in poverty and with limited work opportunities. Inevitably, under such circumstances, social breakdown and decay have taken place. However, a similar account could be written about the poor quarters in virtually any Third World city. But the difference is that in Havana, and Cuba generally, even the most wretched members of society have access to health care, education, and basic sustenance. They also have relative freedom from the horrors of gang warfare that have taken over many cities in Latin America and the Caribbean; with particular reference to El Salvador (Unreported World 2002) and Jamaica (Moser & Holland 1997) where murders are reported every year in the thousands. One should further consider the systematic state violence that still exists in many countries in the region, whereas the Cuban state, despite its problems, is benign towards the population, and its objective remains to provide a reasonable existence for all. It has not abandoned the people to the tyranny of the unregulated market, nor simply become a mechanism for facilitating the interests of foreign capital and its own transnationalising elites. Besides, if one were to write an insider's account of life in the poor quarters of virtually any British inner-city neighbourhood or council estate, or their equivalents in most developed countries, the vision might be even more hopeless than Gutierrez's representation of 'low-life Cuba'.

It is a vital matter that young people become engaged in shaping Cuba's future, but if their main desire is to be like their counterparts in the developed capitalist nations, they should think again. It is understandable that, having limited access to Western consumer culture, its attractiveness and perceived benefits have become mythologised. But what many young Cubans may not realise is that such a lifestyle is not available to all, and carries heavy social, physical and psychological costs. Young people in the capitalist world, and principally in the rich countries, may consume more products than ever before, and have a virtually infinite choice of material goods, but on the whole this has not made them happier, healthier, more confident, or given them better opportunities or future security. Drug culture, alcohol abuse, tobacco-related diseases, promiscuity, eating disorders, obesity, unemployment and violence are pervasive problems which are regularly reported in the media. However, perhaps a more serious malaise, out of which these issues emerge, is that social life in general has begun to decay with growing tribalism often stimulated by lifestyles-type consumerism (Goldberg et al. 2003); possessive individualism; deep class divisions (Blanden et al. 2005); desire for immediate gratification; de-politicisation (Edwards 2007); and little or no interest in the world outside of the immediate environment. It is sad that this is a generation which would rather watch *Big Brother*, the intense personal relations show that is broadcast on Western television, and read accounts of the self-absorbed and dysfunctional lives and relationships of celebrities, than take any interest in fellow human beings at home and abroad who are poor and destitute, or the workings of the economic and political system that in reality offers them an uncertain future. Some imagine themselves to be 'free', but they are in fact an example of 'coercion by consent', with significant areas of their lives designed, controlled and managed by the transnational corporations and the media (Wayne 2003). To this ought to be added education systems, especially at the higher level, which have fallen into the 'End of History' groove, and no longer seek to question or challenge the prevailing order.

Of course many young people in the West, especially from middle-class and wealthy families, have enjoyable and successful lives, but the environment of globalisation and mass consumerism in which they exist is unsustainable, and the mindsets it creates are inadequate to deal with emerging crises and change. One should also remember, as suggested in Chapter 1, that it is not only in the developing world that poverty is prevalent, but also in the advanced nations. In the US, for example, out of a population of approximately 309 million, an estimated 36.5 million are classed as living in poverty, and millions more struggle to get by every month. Among these, 13 million young people do not have enough to meet their basic needs (World Vision 2010). According to UNICEF (2007), the United States ranks 24th of 25 countries when measuring the number of children living below the national poverty line. This is the product of a society in which, in 2005, the wealthiest 1 per cent of Americans had its largest share of the nation's income (19 per cent) since 1929, while the poorest 20 per cent held only 3.4 per cent (Center for American Progress 2007). For those who are poor, life chances seen in terms of economic mobility are abysmal. In a middle-income country like South Africa, the number of people living in poverty has nearly doubled between 1981–2005, from 200 million to 380 million (World Bank, cited in BBC News 2008). Over 25 per cent of South Africans of working age are unemployed. The lives of millions of poor youth are ruined by drugs, unemployment, violence and lack of hope for a better future.

Cuban youth, when looking out at this global system, only really have two possibilities, depending on the route Cuba takes in the future. If it were to embrace the market system and abandon the Revolution, then consumerism would be rife, but, like in other Third World countries, only a small percentage of young people would enjoy its dubious advantages as most of them would remain poor and lacking in opportunities. On the other hand, if the Revolution deepens and extends its project, while Cuban youth may never become mass consumers, they will be part of a country that is preparing for a different and more realistic future: one in which they could play a vital role that would be at least equally important to that of the previous generation. As Cuba's then Foreign Minister Felipe Pérez-Roque stated, in a presentation to Cuban students at the University of Havana, it would be unforgivable for Cuban youth 'to allow the Revolution to be snatched from their hands' (*Granma*, 4 October 2007). Besides, now that globalisation faces a structural crisis, as discussed in Chapter 1, which is leading to deepening recession, Cuban youth may become a beacon of hope for disenchanted and disillusioned young people around the world. Indeed, many in Cuba, and not just Party members or the voices of *Juventud Rebelde*, understand this and are engaging with the Revolution, and with the task of constructive criticism, to create a better future. In a letter issued by the Young Communist League (UJC) in June 2007, Fidel Castro stated, 'If the young people fail, everything will fail. It is my profound conviction that the Cuban youth will fight to stop that. I believe in you' (Weissert 2007). More recently, José Ramón Machado Ventura (*Cuba Briefing* 2009, Issue 470), First Vice-President of the Councils of State and Ministers, speaking at the 10th Plenum of the UJC, stated that Cuba faced a critical moment in its history,

> when young Cubans have to rise to the occasion. We have to rely on the youth. More than just slogans, what we need is analysis, discussion, conviction and above all, the personal example of the activist ... everything we are doing today is to guarantee the future of the Revolution, to make it last; improving our socialism, not distorting it.

The growing global recession will close off many materialist aspirations of Cuban youth, but it is still to be seen if they will follow the exhortations of the previous generation, and its certainty in the historical destiny of the Revolution.

5
Defending Cuban Socialism Against Global Capitalism: Internal Dynamics and External Opportunities

Chapter 1's analysis of the neo-liberal globalisation process revealed material and ideological trends that, far from resolving capitalism's problems as suggested by the utopian 'End of History' thesis, serve to compound them. In its current form globalisation is unsustainable, as has been accepted by actors deep within its establishment such as Stiglitz and Soros, and made clear by a global financial crisis and recession which cannot be resolved without systemic change. Set against this backdrop, the battle for an alternative has begun. However, the form it takes is unlikely to be decided or controlled by wise men in the global matrix, but rather by social forces taking a conscious stand against the constraints neo-liberalism places on their perceived rights and potentials as human beings in a modern world. In this battle the Cuban Revolution, which against all odds has survived the collapse of Communism, is now actively engaged in projecting its ideas and practices onto the resistance forming against the global order.

Nevertheless, as we saw in the previous chapter, Cuba itself faces many internal challenges, largely due to the pressure of global forces on its revolutionary integrity. During the past two decades, Cuban socialism has been compromised by several factors: the influence of limited competitive insertion in the global economy; markets; the inability of elements of the old state socialist system to cope with the loss of Soviet Communism's protective carapace; and the influx of Western influences such as tourism, leading to such negative trends as corruption and materialistic values. The Revolution's internal inadequacies compound these problems. Furthermore, Cuba's new leader Raúl Castro may now be more willing to undertake deeper reforms than his brother Fidel. Is this a temporary stage in the process of building socialism, driven by pragmatism, or the beginnings of a transformation? If it is the former, then perhaps as in the 1980s, when Soviet-style planning prevailed, it will lead to a material improvement in the lives of many Cubans without undermining revolutionary commitment. If it is the latter, then Cuba's relevance for future struggles against globalisation's hegemony will diminish as it strives to become another Dominican Republic.

Ultimately, Cuba's revolutionary future will not be decided by how hard it can bang the socialist drum in the midst of the growing crises within globalisation, nor by its pragmatic, and perhaps necessary, attempts to provide more economic opportunities for the population. Rather, it will be determined by its ability to contain and consciously resist those influences that are diluting the Revolution. This process requires a unity of purpose between masses and leaders that seeks not just to resolve problems, but to transcend corrosive forces by drawing on socialist strengths which have already been proven, and adapting to new circumstances through measures based on increased popular empowerment. This offers the only future with dignity, one that belongs not to Cuba alone, but also, for the first time, coincides with the growing aspirations of many ordinary people in the world. At no other time has Cuba had a better opportunity to integrate the Revolution with external forces that are both sympathetic to, and willing to learn from, its experience of constructing socialism.

In the context of the above statements, this chapter analyses three main issues: the retirement of Fidel Castro and the new leadership of his brother Raúl; Cuba's export of health care; the rise of popular anti-neoliberal movements in Latin America and the governments claiming to represent their interests; and the engagement of Cuba with these counter-hegemonic forces. This will be followed by an assessment of the options open to Cuba.

FIDEL CASTRO RETIRES: THE END OF AN ERA?

When President Fidel Castro retired on 19 February 2008, all Cuba observers, detractors and advocates alike, knew that the Revolution would change in some ways. On the Right, those who emphasise Fidel's personal style and believe that everything was mediated by his rule feel that transition is inevitable, even if Raúl seeks to cling to the old order (Latell 2005, 2008). Moderates expect that Raúl will be more 'pragmatic' and reformist than his brother, and some recent changes suggest that this may be the route he is taking. Given that since 1959 he has been head of the Armed Forces (FAR), an organisation which has consistently been one of the most efficient and practically orientated in Cuba, this perception is not unfounded. Supporters of the Revolution hope that his reforms will not undermine the socialist direction of the island.

Those seeking to identify rifts in the Cuban leadership, especially at the level of the Castro brothers, the Politburo, the Council of State, key trusted individuals and the intelligence services, should be cautious, because despite recent corruption scandals it appears that the government is preparing for a new phase which will require national unity. Although Fidel Castro has relinquished most of his official roles, he remains leader of the Communist Party, and is still a significant player in the 'Battle for Ideas', as indicated by the reflections and writings (Castro 2008) from his sickbed and during his subsequent convalescence and retirement. It is also unlikely that such a tightly organised and well-managed state should not have prepared in full for a future without the 'Maximum Leader'.

Consistent with the foregoing analysis of this book, which examines international political economy, the ideological underpinnings of democracy, hegemony and social processes, the author does not accept that single human beings can shape history, although they can influence events. Leaders may be seen as eminent advocates of a set of ideas and processes that accord with a plausible logic, one which is often part of a hegemonic construct. In some exceptional circumstances, they can become counter-hegemonic intellectuals, whose vision pre-empts the emergent future and helps inform the consciousness of the masses. These 'organic intellectuals', to use Gramsci's terminology, can take many forms and hold various ideological perspectives. Both Margaret Thatcher and Ronald Reagan were in some ways such leaders, as they popularised the hegemony of the ascendant transnational elites by introducing neo-liberal ideas to populations looking for explanations and alternatives to the failing post-war Keynesian social consensus. Fidel Castro is an organic intellectual, but he has not sought to beguile the people on behalf of elites. Instead he has acted as champion of the masses in Cuba and the rest of the world. In a speech made in 1998, Fidel (cited in Valdés 2008:31–32) stated:

I concede that at certain times, certain people can play a certain role. However ... I believe the role that any man has played at any time has always depended on circumstances and had nothing to do with the man himself ... Previous conditions are required for which no man can take credit ... the association of historical events with specific people has long been rooted in the propaganda and even the conception of reactionaries, imperialists and enemies of the Revolution. They speak about Castro's Revolution, they personalise it: Castro did this, Castro did that.

Nevertheless, Fidel is seen to hold special qualities as an individual and as one Cuban academic (interview with Garcia 2007) suggested, rather romantically, 'Fidel has come from the future to lead us there'. Then Minister Felipe Pérez Roque commented (*Cuba Briefing*, Issue 337) in 2006, responding to questions about Cuba without Fidel:

> [W]e promise that we will continue struggling for the ideas and dreams that Fidel has dedicated his life to. When he and the men of his generation are no longer with us, we have the conviction that our people will have made those ideas and principles theirs forever.

Some Western observers also acknowledge Fidel's special qualities and enduring influence. For example, according to Saul Landau (2008:41):

> Fidel remains a larger-than-life leader who never relied on TV spots or political 'handlers' to preach his messages to Cubans and millions of others around the world. People listen because he has something to say. His agenda – justice, equality, ending poverty, facing the perils of environmental erosion – retains urgent cogency. Compare his presentation to the 'lite ideas' offered by major power heads of state!

The 5 November 2006 edition of the Cuban newspaper *Granma* carried a weekend supplement with a picture of Fidel on its front page under the caption, 'Absolved by History'. We will see.

In the first few months after Raúl took over as leader, the main concessions and reforms which were instigated, in approximate chronological order, were: the signing of two UN human rights treaties that were long resisted by Fidel; Raúl's meeting with a Vatican Cardinal to discuss the release, with conditions, of political prisoners; the lifting of restrictions on the purchase and ownership of certain electrical goods; the permitting of farmers to decide what crops to plant, to buy their own equipment, and to sell produce locally (state debts to farmers are also to be promptly repaid); the launch of an emigration website after a conference with Cubans living abroad; announced plans to decentralise Cuban agriculture with power shifting from the Ministry of Agriculture to local delegations; the closing down of inefficient farming co-operatives; the lifting of restrictions on pharmacy sales, and the freedom to buy from an outlet of their choosing; permitting Cubans to own mobile phones; allowing Cuban citizens to stay in tourist hotels; the granting of leases to farmers for unused land in order to increase agricultural production; a proposal to restructure the family doctor programme; the granting of ownership to residents of state housing including the ability to pass the property on to their heirs (over 80 per cent of Cubans already own their own houses); death sentences to be commuted, except for cases such as terrorism. Other reforms being considered or implemented include: a restructuring of wages and salaries, which involves the lifting of limits on what can be earned; an extension of material incentives and some programmed increases; permission to buy and sell cars as well as private houses; the opening of the farming sector to foreign investment; and an end to the dual currency.

There is not space here to analyse the implications of these changes, but it is clear that they are in some respects a departure from the past. However, they should not simply be seen as an incremental move towards the market, which is the interpretation of most outside observers. Firstly, in the area of most radical and far-reaching reform, agriculture, the driving force does not seem to be ideological but pragmatic: to find any controllable method which will increase production. Extensive popular consultations have identified the shortages, quality and price of food as the most pressing of concerns, and the government must act accordingly. Recent reports on the agricultural reforms suggest there has been an enthusiastic response to the increasing availability of state land for private farming. However, weed-infested fields, lack of experience in agriculture and shortages of support mechanisms and equipment are restricting improvements in production (*Cuba Briefing* 2009, Issue 438). Between 2000 and 2007, Cuba's foreign food purchases averaged $1.6 billion per annum, making it the third biggest import after machinery and fuel (EIU 2007). In early 2009 it was estimated that a combination of internal demand, the devastation caused by three recent hurricanes and a looming world food crisis will make import bills rise to over $2 billion (*Cuba Briefing* 2009, Issues 431 & 432). Later in the year it was revealed that food imports for 2008 were $2.2 billion, an estimated 70 per cent of total food consumed in the island (*Cuba Briefing* 2009, Issue 464). This high figure may not fully take into account the local and micro-level food production that was discussed in the previous chapter, but even with an adjustment of 10 per cent the general trend suggests a deterioration rather than an improvement in national food security. As the global crisis deepens, both developing and developed countries will face increasing problems with food production and supplies. With land in Cuba either owned by the state or small private producers, rather than being controlled by transnational corporations, large-scale agribusiness or big private landowners as in nearly all other countries, the island should be in an advantageous position to move towards a higher level of agricultural self-sufficiency. Those who advocate more private agriculture based on small producers must remember that capitalist agriculture under globalisation is becoming monopolised by transnational corporations. Where it does exist in the form of small and medium-sized farms competing mainly in local areas, as in parts of rural France, it is under tremendous pressure to conform to the transnational imperatives of the WTO and the big corporations who dominate its policy making. As for historical socialist models of agricultural production, there are no examples that Cuba could adopt with confidence, although the continuing state and collective farms in Belarus have been reasonably successful and may prove indispensible if there is a world food crisis. Cuba's developments in peri-urban horticulture described in the previous chapter were important beginnings in an integrated and popular approach to food production, but this kind of initiative needs to be sustained and expanded. It must also be complemented with improvements in large-scale production that could co-ordinate closely with Cuba's democratic and participative structures. This is no easy matter and there is no one 'correct' approach. The state import agency *Alimport* warned in 2007 that Cuba would be committing 'suicide' if it failed to reduce its reliance on foreign food supplies (*Cuba Briefing* 2008, Issue 392). Today that task is even more pressing as the global crisis makes food security a crucial issue.

Concerning other areas of reform implemented and proposed by the Cuban government, none constitute a significant reversal of the socialist project. The notion of material incentives is not alien to the Cuban experience and they have been controlled and managed before. The granting of ownership to those living in state housing is also important for instilling a sense of security in the future, but opening up a housing market based on this principle may be divisive and unfair. As for the permission to own mobile phones, stay in tourist hotels and buy expensive consumer items, which the Western press seems so excited about, these changes are unlikely to affect more than a small percentage of the population. Measures to ease restrictions on consumer purchases are also a means, through taxation, to capture more of the hard currency in circulation.

While these reforms do not suggest the beginnings of a wider market orientation, they are not in line with 'revolutionary' objectives and the formation of a socialist consciousness. As Fidel has noted from his retirement, 'everything that ethically fortifies the Revolution is good, everything that weakens it is bad ...', but such adjustments may be necessary in the short term to ameliorate immediate problems. Taking Raúl at his word, his purpose and that of the forthcoming 6th Congress of the Communist Party is to, 'confront the challenges of the future' and 'guarantee the continuity of the Revolution when its historic leaders are no more' (*Cuba Briefing* 2008, Issue 396). On 1 August 2009 he also told the National Assembly, 'I was not chosen as President to restore capitalism to Cuba or renounce the revolution ... I was chosen to defend, maintain and continue to perfect socialism, not to destroy it' (*Daily Telegraph* 2009).

In his presentation to the 6th Plenary of the Central Committee of the Communist Party in April 2008, Raúl emphasised 'strong institutions', 'discipline', 'order' and 'continuity' (MINREX 2008). The transfer of leadership has also involved some political changes including the election by the National Assembly on 24 February 2008 of a new seven-member leadership of the Council of State (executive body of the Cuban legislature). This body is composed of individuals who are all experienced revolutionaries. The President is Raúl Castro, the First Vice-President is José Ramon Machado Ventura, a 78-year-old physician who fought with Fidel and Raúl in the Sierra. The Vice-Presidents named in this first restructuring were: Juan Almeida Bosque (80), who was also in the Sierra and is a trusted revolutionary (deceased September 2009); Abelardo Colomé Ibarra (68), a diehard revolutionary who has served the Castro brothers over many years, and is reputedly Raúl's right-hand man; Carlos Lage Davila (56), a paediatrician turned economist, a reformer and key player since the 1990s in the development of Cuba's economic strategies (now replaced); Juan Esteban Lazo Hernández (63), another long-time supporter of the Castro brothers; and Julio Casas Regueiro (72), who is now Raúl's Minister of the Revolutionary Armed Forces (FAR). Most of these individuals are also members of the Politburo. In December 2009 two Ministers were elevated to the position of Vice-President of the Council of

State; Ramiro Valdés Menéndez (78), another revolutionary from the Sierra days, and Gladys Bejerano Portela (62), who is also Comptroller General of the Republic.

Outside of this group there are other important officials including: Ricardo Alarcon (73), the President of the National Assembly since 1993; Francisco Soberón Valdés (65), the influential President of the Central Bank of Cuba; Ricardo Cabrisas (73), Vice-President of the Council of Ministers; and Major Luis Alberto Rodríguez López-Callejas (47), who runs the military's powerful Enterprise Management Group Inc. (GAESA).

The dismissal in March 2009 of two key Politburo members, Carlos Lage and Felipe Pérez Roque, caused much speculation concerning a possible rift in the leadership, perhaps based on a Fidel–Raúl split. Fidel hinted however that this was not the case when he stated, 'the honey of power, for which they had made no sacrifices, awoke in them ambitions that led them to play an undignified role ... the external enemy was filled with illusions for them' (*Cuba Briefing* 2009, Issue 440). It transpired later, based on video evidence, that Lage and Pérez Roque had been involved in unofficial conversations with foreign diplomats and business-people, in which they speculated on the prospects for change in Cuba. During these secretly recorded sessions they also criticised the Castro brothers and some of the military personnel who were in positions of power (*Cuba Briefing* 2009, Issue 455). This is a worrying trend because it indicates an erosion of solidarity at the highest levels. More recently it was suggested in an article entitled 'Corruption: the True Counter-Revolution', by Cuban academic Esteban Morales (2010), that corruption in government and administration is prevalent at all levels. This he felt was an even greater danger to the Revolution than internal dissent. He further claims that there were people in the state apparatus preparing for a transition to capitalism, just as some in the Soviet Union had done before its collapse. There were individuals, he claimed, who were already 'receiving kickbacks and opening bank accounts in other countries'. Even more astonishing in an article that was published on an official Cuban website (that of National Union of Cuban Writers and Artists – UNEAC) were calls by the author for the government to reveal the reason for the dismissal of General Rogelio Acevedo, the Director of Civil Aviation, on 9 March. It is rumoured that he was involved in one of the most audacious and lucrative corruption scandals in the history of the Revolution. Commenting on the fall from power of Lage and Pérez Roque, Morales refers to the 'weakness of a group of very senior officials' who were involved in 'favouritism, cronyism ... acts of corruption'. Official permission to openly publish this frank and revealing article, especially in a society where information is carefully controlled for reasons of state security, suggests that the core group around the Castro brothers feel they should make it clear to the population and foreign observers that they are aware of the problem and are taking appropriate measures. It is interesting in this context how Raúl is placing in positions of authority greater numbers of senior personnel from his trusted military. As Morales suggests, rogue elements in the state apparatus are the biggest threat to the Revolution, and if they were allowed to consolidate their power, they would, with the eager help of foreign interests, seek a transition along the lines of their counterparts in the former Soviet Bloc.

These recent developments, which threaten the core structure of the Revolution, give a special significance to Raúl's earlier call for the population, and especially the young, to 'fearlessly engage in public debate and analysis'. Ultimately it is not removing and punishing senior officials that will solve the problem of dissent and corruption at the higher levels, but convincing the population that the defence of, and active and critical engagement with, 'their' Revolution is in their interests. If ordinary people observe a system which appears increasingly corrupt, while seeing their own circumstances remain the same or deteriorate, it becomes unsustainable in revolutionary terms. Hence Raúl's statement in 2006 at the beginning of the anti-corruption campaign: 'One of the most difficult challenges in this ideological work is succeeding in making the worker feel like a collective owner of society's riches – and act accordingly' (*Cuba Briefing* 2006, Issue 238). Not surprisingly, it is the need to improve living standards that has produced the loudest cry from the masses. Under such circumstances Raúl has had no option but to instigate a number of strategic adjustments. But one should not automatically assume that this marks a new direction for the Revolution, perhaps along Chinese or Vietnamese lines. Indeed, in 2007 Alarcón specifically ruled out such options (Voss 2007), and there is no reason to assume that they are now being reconsidered. The market, as adopted by these countries, offers no solution for Cuba, especially as globalisation enters crisis. More than its practical unfeasibility, subjugating Cubans to the 'pitiless law of value' (Guevara 1965, cited in Cole forthcoming) would destroy the Revolution.

The author believes that fundamental to Raúl's strategy is the role of the military (FAR) in society, and especially the hard currency sector of the economy (Lambie 2009b). As we have seen, the FAR has a deep symbiotic link with the Revolution and this is understood and internalised by the population. Like the leadership, the military is also largely above corruption. It is, as one author (Klepak 2005:51) suggests, 'the "last bulwark" of the state in times of crisis'. As indicated in the previous chapter, the reforms of the 1990s not only opened up spaces for small-scale private enterprise, but also gave aspirations to an emergent bourgeoisie who, if given the opportunity, would scarcely hesitate to follow the route taken by their counterparts in former Communist countries, as Morales suggests above. The necessary economic transition for this to occur did not take place in Cuba, but aspects of internal and external market relations still exist. However, instead of letting a new bourgeoisie consolidate an influence over these processes, military organisations like GAESA (dollar-orientated operations), GAVIOTA (tourism), CUBANACAN (tourism chain) and ETECSA (telecoms joint venture with Italy) were formed to co-ordinate new economic activities. Sections of the military high command were put in charge and have now begun to act as an alternative power structure to the rise of a new entrepreneurial class, which would have eventually undermined the Revolution. With the 'commanding heights' of the economy in safe and trusted hands, Raúl can afford to experiment with various incentives and material stimuli to raise production at the micro level. This is not a progressive socialist solution, as envisaged by Guevara, but it does not compromise the Revolution in ways presumed by its detractors.

By early 2009 it appeared that the unfolding global crisis was starting to impact on Cuba, and some of the planned reforms were postponed. In May of the same year forecasts for economic growth were predicted to be as low as 1 per cent, from over 7 per cent in the previous year, and it became clear that rather than an improvement in living standards there would be a deterioration (*Cuba Briefing* 2009, Issue 450). It is interesting that in the light of this setback in the reform process, Professor Lazaro Gonzalez from the University of Havana criticised (*Cuba Briefing* 2009, Issue 459) the lack of progress in the restructuring of the workplace, speaking of 'antiquated norms, exaggerated plans, waste, theft, corruption and ... every day more central rules and regulations, procedures ... therefore less participation from below'. He continued, 'participation is not just about being informed, it is not just giving your opinions

– these are often lost in a void. Participation, more than anything, is to take part in making decisions ... we have not been able to formulate the design of a labor policy that integrates all aspects of participation'. Maybe continuing crisis will give credence again to this socialist option.

INTEGRATING THE IDEALS OF THE REVOLUTION WITH A WIDER COUNTER-HEGEMONIC PROCESS

Cuba's leaders have always realised that no matter how popular the Revolution, nor how well defended, 'socialism in one country' is unsustainable in a world capitalist system, let alone a globalised order. Consequently, in the 1960s Cuba promoted armed struggle abroad. In the 1970s and 1980s it continued military intervention in Africa, and supported revolutionary movements in Central America; but it shifted emphasis, with Soviet encouragement, towards exporting its successes in health care and social provision. During the first 30 years of the Revolution, Cuba played an international role far out of proportion to its small size (Dominguez 1989). In the 1990s, despite continuing attempts to maintain its symbolic stance as a successful revolutionary state, the main issue Cuba faced was survival. However, once the imminent threat of collapse had passed, it again began to project its revolutionary image onto the world stage. One form this has now taken is the resumption, and expansion, of the export of health care, which besides its practical value is also seen as 'medical diplomacy'. A second, which will be analysed later, is the attempt to support the counter-hegemony to neo-liberalism that is forming in Latin America.

Exporting Health Care: The 'Politics of Symbolism'

In 1978, a few years after Cuba's foreign health care initiative was launched, Fidel Castro claimed that Cuba intended to become 'a champion of Third World Medicine' and a 'world medical power' (Feinsilver 1989:1). In practice Cuba's foreign policy in health care provision takes the form of strategic humanitarian aid, and what Feinsilver has termed the 'politics of symbolism'. In 1985, less than ten years after this statement was made, the *New York Times* (22 January) reported that Cuba sponsored 'perhaps the largest Peace Corps style programme of civilian aid in the world', in which 16,000 doctors, teachers, construction engineers, agronomists, economists and other specialists were serving in 26 foreign countries. Even then, the Cuban contribution of doctors to the Third World exceeded that of the World Health Organization and most developed nations. Unlike its former Soviet and socialist allies, and indeed any other country in the world, Cuba has adopted a policy of training a surplus of doctors and medical personnel specifically for export overseas. Despite the 'political' dimension of Cuba's health mission abroad, its aid is usually very impartial. It does not interfere with the affairs of sovereign states, making its contributions very popular and well received, even with right-wing governments (Hammett 2004:11). This is in sharp contrast to much development aid from the major Western donors, which is often tied to some form of conditionality such as economic transition, reforms, other foreign policy initiatives, or simply delivered as 'charity' or with a 'West is best' attitude. Compounding these problems, many health care systems in developing countries have followed practices and ideas that were generated and encouraged by the former colonial powers. These include a focus on treatment rather than promoting everyday health, on curative rather than preventative medicine, and large expenditures on hospitals, imported drugs and high-tech equipment. This has tended to favour the modernised sectors of the population in the cities more than the rural and urban poor. Cuba, on the other hand, as already noted in the previous chapter, has a more holistic and participatory approach to health based on low-tech solutions, preventative measures, health education and non-health determinants, such as housing and diet, which would seem more appropriate for Third World environments, and especially if the goal is to assist the poor majority.

Almost all Third World countries have received the assistance of Cuban doctors in the past 30 years, and some countries such as Nicaragua, Angola, Ethiopia, Congo, Mali, Tanzania, Iraq, Venezuela and Haiti have, during certain periods, had a predominance of Cuban medical personnel exceeding the combined contributions of other nations. In some cases Cubans have provided a larger proportion of health care than domestic medical services. For instance, after ten years of co-operation with Haiti, by 2007 Cuban medical staff were caring for 75 per cent of the population (Kirk & Kirk 2010). In the same period, infant mortality per 1000 live births fell from 80 to 33, child mortality under five years per 1000 from 135 to 59.4, and life expectancy rose from 54 to 61 (ibid.). Cuban medical personnel have also worked in the most remote parts of the world under difficult conditions, and in doing so have gained valuable experience of addressing the needs of marginal communities. Cuba's policy is, however, where possible, to train local people to take over their work which is mainly focused in primary care. In some countries this has been extended to the setting up of a domestic medical school to provide the necessary training. Once such a facility is established, Cubans can put more effort into providing secondary and tertiary care and further improving training, which is also developed with a view to eventually being transferred to domestic management. This accords with Cuba's emphasis on capacity building rather than support for larger infrastructure.

Training for foreign medical students and qualified personnel is also provided in Cuba itself, and by the 1980s a mass education programme was functioning. In the academic year 1984/85, 22,000 scholarship students from 82 developing countries were studying in Cuba, many of whom were dedicated to medicine (*Granma Weekly Review*, 11 November 1984). One condition of these scholarships is that the students return to their country of origin after their studies and work there for at least five years. This meets an important objective which seems to have been overlooked, or not promoted, in the training provided in the developed countries for Third World students, as many decide to stay in their wealthier host nation. Moreover, Cuba's international aid often provides opportunities for patients needing complicated medical procedures or lengthy intensive treatments to be taken to Cuba to receive the attention they require. A further dimension to Cuba's comprehensive health export portfolio is the training and equipping of a rapid reaction force to deal with natural disasters, such as the devastating earthquake in Haiti in 2010.

Besides providing personnel, training and treatment, Cuba also supplies medical equipment and pharmaceuticals, and helps adapt and construct buildings for health care use. Another area of support and integration in its foreign aid is sponsorship of international medical conferences during which participants are given the opportunity to study the island's successful domestic health system. A further connection to its international health mission is the development of high-tech medical research, especially in genetic engineering, biotechnology, nanotechnology and immunology. The benefits of this work, and the drugs and treatments which it produces, are included extensively in Cuba's foreign aid programmes.

While Cuban 'medical diplomacy' has at its core the goal of a humanitarian mission, it is strongly imbued with the 'politics of symbolism', which promotes socialism, and Cuba's understanding of what that means, through example and demonstration. Because of these prime objectives, the economic and commercial aspects of

Cuba's health aid are subsumed to ideology and discretion, although, as stated previously, in its delivery it remains impartial. Initially, Cuba gave most of this support for free, and even today very poor countries do not pay, or make token contributions. However, as the scale of aid increased and demand grew, it became normal for wealthier countries like Libya, pre-war Iraq and Algeria to pay at set rates or, as in the case of Venezuela, through special barter arrangements. But even during the difficulties of the 'Special Period' and the growing need for hard currency, Cuba has maintained its image of selflessness and humanitarian internationalism. As Mali's health minister noted in a recent debate on Cuba in the European Parliament (EP 2008), 'Cuba does not give, as it often happens with other Northern counties, her leftovers. She shares what she has, which is sometimes not enough to cover her own needs.' In his 1991 speech in Havana thanking the Cuban people for the role they played in putting an end to apartheid in South Africa (through their success in defending the Angolan liberation movement against UNITA and South Africa at the battle of Cuito Cuanavale), Nelson Mandela expressed similar sentiments about Cuba's selflessness in its foreign assistance (Hammett 2004:23).

With the collapse of its Cold War Communist allies, Cuba's desire to export the example of its Revolution through the 'politics of symbolism' became even more important and, despite major economic difficulties, health care at home and abroad was given special priority. Moreover, with all the major powers, including its former allies now in the capitalist camp, it felt the need to intensify its promotion of 'South–South co-operation', with the conviction that globalisation was not a solution to underdevelopment (Castro 2007:397–400 passim). For example, Cuban health support for Africa increased throughout the 1990s and into the new millennium (Blunden 2008), as indeed it has in Latin America and many parts of the world. In 1999 the Latin American School of Medicine (ELAM) was established in Havana to increase training opportunities for foreign students. The school is now educating over 10,000 students from 55 countries, with 75 per cent from working-class and farming families (*Granma International* 2010). According to one source (Blunden 2008), 'Cuba's international contribution to the capacity building of health workers is on a scale exceeding that of all members of the G8 group of leading advanced countries combined.' As globalisation fails to ensure a future for the majority of the world's population and inequality increases, the inability of the Western powers to provide relevant and appropriate health aid has become a key issue (Crisp 2007). It is interesting that some major donor agencies are looking to Cuba for examples of how to deliver effective health care in the developing world. For example, the European Commissioner for Development and Humanitarian Aid, Louis Michel, and other senior officials from the European Commission, recently adopted this view in a debate on Cuba in the European Parliament (EP 2008). In 2006 Feinsilver provocatively suggested, 'The fact that the Bush administration is trying to destroy Cuba's medical diplomacy program indicates that the program works. Rather than attempt to destroy it, the Bush administration should emulate it.' With regard to health care and its export abroad, Cuba is deeply integrated into the counter-hegemony that is forming against globalisation.

Failure of an Experiment: Latin America Turns Against Neo-Liberalism

In the late 1990s not only did Cuba begin to experience some internal recovery, but the global situation, especially in Latin America, began to change in Havana's favour as neo-liberal experiments faced increasing resistance. This took two interrelated forms: the growing power and confidence of anti-establishment popular movements; and support for populist-style political leaders generated by the previously disengaged masses that formed such movements. These democratically elected leaders promised to dismantle the pro-elite polyarchic systems that were in place, and to undertake reforms responsive to the needs of the people. Not surprisingly, Cuba, with its long and distinguished revolutionary heritage, practical social achievements and David-versus-Goliath stance against the US, began to assume a symbolic and practical relevance which it had not enjoyed in the region since the 1960s. While revolutionary Cuba has always maintained an active interest in Latin America, the twenty-first century presents an unprecedented opportunity to link with forces that are beginning to share some of its own values and ideals.

Latin America is the developing area most integrated with global capitalism. This is partly a consequence of the historical trajectory of the region, beginning with its early colonial experience in which indigenous civilisation was marginalised, and European and later North American influences became particularly profound. A problem stemming from this legacy is that, in all of Latin America except for Cuba, internal oligarchies have largely shunned national development for the more lucrative role as domestic facilitators for the interests of international capital. Therefore, attempts to pursue national objectives and restructuring strategies during the post-1929 era, based on the 'structuralist' ideas of economic theorists like Raul Prebisch and sympathetic politicians such as Juan Perón, largely failed (Lambie 1983). As we have seen in Chapter 1, these experiments came to a close in the 1980s because of the debt crisis, which allowed the IMF and transnational capital to integrate Latin America into their new global project. This shift from attempts at national modernisation to deregulated exposure to market-driven capital flows led to a dramatic increase in poverty. Between 1980 and 1995 the number of people living in this category, according to calculations made by the Economic Commission for Latin America and the Caribbean (ECLAC), rose from 136 million to 230 million, from 41 to 48 per cent of the population in the region (cited in Robinson 1998/99:118). More recently, ECLAC's influential Social Panorama of Latin America (2005) claimed that between 2003 and 2005 poverty decreased in the region by 13 million to 213 million, or 40.6 per cent of the population. This may be largely the result of increasing remittances from emigrant workers abroad, and some temporary economic growth based on rising commodity prices, rather than a structural change leading to sustainable development. The latest Social Panorama report, published in 2009 and covering 2008, indicates that poverty is again on the increase mainly because of the global financial crisis. Such statistics however tend to detract from the transition that has occurred in Latin America through its integration into a system of global accumulation in which a dramatic restructuring is taking place in production, finance and social relations (Robinson 2008). While these new processes are materially benefiting those members of the population who can engage on a managerial, financial, commercial or technical level with modernising sections of the economy, the whole project is based on increasing disempowerment of the masses, and a faith in continuous expansion based on global dependency. In crisis this model will produce disproportionate negative effects, as people are obliged to survive in an impoverished and dismantled 'national' economy.

During the Latin American 'transition', all nations in the region, except Cuba, became 'democracies', but as we have seen in earlier chapters this cannot be understood in terms of popular empowerment. As Green (1995:164) suggests, the implementation of neo-liberal reforms has 'ripped the heart out of democratisation, turning what could have been a flowering of political and social participation into a brand of "low intensity democracy"'.

By the late 1990s, many Latin Americans viewed democracy with cynicism and disappointment. In 2004 the conservative *Latinobarómetro* calculated that only 35 per cent of Latin Americans are satisfied with democracy, with some countries like Peru and Paraguay registering only 7 per cent and 13 per cent approval respectively. Interestingly, the same source notes that over 70 per cent of Latin Americans believe their countries, despite the establishment of formal democracy, are still run by a minority elite who hold power principally to serve their own interests. Discontent with democracy, periods of increasing poverty and the restructuring of social relations along the lines of market-driven ideology have produced the beginnings of a counter-hegemony. As Naomi Klein (2007:458) concludes, 'It stands to reason that the revolt against neo-liberalism would be in its most advanced stage in Latin America – as inhabitants of the first shock lab, Latin Americans have had the most time to recover their bearings.'

Most significant in this new political configuration, at the level of government, was the 1998 election of Hugo Chávez as President of Venezuela. Once in power, he launched a populist/socialist programme which, with valuable Cuban support in areas of social development and security, has now become the most embedded counter-hegemonic process in the region. In Brazil, the Workers' Party came to power in 2002 under the leadership of Luiz Inácio 'Lula' da Silva, who received support not just from the poor, but also from sectors of the middle classes who are being pushed into an increasingly uncertain future by neo-liberal reforms. In 2003, Lucío Gutiérrez was elected President of Ecuador with significant support from indigenous movements, as well as the poor. The Uruguayan election in March 2005 brought to power Tabare Vazquez of the Broad Front coalition, who has promised to make poverty alleviation his primary task, and also openly declared a rapprochement with Cuba. In Bolivia, Evo Morales, the Aymara Indian leader of the Movement Towards Socialism (MAS), won the presidential election in December 2005 to become the country's first indigenous president. He was returned to office in December 2009 with 63 per cent of the vote, a 10-point increase on his earlier victory. All these leaders have come to power partly due to popular reactions against neo-liberalism. In the case of Gutiérrez in Ecuador, the radical programme on which he was elected was all but abandoned, and he reverted to the disciplines of the Washington Consensus. As a consequence, he was deposed in April 2005, largely by the efforts of the same forces that put him into power. His successor Rafael Correa appears to be more responsive to popular demands, and since his election he has introduced a number of progressive reforms that constitute Ecuador's 'Citizens' Revolution'. Lula, in Brazil, has accepted the financial disciplines of the global system, but so far has managed to remain in office despite much discontent. As Robinson (2004b:147) suggests, 'These popular electoral victories [symbolise] the twilight of the reigning neo-liberal order but also the limits of parliamentary changes in the era of global capitalism.'

Some analysts, including Robinson (2008), Petras (2007), Arnson (2007), and Birns and James (2002), are rightly sceptical of the possibilities for change in the region, despite the emergence of 'New Social Movements' (see below) and governments willing to question mainstream 'fundamentals' or even, as in the case of Venezuela, reject the whole neo-liberal doctrine. They believe that while these 'Pink Tide' governments have become very visible and prompted much speculation about change in Latin America, in practice they have done little to challenge the dominant order. It may also be argued that the leaders of the 'Pink Tide', such as Lula in Brazil, Kirchner in Argentina, Ortega in Nicaragua and others, are potential recruits for a new modified form of neo-liberalism as proposed by reformist globalisers. In a series of articles, Paul Cammack (2002a, 2002b, 2003, 2004) has analysed what he terms 'the Wolfensohn-Stiglitz project', which he claims is designed to 'operationalise' a blueprint for global neo-liberal political economy that incorporates 'a new politics of development' (2002a:178). Indeed, rather like the Labour Party in the UK, the use of a 'soft left' option to repackage the neo-liberal agenda, and disarm and undermine potentially radical forces, is a well-tried formula. In Brazil, for instance, despite some radical posturing by Lula, inequality has increased during the period he has been in office. Globally, in 2005 the wealthy grew by 6.5 per cent and in Latin America by 9.5 per cent, but in Brazil this group grew by 11.3 per cent (Merrill Lynch & Capgemini 2006). While sections of the reformist 'Pink Tide' may be falling in line with the kind of policy shift envisaged by the World Bank, which, in the case of Mexico, Cammack (2002a:178) believes has 'succeeded brilliantly', the more radical leaders like Chávez in Venezuela, Morales in Bolivia and Correa in Ecuador imagine an alternative programme that is in direct opposition to the Bank's vision of neo-liberal adjustment and the strictures of the IMF. The policies of these governments also seem to be more responsive to, and in tune with, popular demands in the region. This process is being articulated through the Bolivarian Alternative for Latin America and the Caribbean (ALBA), which seeks continental co-operation to resolve problems of poverty and inequality, a topic that will be addressed later in this chapter.

Even some 'Pink Tide' governments have been obliged to undertake significant reforms. For example, at the end of 2003, after two years of chaos, Argentina's President Nestor Kirchner set out to find an 'Argentine' solution to the country's economic crisis, regardless of international demands and prescriptions; the position was undoubtedly influenced by knowledge of the IMF's failure in Southeast Asia in the late 1990s. In September 2003, Argentina temporarily defaulted on its IMF loans, a rare and dramatic occurrence for a middle-income country. But with the Fund facing large-scale popular resistance to its policies, and a government determined not to acquiesce, it did not cut off credit as might have been expected, but rather rolled over the debt and agreed to new terms and conditions. Three months after the default, the Argentine economy began to recover, stimulated by policies which ran against the current of mainstream advice. These policies included: Central Bank intervention and management of the exchange rate; encouragement of import substitution; a tightening up of the tax collection system; a freeze on utility price increases; and an increase in social expenditure. These are general lessons that today's (2010) failing European economies such as Greece, Spain, Portugal and Ireland, as well as most Eastern European countries, may eventually have to follow. A detailed analysis of the agreement reached between Argentina and the IMF does not however suggest a dramatic departure from IMF policy (Cibils 2003), yet Argentina's resistance was seen by many as a victory over the Fund. In fact, the deal was a compromise on both sides, but great pressure was kept on Argentina to adopt orthodox neo-liberal policies. This prompted President Kirchner to suggest, in a speech at the UN General Assembly in 2004, that it was not Argentina that needed structural reform, but the IMF (Rush 2004). Alluding to the Fund's original role under the Bretton Woods agreement, he stated that it must 'change that direction which took it from being a lender for development to a creditor demanding privileges' (ibid.). Moreover, the IMF's authority has been further challenged by a newly available source of finance in Latin America through Venezuela and the ALBA arrangements for regional support.

While the most widely reported and visible resistance to neo-liberal orthodoxy in Latin America is at the government level, those politicians who seek to break the mould are supported by vast and diverse popular movements. The electoral 'victories' are therefore indications of deeper social stirrings in Latin America. These 'New Social Movements' constitute a spectrum of forces emerging, sometimes spontaneously, from civil society, and may be the real threat to the established order in the region; they express demands, hopes and aspirations which the prescribed democratic model is not designed to address (Foweraker 1995). Robinson (2004b:144) notes:

> Almost every Latin American country [has] experienced waves of spontaneous uprisings generally triggered by austerity measures, the formation in the shantytowns of urban poor movements of political protest, and a resurgence of mass peasant movements and land invasions, all outside of the formal institutions of the political system, and almost always involving violent clashes between states and paramilitary forces and protesters.

There is not space here to deal in detail with the popular response to globalisation and neo-liberal reforms in Latin America, but it is important to identify some of the grassroots organisations that have emerged and the strategies they have adopted. The range of oppositional forces and forms of resistance is vast, and includes movements of workers, women, youth, environmentalists, indigenous groups, ethnic minorities, the urban poor, community organisations and many more. The types of struggle they have engaged in are also extremely varied. To name a few: anti-privatisation; agrarian reform; the claiming of urban spaces; ethnic rights; labour rights; and defence of the environment. Examples include: in Brazil, the Landless People's Movement (MST) (Branford & Rocha 2002; Harnecker 2003), and, in Porto Alegre (Rio Grande do Sul), direct democracy and the participatory budget system (Bruce 2004); in Argentina, '*asambleas populares*' (Bielsa 2002); in Venezuela, '*circulos bolivarianos*' (Chavez 2005; McCaughan 2004); in Cochabamba, Bolivia, the popular resistance to water-privatisation (The Democracy Centre 2000); in Mexico, the movement of the Zapatistas in Chiapas (Holloway 2002; Chiapaslink 2000; Capital & Class 2005) and workers' movements for improved rights in the *maquila* industry (Carty 2003); and peasant protests against land expropriations and other policies of globalisation in the rural sectors in Central America and the Caribbean. Chavez and Goldfrank (2005) identify many other examples of the growth of independent initiatives in local participatory democracy outside the 'mainstream' of national and local politics. Although most of these social movements have emerged from poor grassroots sectors of society, they are modernising their resistance in line with the national and global challenges they face. For example, even some of the minor groups have made use of the internet to promote their objectives, and many have their own websites (León et al. 2001). They also tend to blend old-style labour protest with community struggles, which has been described as 'social movement unionism' (Moody 1997). The decline of traditional working-class bases in industry and the rise of unemployment, informality and flexibility, has undermined the effectiveness of forms of protest such as the withdrawal of labour (strikes). This has given rise to such new initiatives as the methods used by unemployed *piqueteros* in Argentina, who have taken their struggle to the streets with the intent of gaining visibility and disrupting the system.

Perhaps the most profound of the social movements in Latin America has been the growing resistance by indigenous peoples to global restructuring in the region. In 2000, native Latin Americans officially numbered approximately 10 per cent of the population. This figure is probably higher, but sometimes indigenous people do not register their descent or are not included in the census, as in Chile. In Andean countries, the Amazon and Mesoamerica, they form a much higher percentage of the population, and in Bolivia and Guatemala they constitute the majority. Since colonial times they have always been a marginalised and exploited group, and their poverty rates in many countries, even today, range from 65–85 per cent (Psacharopoulos & Patrinos 1994:207). The first attempts to include the 'Indian' in projects of nation building began in the 1920s and were particularly prominent in Peru, where an *indigenista* movement grew which was supported and encouraged by progressive elites. The most notable example was the initiative of Víctor Raúl Haya de la Torre, the American Popular Revolutionary Alliance (APRA), which sought to include the majority native population in a nationalist programme designed and run by minority whites and mestizos. A more radical vision of the Indian's role in society was formulated by the Peruvian Marxist José Carlos Mariátegui (1929), who believed that native peoples had never been fully incorporated into the Western capitalist project and still retained a practical and conscious attachment to communal life. This pre-formed consciousness, he believed, could provide a basis for the building of socialism, bypassing the Communist Moscow-line 'stages of history' formula (in which the working class in capitalism had to reach sufficient maturity before it could begin to realise socialism). He knew that the mechanistic Communist formula for the region was an illusion because of the compromise and weakness of the working class in Peru, and in Latin America in general. Consideration of the 'Indian question' never regained the level of analysis proposed by Mariátegui, until the indigenous peoples themselves began to enter the political stage on their own terms. Neo-liberalism intensified this process, and towards the end of the twentieth century native peoples began to organise to resist this further degeneration of their existence. The Zapatistas and the Indigenous National Congress (CNI) of Mexico, the Confederation of Indigenous Nationalities of Ecuador (CONAIE) and the pan-Maya movement in Guatemala, along with Quechua and Aymara groups in Bolivia, to name a few such organisations, have become perhaps the most dedicated and powerful popular force to challenge global capitalism in Latin America. CONAIE, for instance, forced the Ecuadorian state to give land to indigenous communities and precipitated the fall of three governments (1997, 2000 and 2005) which attempted to implement neo-liberal reforms. In Bolivia the sustained action of indigenous groups led to the election of Evo Morales, the second native president in Latin America (after Peru's Alejandro Toledo) since the conquest.

It would seem, contrary to postmodern perspectives, that the indigenous struggle in Latin America has to do with much more than issues of identity, and manifests itself as a direct challenge to the logic of capitalism. The fight for land and the right to communal ownership is a specifically native struggle rooted in centuries of resistance, but the contemporary form of this phenomenon is directly linked to the negative impact of globalisation. This material and social dimension of the indigenous struggle was theorised by Mariátegui (1929:31) who stated:

> The possibility of the Indian improving their material and intellectual position depends on a change of economic and social conditions. This is not determined by race but by economics and politics. Race alone has not awoken, and will not awaken, an emancipatory consciousness. Above all, it will never give the power to impose and realise it. That which will assure their emancipation is the dynamism of an economy and a culture that has at its source the seed of socialism. [author's translation]

In Latin America over the past few decades, there has been a shift from clientelist and traditional party politics, based on authoritarian populism and legitimised by promises of 'development' and 'modernisation', to a new form of change led by grassroots activism. When old-style populists like the Peronist Ménem in Argentina revealed themselves as promoters of neo-liberalism, they lost the trust of the people. The new breed of populist can no longer rely on tradition and party loyalty from an organised working class, but must respond to spontaneous and collective demands generated by the masses. Unlike the formal proletariat of the 'structuralist' period of development, the new 'informal proletariat' has no party and only appeals to traditional power structures if they commit to serving its interests. The catalyst of this change is neo-liberal globalisation. The popular movement is becoming a 'class in itself' and moving in the direction of a 'class for itself': a collective agent that changes history rather than simply being a victim of the historical process. This tendency, still fluid and not yet clearly articulated, continues to interact strongly with traditional structures and especially the state. A key question is: Will the new left-leaning governments encourage this popular tide, or seek its containment? This is essentially an interactive process, highly dependent on historical circumstances. In Brazil, for instance, Lula's 'Workers' Party' (PT) took power without the support of a clear mass mobilisation, conscious of its political objectives and willing to press for a programme of confrontation with global capital and support for popular reforms. It is not surprising, in the absence of such pressures from below, that Lula has been pushed along a traditional political line by the 'conscious' forces of elites and foreign capital.

In Venezuela it is a different story. Here sections of the masses have a long history of popular resistance with a defined political purpose, and the elites are clearly identified as a parasitic group largely dependent on oil revenues. A defining moment in the struggle between masses and elites came with the huge protests and strikes against the neo-liberal reforms of *Acción Democrática* leader Carlos Andres Pérez in 1989. This period of turbulence, known as the *Caracazo*, was the first popular response to globalising forces in Latin America, and etched in the minds of the protestors and elites alike the nature of the contest for power that lay ahead. This event and subsequent struggles helped to propel Hugo Chávez to the presidency in 1998. Since then Chávez has fought an internal battle, with the support of the masses, to take political and greater economic control of the state with the intention of diverting resources to the poor, who constitute 80 per cent of the population. His capture of the state oil company PDVSA in defiance of the privatising ambitions of the elites and their foreign allies, along with the remarkable defeat of the coup attempt by his enemies in 2002, has helped to consolidate the power of Chávez's Bolivarian Revolution. In 2005, he proclaimed that the Revolution would seek to build 'twenty-first-century socialism' in which the masses will be the key actors (Forero 2005). The developments in Venezuela are the most advanced in Latin America towards realising the ambitions of the poor majority, and the state is being remodelled to serve this purpose, including the introduction of a progressive popular constitution. As Klein (2007:453–454) notes:

> Despite the overwhelming cult of personality surrounding Chávez, and his moves to centralise power at state level, the progressive networks in Venezuela are at the same time highly decentralised, with power dispersed at the grass roots and community level, through thousands of neighbourhood councils and co-ops.

In March 2010 Chávez stated, partly in response to continuing and growing threats from internal elites and foreign interests, 'the free sovereign and independent homeland of our dreams will only come true if we radicalise the process and speed up the transition to socialism' (Fuentes 2010). In practice this will involve a greater transfer of power to 'communal councils', composed of groups of 200–400 families in urban areas and 20–50 in rural areas. These grassroots bodies are run by citizen assemblies and encourage participation from the whole community. They have grown around the new health, education, water, electricity and agricultural initiatives that are being developed in poor areas. There are also indications that the government is seeking to increase workers' control in state-run industries, such as electricity generation and distribution. Newly nationalised industries are now strong candidates for more worker participation in management (ibid.).

Despite these bold revolutionary objectives, and some practical results, huge challenges remain, especially in the form of the continuing power of the elites and their foreign allies. Key for this attempted process of transformation will be the ability of the Bolivarian movement, and the state, to guide – but ultimately subordinate itself to – mass mobilisation from below. This point was seemingly accepted by Chávez when he stated, of the moves to encourage participation and worker control, 'This is about legislating in accordance with socialist praxis and obeying the people. Those who do not understand it must choose another path' (ibid.).

If viable progressive change is to take root in Latin America, then traditional structures like the state, the party, and the leadership will have to take a lead from the new grassroots forces. It was the failure, and unwillingness, of these elements of power to respond to social pressures, acquiescing to neo-liberalism instead, that generated the reaction of the masses. Can the former instruments of class oppression become the facilitators of liberation?

Concerning the popular resistance that is forming in Latin America, it would seem that the conservative Right in the US are less concerned with maintaining the 'hegemony' and 'coercion by consent' that are being promoted through the neo-liberal reformist agenda, and are considering instead a return to 'straight power concepts' (Kennan, cited in Robinson 1996a:1). In 2004, after several unconvincing attempts to raise the spectre of terrorism in Latin America, the US Army's Southern Military Command (SOUTHCOM), based in Miami, issued a Posture Statement claiming that 'radical populism' was a major threat to stability in the region (Berrigan & Wingo 2005). The Castros, Chávez and now Morales in Bolivia are seen as the principal perpetrators of this 'backslide away from democratic principles'. This can, perhaps, be interpreted as indicative of polyarchy's inability to contain the devastating effects of neo-liberalism, and the consequent need to find more draconian solutions. US military aid to friendly governments in Latin America such as Colombia, Paraguay and El Salvador has also increased in the last few years. Besides direct military assistance to allies, traditional intervention and destabilisation tactics are also being used against new Left governments, and in particular Venezuela's (Kumar & Sharma 2004).

Latin America is at a crossroads, and the direction it will take is unknown. What is fairly certain, however, is that the neo-liberal experiment has failed, at least in terms of serving the majority of the population, and is facing increasing opposition. How the globalising elite deal with this problem is crucial: the reformist route offers the possibility of restoring the myth of autonomous and classless national development, and may indeed succeed in wringing from capital a greater concession to social welfare and increased state control. This might work for a while, especially if it becomes part of a global initiative with proper regulatory structures. But it is an option that now seems unlikely as the global economy descends into recession.

The response of the global elites, the US and the transnational agencies, could nevertheless be overtaken by the growing dynamic of popular movements in Latin America and those recently elected left-leaning governments with radical agendas. As the US foreign policy strategist Zbigniew Brzezinski has acknowledged, there has been a 'global awakening' of the world's poor and marginalised (cited in Watson forthcoming). This emerging consciousness has become an 'integral part of the shifting global demographic, economic, and political balance', and has been stimulated by the elitist global structure which produces 'resentments, emotion and quest for status of billions ... a qualitative new factor of power'. Nowhere is this process more pronounced than in Latin America.

Cuba and Latin America: Building a Hemispheric Challenge to Neo-Liberalism

The most powerful examples of Cuba's direct support for the forces challenging globalisation are, as noted previously, in Latin America, and particularly in Venezuela. Nothing could have been more fortuitous for Cuba than the electoral victory in 1998 of the Fifth Republic Movement (MVR) of Hugo Chávez, who came to power in the largest oil-producing country in the region. Despite Venezuela's wealth, after decades of inequality and neo-liberal policies it had severe social needs which could only be addressed with outside support. In October 2000, Presidents Castro and Chávez signed the Integral Cooperation Accord, which was an arrangement whereby, in exchange for oil, Cuba would launch a massive programme to address Venezuela's deficiencies in welfare and social development, and provide support with military and intelligence matters. The relationship was further cemented when the Cubans played a major role in helping Chávez to survive the coup attempt in 2002, instigated by Venezuela's elites, sections of the military high command and covert US operations (Naim 2003).

By 2005 there were almost 40,000 Cuban personnel working in Venezuela (Yanes 2005), and there are daily flights between Havana and Caracas. Cuba's contribution to the co-operation arrangement is primarily its support for a number of '*Misiones*' (missions) which the Chávez government has created to promote social, economic and political change (interview with González 2004). *Misión Barrio Adentro* (Mission in the Neighbourhood) promotes and develops publicly funded health care, dental treatment and sports training for the poor. *Misión Robinson* uses volunteers and professionals to provide basic education in deprived areas, in which live 1.5 million illiterate adults. *Misión Sucre* presents learning opportunities to those who have been unable to complete their higher education. *Misión Ribas* encourages high school drop-outs to return to education. *Misión Habitat* is tasked with the construction of social housing and *Misión Mercal* establishes subsidised grocery stores for the poor. Other *Misiones* include: *Guaicaipuro* defends and secures the rights of indigenous people; *Miranda* has created a civilian military reserve; *Vuelta al Campo* (Return to the Countryside) encourages and provides support for people to move from poor urban areas to the countryside; *Vuelvan Caras* (About Face) attempts to foster economic and social development based on participation and non-material reward; *Piar* promotes sustainable development in mining communities; *Zamora* facilitates land reform and redistribution; and *Identidad* issues identity cards, partly to provide access to other *Misiones*.

Although Cuban support is probably received by all of these *Misiones*, its assistance is most visible, and on the largest scale, in *Barrio Adentro*. The immediate background to this *Misión* was *Plan Bolivar 2000*, launched in 1999, in which 40,000 Venezuelan soldiers became engaged in a country-wide campaign to bring basic health care, food and education to the poorest citizens. Cubans co-operated in this plan and gained experience in preparation for taking up a major role in the formation of *Barrio Adentro*, which was inaugurated in March 2003. Legally, the programme is sanctioned in the new Venezuelan Constitution (2000:Article 84), which states that free health care is a right of all citizens. Cuban co-operation principally takes the form of providing medical staff, statistical and organisational support and planning. With assistance from the Venezuelan and Cuban authorities, the author visited a number of poor areas around Caracas in June 2004. Most of the subsequent analysis includes personal observations and interviews.

From the first meeting with Cuban officials in the Anauco Hilton Hotel in Caracas, where many Cuban personnel in Venezuela have been based, it became clear that the *Barrio Adentro* programme was a vast project including thousands of people and massive material resources. Initial briefings indicated that the project involved not only the delivery of health care, but also addressed longer-term issues such as constructing a statistical database and medical records for millions of patients, many of whom had no previous regular access to a doctor (interview with Pérez 2004). The author's visits to '*consultorios*' (clinics) were arranged by the mayor's office in the municipality of Sucre and took place mainly in Petare, an urban area of Caracas located in the hills (*cerros*) to the east of the city. It is largely composed of shanty towns and is home to 1.5 million people, most of whom are poor. Clinics are usually new buildings constructed in the form of an octagon, with a steel frame painted blue and red brickwork walls. These bright structures stand out in the rather drab shanty towns and are often found in prominent locations, with most major '*cerros*' marked by a '*consultorio*'. Clinics are normally staffed by two Cuban doctors and one dentist, who have living quarters above or beside the main building. Their services are available 24 hours a day in the case of emergencies. All equipment appears to be modern, and professionalism is of the highest levels. Many of the personnel have had previous experience working abroad, sometimes in remote parts of the world and in difficult conditions. In Venezuela, Cuba has established clinics and support for indigenous peoples in jungle areas, and the programme was operational at that time in 16 of Venezuela's 24 states (interview with Alvarez-Escobar 2004). Many statistics have been issued concerning the numbers of people that have been treated in the clinics, including the claim by the Cuban newspaper *Granma International* (Ventura de Jesus 2005:1) that *Barrio Adentro* 'has brought medical attention to more than 17 million Venezuelans (approximately 66 per cent of the population) through 142 million doctor's visits and medical procedures that have saved more than 29,000 lives'. Such figures are disputed but, as acknowledged by UNICEF (2005), there can be no doubt that medical care for the masses has significantly improved since *Barrio Adentro* was introduced.

What is even more difficult to quantify are the social and political impacts of programmes like *Barrio Adentro*. But this is perhaps the most important measure of the synchronisation of Cuban socialism with reactions against neo-liberalism, and with the popular quest to secure basic needs and a fundamental human dignity. In meetings with representatives of the local community, it was revealed that '*consejos locales*' (local councils) are involved in the co-management and administration of the system. Another popular structure that has active contact with *Barrio Adentro* and other *Misiones* are the Bolivarian Circles (which were mostly formed after the failed coup against Chávez in 2002, and in some ways resemble Cuban CDRs). The *Misiones* are also linked to public planning councils, urban land committees, water management groups and many other organisations involved in neighbourhood decision making. In the barrio *La Dolorita* (Petare) there was a strong sense of involvement by the community, which seemed to have taken ownership and responsibility for the health project. This included encouraging people to attend the clinic for vaccinations and basic treatment, especially for dentistry which was something most people rarely had access to previously. Cuban dentists spoke of some people presenting themselves being very nervous about treatment, which they did not understand and had never received before.

A less tangible measure was the general feeling of respect and gratitude that the new patients showed to the Cuban health personnel. This was not so much in thanks for the free service they provided, but for their part in a co-operative empowerment project that was running through society. In a visit to the barrio *Montañita* (one of the poor areas of Petare, whose inhabitants marched *en masse* to central Caracas to call for the re-instatement of President Chávez during the coup attempt in 2002), this feeling was expressed in a '*circulo de abuelos*' (grandparents' club) which, along Cuban lines, had organised older people to gather together for medical checks, exercise and meeting as a social group. Some of the elderly people attending were not only pleased that this was the first time they had access to regular health care, but also enjoyed getting to know people they had never met before, often from their own streets or communities. One woman (Rosa 2004) said that she used to stay indoors most of the time because it was dangerous to venture out, and theft and house break-ins were very common. But she claimed that the 'streets are now safer and people are working together to improve their lives'. Even the foreign press, often hostile to the Chávez government, acknowledges that the *Barrio Adentro* programme is popular with the Venezuelan poor. The *Washington Post* (Forero 2007), for example, interviewed a poor mother in Caracas who informed the reporter that health care was virtually non-existent in her district before the Cubans arrived, but now there was a free and accessible 24-hour service based on need. When asked how people got by before Cuban doctors arrived, she stated, 'You had to buy the medicines. You had to go to the clinics and pay high prices. The doctors didn't want to come to the barrios.' There are also many anecdotes, such as the shopkeeper (interview with Gonzálo 2004) who said local thieves had attacked a motorcyclist and stolen the motorbike late one night, but the following day when the news went out that the rider was a Cuban doctor on his way to attend a patient, the bike was returned to the local *consultorio* by the thieves.

The excitement of local people was complemented by Cuban medical staff who showed dedication and enthusiasm, with one commenting that the *Barrio Adentro* project was 'not just a huge initiative in public health but part of a rebirth of society which gives priority to human dignity' (interview with Manolo 2004). While all Cubans seemed motivated by their work, some younger personnel expressed the view that things could be boring at times in the evenings when they were not busy, but it helped that they were making new friends and had internet access to family in Cuba. The author was also told that medical staff are paid between $100–200 US (hard currency) a month, part of which is transferred to accounts in Cuba and part used for living expenses in Venezuela, but food and accommodation are free. This contrasts favourably to the $15–20 a month doctors are paid in Cuba. Most Cubans are highly dedicated and see working in Venezuela as a privilege and career opportunity. But a few are dissatisfied, and there have been reports of some attempting to defect by seeking asylum at the US Embassy, or crossing the border into countries like Colombia (Forero 2007). Many, however, are disappointed because they are left in limbo and unable to return, yet also have no guarantee of being accepted into the US.

The middle-class response to Cuban assistance was difficult to assess. On the one hand, conversations with well-off Venezuelans working for and around the British Council in Caracas revealed a distrust and dislike of Cuban involvement in Venezuela, and graffiti around the city confirmed these views. Speaking with a middle-class patient who had attended a *consultorio* in *La Lucha Barrio* (Petare) (interview 2004), she indicated satisfaction with the treatment she was receiving, which was good and free, but whispered as she was leaving that she did not trust the Cubans. This is in contrast to a visit made to the home of a middle-class businessman (interview with Ferreira 2004) and his family, who expressed the view that the Chávez government had reinvigorated the Venezuelan economy, and that Cuban support was vital and necessary to help rebuild social trust in the state.

However, there is some evidence to suggest that overall health care in Venezuela is not improving in line with the exceptional achievements of the *Barrio Adentro* programme. According to a 2008 study (Kraul), the country's parallel public health care system is failing because of lack of resources, funds, staff shortages and corruption. As a consequence, it is claimed, the figures are rising for some indicators such as infant mortality rates and incidences of diseases like dengue fever. This problem may be overstated by the *LA Times* source from which the information is taken. Naturally the rich minority are protected from such problems by their access to the private health sector.

The author also visited very poor areas sometimes called *'Invasiones'* (Invasions), which were usually in outlying areas and were inhabited by recent arrivals, often foreigners from Colombia, Peru and other Latin American countries. People here lived in makeshift dwellings with limited access to basic services. Two such barrios, *El Milagro and El Carmen* in the *Caucaguita* area beside the *'autopista'* Caracas-Guarenas, had a new *consultorio*, and basic education was being delivered through *Misión Robinson*. People were retiring and suspicious, and many had clearly endured great hardship in their lives. One elderly black man (Santos 2004) who was willing to speak said he had arrived a year ago from Colombia, and came because he had heard that 'people were being respected in Venezuela'.

Besides visits to *consultorios* and groups linked to the *Barrio Adentro* project, a visit was also made to a *'cocina comunitaria'* (community kitchen) in *La Montañita Pequeña* in northeast Petare. The local staff who ran the kitchen said that it was used mainly by those with limited economic means. They referred in particular to the unemployed, the semi-employed and the young not in school, who were encouraged to help with various duties and inform other disadvantaged people that this facility existed, especially poor young families and pregnant women. When people came to the canteen for the first time, they were alerted to other programmes such as *Barrio Adentro* by posters on the wall of the dining room. One user of the kitchen said that working people came to eat there sometimes, but they usually made a donation or paid a small tariff.

Another example of community action was a project to lay water pipes in an *Invasion* near to the barrio *5 de Julio* in the sector *Las dos Bodegas* (Petare). This was apparently organised by a community committee, and resources were supplied by the local government. Many of the workers were from the *Invasion*, and one commented that he had never before lived anywhere that had running water. In some of the barrios, and especially on the more inaccessible land unsuitable for building, there was a land distribution programme, as well as projects of peri-urban agriculture that were run by local people and communities along the lines of Cuban *organopónicos* (Raby 2004). The author was informed that these initiatives were receiving Cuban support and advice (interview with Rodríguez Nodals 2005).

Regarding the management of the various *Misiones*, personnel who worked for the mayor's office of Sucre indicated that they were involved at various levels of organisation. But because of previous lack of government commitment to the poor, and two decades of neo-liberal reform, local government was weakened, and they had much catching up to do in providing services and implementing the new constitution. Some staff expressed concern about the direct links that had been established between central government and the grassroots communities to deliver various programmes, bypassing local administrations.

Although travelling through the shanty towns around Caracas was visually similar to visiting the equivalent areas in any Latin American city, the difference was apparent when one spoke to local residents. Clearly, in a visit prepared by those who are organisers and advocates of the projects studied, the aim is to give the observer a favourable impression. However, the author was free to wander and talk to people, and it would have been obvious, even to the hardest sceptic, that this was not a few showcase experiments but a massive participatory social project that was alive and engaged with the whole community. This view was shared by taxi drivers, gardeners, hotel porters and many other workers with whom chance conversations were had. The author felt safe visiting the poor areas around Caracas, either accompanied by Cuban and Venezuelan personnel and/or because local activists were alerted to his role and prepared to offer support and information. However, it would be unwise for foreigners to go to such areas alone.

Since the author's study of the *Barrio Adentro* programme in 2004, co-operation between Cuba and Venezuela has strengthened and expanded. An Associated Press report in 2010, which was cited by many newspapers including the *Guardian* and the *New York Times*, reported that trade between the two countries reached $7 billion per annum in 2009, comprised mainly of 100,000 barrels of Venezuelan oil sent to Cuba daily in exchange for services. The same report suggests that Cubans are now working with Venezuela to provide not just health and educational support but also extensive military training, including defence and communication systems; computerisation of passports and identification cards; increased co-operation in agriculture, policing, sports and culture. Cuba's Deputy Health Minister, Joaquin Garcia Salavarria, in charge of medical co-operation with Venezuela, estimates that there have been over 408 million consultations in neighbourhood health clinics since 2003: an average of 14 medical visits for each of a population of 28 million people (ibid.). In response to accusations from abroad and by some Venezuelans that Cuba is taking over the country, and especially its defence and military capabilities, the Cuban director of the National Genetic Medicine Centre near Caracas, Dr Reinaldo

Menendez, stated: 'What we do is science ... Our weapons ... are our mind, our work, our coats, our stethoscopes. We are internationalists by conviction' (ibid.). Countering [economically justified] claims that Venezuela is bankrolling the Cuban Revolution in a similar fashion to its previous benefactor, the Soviet Union, President Chávez responded, 'Cuba's assistance is worth 10 times more than the cost of oil we send' (ibid.).

In many ways, Venezuela, with its Bolivarian Revolution, is an ideal location for a large-scale expansion of the Cuban strategy to export its experience and ideals. The Chávez government, in the absence of adequate social services, and facing the ravages of decades of neo-liberalism, needs Cuban support and expertise. The Venezuelan popular classes are experienced in organising themselves and have a tradition of being strongly anti-neoliberal, as suggested by the rebellion against an IMF restructuring programme in 1989, the *Caracazo*; and the same groups in society were also capable of seeing the limitations of traditional political parties and the advantages of supporting Chávez. Added to this, Venezuela has oil reserves, which, now saved from privatisation, can serve the material demands of the Chávez Revolution and supply the Cubans with a vital resource. But despite the centrality of Venezuela in Cuba's Latin America strategy, it is only one, albeit key, ally in a much wider programme of integration with progressive movements on the continent.

As Fidel Castro noted in 2004, Latin America is an 'extremely fertile ground for revolutionary change' (BBC World). Perhaps of greatest significance to Cuba, after its deep involvement in Venezuela, are Bolivia's prospects after the 2005 election victory of the anti-neoliberal indigenous leader Evo Morales. As early as 1995, when Morales was establishing his political platform, he declared (Executive Intelligence Review 1995) at a rally in Buenos Aires:

If we want to be free in Latin America there should be not one Cuba but several Cubas ... What do we need for that? Heroic figures. And for me, Fidel Castro is such a figure. I am ready to proclaim him commander of the liberation forces of America.

As in Venezuela, sectors of the Bolivian popular classes have a well-developed anti-neoliberal popular consciousness, and the country is sitting on a vast resource in the form of natural gas that could potentially pay for its planned social and political transition. The victory of Morales in some ways vindicates the struggle and sacrifice of Guevara in Bolivia, and spirits were high in Cuba when news of the election result was announced.

Although the constraints on Luiz Inácio 'Lula' da Silva in Brazil are well understood by the Cubans, having a friendly leader in such a powerful Latin American nation is a comfort to Havana. Lula supports Cuba in various international forums, and has encouraged trade and co-operation agreements between the two countries. Some of his key advisers also have Cuban connections.

Argentina is another major Latin American country that has moved closer to Cuba with the election to the presidency of Nestor Kirchner in 2003, and of his wife Christina Fernández in 2007. Since the 1980s, reaction against neo-liberal reforms had been growing in Argentina, and by the 1990s the unemployed caught international headlines as '*piqueteros*' (picketers) blocked major highways demanding jobs. These groups joined with many others in popular assemblies, people's councils, workers' councils and a national movement of factories rescued by workers' takeovers. Many ordinary people also participated in local barter gatherings called '*nodos*' where various goods could be exchanged. All of these popular reactions against neo-liberalism have been exacerbated by, or took root, during the 1998–2001 recession, which climaxed with the bankruptcy of the Argentine economy (Valante 2005). As we have seen earlier in this chapter, because of dogmatic IMF policies which precipitated resistance from the Kirchner government, Argentina is now taking a successful semi-independent stand against the Fund.

Also noted earlier were the elections in Ecuador and Uruguay of left-leaning presidents who have sought to establish closer ties with Cuba. In Ecuador particularly there is a powerful indigenous movement that is strongly anti-neoliberal. The election in December 2006 of US-educated economist Rafael Correa has not only strengthened the position of these popular domestic forces, but also contributed to the expansion of the Cuban–Venezuelan project in the region. Importantly, in September 2008 Correa won a popular mandate for a strongly anti-neoliberal new constitution.

Over the decades, Cuba has also had a powerful influence in Central America, and particularly Nicaragua and El Salvador in the 1980s. During the civil war in El Salvador, it supported the Farabundo Marti National Liberation Front (FMLN). Its leader, Jorge Schafik Handal (Comandante Marcelo), contested the 2004 presidential elections, which indicated a growing popular support for radical change. The point was not lost on Washington, which gave firm support to the right-wing candidate Tony Saca from ARENA. In 1995, at the fifth São Paulo Forum, Handal had stated, 'Cuba is the hope ... There will be Cuban socialism and revolution forever' (*Executive Intelligence Review* 1995). Handal died in January 2006, but the popular resistance to neo-liberalism in El Salvador continues.

Although Cuba has connections with various radical governments and movements in Latin America, it also has a wider regional strategy to draw these forces together to produce a Latin American alternative to the Washington Consensus. As we have seen, with the demise of its Soviet ally, Cuba was left vulnerable and highly exposed in a changing and hostile world. This, along with the regressive policies of neo-liberalism in Latin America, makes the promotion of a socialist alternative imperative for Cuba's survival and the future of the region. Interestingly, this relies less on armed struggle and more on hegemonic strategy, such as its extensive programme of 'health diplomacy' and 'the politics of symbolism'.

The beginnings of Cuba's post-Cold War Latin American initiative can be linked to the convening of the São Paulo Forum (FSP), which held its first conference in 1990. Instrumental in organising this event was Lula and the Brazilian Workers' Party, which sought, with encouragement from Havana, to create a movement that could protect and promote Cuban and Latin American socialism. From its first meeting, those in attendance constituted a roll call of the Latin American Left (*Executive Intelligence Review* 1995). In 1992, the Forum launched the journal *América Libre*, published in Argentina. At its fourth conference in Havana in 1993, the demoralisation caused by the collapse of the Soviet Union was reversed, as opportunities were seen to open up with 'the rupture of the neo-liberal project' in Latin America (ibid.). It has been claimed that the Forum represents an attempt by Cuba to rebuild something like the old Communist International, but in Latin America and under Cuban guidance, an idea which was first conceived at the Tricontinental Congress held in Havana in 1966 (ibid.).

A Bolivarian Alternative for the Americas?

The desire for Latin American integration has a long history and was central to the thinking of Bolivar and Martí, both of whom spent time in the US and realised that the emerging colossus would seek to divide and rule its southern neighbours if they did not unite in solidarity against such a threat. This concern was immortalised in Bolivar's (1951:732) statement, 'The United States ... seem[s] destined by Providence to plague America with torments in the name of freedom', and his concrete proposal for the formation of a 'League of Latin American Nations' integrated around a common economic policy, unified armed forces and a regional political authority responsible for international negotiations. Concerning the possibility of regional integration, the Cuban scholar Osvaldo Martínez (2006) points out that Latin America, despite its diversity, does have a similar colonial heritage and developmental trajectory. It also shares two common languages, Spanish and Portuguese, making it a better candidate for integration than most other areas of the world, which are far more fragmented and diverse. The same author argues, however, that a combination of US hegemonic influence and internal elites, compromised by foreign capital and imperial interests, have served to undermine the region's potential for co-operation. This has been particularly true in the neo-liberal period, in which talk of co-operation is a chimera because economic and financial deregulation, and the opening up of national economies to the global market (SAPs), are totally contradictory to any form of regional unity. Advocates of regional integration under global capitalism have produced statistics to indicate growing interregional commerce, but these are questionable. The problem is that much of the trade included in such statistics consists of movements of goods *within* transnational companies to evade taxes, or as part of the necessary operation of these giant enterprises (Martínez 2006). Even if this error is adjusted for, in 1997 interregional trade accounted for only 21.1 per cent of total trade, and by 2003 had fallen to 16 per cent (ibid.). A further problem with neo-liberal conceptions of regional trade is that by relying solely on the market as arbiter, the rich countries tend to get richer and the poor poorer. To redress this imbalance it would be necessary to introduce strong preferential arrangements to assist the weaker nations, but according to the theory of perfect competition that determines the economic relations that Latin America is obliged to endure, this is unacceptable.

Closely connected with the leftist grouping around the São Paulo Forum is an attempt to create an alternative model of Latin American integration, the Bolivarian Alternative for the Americas (ALBA), of which Venezuela and Cuba are the main proponents. The central objectives of ALBA are to derail the Washington-led Free Trade Area of the Americas (FTAA – ALCA) and to establish 'a socially orientated trade block rather than one strictly based on the logic of deregulated profit maximisation' (Arreaza 2004). As Klein (2007:454–455) observes, the economic underpinning is 'that

ALBA is essentially a barter system, in which countries decide for themselves what any given commodity or service is worth'.

The Alternative's more specific objectives include: plans for a 'Compensatory Fund for Structural Convergence', which would seek to raise social and economic levels in poorer countries in the region; encouragement of self-sufficiency in food production; an equalisation of business legislation that would favour smaller domestic enterprises; a reversal of privatisations, especially of public services; and opposition to intellectual property rights, so that generic medicines and other national products can be developed without fear of retaliation from the big multinationals that control pharmaceuticals and other necessary products. In its first practical manifestation, in April 2005 a raft of economic and trade agreements were signed between Cuba and Venezuela (*Cuba Briefing* 2005, Issue 263), coinciding with the Fourth Hemispheric Conference against the FTAA in Havana. Other strategic elements linked to ALBA include a Bank of the South to challenge the power of the IMF, and a Latin American news and cultural television initiative, TELE SUR, to provide a regional alternative to US-based CNN. In this context then President Castro advocated 'using all forms and means of mass media to bring [anti-FTAA] ideas to the masses, to educate and mobilise them' (Mayoral & Rivery 2004).

The ALBA initiative is the first time (excepting perhaps the ill-fated American Popular Revolutionary Alliance (APRA) of Haya de la Torre in the 1920s, and Bolivar's League of Latin American Nations) that a concrete plan has been devised for the region, whose objective is more than an economic and commercial accord between governments, and which recognises social and cultural issues. It seeks to be inclusive of marginal groups, such as social movements and indigenous peoples, and to use regional unity to oppose and reverse those forces that exacerbate poverty and inequality. This is the beginning of the realisation of the vision that Castro (1962:21) proclaimed in 1962, during the Second Declaration of Havana:

> No nation in Latin America is weak – because each forms part of a family of 200 million brothers, who suffer the same miseries, who harbour the same sentiments, who have the same energy, who dream about the same future and who count upon the solidarity of all honest men and women throughout the world.

In connection with the emerging 'Bolivarian Alternative', at the Havana conference in 2005 it was decided to mount resistance to the next round of discussions of the FTAA, which were to be held in Mar del Plata, Argentina, in November 2005 at the fourth Summit of the Americas (under the auspices of the Organisation of American States (OAS), from which Cuba is excluded). The opposition was organised in the form of the Third Summit of the Peoples of the Americas (previously held in Santiago in 1998 and Quebec City in 2001). To the chagrin of President Bush and members of the US administration who attended the official summit, Chávez was able to promote his alternative vision for the region, and his views were broadcast by the world media. With Bush's growing unpopularity at home due to the Iraq war and the manipulations that surrounded its justification, combined with the failures of neo-liberalism in Latin America, the position of the US was weak and the opposition played on this to the full. In a cleverly engineered media event, the Argentine football hero Diego Maradona, now a television personality, embraced Chávez on the rostrum as he addressed the 'alternative summit' and proclaimed, 'Argentina has its dignity! Let's throw Bush out of here!' (Borger & Goni 2005). On returning to Caracas, Chávez claimed, 'In the future, we will speak of US–Latin American relations in terms of the era before Mar del Plata, and the era after it' (James 2005). It has been argued that, in Chávez's 'strategic map' of Latin America, there is an emerging 'Bolivar Axis' which seeks to challenge the pro-Washington 'Monroe Axis' (Yanes 2005). The former is composed of Cuba, Venezuela, Ecuador, Brazil, Argentina, and Bolivia. This would leave the so-called 'Monroe Axis', consisting principally of Mexico and Colombia, looking very isolated. Cuba is managing this game of allegiances carefully, and is eager to 'enlist' countries that 'comprehend the revolutionary process' (*Cuba Briefing* 2007, Issue 345).

Although Cuba is playing for high stakes which are overtly political, its role has been viewed as pragmatic and responsive to the situation in Latin America. According to Wayne Smith, a North American Cuba analyst and former special envoy to Havana under the Carter Administration, Fidel Castro himself is also 'enjoying more support [today] than in the [previous] 47 years he has been in power' (*Miami Herald* 2006). He has even been described by one Caribbean politician as a 'stabilising force' in the region (ibid.). That role has been passed on to his brother Raúl, although the latter may not carry the semi-mythical status of his brother. One US diplomat (Rocha) noted, referring generally to the role of Cuba and Venezuela in Latin America, 'the US left a void – and it is being filled' (ibid.). However, underlying this support is not just a reaction to the 'void', but also Cuba's active and positive participation in the region, in response to real needs and concerns, which has become highly ideological. In this context, Cuba's 'Operation Miracle', an initiative using Cuban doctors to improve the sight of poor people throughout the developing world, especially in Latin America, is not just a humanitarian act but an example of the 'politics of symbolism'. The restoration of the sight of 500,000 people from 28 countries (*Granma International* 2006) is therefore, besides its obvious medical value, an important action in support of the 'Battle for Ideas'. Cuba has also organised an international contingent of doctors specialising in disaster situations and serious epidemics, called the Henry Reeve Contingent. In the disaster-prone year of 2005, the Contingent played a crucial role both in Central America, which was struck by Hurricane Stan, and in Kashmir in Pakistan after the earthquake. Cuba offered its expertise to the US in 2005 after Hurricane Katrina hit the southern American states, which led to the catastrophe in New Orleans. Needless to say, the offer was refused by the Bush administration, despite the fact that its own resources and experience proved totally inadequate.

It would be inaccurate, however, to see the emerging coalition of governments opposed to the FTAA and neo-liberalism as the main thrust of the resistance that is forming in the region. All leaders know that, perhaps like never before in Latin America, there is a conscious popular upsurge among the masses that is propelling the process of change. This is clearly indicated in the call to attend the People's Summit in Mar del Plata, which states:

> In recent times popular movements throughout the Americas have waged diverse and extraordinary struggles against the imposition of a neo-liberal economic and social model. The deepening and strengthening of popular resistance has already brought change to the socio-political landscape in our hemisphere ... our common struggle to make another America possible: the America of popular creativity, and of the many faces of resistance; the America of alternatives to neo-liberalism and war; the America of our original peoples, of women in struggle, of farmers, of workers, of young people; the America of sexual, cultural and religious diversity – a people's America. (Cumbre de los Pueblos 2005)

The emergence of a new popular consciousness in Latin America is no ordinary hegemonic shift (the change of class forces within a region or nation), nor even an international reconfiguration within capitalism, but a challenge emerging from within the specific conditions that globalisation has produced. As Klein (2007:450) observes, 'In Latin America ... the backlash [against neo-liberalism] takes a distinctly more hopeful form. It is not directed at the weak or the vulnerable but focuses squarely on the ideology at the root of economic exclusion.'

Cuba's role in this process is to act in ways which support these popular forces, especially through representative governments. This is not a case of exporting revolution but one of integration with an emerging counter-hegemony for which Cuba can act as guide by example. A role in which the 'Battle for Ideas' is not just a struggle within the Revolution to preserve socialism, but part of a Latin American transition based on increasingly conscious popular actors taking control of their environments to design a different and more egalitarian future. As Fidel Castro stated (cited in Cole forthcoming) in 2003:

> I believe firmly that the great battle to liberate ourselves will be in the field of ideas and not in armed conflict ... every force, every armament, every [military strategy] and tactic has its antithesis in the inexhaustible consciousness of those who fight for a just cause.

CUBA: THE OPTIONS

Having considered the nature of the global order, the distinctive forms of Cuban socialism, the ways in which Cuba has sought to deal with its own internal crisis and its attempts to integrate its socialist principles with international forces of resistance to globalisation, it is necessary to consider the possible options that may be available to Cuba in the future. One thing is clear, it is impossible to return to the conditions which existed during earlier decades of the Revolution, or sustain the economy by clinging to the remnants of the old economic system. Change is inevitable, but the form it should take is the subject of much dispute both inside and outside Cuba.

For those who believe in a neo-liberal solution to the island's predicament, which forms by far the largest component of external opinion, reforms simply signal the inevitable birth pangs of the market, in which a nation of individuals is seeking freedom to engage in private enterprise backed by a representative democracy (Centeno & Font 1997; Domínguez 1996). In this context, local initiatives in agricultural production and so on are seen in terms of self-help, not participation. Given the above views, it is assumed that the acquisitive and self-seeking nature, which Cubans are presumed to share with all other human beings, can no longer be held back by state manipulation and oppression. From this perspective, it was the favourable trade and aid relationship with the CMEA which allowed the Castro government to project the illusion of socialist 'development' and rising living standards, and thus to buy the political acquiescence of the Cuban people. The conclusion is that Cuba will have to face economic 'realities', and can no longer deal with problems by turning to ideology. For example, referring to the Rectification Campaign, Eckstein (2003:77) states, 'there were underlying economic reasons for reforms rooted in the domestically orientated economy that the state justified ideologically in the name of rectification'. Such thinking, and the 'realities' it identifies, are themselves not ideologically neutral however, but based on untested and unproven assumptions about human behaviour. The only sense in which they are 'real' is that they concur with a dominant mode of thought and a prevailing economic system, which will inevitably effect, but need not necessarily determine, Cuba's development.

In practice, the difficulty with the market prescription, and with the establishment of representative democracy and political pluralism as experienced in most of the Caribbean and in Central and South America, is that it does not seem to have brought improvements in the standards of living of the masses and, in contrast to Cuba, the concept of growth with equity has been abandoned. One could argue that with the end of the US embargo, capital would flood into Cuba and stimulate growth; however, the island's 'Cinderella' status may not last for long. The current advantages it offers to investors in the form of a skilled workforce, viable exports and tourism, once exploited and exhausted, would leave Cuba little opportunity but to compete with very low-wage economies like Haiti and Vietnam. It is also worth remembering, as indicated in Chapter 3, that in the pre-revolutionary period Cuba received a vast amount of US investment in proportion to the rest of Latin America, but this did not resolve the problem of inequality; indeed, it exacerbated it. As we have seen in Chapter 1, it is also clear that under globalisation it is difficult, if not impossible, to maintain nationally orientated strategies in an increasingly integrated world. The imperative of global competition for foreign direct investment and markets serves to enrich those local groups that are linked to the circuits of transnational accumulation, whose interests are often distinct from the majority of the national population.

Moreover, democracy in the region is weak. In Chapter 2, it was argued that neo-liberalism has shifted power away from the state and to non-elected agencies that represent the interests of capital. The move from an international system of nation-states to a trans-nationalised matrix of accumulation has weakened the economic and political control of nations over their resources, which are increasingly managed on a globalised level. Now, a transnational elite and their representative agencies make many of the decisions that affect individual countries, instead of leaving those choices to national constituencies. In Cuba, a neo-liberal solution would also divert participation into the market, in which it (participation) would lose its function as a process of interaction between organisations and individuals. Political parties would become defenders of free-market ideology and 'representative democracy'. Given such a scenario, the revolutionary ideals of Cuba as an independent, nationalist and equitable nation would dissolve, as the economy and society were refashioned to suit the needs of international capital and the emerging elites in a new class structure. As this book was being finalised in June 2010, the world was facing the second wave of a global financial and economic crisis, which began in 2008 with the failure of underlying assets to support an overleveraged banking system. Why should Cuba now buy tickets for a train that has been derailed and is unlikely to be put back on track in the foreseeable future?

Alternatively, for a number of economists within Cuba and a minority of foreign observers, the solution lies in a form of market socialism in which the state retains firm control over key sectors of the economy, while allowing private enterprise and foreign investment to function in the less vital areas (Carranza et al. 1995). This perspective assumes that the Cuban population should continue to receive substantial levels of state guidance and protection, but private initiative could be used as a managed stimulant to increase choice, improve delivery and quality, and encourage greater efficiency. As we have seen in Chapter 2, for the market socialists or structuralists, economies are not mechanisms in which individuals compete to consume and maximise utility, as neo-liberals believe, but systems in which producers and the state are interdependent. The underlying assumption of this model is that humans are shaped by their environments, and it is the role of states to manage that environment. From the structuralist perspective, emphasis is also placed on technical specialisation rather than political consciousness, because development, even when seen in a socialist context, is perceived as requiring management and organisation rather than participation and ideological formation. As noted in Chapter 3, this is a position that was supported in the 1960s and 1970s by economists like Bettelheim. This model would also pursue an extension of 'representative democracy' and eventually political pluralism, perhaps with a bias towards an 'associative' democratic model. In this respect, it is an attractive 'soft option', and some analysts felt that Cuba was moving in this direction in the 1990s; many believe it is re-engaging with this possibility since the transfer of the presidency to Raúl Castro. It could be argued that his attempts to 'de-paternalise' the economy, by withdrawing some state control from micro-level enterprises and social welfare, are an initiative that falls in line with the above model. However, as Minister of Economy and Planning Marino Murillo stated in March 2010, 'the gigantic paternalistic state can no longer be, because there is no longer any way to maintain it' (*Cuba Briefing* 2010, Issue 489), indicating that it is not ideological conviction driving these decisions but economic necessity. Apart from the theoretical weaknesses of attempting to blend socialism and the market, this essentially radical Keynesian strategy may no longer be feasible in a globalising world economy in which capital reigns supreme, diminishing the powers and controls available to the nation-state. Commenting on this problem, one Cuban analyst perceptively notes, 'The market is too powerful a mechanism to incorporate as a docile instrument of socialist construction' (Dilla et al. 1993:25). In a study of financial strategies open to Cuba, an international specialist in fiscal policy arrived at a similar conclusion:

> The more Cuba enters the international economy, and the more dependent it becomes on international markets to rebuild its economy, the more control that these market actors will have on the nature of Cuban development. As these actors tend to harbour an underlying bias against socialist economic designs, and they have fairly narrow (and short-term) conceptions of what constitutes 'healthy economic fundamentals', this market control will be in sharp contrast to the ambitions of Cuba's current policy makers. (Moses 1996)

One could conclude, therefore, that the ultimate result for Cuba of taking the structuralist option would be the same as that offered by the market route: loss of national control, and integration into the international system dominated by the rule of money and its concomitant (global) class divisions. Indeed, poor results can be seen even in developed nations which have attempted to maintain a social democratic Keynesian model in the period of neo-liberalism and globalisation. In every case, the role of the state in guaranteeing minimum standards of social welfare and employment has been compromised because of pressures to maintain the profitability of enterprises and to satisfy the demands of currency speculators and global capital. The prospects, therefore, look bleak for a small developing country entering the same system. Then President Castro (2007:623), always an opponent of market-style reforms, claimed, referring to those who proposed such measures, and, perhaps, on an international level, countries like China: 'There were those who thought that capitalist methods would allow them to construct Socialism. That is one of the great errors in history.'

While the two options above offer few prospects for defending the achievements of the Revolution, a third option may exist based on revolutionary continuity: a strategy which appeared to be emerging as the immediate crisis caused by the collapse of Soviet-style Communism was brought under control in the late 1990s. This third option should not be understood as socialist dogma driven by a headstrong leadership, particularly referring to retired president Fidel Castro, but as part of an evolutionary process with which the majority of the Cuban population is engaged. The dialectical interaction between material existence, societal formation and consciousness is in sharp contrast to the 'models' of development and democracy proposed by liberals and structuralists. As we have seen in Chapter 2, free markets and democracy cannot be contained within a single model – some kind of 'End of History' mindset – based on a presumed best possible system. Democracy, especially under neo-liberalism, is seen as an extension of individual choice, exercised by selecting representatives in a given and unquestioned order, in which procedure takes precedence over participation, and civil society and the state are held to be separate entities. In Cuba, the rhythm of life and development is different. There is no dominant market that conditions social, economic and political life, but rather a complex fusion of state and civil society in a creative dynamic that opens up different avenues for individuals to realise opportunities and potentials. This process is intimately linked with social co-operation rather than individual competition. As the Cuban social scientist Martínez Heredia (1992:75–76) notes, participatory democracy is central to the building of socialism. He continues by suggesting that the problem for Cuba is not finding a transition route to the market:

> Decisive as the Revolution has been ... it has not produced an effective system of participation ... with respect to the deficiencies of the existing regime, the debates and preoccupations with it reflect a need not to replace the regime but to improve it by deepening its ideals and its socialist project.

Although coming from a different ideological stance, López (1997:34) arrives at a similar conclusion when he states, 'Participation is the criteria against which Cuban civil society should be judged.' As we have seen, for Martínez Heredia (1992) it is a conscious revolutionary project in which Cuba remains 'a gigantic school through which people learn to direct social [and economic] processes'.

If Cuba were to integrate its economy into a globalising world, one which gives priority to the interests of capital over economic development, equality and democracy, then the island would have little hope of continuing the nationalist and revolutionary project on which it has embarked. Perhaps, however, the option still exists to seek survival through a continuation of the Revolution, which Guevara believed to be 'the skeleton of total liberty' which had to be given flesh and blood (Bengelsdorf 1994:66), and through its synchronisation with a conscious international counter-hegemony to globalisation.

Conclusion

This book argues that to understand the Cuban Revolution, especially at the beginning of the twenty-first century, it is necessary to go beyond analyses of Cuba itself and locate its revolutionary process in the wider context of a globalising world system. Nearly all studies of Cuba since the Insurrection of 1959 have dealt with the internal workings of the island, or made assessments of its external orientations in the area of foreign policy. Before the era of globalisation these approaches were perhaps logical and adequate, because despite Cuba's considerable symbolic status as a revolutionary alternative and its practical foreign policy successes, such as the victorious battles in the Angolan liberation struggle, it was only a sideshow in the wider conflict between the superpowers. The rise of neo-liberalism and the collapse of Soviet-style Communism have, however, dramatically changed the configuration of world economics and politics. Today we no longer live in a system of independent nation-states organised in an international order divided by ideologies, but in a world of transnational integration whose advocates proclaim an 'End of History' and, by the same measure, an end of ideology. As Colburn (2002:12) states, referring to the 1990s, 'A century of ideological contestation, which was fanned by the Cuban Revolution ... came to a quiet close'. However, Cuba may be able to find a new role as the certainties of the global age begin to lose their credibility in the face of growing inequality and crisis.

Despite the current global financial and economic problems, few scholars and policy makers believe that Cuba is anything but a curious anomaly, especially as the last remaining Communist power, China, surges towards market integration. In this context, contemporary writers on Cuba seem to be recording the Revolution's history for posterity, or conducting studies which presume that the island's resistance is untenable. Some analysts seek to defend Cuba's achievements, especially in welfare provision, and juxtapose the emphasis on social justice with the inequalities that exist in many parts of the modern world, particularly in other developing countries. Such observations are mostly astute, but the logic of these arguments holds no sway in a transnationalised system dominated by an elitist conception of markets and individualism, which does not prioritise social needs. This incompatibility is starkly described by Robinson (1996b:13–14), who claims, 'Capitalist globalisation denotes a world war ... It is a war of a global rich and powerful minority against the global poor, dispossessed and outcast majority ... it involves all people around the world, and none can escape its involvement'. This battle may become more intense as the global crisis deepens.

Whether globalisation is ultimately considered as a positive process for humanity, one that, with time, will resolve its crises through deeper integration (Barnevik 2001; Wolf 2004; Ohmae 1990), or viewed with the pessimism of Robinson and others, the reality is that at this current conjuncture it appears to be failing to respond to the needs of the majority of humanity. This is represented less by statistics on poverty, inequality and exclusion, which can be assembled to reflect different perspectives, but by the conscious reactions of people around the world to what they perceive to be the unfairness of the current neo-liberal order. Cuba's reaction to this popular resistance, especially in Latin America, is to act as it always has towards selective cases of injustice, by providing support and seeking a degree of reciprocal (ideological) commitment to its cause. However, in the new global environment, it is not engaging so much with small resistance groups, or even with countries fighting for liberation, but more with a growing mass opposition to neo-liberalism that transcends specific ideologies, institutional politics, geographical borders and traditional revolutionary logic. These are not isolated struggles, but an emerging mass counter-hegemony against the global system, with which the Cuban Revolution is integrating. It is this symbiotic relationship based on a commonality of purpose, driven by resistance to the effects of globalisation, that is giving Cuba new energy; the process is transformative and creative for both sides (Lambie 2009b:73). There is a renewed poignancy and some truth in Guevara's (1967) observation, 'We [Cuba's leaders] are the head of the people that is at the head of America.' This point was again emphasised by Bolivia's President Evo Morales, who stated in a ceremony commemorating Guevara in Vallegrande (the town in central Bolivia where the revolutionary's body was displayed after his execution on 8 October 1967), that Che was 'invincible in his ideals ... and in all this history, after so many years, he inspires us to continue fighting, changing not only Bolivia, but all of Latin America and, better, the world' (Associated Press 2009).

In the author's view, to present Cuba's current position as one of creative flux linked to a wider global dynamic of resistance requires more than a simple assertion. This argument must be premised on a critical analysis of the global environment which Cuba, the New Social Movements and radical governments (especially in Latin America) are engaged in resisting. It is widely accepted, even among some of globalisation's advocates, that inequality is growing, but rarely are the deep internal workings of the system that produces such conditions explored. Only by understanding the nature of globalisation, driven by the imperatives of transnational accumulation, the class forces central to its operation and the deep contradictions that it is creating, can the reactions against it be fully comprehended. Globalisation is also much more than an economic phenomenon, and involves a complex process of hegemony which seeks to legitimise its existence as the sole and inevitable world system. This includes fomenting a culture of mass consumption, individualism, competition and slavish adherence to the alienating 'laws' of the market and the 'end of politics'. Within this matrix of persuasion, modern democracy plays a key role; it is a constructed pseudo-freedom that limits resistance to an increasingly unequal world. In this way it is not just 'hollowed out', but also becomes an instrument of manipulation and disempowerment – a form of 'polyarchy' designed and promoted to produce coercion by consent. The above trends are being resisted most visibly today in Latin America, and it is difficult to comprehend what is happening in the region without first understanding the global-level developments that have led to this juncture.

As for the internal workings of Cuba, its form of democracy is a process, and it would be inaccurate to suggest that the island has developed some form of 'ideal' democratic system that could be copied and implemented in other parts of the world. The collapse of the Soviet Bloc caused Cuba enormous difficulties and it still faces problems, most of which are economic but can only be considered politically. All forms of democratic governance are historically contingent, being more or less partial, and the Revolution is not a perfectly functioning system reaching seamlessly from bottom to top, expressing the unmediated will of the people. Just as in representative democracies, much decision making in Cuba is by dictat (perhaps inevitable while the sovereignty of the island is precarious in the face of real external hostility). But within the socialist process there are interesting democratic 'spaces' which are expanding, as the institutionalisation of the popular will evolves through participatory social and political experience. Opportunities and possibilities are also emerging from community action; these are generated by attempts to resolve economic and social questions that state mechanisms alone are not coping with, have not fully addressed, or are not yet asking.

This community action is exemplified by the movement in peri-urban organic horticulture in response to food shortages. In such instances the state often responds in a positive way, in this case by supplying land, outreach workers, seeds and so on, but in most cases it does not direct the activities. Democracy in Cuba is based on complex interactions between state and civil society, in which it is not possible, nor helpful, to draw a delineating line between the two, as seems to be the theoretical preference of analysts of contemporary democracy. Indeed, much study of Cuba is misguided because it is assumed that civil society is an independent space; which in typical neo-liberal reasoning is the instrument which pressures the state to support markets, 'democracy' and 'freedom'. What makes Cuba different in this respect is not only its democratic practices, but also the relative absence of both competitive markets and the rationalisation of social experience from the point of view of individuals as consumers. The author would argue that the market is such an overbearing factor in capitalist society, and especially under globalisation, that it restricts the range of social (participatory) democratic potentials, rather than allowing them to flourish. Democracy cannot be reduced to a reflection of market relations, because by doing so we are limited to seeing people as consuming individuals. Such a view assumes we choose political leaders and make important decisions as though we were buying a packet of soap powder, which is individually alienating and denies effective political participation.

What the Cuban experience can perhaps demonstrate is that democratic 'space' is much broader than the parameters set by mainstream conceptions of democracy. It is important in this respect that academics attempt to look beyond the simplistic neo-liberal 'holy trinity' of individualism, democracy and markets, which is conditioned by the 'End of History' mindset and the economic imperatives of globalisation. They must conceive of ways in which democracy can be realised more as an expanding social process, encompassing human existence, rather than a polyarchic system which limits human development. It is also misleading to simply talk of 'participation', 'social inclusion', and 'stakeholder involvement' only in the context of the narrow spectrum of activity that 'democracy' can influence in its current form. To address the 'democratic deficit', one needs to theoretically challenge the limiting intellectual parameters within which democracy itself is conceived and enacted, and acknowledge the legitimacy of social activism that rejects this impoverished ideological construct. Mainstream academia may shy from this task, but ordinary people, whose daily lives are constrained and controlled by the restrictions imposed on them by representative democracy, will not. As we are seeing in many of the New Social Movements, the first task is to build their own participatory democratic processes that seek to liberate, not control.

Cuba stands at a critical juncture not only in terms of its own history, but also in the wider context of an emerging resistance to neo-liberalism. There is no guarantee that the Revolution will survive, but it is unlikely, as some suggest, that it will implode when either Fidel or Raúl Castro dies. Nevertheless, Cuba still endures many internal and external pressures for change, as well as seemingly intractable problems: corruption, increasing materialism, inequality, continuing shortages, the disenchantment of some young people, and migration of the skilled and disillusioned. For the Revolution's detractors, these are the green shoots of a transition to a market society, which can only grow and become more powerful. Alternatively, as argued in Chapter 4, Cuba's historical and revolutionary experience runs deeper than indicated by the superficial manifestations of internal problems, and external pressures and temptations. Rather than economic indices, 'models' of development and democracy, the Revolution is about the evolution of a socialist consciousness based on participation and experience. Therefore there is no clear way forward for Cuba, no prescriptive set of actions that will produce 'authentic' socialism. At present Cuba is a mixture of Soviet-style planning and paternalism, socialist participation and consciousness building, and tentative market reforms. The Revolution, however, still seems to retain a unity of purpose, which cannot be said for most other countries that are divided by inequality, exposure to global forces and neo-liberal divisiveness. Cubans also continue to have access to good health care, education and some protection from outright poverty and destitution, privileges not enjoyed by a large number of the world's population. But the island's greatest strength is its apparent determination to pursue a revolutionary course, based on a belief in socialism. An amendment to Article 3 of the Cuban Constitution in 2002 states:

Socialism and the revolutionary political and social system established in the Constitution and proven through years of heroic resistance to aggression of all kinds and economic warfare waged by the successive administrations of the most powerful country that has ever existed, and having demonstrated their capacity to transform the country and create an entirely new and just society, are irrevocable; and Cuba will never again return to capitalism.

Robinson (2009) sums up these views when he states:

[T]he global meaning of its revolution is to be found not in its material achievements (such as universal health care), no matter how significant they are, but in the ideological and psychological impact of its survival and defiance in the face of a relentless world capitalist system whose leading agents have from the start been bent on its destruction.

The Revolution represents therefore an ideological and a practical conviction in which 'material achievements', despite their direct value, are also part of the process of defending and constructing socialism in Cuba, and, through their export abroad, contribute to the 'politics of symbolism'. In its attempts to build socialism, the Cuban Revolution has had many successes: engagement of the population at various levels in the activities that shape their lives; a willingness on the part of the leadership to admit their mistakes; experimentation to improve society for the many rather than for the few; provision of high levels of equality and support for basic needs; free health care and education in Cuba, and their delivery to millions of people around the world with the humanity, 'to share what she has, which is sometimes not enough to cover her own needs' (EP 2008). In this, Cuba and its socialist path have already been 'absolved by history'. It remains to be seen if the global crisis will propel these achievements to a higher level in the minds of Cubans and of those in other countries whose life chances and resources are diminishing. To repeat the statement by Fidel that was cited in Chapter 1: 'The objective conditions, the suffering of the immense majority of those people create the subjective conditions for the task of awareness building ... the battle for ideas is what we are doing'.

Ultimately, Cuba alone is unlikely to survive in the long term, but, as this book has argued, the Revolution is not alone: its social achievements, its participatory democracy, its revolutionary pedigree and its dignity are finding wider processes with which to integrate, reviving its legitimacy and relevance. These processes represent a mass movement born out of the deep contradictions of global capitalism. This struggle is unlike any previous resistance or war against an enemy, because it is all encompassing – it is a transnational conflict and its outcome will do nothing less than decide the fate of humanity. Perhaps at no time has Mariatigui's (1928 vol. 1:158) statement on social change been more poignant: 'The revolution of the poor is not just about the conquest of bread, but also the conquest of beauty, of art, of ideas and all the pleasures of the spirit' (author's translation). Globalisation, not imperialism, is the highest stage of capitalism – the stage at which its fate will be decided. For the Cuban leadership, and many of its citizens, they are engaged in more than a struggle for national survival; this is the endgame. The destiny of the Cuban Revolution is now inextricably linked to the mounting resistance to neo-liberal globalisation.

Bibliography

BOOKS

Acanda, J., 2002. *Sociedad Civil y Hegemonía* (La Habana: Centro de Investigación y Desarrollo de la Cultura Cubana, 'Juan Marinello').

Adiga, A., 2008. *The White Tiger* (London: Atlantic Books).

Adorno, T., 1974. *Minima Moralia: Reflections from a Damaged Life*, trans. Jephcott, E. (London: Verso).

Aglietta, M., 1979. *A Theory of Capitalist Regulation: The US Experience*, trans. Fernbach, D. (London: New Left Books).

Ajami, R., et al., 2006. *International Business: Theory and Practice* (London: M.E. Sharpe).

Albertoni, E., 1987. *Mosca and the Theory of Elitism* (Oxford: Basil Blackwell).

Amin, S., 1996. *Capitalism in the Age of Globalisation* (London: Zed Press).

Anweiler, O., 1974. *The Soviets: The Russian Workers, Peasants, and Soldiers Councils, 1905–1921* (New York: Random House).

Arblaster, A., 1994. *Democracy* (Buckingham: Oxford University Press).

Aristotle, 1958. *The Politics of Aristotle*, trans. & ed., Barker, E. (New York: Oxford University Press).

August, A., 1999. *Democracy in Cuba and the 1997–98 Elections* (Havana: Editorial José Martí).

Avritzer, L., 2002. *Democracy and the Public Space in Latin America* (Princeton: Princeton University Press).

Azicri, M., 1988. *Cuba: Politics, Economics and Society* (London: Pinter).

Bakan, J., 2004. *The Corporation: The Pathological Pursuit of Profit and Power* (Toronto: Penguin).

Bakunin, M., 1974. *Selected Writings*, Lehning, A. (ed.), (New York: Grove Press).

Balanya, B., et al., 2000. *Corporate Europe Inc.* (London: Pluto Press).

Barnet, R. & Muller, R., 1974. *Global Reach: The Power of the Multinational Corporation* (New York: Simon and Schuster).

Bauzon, K. (ed.), 1992. *Development and Democratisation in the Third World: Myths, Hopes and Realities* (New York: Crane Russak).

Bengelsdorf, C., 1994. *The Problem of Democracy in Cuba. Between Vision and Reality* (Oxford: Oxford University Press).

Benjamin, M., et al., 1986. *No Free Lunch: Food and Revolution in Cuba Today* (New York: Grove Press).

Benn, T., 1976. Uncut Diaries. I am grateful to Mr Benn for granting me permission to consult his diaries on a number of occasions (31 August, 20 September, 17 October, 13 December) during 2007 and for the discussions we held.

Bernays, E., 1969. *The Engineering of Consent* (Norman: University of Oklahoma Press).

Bertram, C., 2003. *Rousseau and the Social Contract* (London: Routledge).

Bettelheim, C., 1975. *On the Transition to Socialist Economy* (London: Harvester Press).

Bielsa, R. et al., 2002. *Qué Son Las Asambleas Populares* (Buenos Aires: Ediciones Continente).

Blight, J. & Brenner, P., 2002. *Sad and Luminous Days: Cuba's Struggle with the Superpowers After the Missile Crisis* (New York: Rowman & Littlefield).

Boggs, C., 1980. *Gramsci's Marxism* (London: Pluto Press).

Boggs, C., 2000. *The End of Politics: Corporate Power and the Decline of the Public Sphere* (New York: The Guilford Press).

Bolívar, S., 1951. *Selected Writings of Bolívar*, vol. II (New York: Colonial Press Inc.).

Boron, A., 1995. *State, Capitalism, and Democracy in Latin America* (Boulder, Colorado: Lynne Rienner).

Bottomore, T., 1993. *Elites and Society* (London: Routledge).

Branford, S. & Kucinski, B., 1990. *The Debt Squads: The US, the Banks, and Latin America* (London: Zed Books).

Branford, S. & Rocha, J., 2002. *Cutting the Wire* (London: Latin America Bureau).

Braverman, H., 1974. *Labour and Monopoly Capital: The Degradation of Work in the Twentieth Century* (New York: Monthly Review Press).

Brenner, P., Jiménez, M.R., Kirk, J. & LeoGrande, W. (eds), 2008. *Reinventing the Revolution: A Contemporary Cuba Reader* (New York: Rowman & Littlefield).

Brenner, R., 2009. *The Economics of Global Turbulence* (London: Verso).

Brett, E.A., 1985. *The World Economy Since the War: The Politics of Uneven Development* (London: Macmillan).

Bruce, I., 2004. *The Porto Alegre Alternative: Direct Democracy in Action* (London: Pluto Press).

Brundenius, C., 1984. *Revolutionary Cuba: The Challenge of Economic Growth with Equity* (Boulder: Westview Press).

Burnham, P., 2003. *Remaking the Postwar World Economy: Robot and British Policy in the 1950s* (London: Palgrave Macmillan).

Caballero, M., 1986. *Latin America and the Comintern, 1919–1943* (Cambridge: Cambridge University Press).

Callao, D., 1982. *The Imperious Economy* (Cambridge, MA.: Harvard University Press).

Callinicos, A., et al., 1994. *Marxism and the New Imperialism* (London: Bookmarks).

Carr, E., 1979. *The Russian Revolution: From Lenin to Stalin (1917–1929)* (Basingstoke: Macmillan).

Carr, E., 1982. *The Twilight of the Comintern, 1930–1935* (Basingstoke: Macmillan).

Carr, E., 1985 [1950]. *The Bolshevik Revolution, 1917–1923*, 3 vols. (New York: W.W. Norton).

Carranza, J., Gutierrez, L. & González, P., 1995. *Cuba: La Reestructuración de la Economía: Una Propuesta Para el Debate* (Havana: Editorial de Ciencias Sociales).

Castells, M., 1996. *The Rise of the Network Society* (Oxford: Blackwell).

Casteñeda, J., 1993. *Utopia Unarmed: The Latin American Left after the Cold War* (New York: Knopf).

Castro, F., 1972. *La Revolución Cubana 1953–1972* (Ciudad de México: Editorial Era).

Castro, F., 1975. 'History Will Absolve Me', trans. Álvarez Tabío, P. & Booth, A. (Havana: Editorial de Ciencias Sociales).

Castro, F., 1986. *Nothing Can Stop the Course of History*. Elliot, M. & Dymally, M. (eds), (New York: Pathfinder).

Castro, F., 1991 [1962]. *The Second Declaration of Havana* (New York: Pathfinder).

Castro, F., 2000. *Capitalism in Crisis: Globalisation and World Politics Today* (Melbourne: Ocean Press).

Castro, F., 2004. *War, Racism and Economic Justice* (Melbourne: Ocean Press).

Castro, F., 2007. *My Life: Fidel Castro: One Hundred Hours with Fidel*, Interviews by Ramonet, I. (London: Penguin).

Caute, D., 1988. *The Year of the Barricades '68* (London: Paladin).

Centeno, M. & Font, M., 1997. *Towards a New Cuba: Legacies of a Revolution* (Boulder: Lynne Rienner).

Chanan, M., 1985. *The Cuban Image: Cinema and Cultural Politics in Cuba* (London: British Film Institute Publishing).

Chang, L. & Kornbluh, P., 1992. *The Cuban Missile Crisis, 1962: A National Security Archive Documents Reader* (New York: New Press).

Chavez, D. & Goldfrank, B. (eds), 2005. *The Left in the City: Participatory Local Governments in Latin America* (London: Latin American Bureau).

Chavez, H., et al., 2005. *Chavez, Venezuela and the New Latin America* (Melbourne: Ocean Press).

Chiapaslink, 2000. *The Zapatistas: A Rough Guide* (London: Chiapaslink).

Chomsky, N., 1992. *Deterring Democracy* (London: Vintage).

Chomsky, N., 2003. *Hegemony of Survival: America's Quest for Global Dominance* (New York: Penguin Books).

Chossudovsky, M., 1998. *The Globalisation of Poverty: Impacts of IMF and World Bank Reforms* (Australia: Pluto Press).

Clarke, S., 1988. *Keynesianism, Monetarism, and the Crisis of the State* (Aldershot: Edward Elgar).

Coates, D., 1980. *Labour in Power? A Study of the Labour Government 1974–79* (London: Longman).

Coates, D., 1991. *Running the Country* (Milton Keynes: Open University).

Colburn, F., 2002. *Latin America at the End of Politics* (Princeton: Princeton University Press).

Cole, K., 1998. *Cuba from Revolution to Development* (London: Pinter).

Cole, K., (forthcoming). *The Bolivarian Alternative for the Americas: The Last Putting Themselves First*.

Cole, K., Cameron, J. & Edwards, C., 1991. *Why Economists Disagree* (London: Longman).

Colletti, L., 1972. *From Rousseau to Lenin: Studies in Ideology and Society* (London: New Left Books).

Cox, R., 1987. *Power, Production, and World Order: Social Forces in the Making of History* (New York: Columbia University Press).

Croteau, D., 1995. *Politics and the Class Divide: Working People and the Middle Class Left* (Philadelphia: Temple University Press).

Crowe, M., 1977. *The Changing Profile of the Natural Law* (The Hague: Matinus Nijoff).

Dahl, R., 1971. *Polyarchy: Participation and Opposition* (New Haven: Yale University Press).

De Soto, H., 1989. *The Other Path: The Economic Answer to Terrorism* (New York: Basic Books).

Debray, R., 1967. *Revolution Within the Revolution: Armed Struggle and Political Struggle in Latin America* (London: Penguin).

Deutscher, I., 1963. *The Prophet Outcast. Trotsky: 1929–1940* (New York: Vintage).

Deutschmann, D., 1987. *Che Guevara and the Cuban Revolution: Writings and Speeches of Ernesto Che Guevara* (Pacific and Asia: Pathfinder Press).

Diamond, L. & Platter, M. (eds), 1993. *The Global Resurgence of Democracy* (Baltimore: Johns Hopkins University Press).

Díaz Castañón, M., 2001. *Ideología y Revolución: Cuba, 1959–1962* (Havana: Editorial de Ciencias Sociales).

Dicken, P., 1998. *Global Shift: The Internationalisation of Economic Activity*, 3rd ed. (New York: Guildford Press).

Dilla, H., Conzalez, G. & Vincentelli, A., 1993. *Participación Popular y Desarrollo en los Municipios Cubanos* (Havana: Editora Política).

Domínguez, J., 1978. *Cuba: Order and Revolution* (London: Belknap Press of Harvard University Press).

Domínguez, J., 1989. *To Make a World Safe for Revolution: Cuba's Foreign Policy* (Cambridge, MA: Harvard University Press).

Domínguez, J., Pérez Villanueva, E., & Barberia, L., 2004. *The Cuban Economy at the Start of the Twenty-First Century* (Cambridge, MA: Harvard University Press).

Downs, A., 1956. *An Economic Theory of Democracy* (New York: Harper and Row).

Dumont, R., 1974. *Is Cuba Socialist?* (London: Andre Deutsch).

Eckstein, S., 2003. *Back from the Future: Cuba Under Castro* (New York: Routledge).

Edelman, M., 1999. *Peasants Against Globalization: Rural Social Movements in Costa Rica* (Stanford: Stanford University Press).

Elliot, L. & Atkinson, D., 2007. *Fantasy Island: Waking Up to the Incredible Economic, Political and Social Illusions of the Blair Legacy* (London: Constable).

Elliot, L. & Atkinson, D., 2008. *The Gods That Failed: How Blind Faith in the Market Has Cost Us Our Future* (London: The Bodley Head).

Engdahl, W., 2004. *A Century of War: Anglo-American Oil Politics and the New World Order* (London: Pluto).

Engdahl, W., 2007. *Seeds of Destruction. The Hidden Agenda of Genetic Manipulation* (Quebec: Global Research).

Fagan, R., 1969. *The Transformation of Political Culture in Cuba* (Stanford: Stanford University Press).

Fanon, F., 1967. *Black Skin, White Masks*, trans. Markmann, C.L. (New York: Grove Press).

Feinsilver, J., 1993. *Healing the Masses: Cuban Health Politics at Home and Abroad* (Berkeley: University of California Press).

Foweraker, J., 1995. *Theorising Social Movements* (London: Pluto Press).

Foweraker, J. & Landman, T., 1997. *Citizenship Rights and Social Movements* (Milton Keynes: Open University Press).

Franklin, J., 1997. *Cuba and the United States: A Chronological History* (Melbourne: Ocean Press).

Fraser, R., 1979. *Blood of Spain: The Experience of the Civil War, 1936–1939* (Suffolk: Penguin).

Friedman, M., 1962. *Capitalism and Freedom* (Chicago: University of Chicago Press).

Fukuyama, F., 1992. *The End of History and the Last Man* (London: Hamish Hamilton).

Fukuyama, F., 1999. *The Great Disruption: Human Nature and the Reconstitution of Social Order* (London: Profile Books).

Fuller, L., 1992. *Work and Democracy in Socialist Cuba* (Philadelphia: Temple University Press).

Funes, F. & García, L., 2002. *Sustainable Agriculture and Resistance: Transforming Food Production in Cuba* (Oakland, California: Food First Books).

Galbraith, J. K., 1968. *The New Industrial State* (London: Hamish Hamilton).

García Brigos, J., 1998. *Gobernabilidad y Democracia: Los Organos del Poder Popular en Cuba* (Havana: Editorial de Ciencias Sociales).

George, S., 1992. *The Debt Boomerang: How Third World Debt Harms Us All* (London: Pluto).

Gereffi, G. & Korzeniewicz, M., 1994. *Commodity Chains and Global Capitalism* (Westport: Praeger).

Getzler, I., 2002. *Kronstadt, 1917–1921: The Fate of a Soviet Democracy* (Cambridge: Cambridge University Press).

Ghai, D., Kay, C. & Peek, P., 1988. *Labour and Development in Rural Cuba* (Basingstoke: Macmillan).

Gilderhus, M., 2000. *The Second Century: US Latin American Relations Since 1889* (Wilmington, Delaware: Scholarly Resources Inc.).

Gill, S. & Law, D., 1988. *The Global Political Economy* (New York: Harvester).

Gills, B., Rocamora, J. & Wilson, R. (eds), 1993. *Low Intensity Democracy: Political Power in the New World Order* (London: Pluto).

Glyn, A. (ed.), 2001. *Review of Social Democracy in Neoliberal Times: The Left and Economic Policy since 1980* (Oxford: Oxford University Press).

Glyn, A. & Harrison, J., 1980. *The British Economic Disaster* (London: Pluto).

Gould, C., 1990. *Rethinking Democracy: Freedom and Social Co-operation in Politics, Economy and Society* (Cambridge: Cambridge University Press).

Gould, S., 1996. *The Mismeasure of Man* (New York: Norton).

Gramsci, A., 1958. *El Materialismo Histórico y la Filosofía de Benedetto Croce*, trans. Flaumbaum, I. (Buenos Aires: Lautaro).

Gramsci, A., in Hoare, Q. & Nowell-Smith, G. (eds), 1971. *Selections from the Prison Notebooks of Antonio Gramsci* (London: Lawrence & Wishart).

Green, D., 1995. *Silent Revolution: The Rise of Market Economics in Latin America* (London: Cassel/Latin America Bureau).

Greider, W., 1993. *Who Will Tell the People: The Betrayal of American Democracy* (New York: Simon & Schuster).

Guehénno, J.M., 1996. *The End of the Nation State*, trans. Elliott, V. (Minneapolis: University of Minnesota Press).

Guevara, E., 1967. *Man and Socialism in Cuba* (Havana: Guairas Book Institute).

Guevara, E., 1968. *Venceremos: The Speeches and Writings of Che Guevara* (New York: Simon & Schuster).

Gutierrez, P., 2001. *Dirty Havana Trilogy* (London: Faber & Faber).

Gutierrez, P., 2003. *Tropical Animal* (London: Faber & Faber).

Gwynne, R. & Kay, C. (eds), 1999. *Latin America Transformed: Globalisation and Modernity* (London: Arnold).

Habel, J., 1989. *The Revolution in Peril* (London: Verso Press).

Hacker, J., 2006. *The Great Risk Shift: The Assault on American Jobs, Families, Health Care, and Retirement and How You Can Fight Back* (New York: Oxford University Press).

Hadenius, A., 1992. *Democracy and Development* (Cambridge: Cambridge University Press).

Hahn, J., 1988. *Soviet Grassroots: Citizen Participation in Local Soviet Government* (Princeton: Princeton University Press).

Halebsky, S., et al. (eds), 1992. *Cuba in Transition: Crisis and Transformation* (Boulder: Westview Press).

Harnecker, M., 1979. *Cuba: Dictatorship or Democracy* (Connecticut: Lawrence Hill).

Harnecker, M., 1986. *La Estratégia Política de Fidel* (México: Nuestro Tiempo).

Harnecker, M., 2003. *Landless People: Building a Social Movement* (São Paulo: Editora Expressão Popular).

Harvey, D., 1982. *The Limits to Capital* (Cambridge, MA: Blackwell).

Harvey, D., 1990. *The Condition of Postmodernity* (Oxford: Blackwell).

Held, D., 1993. *Models of Democracy* (Cambridge: Polity Press).

Held, D., McGrew, A. et al., 1999. *Global Transformations* (Cambridge: Polity Press).

Helleiner, E., 1994. *States and the Reemergence of Global Finance* (Ithaca, NY: Cornell University Press).

Hellinger, D., 1991. *Venezuela: Tarnished Democracy* (Boulder: Westview Press).

Hennessy, A. & Lambie, G. (eds), 1993. *The Fractured Blockade: West European-Cuban Relations During the Revolution* (Basingstoke: Macmillan).

Hinkelammert, F., 1990. *Democrácia y totalitarismo* (San José, Costa Rica: Departamento Ecuménico de Investigaciones).

Hirst, P., 1994. *Associative Democracy: New Forms of Economic and Social Governance* (Cambridge: Polity Press).

Hirst, P. & Thompson, G., 1996. *Globalisation in Question: The International Economy and the Possibilities* (Cambridge: Polity Press).

Hobbes, T., 1991 [1651]. *Leviathan.* Tuck, R. (ed.), (Cambridge: Cambridge University Press).

Holden, B., 1988. *Understanding Liberal Democracy* (Oxford: Philip Allen Publishers).

Holland, S., 1975. *The Socialist Challenge* (London: Quartet Books).

Holloway, J., 2002. *Change the World Without Taking Power* (London: Pluto).

Hoogvelt, A., 1997. *Globalisation and the Postcolonial World: The New Political Economy of Development* (Basingstoke: Macmillan).

Horkheimer, M., 1974. *The Eclipse of Reason* (London: Continuum International Publishing Group).

Howells, J. & Wood, M., 1992. *The Globalisation of Production and Technology* (London & New York: Belhaven Press).

Huntington, S., 1991. *The Third Wave: Democratization in the Late Twentieth Century* (Norman: University of Oklahoma Press).

Hutton, W., 2007. *The Writing on the Wall: China and the West in the 21st Century* (New York: Little Brown).

Hymer, S., 1979. *The Multinational Corporation: A Radical Approach* (Cambridge: Cambridge University Press).

Kapcia, A., 2000. *Cuba: Island of Dreams* (Oxford: Berg).

Karol, K.S., 1971. *Guerrillas in Power* (London: Jonathan Cape).

Keynes, J. M., 1980. *The Collected Writings of J.M. Keynes*. Vol. 26., Moggeridge, D. (ed.), (Cambridge: Cambridge University Press).

Kiely, R. & Marfleet, P., 1998. *Globalisation and the Third World* (London: Routledge).

Klein, N., 2007. *The Shock Doctrine: The Rise of Disaster Capitalism* (London: Metropolitan Books).

Klepak, H., 2005. *Cuba's Military 1990–2005: Revolutionary Soldiers During Counter-Revolutionary Times* (New York: Palgrave Macmillan).

Korton, D., 1995. *When Corporations Rule the World* (Connecticut: Kumarin Press).

Kropotkin, P., 1989. *Memoirs of a Revolutionist (Collected Works of Peter Kropotkin).* Woodcock, G. (ed.), (Montreal: Black Rose Books).

Lambie, G., 1993. *El Pensamiento Político de César Vallejo y la Guerra Civil Española* (Lima: Editorial Milla Batres).

Latell, B., 2005. *After Fidel: The Inside Story of Castro's Regime and Cuba's Next Leader* (London: Palgrave Macmillan).

Le Bon, G., 1895. *La psychologie des foules*. English trans. 1896. *The Crowd: A Study of the Popular Mind* (New York: Macmillan).

Lenin, V.I., 1972. *Selected Works*, 45 vols. (Moscow: Progress Publishers).

Lenin, V.I., 2004 [1917]. *The State and Revolution* (Whitefish: Kessinger Publishing).

León, O., Burch, S. & Tamayo, E., 2001. *Movimientos Sociales en la Red* (Quito: Agencia Latinoamericana de Información).

Leval, G., 1975. *Collectives in the Spanish Revolution* (London: Freedom Press).

Leys, C., 1996. *The Rise and Fall of Development Theory* (Bloomington: Indiana University Press).

Linz, J. & Stepan, A., 1996. *Problems of Democratic Transition and Consolidation* (Baltimore: Johns Hopkins University Press).

Lipietz, A., 1992. *Towards a New Economic Order: Postfordism, Ecology and Democracy* (London: Polity Press).

Lippmann, W., 1922. *Pubic Opinion* (New York: Macmillan).

Locke, J., 1987 [1689]. *Two Treatises of Government* (Boston: Unwin Hyman).

López, J., 2002. *Democracy Delayed: The Case of Castro's Cuba* (Baltimore: Johns Hopkins University Press).

Macpherson, C., 1962. *The Political Theory of Possessive Individualism: Hobbes to Locke* (Oxford: Clarendon Press).

Maddison, A., 1982. *Phases of Capitalist Development* (Oxford: Oxford University Press).

Mandel, E., 1978. *Late Capitalism* (London: Verso).

Mannheim, K., 1936. *Ideology and Utopia: An Introduction to the Sociology of Knowledge*, trans. Wirth, L. & Shils, E. (London: Routledge).

Marcuse, H., 1992 [1964]. *One-Dimensional Man: Studies in the Ideology of Advanced Industrial Society* (Boston: Beacon Press).

Mariátegui, J.C., 1959 [1927]. 'La Escena Contemporánea', in *Obras Completas*, edited and reprinted by Sandro, S., Carlos, J. & Chiappe, J.M. (20 vols.), vol. 1 (Lima: Biblioteca Amauta).

Mariátegui, J.C., 1959 [1927]. Siete Ensayos de Interpretación de la Realidad Peruana, *Obras Completas*, op. cit., vol. 2.

Mariátegui, J.C., 1959 [1927]. 'Peruanicemos al Perú', *Obras Completas,* op. cit., vol.11.

Marshall, P., 1987. *Cuba Libre. Breaking the Chains* (London: Gollancz).

Martin, H.P. & Schumann, H., 1997. *The Global Trap: Globalisation and the Assault on Democracy and Prosperity* (London: Zed Books).

Martínez Puentes, S., 2003. *Cuba: Más Allá de los Sueños* (Havana: Editorial José Martí).

Martínez-Alier, J., 1977. *Haciendas, Plantations, and Collective Farms: Agrarian Class Societies, Cuba and Peru* (London: Frank Cass).

Marx, K., 1926. *The Poverty of Philosophy* (London: Lawrence & Wishart).

Marx, K. & Engels, F., 1968. *Selected Works*, 50 vols. (Moscow: Progress Publishers).

Marx, K., 1972. *Capital*, vol. 3 (London: Lawrence & Wishart).

Mason, P., 2007. *Live Working or Die Fighting: How the Working Class Went Global* (London: Harvill Secker).

McCaughan, M., 2004. *The Battle of Venezuela* (London: Latin America Bureau).

McNally, D., 1993. *Against the Market: Political Economy, Market Socialism and the Marxist Critique* (London: Verso).

Mendez-Tovar, C., 1995. *¿Democracia en Cuba?* (Havana: Editorial José Martí).

Mesa-Lago, C., 1978. *Cuba in the 1970s: Pragmatism and Institutionalistion* (Albuquerque: University of New Mexico Press).

Mesa-Lago, C. (ed.), 1993. *Cuba after the Cold War* (Pittsburgh: University of Pittsburgh Press).

Midgley, M., 1978. *Beast and Man: The Roots of Human Nature* (Ithaca: Cornell University Press).

Milward, A., 1984. *The Reconstruction of Western Europe, 1945–51* (London: Methuen).

Moffitt, M., 1983. *The World's Money: International Banking from Bretton Woods to the Brink of Insolvency* (New York: Simon & Schuster).

Moore-Lappe, F. & Du Bois, P., 1994. *The Quickening of America: Rebuilding our Nation, Remaking our Lives* (San Francisco: Jossey-Bass).

Moore-Lappe, F., Collins, J. & Rosset, P., 1998. *World Hunger: 12 Myths* (New York: Grove Press).

Morley, M., 1987. *Imperial State and Revolution: The United States and Cuba 1952–1986* (Cambridge: Cambridge University Press).

Munck, R., 1989. *Latin America: the Transition to Democracy* (London: Zed Books).

Munck, R., 2002. *Globalisation and Labour: The New 'Great Transformation'* (London: Zed Books).

Nwabueze, B., 1993. *Democratisation* (Nigeria: Spectrum Law Publishing).

O'Brian, R., 1992. *Global Financial Integration: The End of Geography* (London: Pinter).

Ohmae, K., 1990. *The Borderless World* (London: Collins).

Ortega y Gasset, J., 1994. *The Revolt of the Masses* (New York: W.W. Norton & Company).

Orwell, G., 1979. *Homage to Catalonia* (London: Penguin Modern Classics).

Paterson, T., 1994. *Confronting Castro: The United States and the Triumph of the Cuban Revolution* (Oxford: Oxford University Press).

Paz, A., 1976. *Durruti: The People Armed* (London: Black Rose Books).

Pérez, L., 1988. *Cuba: Between Reform and Revolution* (Oxford: Oxford University Press).

Pérez, L., 1999. *On Becoming Cuban: Identity, Nationality and Culture* (Chapel Hill: University of North Carolina Press).

Pérez-López, J., 1994. *Cuba at a Crossroads* (Gainesville: University Press of Florida).

Pérez-Stable, M., 1993. *The Cuban Revolution: Origins, Course, and Legacy* (Oxford: Oxford University Press).

Perkins, J., 2005. *Confessions of an Economic Hit Man* (London: Ebury Press).

Petras, J., 2007. *Rulers and Ruled in the US Empire: Bankers, Zionists, Militants* (Atlanta, GA: Clarity Press).

Petras, J. & Morley, M., 1992. *Latin America in the Time of Cholera. Electoral Politics, Market Economics, and Permanent Crisis* (New York: Routledge).

Petras, J. & Veltmeyer, H., 2005. *Social Movements and State Power: Argentina, Brazil, Bolivia, Ecuador* (London: Pluto Press).

Pinkney, R., 1993. *Democracy in the Third World* (Oxford: Oxford University Press).

Piore, M. & Sabel, C., 1984. *The Second Industrial Divide* (New York: Basic Books).

Poppino, R., 1964. *International Communism in Latin America: A History of the Movement, 1917–1963* (Toronto: Free Press of Glencoe).

Pourgerami, A., 1991. *Development and Democracy in the Third World* (Boulder: Westview Press).

Raby, D., 2006. *Democracy and Revolution: Latin America and Socialism Today* (London: Pluto Press).

Redwood, J., 1994. *The Global Marketplace* (London: HarperCollins).

Reich, R., 1991. *The Work of Nations: Preparing Ourselves for 21st. Century Capitalism* (New York: Vintage Books).

Ritter, A. (ed.), 2004. *The Cuban Economy* (Pittsburg: University of Pittsburg Press).

Robinson, W., 1996(a). *Promoting Polyarchy: Globalisation, US Intervention and Hegemony* (Cambridge: Cambridge University Press).

Robinson, W., 2003. *Transnational Conflicts: Central America, Social Change, and Globalisation* (London: Verso).

Robinson, W., 2004(a). *A Theory of Global Capitalism: Production, Class, and State in a Transnational World* (Baltimore: Johns Hopkins University Press).

Robinson, W., 2008. *Latin America and Global Capitalism: A Critical Globalisation Perspective* (Baltimore: Johns Hopkins University Press).

Roca, S., 1976. *Cuban Economic Policy and Ideology: The Ten Million Ton Sugar Harvest* (New York: Sage).

Rodríguez, J. & Carrizo Moreno, G., 1987. *Eradicación de la pobreza en Cuba* (Havana: Editorial de Ciencias Sociales).

Rodrik, D., 1999. *The New Global Economy and Developing Countries: Making Openness Work* (Baltimore: Johns Hopkins University Press).

Roelofs, M., 1992. *The Poverty of American Politics* (Philadelphia: Temple University Press).

Roland, R., 1915. *Au-dessus de la Mêlée* (Paris: Société d'Éditions Littéraires et Artistiques)

Roman, P., 1999. *People's Power: Cuba's Experiment with Representative Government* (Boulder: Westview Press).

Rose, S., Kamin, B. & Lewontin, R., 1984. *Not in Our Genes* (Harmondsworth: Penguin).

Rosset, P. & Benjamin, M. (eds), 1994. *The Greening of the Revolution: Cuba's Experiment with Organic Agriculture* (Melbourne: Ocean Press).

Rostow, W.W., 1960. *The Stages of Economic Growth: A Non-Communist Manifesto* (Cambridge: Cambridge University Press).

Rothkopf, D., 2008. *Superclass: The Global Power Elite and the World They Are Making* (New York: Farrar, Straus & Giroux).

Rousseau, J.-J., 1978 [1762]. *On the Social Contract with Geneva Manuscript and Political Economy* (New York: St Martin's Press).

Rousseau, J.-J., 1979 [1762]. *Emile, or On Education.* (New York: Basic Books).

Rousseau, J.-J., 2009 [1755]. *Discourse on Political Economy and the Social Contract* (Oxford: Oxford University Press).

Rueschemeyer, D., Huber Stevens, E. & Stevens, J., 1992. *Capitalist Development and Democracy* (Cambridge: Polity Press).

Saney, I., 2004. *Cuba: A Revolution in Motion* (London: Zed Books).

Scheer, R. & Zeitlin, M., 1964. *Cuba: An American Tragedy* (Harmondsworth: Penguin).

Schiller, H., 1996. *Information Inequality* (New York: Routledge).

Scholte, J.A., 2000. *Globalisation: A Critical Introduction* (London: Palgrave).

Schulkind, E. (ed.), 1974. *The Paris Commune of 1871: The View from the Left* (New York: Grove Press).

Schumpeter, J., 1942. *Capitalism, Socialism and Democracy* (New York: Harper).

Servan-Schreiber, J.J., 1968. *The American Challenge* (London: Hamish Hamilton).

Shafer, D., 2005. *The Paris Commune* (London: Palgrave Macmillan).

Shearman, P., 1987. *The Soviet Union and Cuba* (London: Routledge & Kegan).

Siekmeier, J., 1999. *Aid, Nationalism, and Inter-American Relations: Guatemala, Bolivia and the United States, 1945–1961* (New York: The Edward Mellon Press).

Silverman, B., 1971. *Man and Socialism in Cuba* (New York: Atheneum).

Sinclair, A., 1970. *Guevara* (London: Fontana).

Singh, K., 1998. *The Globalisation of Finance: A Citizen's Guide* (London: Zed Books).

Skidmore, T. & Smith, P., 2005. *Modern Latin America* (London: Oxford University Press).

Sklair, L., 1995. *Sociology of the Global System* (Baltimore: Johns Hopkins University Press).

Sklair, L., 2001. *The Transnational Capitalist Class* (London: Blackwell).

Smith, A., 1904 [1776]. *An Inquiry into the Nature and Causes of the Wealth of Nations*, vol. I. Cannan, E. (ed.), (London: Methuen).

Smith, A., 2007. *The Theory of Moral Sentiments* (Mineola, NY: Dover Publications)

Soros, G., 1998. *The Crisis of Global Capitalism* (London: Little, Brown and Company).

Stiglitz, J., 2002. *Globalisation and Its Discontents* (London: Allen Lane).

Strange, S., 1988. *States and Markets: An Introduction to International Political Economy* (London: Pinter).

Strange, S., 1996. *Casino Capitalism* (Oxford: Basil Blackwell).

Stubbs, R. & Underhill, G., 1994. *Political Economy and the Changing Global Order* (Basingstoke: Macmillan).

Taber M. (ed), 1983. *Fidel Castro's Speeches*, vol. 2 (New York: Pathfinder Press).

Talmon, J., 1970. *The Origins of Totalitarian Democracy* (New York: W.W. Norton).

Thomas, H., 1971. *Cuba: or the Pursuit of Freedom* (New York: Harper & Row).

Thomas, H., 1979. *The Spanish Civil War* (Middlesex: Penguin).

Thomson, R., 1998. *Apocalypse Roulette: The Lethal World of Derivatives* (Basingstoke: Macmillan).

Tombs, R., 1999. *The Paris Commune 1871* (London: Longman).

Toynbee, P., 2003. *Hard Work: Life in Low Pay Britain* (London: Bloomsbury).

Tucker, R., 1992. *Stalin in Power: The Revolution from Above, 1928–1941* (New York: W.W. Norton & Co.).

Vallejo, C., 1938. *España, aparta de mí este cáliz*, in Eshleman, C. (ed.), 1978. *César Vallejo: The Complete Posthumous Poetry* (Berkeley: University of California Press): 221–286.

Van der Pijl, K., 1999. *Transnational Classes and International Relations* (London: Routledge).

Watson, H. (ed.), 1994. *The Caribbean in the Global Political Economy* (Boulder: Lynne Rienner).

Wayne, M., 2003. *Marxism and Media Studies: Key Concepts and Contemporary Trends* (London: Pluto Press).

Weber, M., 1978. *Economy and Society*, 2 vols. (Berkeley: University of California Press).

Webster, F., 1995. *Theories of the Information Society* (London: Routledge).

Weiss, L., 1998. *The Myth of the Powerless State* (Ithaca, NY: Cornell University Press).

White, S., Gardner, J. & Schopflin, G., 1987. *Communist Political Systems: An Introduction* (London: Macmillan Education).

Wickham Jones, M., 1996. *Economic Strategy and the Labour Party: Politics and Policy-Making 1970–1983* (Basingstoke: Macmillan).

Wilkinson, R., 2005. *The Impact of Inequality: How to Make Sick Societies Healthier* (New York: New Press).

Wolf, M., 2004. *Why Globalization Works* (New Haven: Yale University Press).

Wriston, W., 1992. *The Twilight of Sovereignty* (New York: Charles Scribner & Sons).

Zimbalist, A. & Brundenius, C., 1989. *The Cuban Economy. Measurement and Analysis of Socialist Performance* (Baltimore: Johns Hopkins University Press).

ARTICLES

Aguirre, B., 1998. 'Culture of Opposition in Cuba', *Cuba in Transition*, no. 8: 326–343.

Alarcón, R., 1999. 'The Cuban Miracle and its Future', *Tricontinental*, no. 141:15–17.

Alvarez, J., 2004. 'The Issue of Food Security in Cuba', Institute of Food and Agricultural Sciences, University of Florida.

Amaro, N., 1996. 'Decentralization, Local Government and Citizen Participation in Cuba'. *Cuba in Transition*, no. 6: 262–282.

Anderson, B., 2004. 'In the World-Shadow of Bismarck and Nobel', *New Left Review*, no. 28, July–August: 85–129.

Arnson, C., 2007. 'Introduction' in *The New Left and Democratic Governance in Latin America*, Arnson, C. & Perales, J. (Washington, DC: International Center for Scholars, Latin American Program).

Arreola, G., 2007. 'Abren el debate en Cuba sobre la censura de los 70', *La Jornada* (Mexico) 6 February.

Axworthy, T., 1992. 'Democracy and Development: Luxury or Necessity?', in Bauzon, K. (ed.), *Development and Democratisation in the Third World* (London: Taylor & Francis): 111–118.

Barnevik, P., 2001. 'Growth Spur', *World Link: The Magazine of the World Economic Forum*, September/October: 36–39.

Barry, M., 2000. 'Effects of the U.S. Embargo and Economic Decline on Health in Cuba', *Annals of Internal Medicine*, 132 (2): 151–4.

Berrigan, F. & Wingo, J., 2005. 'The Bush Effect: U.S. Military Involvement in Latin America Rises, Development and Humanitarian Aid Fall', *World Policy Institute*, 5 November.

Binns, P. & González, M., 1980. 'Cuba, Castro and Socialism', *International Socialism*, 2:8 (Spring): 1–36.

Birns, L. & James, M., 2002. 'Is the "New Left" Simply More of the Same, or a New Political Force in Latin America?' (Washington, DC: Council on Hemispheric Affairs), November.

Blackburn, R., 1963. 'Prologue to the Cuban Revolution', *New Left Review*, 1/21, October: 52–90.

Blackburn, R., 1980. 'Class Forces in the Cuban Revolution. A Reply to Peter Binns and Mike González', *International Socialism*, 2:9 (Summer):81–93.

Boadle, A., 2003. 'Cuba Necesita Crecer para Mantenerse Socialista', *Reuters*, 25 July.

Borger, J. & Goni, U., 2005. 'Bush Feels Hand of God as Poll Ratings Slump', *Guardian*, 5 November.

Borosage, R., 2000. 'Beneath the Divide', *The Nation*, November.

Brundenius, C., 1985. 'Cuba: Redistribution and Growth with Equity', in Halebsky, S., & Kirk, J.M. (eds), *Cuba: Twenty-Five Years of Revolution, 1959–1984* (New York: Praeger): 43–58.

Burchardt, H., 1995. 'La Economía Submergida: ¿De la Ileglidad al Programa?', in Kohut, K. & Mertins, G. (eds), *Cuba en 1995: Un Diálogo entre Investigadoes Alemanes y Cubanos* (Augsburg): 13–19.

Burnham, P., 1991. 'Neo-Gramscian Hegemony and the International Order', *Capital and Class*, 45:73–93.

Cammack, P., 2002(a). 'Neoliberalism, the World Bank, and the New Politics of Development', in Kothari, U. & Minogue, M. (eds), *Development Theory and Practice: Critical Perspectives* (London: Palgrave): 157–178.

Cammack, P., 2002(b). 'The Mother of all Governments: The World Bank's Matrix for Global Governance', in Hughes, S. & Wilkinson, R. (eds), *Global Governance: Critical Perspectives* (London: Routledge): 36–53.

Cammack, P., 2003. 'The Governance of Global Capitalism', *Historical Materialism*, vol. 2, no. 2: 37–59.

Cammack, P., 2004. 'What the World Bank Means by Poverty Reduction and Why it Matters', *New Political Economy*, vol. 9, no. 2: 189–211.

Cancio Isla, W., 2006. 'En crisis la salud en Cuba por misiones de médicos', *El Nuevo Herald*, 6 January.

Capital & Class, 2005. Special edition 'Change the World Without Taking Power', no. 85, Spring.

Carr, B., 1998. 'From Caribbean Backwater to Revolutionary Opportunity: Cuba's Evolving Relationship with the Comintern, 1925–34' in Rees, T., & Thorpe, A. (eds), *International Communism and the Communist International 1919–43* (Manchester: Manchester University Press): 234–253.

Carty, V., 2003. 'New Social Movements and the Struggle for Workers' Rights in the Maquila Industry', *Theory and Science*, International Consortium for the Advancement of Academic Publication (ICAAP).

Castro, F., 1987. 'A Historic Moment, Two Speeches by Castro', in *New International*, issue 6: 220–226.

Castro, F., 2008–2010. 'Reflections of President Fidel Castro', *Granma*, various issues.

Cerny, P., 1996. 'International Finance and the Erosion of State Policy Capacity', in Grummett, P. (ed.), *Globalisation and Public Policy* (Cheltenham: Edward Elgar, Studies in International Political Economy): 83–104.

Chanan, M., 2001. 'Cuba and Civil Society, or Why Cuban Intellectuals are Talking About Gramsci', *Nepantla: Views from the South*, 2: 387–406.

Cibils, A., 2003. 'Argentina's IMF Agreement: The Dawn of a New Era?', *Foreign Policy in Focus*, Washington, DC, October.

Claudio, L., 1999. 'The Challenge for Cuba', *Environmental Heath Perspectives*, 107 (5): 246–251.

Collier, D. & Levitsky, S., 1997. 'Democracy with Adjectives: Conceptual Innovation in Comparative Research', *World Politics*, 49 (3): 430–451.

Constant, B., 1988. 'Principles of Politics Applicable to all Representative Governments', in Fontana, B. (ed.), *Constant: Political Writings*, (Cambridge: Cambridge Texts in the History of Political Thought): 169–305.

Cornia, G., 2001. 'Globalization and health: results and options', *WHO*, 79 (9): 834–841.

Cox, R., 1981. 'Social Forces, States and World Orders: Beyond International Relations Theory', *Millennium: Journal of International Studies*, 10 (2): 126–155.

Cox, R., 1983. 'Gramsci, Hegemony and International Relations', *Millenium: Journal of International Studies*, 12 (2): 162–175.

Cox, R., 1993. 'Structural Issues of Global Governance: Implications for Europe' in Gill, S. (ed.), *Gramsci, Historical Materialism and International Relations* (Cambridge: Cambridge University Press).

Cushion, S., 2009. 'Organised Labour Under Batista', *The International Journal of Cuban Studies*, 3 (2), 1.

Daily Telegraph, 2009. 'Raul Castro: Cuba will Never Renounce the Revolution', 2 August.

Daily Worker, 1953. (New York) 10 August.

De Vos, C., & Wim De Stuyft, P., 2006. 'Colombia and Cuba, Contrasting Models in Latin America's Health Sector Reform', *Tropical Medicine & International Health,* vol. 11, no. 10, October: 1604–1612.

Dilla, H., 1999. 'Comrades and Investors: the Uncertain Transition in Cuba', *Socialist Register*, 35.

Dilla, H., 2000. 'The Cuban Experiment. Economic Reform, Social Restructuring, and Politics'. *Latin American Perspectives* 27(1): 33–44.

Dilla, H., 2002. 'The Virtues and Misfortunes of Civil Society in Cuba', *Latin American Perspectives*, 29(4): 11–30.

Dollar, D., 2002. 'Is globalization good for your health', *Bulletin of the World Health Organisation*, 79: 832–833.

Dominguez, J., 1996. 'La Democracia en Cuba: ¿Cuál es el Modelo Deseable?, in Dilla, H. (ed.), *La Democracia en Cuba y el Diferenciado con los Estados Unidos*, (Havana, Editorial de Ciencias Sociales): 117–129.

Drucker, P., 1983. 'Schumpeter or Keynes'?, *Forbes*, 23 May: 124–128.

Eberstadt, N., 2008. 'Rising Ambitions, Sinking Population', *New York Times*, 28 October.

Eckstein, S., 1997. 'The Limits of Socialism in a World Capitalist Economy: Cuba Since the Collapse of the Soviet Bloc', in Centeno, M. & Font, M. (eds), *Toward a New Cuba? Legacies of a Revolution* (Boulder: Lynne Rienner): 193–217.

The Economist, 1997. 'Global Investment Banks', 13 December.

The Economist, 2008(a), 'Castro's Legacy', 23 February.

The Economist, 2008(b). 'Eastern Europe. Who's Next'?, 23 October.

Espina Prieto, M., 1997. 'Transformaciones Recientes de la Estructura Socioclasista Cubana', *Papeles*, 52, Universidad Autónoma de Barcelona : 83–99.

Espinosa, J. C., 1999. 'Civil Society in Cuba: the Logic of Emergence in Comparative Perspective'. *Cuba in Transition*, 9: 346–367.

Executive Intelligence Review, 1995. 'The São Paulo Forum. Castro's Shocktroops', 10 November.

Fawthrop, T., 2006. 'New Face of Cuba's Castro Dynasty', *The Scotsman*, 9 December.

Feinsilver, J., 1989. 'Cuba as a "World Medical Power": The Politics of Symbolism', *Latin American Research Review*, vol. XXIV, no. 2: 1–34.

Fernández, H. & Ortazo, R., 1996. 'Comunidad, Autogestión, Participación y Medio Ambiente', in Dilla, H. (ed.), *La Participación en Cuba y los Retos del Futuro* (Havana: Ediciones CEA): 225–239.

Forero, J., 2005. 'Chávez Restyles Venezuela with "21st-Century Socialism"', *New York Times*, 30 October,

Forero, J., 2007. 'Cubans on Medical Aid Mission Flee Venezuela, but Find Limbo', *Washington Post*, 20 February.

Frank, M., 2004 (a). 'Havana Plans Crackdown on Army of Self-Employed', *Financial Times*, 2 June.

Frank, M., 2004(b). 'Anti-Corruption Drive Signals Change in Cuba', *Financial Times*, 6 July.

Fuentes, F., 2010. 'Venezuela: New Moves to Build People's Power', *Green Left Weekly* (Australia), 24 March.

Fukuyama, F., 1989. 'The End of History', *The National Interest*, Summer: 3–18.

Goldberg, M., Gorn, G., Peracchio, L. & Bomossy, G., 2003. 'Materialism Among Youth', *Journal of Consumer Psychology*, vol. 13, no.3: 278–288.

Goldfrank, W., 1977. 'Who Rules the World? Class Formation at the International Level', *Quarterly Journal of Ideology*, 1/2: 32–37.

Gordon, J., 1997. 'Cuba's Entrepreneurial Socialism', *The Atlantic Monthly*, January.

Granma International, 2006. 'Almost Half a Million Patients Benefit from Operation Miracle', 20 November.

Granma International, 2010. 'Latin American School of Medicine Enrollment in Cuba Reaches 10,000', 16 March.

Greenwood, J. & Lambie, G., 1999. 'Local Government in Cuba: Democracy Through Participation', *Local Government Studies*, vol.25, no.1 (Spring): 55–74.

Guevara, E., 1960. 'Speech to Medical Students and Workers', in Deutschemann, D. (ed.), 1994. *Che: A Memoir by Fidel Castro* (Melbourne: Ocean Press).

Gunn, G., 1995. 'Cuba's NGOs: Government Puppets or Seeds of Civil Society'? *The Caribbean Project*, Washington, Georgetown University, Center for Latin American Studies.

Hansen, J., 1962. 'Trotskyism and the Cuban Revolution', *The Militant*, October.

Harris, J., 1998/99. 'Globalisation and the Technological Transformation of Capitalism', *Race and Class*, 40, 2/3: 21–34.

Hart, A., 1996. 'Socialismo, Democracia y Sociedad Civil'. *Habanera*, 3:15–21.

Hartlyn, J., 2003. 'Contemporary Latin America: Global Changes and Democratic Disenchantment', *Asian Journal of Latin American Studies*, vol. XVI, no. 2, December: 235–261.

Hennessy, A., 1963. 'The Roots of Cuban Nationalism', *International Affairs* (Royal Institute of International Affairs), vol. 39, no. 3 (July): 345–359.

Hennessy, A., 1964. 'Cuba, the Politics of Frustrated Nationalism', in Needler, J. (ed.), *Political Systems of Latin America* (Princeton: Van Nostrand Reinhold): 183–205.

Hennessy, A., 1988. 'Cuba: a Client State'?, in Calvert, P. (ed.), *The Central American Security System: North-South or East-West?* (Cambridge: Cambridge University Press), 75–91.

Hennessy, A., 1993. 'Cuba, Western Europe and the US: An Historical Overview', in Hennessy & Lambie (eds), *The Fractured Blockade*, op. cit.: 11–63.

Hernández, R., 1969. 'La Atencion Medica en Cuba Hasta 1958'. *Journal of Inter-American Studies*, vol XI, no. 4: 533–557.

Hernández, R. , 1994. 'La Sociedad Civil y sus Alrededores', *La Gaceta de Cuba*, enero-febrero.

Hernández, R., 2003. 'Looking at Cuba'. *Essays on Culture and Civil Society* (Gainesville: University Press of Florida).

Hernández, R., 2008. 'On Cuban Democracy: Cuba and the Democratic Culture', in Brenner et al., *Reinventing the Revolution, op. cit.*: 74–78.

Hernández, R. & Dilla, H., 1990. 'Cultura Política y Participación Popular en Cuba', in *Cuadernos de Nuestra América*, vol.VII, no.15, July–December: 101–115.

Hilary, J., 2008. 'Which India, Mr Brown?', *Guardian*, 21 January.

Huntington, S., 1975. 'The Democratic Distemper,' *The Public Interest*, Fall: 9–38.

Huntington, S., 1984. 'Will More Countries Become Democratic', *Political Science Quarterly*, 99, no. 2: 193–218.

Ibarra, J., 1995. 'Historiografía y Revolución', *Temas*, no. 1:5–17.

Kapcia, A., 1996. 'Politics in Cuba: Beyond the Stereotypes', *Bulletin of Latin American Research*, 15/2.

Keller, B., 1989. 'Gorbachev–Castro Face-Off: A Clash of Style and Policies', *New York Times*, 8 April.

Khrushchev, S., 2002. 'How my Father and President Kennedy Saved the World: The Missile Crisis as seen from the Kremlin', *American Heritage*, October.

Kirk, J., 1984. 'José Martí: Mentor of the Cuban Nation, *The Hispanic American Historical Review*, vol. 64, no. 2 (May): 388–389.

Kirk, J. & Kirk, J.M., 2010. 'Cuban Medical Co-operation in Haiti: One of the World's Best-Kept Secrets', *International Journal of Cuban Studies*, vol. 2, nos, 1 and 2, Spring/Summer.

Klebnikov, P., 2004. 'The 100 Richest Russians', *Forbes*, 23 July.

Kohan, N., 1997. 'El Che Guevara y la Filosofía de la Praxis', *America Libre* (July): 59–75.

Koont, S., 2004. 'Food Security in Cuba', *Monthly Review*, vol. 55, no. 8 (January).

Kraul, C., 2008. 'Healthcare in Venezuela takes Turn for Worse', *Los Angeles Times*, 8 April.

Kumar, S. & Sharma, S., 2004. 'Venezuela – Ripe for US Intervention', *Race and Class*, April–June: 61–74.

Kunz, D., 1994. 'When Money Counts and Doesn't: Economic Power and Diplomatic Objectives', *Diplomatic History*, vol. 18, no.4, Fall: 451–462.

Lambie, G., 1992. 'Marxismo: ¿Una Technología de la Revolución o una Filosophía de Praxis? Un Debate Entre Max Eastman y José Carlos Mariátegui', *Anuario Mariateguiano* , vol. 4, no.4 (Lima: Empresa Editora Amauta S.A.):107–120.

Lambie, G., 1993(a). 'De Gaulle's France and the Cuban Revolution', in Hennessy, A. & Lambie, G. (eds), *The Fractured Blockade*, (Basingstoke: Palgrave Macmillan): 197–233.

Lambie, G., 1993(b). 'Western Europe and Cuba in the 1970s: The Boom Years', in Hennessy, A. & Lambie, G. (eds.), *The Fractured Blockade*, op. cit.: 276–311.

Lambie, G., 1998. 'Cuban–European Relations: Historical Perspectives and Political Consequences', Occasional Papers, *Cuban Studies Association*, University of Miami, vol. 3, no.4: 1–38

Lambie, G., 1999(a). 'Vallejo's Interpretation of Spanish Culture and History in the Himno a los Voluntarios de la República', *Bulletin of Hispanic Studies*, LXXVI: 367–384.

Lambie, G., 1999(b). 'Reinforcing Participatory Democracy in Cuba: An Alternative Development Strategy', *Democratisation*, vol. 6, no.3, Autumn: 30–61.

Lambie, G., 2000. 'Intellectuals, Ideology and Revolution: The Political Ideas of César Vallejo', *Hispanic Research Journal*, vol.1, no. 2, June: 139–169.

Lambie, G., 2009(a). 'Nemesis of "Market Fundamentalism"? The Ideology, Deregulation and Crisis of Finance', *Contemporary Politics*, vol. 15, issue 2, June: 157–177.]

Lambie, G., 2009(b). 'Globalisation and the Cuban Revolution in the 21st Century', *European Review of Latin American and Caribbean Studies*, 86, April: 63–77.

Lambie, G., 2010, forthcoming. 'The Globalisation of Finance: Was there an "Alternative Economic Strategy"?

Landau, S., 2008. 'History Absolved Him. Now What?', in Brenner et al., *Reinventing the Revolution*, op. cit.:41–44.

Lenin, V.I., 1972. 'Lessons of the Commune', in *Selected Works* (Moscow: Progress Publishers), vol. 13: 475–478.

LeoGrande, W., 1989. 'Mass Political Participation in Socialist Cuba', in Brenner, P., LeoGrande, W., et al. (eds), *The Cuban Reader: The Making of a Revolutionary Society* (New York: Grove Press).

Leval, G., 1996. 'The Spanish Revolution: A New World in their Hearts', *Workers Solidarity*, 47, Spring.

Lipset, S., 1959. 'Some Social Requisites of Democracy: Economic Development and Political Legitimacy', *American Political Science Review*, vol. 53, issue 1 (March): 69–105.

Lipset, S., 1968. 'Robert Michels and the "Iron Law of Oligarchy", chapter 12 in *Revolution and Counterrevolution: Change and Persistence in Social Structures* (New York: Basic Books).

López, V., 1997. 'Sociedad Civil en Cuba', *Envio*, no. 184:17–40.

Lutjens, S., 1992. 'Democracy and Socialist Cuba', in *Cuba in Transition: Crisis and Transformation*, Halebsky, S., ct al. (eds), op.cit. : 55–76.

Mariátegui, J.C., 1959 [1929]. 'El problema de las razas en America Latina', in *Ideologia y Politica, Obras Completas*, op. cit., vol. 13: 21–86.

Martí, J., 2006 [1895]. 'The Revolution Desires Complete Freedom', Letter to Manuel Mercado, *Granma International*, Havana, 19 May.

Martínez Heredia, F., 1992. 'Cuban Socialism: Prospects and Challenges', in *The Cuban Revolution into the 1990s*, edited by Centro de Estudios Sobre América, Latin American Perspectives Series, no. 10 (Boulder: Westview Press): 61–78.

Martínez, O., 2006. 'ALBA y ALCA: El Dilemma de la Integración o la Anexión', Centre for the Study of the World Economy, *Centro de Investigaciones sobre la Economia Mundial* (CIEM), Havana.

Marx, K., 1968(a) [1871]. 'The Civil War in France', in *Marx & Engels, Selected Works* (Moscow: Progress Publishers), vol. 22: 252–311.

Marx, K., 1968(b) [1881]. Letter [22 Feb] to 'Domela Nieuwenhuis' in the Hague, in *Marx & Engels, Selected Works, op. cit.*, vol. 46.

Marx, K., 1968(c). 'Private Property and Communism', Economic and Philosophical Manuscripts of 1844, in *Marx & Engels, Selected Works*, op. cit., vol. 3: 293–305.

Marx, K., 1968(d) 'Critique of the Gotha Programme', in *Marx & Engels, Selected Works*, op. cit., vol. 3: 13–30.

Massardo, J., 1999. 'Antonio Gramsci, Ernesto Guevara: Dos Momentos de la Filosofia de al Praxis', *International Gramsci Society Newsletter*, no. 9, March.

Mayoral, M. & Rivery, J., 2004. 'Habra Muchas Alternativas para un Mundo Mejor', *Granma*, Havana, 30 January.

Mehta, S., 2007. 'Carlos Slim, the richest man in the world', *Fortune*, 20 August.

Mesa-Lago, C., 1981. 'Economics: Realism and Rationality' in Horowitz, I. (ed.), *Cuban Communism* (4th ed.), (New Brunswick: Transaction Books).

Miami Herald, 2006. 'Castro's Standing Tied to Leftists' Rise. The Cuban President's Stature Appears to be at its Highest in at Least 15 years, Elevated by Left-Leaning Latin American Presidents'. 4 June.

Miller, D., 1993. 'Deliberative Democracy and Social Choice', in Held, D. (ed.), *Prospects for Democracy: North, South, East and West* (Cambridge: Polity Press): 74–92.

Miller, N., 2003. 'The Absolution of History: Uses of the Past in Castro's Cuba', *Journal of Contemporary History* 38 (1):147–162.

Milne, D., 2007. 'America's Rasputin lives again', *Los Angeles Times*, 2 September: M4.

Moody, K., 1997. 'Towards an International Social Movement Unionism', *New Left Review*, 1/225, September/October: 52–72.

Moser, C. & Holland, J., 1997. 'Urban Poverty and Violence in Jamaica', *World Bank Latin American and Caribbean Studies*, Viewpoints, Washington, DC.

Murphy, C., 2000. 'Cultivating Havana: Urban Agriculture and Food Security in the Years of Crisis', *Development Report*, no. 12, Institute for Food and Development Policy (Oakland: Food First).

Nye, J. S. Jr., 2001. 'Globalization's Democratic Deficit: How to Make International Institutions More Accountable', *Foreign Affairs*, July-August: 37–47.

Palmisano, S., 2006. 'Multinationals Have Been Superseded', *Financial Times*, 12 June: 19.

Petras, J., 1973. 'Cuba, Fourteen Years of Revolutionary Government', in Thurbur, C. (ed.), *Development Administration in Latin America* (Durham, N.C: Duke University Press): 281–293.

Pollock, A. & Price, D., 2006. 'Privatising Primary Care', *British Journal of General Practice*, vol. 56, no. 529, August: 565–566.

Pratley, N., 2008. 'The Day the Ticking Time Bomb Went Off', *Guardian* (London), 16 September: 1–2.

Psacharopoulos, G. & Patrinos H. (eds), 1994. 'Indigenous People and Poverty in Latin America: An Empirical Analysis' (Washington: World Bank).

Raby, D., 2004. 'The Greening of Venezuela', *Monthly Review*, vol. 56, no. 6: 49–52.

Ramonet, I., 1998. 'The Politics of Hunger', *Le Monde Diplomatique*, November.

Recio Silva, M., 1999. 'Sociedad civil en los 90: el debate cubano', *Temas*, 16–17: 155–176.

Reddy, S. & Pogge, T., 2005. 'How Not to Count the Poor', in Anand, S. & Stiglitz, J. (eds), *Measuring Global Poverty* (Oxford: Oxford University Press).

Revolución, 1959. 'Esta Revolución no es Roja ... es "Verde Olivo", en Hicimos la Revolución para Arrancar Todos los Males, 22 May: 1–2.

Ritter, A., 1995. 'The Dual Currency Bifurcation of Cuba's Economy in the 1990s: Causes, Consequences and Cures', *Cepal Review*, 57:113–131.

Robinson, W., 1995. 'Pushing Polyarchy: the US–Cuba Case and the Third World', *Third World Quarterly*, vol. 16, no. 4: 643–659.

Robinson, W., 1996(b). 'Globalisation: nine theses on our epoch', *Race and Class*, 38/2: 13–30.

Robinson, W., 1998/99. 'Latin America and Global Capitalism', *Race and Class*, 40, no. 2/3: 111–131.

Robinson, W., 2004(b). 'Global Crisis and Latin America', *Bulletin of Latin American Research*, vol. 23, no. 2: 135–153.

Robinson, W., 2009. 'Cuba! Cuba! Cuba!', *Latin American Perspectives*, no. 36 January: 134–135.

Robinson, W. & Harris, J., 2000. 'Towards a Global Ruling Class? Globalisation and the Transnational Capitalist Class', *Science and Society*, vol. 64, no. 1, Spring: 11–54.

Roca, B., 1935. 'Forward to the Cuban Anti-Imperialist People's Front!', *The Communist* (New York), vol. 14, no. 10, October.

Rodríguez, J., 1988. 'Cubanology and the Provision of Basic Needs in the Cuban Revolution', in Zimbalist, A. (ed.), *Cuban Political Economy. Controversies in Cubanology*, (New York: Westview Press): 23–38.

Roman, P., 1995. 'Worker's Parliament in Cuba', *Latin American Perspectives*, 22/87: 43–58.

Rousseau, J.-J., 1993 [1754]. 'A Discourse on the Origin of Inequality' in *Jean-Jacques Rousseau. The Social Contract and Discourses*, trans. Cole, G.D.H. (London: Campbell Publishers): 31–125.

Rush, C., 2004. 'IMF Needs "Structural Reform"- Not Argentina', *Executive Intelligence Review*, 15 October.

Ryan, A. (ed.), 1993. 'Introduction' to Rousseau, J.-J., *The Social Contract and Discourses*, op. cit.: xiii–xlix.

San Martin, N., 2007. 'Cuba Seems to Urge Freer Press', *Miami Herald*, 16 January.

Schenk, C., 1998. 'The Origins of the Eurodollar Market in London: 1955–1963', *Explorations in Economic History*, 35: 221–238.

Sengupta, S., 2008. 'Inside Gate, India's Good Life; Outside, the Slums', *New York Times*, 9 June.

Silva, E., 1999. 'Authoritarianism, Democracy and Development' in Gwynne, R. & Kay, C. (eds), *Latin America Transformed, op. cit.*: 32–50.

Sklair, L., 1998. 'Social Movements and Global Capitalism', in Jameson, F. & Miyoshi, M. (eds), *The Cultures of Globalisation* (Durham: Duke University Press).

Smith, G., 2008. 'The Cuban Economy: After the Smoke Clears', *Business Week*, 10 March: 52–55.

Snow, A., 2006(a). 'Cuba's Raul Castro Signals More Openness', Associated Press, 21 December.

Snow, A., 2006(b). 'Raul Castro Speaks About Cuba Food Woes', Associated Press, 23 December.

Soros, G., 2010. 'The Full Soros Speech on 'Act II' of the Crisis', *New York Times* (Dealbook), 10 June.

Spiegel, J. & Yassi, A., 2004. 'Lessons from the Margins of Globalization: Appreciating the Cuban Health Paradox', *Journal of Public Health Policy*, 25:85–110.

Stein, B., 2006. 'In Class Warfare, Guess Which Class Is Winning', *New York Times*, 26 November.

Stiglitz, J., 2009. 'The Economic Crisis. Capitalist Fools', *Vanity Fair*, January.

Strange, S., 1990. 'The Name of the Game', in Rizopoulos, N. (ed.), *Sea Changes: American Foreign Policy in a World Transformed* (New York: Council on Foreign Relations): 238–273.

Sweig, J., 2007. 'Fidel's Final Victory. Cuba After Castro', *Foreign Affairs*, vol. 86, no. 1, Jan/Feb.

Traynor, I., 2003. 'The Privatisation of War', *Guardian* (London), 10 December.

UNICEF, 2005. 'Venezuela's Barrio Adentro: a Model of Universal Primary Health Care', *Immunization Plus Quarterly*, vol. 1, issue 1, Regional Office for Latin America and the Caribbean, July/March: 1–2.

Valante, M., 2005. 'Labour-Argentina: Working Without Bosses', Inter Press Service News Agency, Buenos Aires, 14 September.

Valdés, N.P., 2008. 'The Revolutionary and Political Content of Fidel Castro's Charismatic Authority', in Brenner, P., et al., *A Contemporary Cuba Reader*, op. cit.: 27–40.

Vallejo, C., 1937. 'Los Enunciados Populares de la Guerra Española', in Merino & Vélez (eds), *España en César Vallejo*, 1984, vol. 2. (Madrid: Fundamentos): 32–37.

Ventura de Jesus, 2005. 'Cuba and Venezuela: Cooperation Projects worth more than $800 million', *Granma International*, Havana, 6 October: 1–2.

Walzer, M., 1989. 'Citizenship', in Ball, T., et al. (eds), *Political Innovation and Conceptual Change* (Cambridge: Cambridge University Press): 211–220.

Warren, E., 2006. 'The Middle Class on the Precipice', *Harvard Magazine*, January–February.

Watson, H., forthcoming. 'Imperialism or Transnational Capitalism: Global Capitalism, Rogue State, and Latin America and the Caribbean'.

Weissert, W., 2007. 'Castro: If Youth Fail Everything Will', *Washington Post*, 24 June.

Wolf, M., 2000. 'The Big Lie of Global Inequality', *Financial Times*, 9 February.

Yaffe, D., 1973. 'The Crisis of Profitability: a Critique of the Glynn-Sutcliffe Thesis', *New Left Review*, 80 (July–August): 45–62.

Yanes, H., 2005. 'The Cuba–Venezuelan Alliance: "Emancipatory neo-Bolivarismo" or Totalitarian Expansion?', *Institute for Cuban & Cuban-American Studies*, Occasional Paper Series (University of Miami), December.

Zeitlin, M., 1969. 'Cuba: Revolution Without a Blueprint', *Transaction*, vol. 6, no. 6, April.

Zeitlin, M., 1970. 'Inside Cuba: Workers and Revolution' [interview conducted 1961], *Ramparts*, March: 31–42.

Zimbalist, A., 1992. 'Teetering on the Brink', *Cuba Business*, February: 8–10.

REPORTS

Anderson, S. & Cavanagh, J., 2000. 'Top 200: The Rise of Corporate Global Power', *Institute of Policy Studies* (Washington, DC.).

Associated Press, 2009. 'Bolivian Leader Joins in Tribute to Che Guevara' (La Paz), 9 October.

Associated Press, 2010. 'Cuba Trains Venezuela in Military', *Communications*, 1 June.

BBC News, 2008. 'South Africa Poverty "emergency"', 23 October.

Blanden, J., Gregg, P. & Machin, S., 2005. 'Intergenerational Mobility in Europe and North America', *Centre for Economic Performance*, London School of Economics.

Center for American Progress, 2007. 'The Poverty Epidemic in America, by the Numbers', 24 April.

Cuba Briefing, 2004–2010 (various issues, see text). A Caribbean Insight Publication (London).

Crisp, N., 2007. 'Global Health Partnerships. The UK Contribution to Health in Developing Countries', Department of Health, UK Government, London.

Economic Commission for Latin America and the Caribbean (ECLAC), 2004(a). 'Preliminary Overview of the Economies of Latin America and the Caribbean', December.

Economist Intelligence Unit (EIU), 2006–2009, Cuba Country Reports (London: The Economist).

Focus on Cuba, 2003. 'The Cuban Military in the Economy'. An Information Service of the Cuba Transition Project [US government funded], University of Miami, issue 46, 11 August.

González, A., et al., 2000. 'El Sector Agropecuario y las Política Agrícolas Ante los Nuevos Retos', Ministry of the Economy (Havana).

Latell, B., 2008. 'Raul's Mounting Crisis', The Latell Report, September, Institute for Cuban and Cuban American Studies, Miami.

Latinobarómetro, 2004. 'Una Década de Mediciones' (Santiago de Chile: Corporación Latinobarómetro)

Merrill Lynch & Capgemini, 2005 - 2007. 'World Wealth Report(s)' (New York).

Ministry of Finance and Prices, 1997. 'Cuba's Economic Reforms: Results and Future Prospects 1997', Havana. English edition Jenkins, G. (ed.), *Cuba Business* (London).

Organisation for Economic Co-operation and Development (OECD), 1996. Financial Market Trends 1992–1996 (Paris).

OECD, 1992. International Direct Investments: Policies and Trends in the 1980s (Paris).

Power Enquiry, 2006. 'Power to the People: the report of Power, an Independent Enquiry into Britain's Democracy' (London), February.

Soros, G., 2008. 'Statement before the U.S. House of Representatives Committee on Oversight and Government Reform', 13 November.

United Nations Development Programme (UNDP), Human Development Reports 1986– 2008 (New York).

UNDP 1996. Habitat II Report, Conference on Human Settlements (Istanbul), June.

United Nations International Children's Fund (UNICEF), 1997. 'The State of the World's Children'.

UNICEF, 2007. Child Poverty in Perspective. An overview of child well-being in rich countries (Florence: Innocenti Research Centre).

UNICEF, 2008. Country Statistics, Cuba.

United Nations – Economic Commision for Latin America and the Caribbean (UN-ECLAC), 2005 and 2009. Social Panorama of Latin America.

United Nations University, World Institute for Development Economics Research (WIDER), 2008.

Wan, G., 2008. 'Poverty Reduction in China: Is Growth Enough?', Policy Brief No. 4, United Nations University (WIDER).

Weisbrot, M., et al., 2001. 'The Emperor Has No Growth: Declining Economic Growth Rates in the Era of Globalisation', Center for Economic and Policy Research, Washington, DC.

World Bank, 2005(a). 'Regional Poverty Study. Eastern Europe and the CIS', (Poland).

World Bank, 2005(b). 'World Development Indicators, Latin America and the Caribbean'.

World Bank, 2005(c). 'Investing in Infrastructure: What is Needed from 2002–2010'?

PAPERS

Blaufuss, K., 2005. 'Claiming (neo-liberal?) Spaces: Development NGOs in Cuba', paper presented at IDPM, Manchester, 27–29 June.

Cerny, P., 1997. 'Globalisation and the Erosion of Democracy', paper presented at ECPR conference (Bern: Switzerland), 27 Feb. – 4 March.

Clift, R., 1999. 'General Agreement on Trade in Services (GATS) and Post-Secondary Education in Canada', Confederation of University Faculty Associations of British Columbia (CUFA/BC), November.

Gourinchas, P.O. & Rey, H., 2005. 'From World Banker to World Venture Capitalist: US External Adjustment and the Exorbitant Privilege', London: Centre for Economic Policy Research (CEPR).

Hammett, D., 2004. 'From Havana with Love: a Case Study of South-South Development Cooperation between South Africa in the Health Care Sector', *Centre of African Studies*, University of Edinburgh, Occasional Papers, No. 97.

Lambie, G., 1983. 'The Failure of Perón's Economic Policies in the Immediate Post-war Years: A Case of Internal Mismanagement or International Manipulation?', MA Dissertation, University of Liverpool.

Lambie, G., 2009(c). 'The Cuban Military and Society', paper presented at the Center for Strategic and International Studies (CSIS) conference, 'Cuba's Armed Forces and Security Aparatus', Washington, DC, 5 February.

Morris, E., 2002. 'What Economists Might Learn from Cuba, 1990–2000', paper presented at Society for Latin American Studies (SLAS) conference, University of East Anglia, 23 May.

Moses, J., 1996. 'Financial Strategies and Consequences for Cuba as it Engages the World Market', unpublished paper, July.

Moskow, A., 1995. 'The contribution of Urban Agriculture to Individual Control and Community Enhancement', Master's Dissertation, International Agricultural Development, University of California, UC Davis.

Padula, A., 1974. 'The Fall of the Bourgeoisie: Cuba, 1959–61', unpublished PhD thesis, University of New Mexico.

Pietroni, P., 2000. 'Cuban Health Care in Perspective', presentation to the Cuba Initiative Committee, 27 June (London: Department of Trade and Industry).

Piketty, T. & Saez, E., 2006. 'The Evolution of Top Incomes: A Historical and International Perspective', NBER Working Paper, 11955.

Raby, D., 2005. 'From Formal to Participatory Democracy: Venezuela Under Chávez', paper presented to the Society for Latin American Studies conference, Derby University, 8–10 April.

Robinson, W., 1999. 'Capitalist Globalisation and the Transnationalisation of the State', presented at a workshop entitled Historical Materialism and Globalisation, University of Warwick, 15–17 April.

Underhill, G., 2001. 'States, Markets and Governance: Private Interests, the Public Good and the Democratic Process', Inaugural Lecture (Professorship of International Governance), University of Amsterdam, Faculty of Social and Behavioural Sciences.

Watson, H., 1996. 'The Caribbean, Western Hemisphere Integration and Global Transformation', presented to the 20th Annual Conference of the Society for Caribbean Studies, London, 3–6 July.

Wilson, D., 1999. 'Exploring the Limits of Public Participation', a working paper based on research conducted for a Department of Education (UK - London) sponsored project entitled Enhancing Public Participation in Local Government.

WEBSITES

American Experience, 2009. 'Timeline: Post-Revolution Cuba'. www.pbs.org/wgbh/ amex/castro /time line/index.html. Accessed 8 June 2007.

Arreaza, T., 2004. 'ALBA: Bolivarian Alternative for Latin America and the Caribbean', Venezuelanalysis.com, 30 January, www.venezuelanalysis.com/analysis/339. Accessed 14 July 2008.

Bardham, P., 2005. 'China, India Superpower? Not so Fast!', *YaleGlobal*, 25 October, www.yaleglobal. yale.edu/display.article?id=6407. Accessed 13 June 2008.

Blunden, M., 2008. 'South-South Development Cooporation', *The International Journal of Cuban Studies*, Issue 1, London Metropolitan University, online, www.cubastudiesjournal.org/issue-1/articles/south-south-development-cooperation.cfm. Accessed 1 December 2008.

Boron, A., 1998. 'Democracy or Neoliberalism?' *Boston Review*, October/November, http://bostonreview.net/BR21.5/boron.html. Accessed 21 July 2008.

Castro, F., 2005. Speech given at the University of Havana, 17 November, www.granma.cu /documento /ingles05/17nov.html. Accessed 18 December 2009.

Cumbre de los Pueblos de América, 2005. '2005 Call to attend the III Peoples' Summit and Mass Mobilisations', 1–5 November, Mar del Plata, Argentina, www.cumbredelospueblos.org/article.php3?id_article=11. Accessed 23 Feb 2009.

Democracy Centre, 2000. 'Bolivia's War Over Water', www.democracyctr.org/waterwar. Accessed 24 July 2006.

Edwards, B., 2007. 'The Rise of Young Fogies', *Liberacion* (New Zealand), 22 August. http://liberation.typepad.com/liberation/2007/08/the-rise-of-the.html. Accessed 19 September 2009.

Farag, E., 2000. 'Cuban Healthcare: An Analysis of a Community-Based Model', The Ambassadors (Online Magazine), Vol.3, Issue 2, July. http://ambassadors.net/archives/issue 8/cuba_select.htm. Accessed 8 November 2007.

Feinsilver, J., 2006. 'Cuban Medical Diplomacy: When the Left Has Got it Right', Council on Hemispheric Affairs, www.coha.org/2006/10/cuban-medical-diplomacy-when-the-left-has-got-it-right/. Accessed 24 April 2009.

Freeman, R., 2005. 'What Really Ails Europe (and America): The Doubling of the Global Workforce', *The Globalist*, June. http://www.theglobalist.com/StoryId.aspx?Story Id=4542. Accessed 15 November 2007.

Freeman, R., 2010. 'Why Obama's Economic Plan Will Not Work – And a Better Plan', *Common Dreams*. http://www.commondreams.org/view /2010/01/17. Accessed 10 June 2008.

Hammond, J., 2009. 'Has the U.S. Played a Role in Fomenting Unrest During Iran's Election?', *Foreign Policy Journal*, 23 June.www.foreignpolicyjournal.com/2009/06/23/ has-the-u-s-played-a-role-in-fomenting-unrest-during-irans-election/. Accessed 21 August 2009.

James, D., 2005. 'Summit of the Americas, Argentina: Tomb of the FTTA', Common Dreams Newscentre. www.commondreams.org/views05/1123-22.htm. Accessed 23 November 2007.

Milanovic, B., 2008. 'Developing Countries Worse Off Than Once Thought – Part 1', *YaleGlobal*, 11 February. yaleglobal.yale.edu/display.article?id=10333. Accessed 13 June 2008.

Ministry of Defense (DCDC), 2007. http://www.mod.uk/NR/rdonlyres/94A1F45E-A830-49DB-B319-DF68C28D561 D/0/strat_trends_17mar07.pdf. Accessed 11 June 2010.

Ministry of External Relations – Havana (MINREX), 2008. http://embacu.cubaminrex.cu/ Default.aspx?tabid=6976. Accessed 2 June 2010.

Morales, E., 2010. ¿Corrupción. La Verdadera Contrarrevolución? (Havana, UNEAC) 9 April. http://www.uneac.org.cu/index.php?module=noticias&act=d etalle&tipo =noticia &id =3123. Accessed 25 May 2010.

Naim, M., 2003. 'A Venezuelan Paradox: How Latin America's Sole Re-maining Dictator Outsmarted the World's Sole Remaining Superpower', www.foreignpolicy.com/articles/2003/03/01/a_venezuelan_paradox. Accessed 10 February 2010.

Pan American Health Organisation 1995–2004, Regional Core Health Data Initiative. http://www.paho.org/English/SHA/coredata/tabulator/newTabulator. htm. Accessed 18 November 2007.

Petras, J., 2009. 'Iranian Elections: The "Stolen Elections" Hoax', *Global Research*, www.Globalresearch.ca/index.php?context=va&aid=14018. Accessed 2 February 2010.

ukpolitical.info, 2010. General election turnout 1945–2010, http://www. ukpolitical. info/Turnout 45.htm. Accessed 14 May 2010.

Voss, M., 2007. 'Cuba Awaits News on Castro's Return', BBC News. http://news. bbc. co.uk/1/hi/world/Americas/6949734.stm. Accessed 8 January 2008.

Voss, M., 2010. 'Cuba liberalises barber shops and beauty salons', BBC News, Havana, 13 April. http://news.bbc.co.uk/1/hi/world/americas/8616858.stm. Accessed 6 May 2010.

Wallach, L., et al, 2002. 'Whither Globalisation and its Architects in a Post-Sept 11, Post-90s Bubble World', Roundtable discussion, New York, 4 Feb. www. cepr.net/meetings/globalization_2002_ 02_ excerpts.htm. Accessed 24 Jan 2006.

Williams, J., 2008. 'Shadow Government Statistics. Analysis Behind and Beyond Government Economic Reporting'. http://www.shadowstats.com/. Accessed 12 February 2008.

World Health Organisation (WHO), World Health Chart 2001, http://www.math. yorku.ca/ SCS/ Gallery/images/WorldHealth2001.pdf. Accessed 7 April 2009.

WHO 2004–2005. World Health Report.http://www.who.int/whr/2004/en/ and http://www.who.int/whr/2005/en/index.html. Accessed 7 April 2009.

Worldvision, 2010. Advocacy for Youth in the United States. http://www.world vision.org/ content.nsf/learn/globalissues-america-youth#sources. Accessed 10 June 2010.

INTERVIEWS

Aguilera, Hilda (MINAG official), 1996. Ministry of Agriculture, Havana, 17 November.

Alvarez-Escobar, Dr Belkis, 2004. Co-ordinator Barrio Adentro. Caracas, 14 June.

Consejo de Administración Matanzas, 1997. Matanzas, 12 November.

Delgado, Ricardo, 1999. Asociación Cubana Technicos Agrícolas Forestales (ACTAF). Ministry of Agriculture. Havana, 18 February.

Dilla, Haroldo, 1996. Academic. Havana, 21 February.

Ferreira, Dário, 2004. Businessman. Caracas, 8 June.

Figueroa, Vilda & Lama, José, 1996, 2000, 2005, 2006, 2007. Havana, various dates.

Fuentes, Alejandro, 1998–99. International Relations Officer. Ministry of Finance and Prices, Havana, various dates.

Garcia, Jesus, 2007. Poder Popular Delegate and academic. Vedado, Havana, 14 March.

González, Alfredo, 1996. Adviser to the Minister of Economics and Planning. Havana, 19 February.

González, Victor, 2004. Public Relations Officer. Alcaldía Municipal de Sucre, Caracas, 3–13 June.

'Gonzalo', 2004. Shopkeeper. Leonceo Martínez, Caracas, 9 June.

Hernández, Iliana, 1996. Director of Local Government Budgets. Ministry of Finance and Prices, Havana, 25 November.

Leon Vega, Juan, 1995, 1996. Director International Relations, Ministry of Agriculture (MINAG). Havana, 27 June, 17 February.

'Manolo', 2004. Cuban medical officer. Caracas, 8 June.

Martínez Heredia, Fernando, 2004. Academic. Havana, 19 November.

Ministry of Finance, 1998. 15 September.

Molina Aeosta, Osmany, 1999. Director, Finance and Prices (Municipal Government) Cruces, Cienfuegos, Cuba, 24 November.

Pérez Vizcano, R., 1997. Vice President, San Miguel del Padron Municipality. City of Havana Province, Havana, 26 November.

Pérez, Juan Carlos, 2004. Statistical Director. Anauco Hilton, Caracas, 17 June.

Ramirez García, Mariano, 1999. Director, Provincial Council of Administration, Cienfuegos, Cuba, 25 November.

Resident, 2004. La Lucha Barrio, Parroquia Leonceo Martínez, Caracas, 10 June.

Rodríguez Nodals, Dr Adolfo, 2005. Director, Instituto de Investigaciones Fundamentales en Agricultura Tropical (INIFAT). Havana, Santiago de las Vegas, 22 November.

'Rosa', 2004. Participant in 'Grandparents' Circle'. Calle Principal del Morro, Caracas, 8 June.

Sánchez Naranjo, Víctor, 1999. Club de Horticultores. Santa Fe, Havana, 15 November.

'Santos', 2004. Resident. La Caucaguita, Caracas, 9 June.

Toledo, Ruben, 1996. Vice Minister, Ministry of Finance and Prices. Havana, 17 September.

Vital Martínez, Juan, 1999. President of Municipal Government. Cruces, Cienfuegos, Cuba, 24 November.

OTHER SOURCES

BBC World, 2004. 'Castro: Morire Combatiendo', 30 January.

BBC-Granada, Ltd, 1986. 'Inside the Revolution', Part Five of a six-part documentary entitled 'The Spanish Civil War'.

Cabrisas, Ricardo, 2005. Minister of Government within the Office of the President, Cuban representative to the Cuba Initiative and counterpart to Lord Moynihan, Round Table, Council of Ministers, Havana, 21 November.

Constitution of the Republic of Cuba, 1976. (Havana: Centre for Cuban Studies).

Constitución de la República Bolivariana de Venezuela, 1999.

Dew, John, 2006. British Ambassador to Cuba. Briefing given to British business delegation, Hotel Parque Central, Havana, 6 November.

European Parliament, 2008. Conference. 'The normalisation of the relations between the European Union and Cuba and the chances in the field of development cooperation', organised by the Group for the Friendship and Solidarity with the People of Cuba and Grupo Sur, Brussels, 26 May.

'Sobre los Organos del Poder Popular', 1976. Tesis y Resoluciónes: Primer Congreso del Partido Comunista de Cuba (Havana).

Unreported World, 2002. 'El Salvador: Killing to Belong; Gang Warfare', Channel 4 Television (London).

Walden, B., 2006. 'Power to the People: A Point of View', BBC News (transcript), 3 March.

Index

Compiled by Sue Carlton